WILLIAM BLIGH

Born 1754 of a Cornish family.   Sailed with Cook on his
third voyage, and subsequently had command of the
Bounty and the *Providence*.   Fought at Camperdown;
specially mentioned at the Battle of Copenhagen,
1801.   Appointed governor of New South Wales in
1805.   After his return to England in 1811 was made
first rear-admiral and then vice-admiral.   Died in
London in 1817.

A Book of the 'Bounty'

William Bligh and Others

Edited by
George Mackaness

New introduction by
Gavin Kennedy PHD

Dent: London, Melbourne and Toronto
EVERYMAN'S LIBRARY
Dutton: New York

© Introduction, J. M. Dent & Sons Ltd, 1981
All rights reserved
Printed in Great Britain by
Biddles Ltd, Guildford, Surrey
for
J. M. DENT & SONS LTD
Aldine House, 33 Welbeck Street, London
First included in Everyman's Library 1938
Reissued 1981

Published in the USA by arrangement with
J. M. Dent & Sons Ltd

No 950 Hardback ISBN 0 460 00950 8

INTRODUCTION

THE pamphlets and letters in this little volume were originally
selected by Dr George Mackaness (1882–1968), the distinguished
Australian scholar, and published in Everyman's Library
in 1938. The purpose was to make available some of the
original sources to those who were interested in the *Bounty*
mutiny but were unable to consult them in the major collections
in London or Sydney, or who could not afford to purchase the
very expensive collections from the Golden Cockerel Press.
Dr Mackaness was the author of *The Life of Vice-Admiral
William Bligh*, RN, FRS (Sydney, 2 vols., 1931), the first
scholarly biography of Bligh. He continued to publish articles
and monographs on aspects of Bligh's career up to 1960 but,
regrettably, these later contributions to the continuing debate
about this most controversial of naval officers have been until
recently only accessible to a very limited audience. The two
most important contributions by Dr Mackaness, consisting of
unpublished correspondence of Bligh and his close relative,
Francis Godolphin Bond, appeared, in 1949 and 1953 respectively, in limited editions of 140 copies only.

Public interest in the *Bounty* affair continues unabated
nearly two hundred years after the mutiny, which took place
on 28 April 1789 about thirty miles off the Pacific island of
Tofoa. A typical bibliography of books and articles on the
Bounty mutiny would contain over 300 items and a fully
comprehensive one a few hundred more. What is it that has
given this mutiny its fascination for each generation? It
cannot possibly be because of its intrinsic importance or
historical relevance. The *Bounty* was a minor ship of the Royal
Navy, specially purchased and fitted for what was effectively
a 'greenhouse' operation. Bligh's mission was to transplant the
breadfruit tree from Tahiti in the Pacific to the colonies in the
West Indies. *En passant* he was to explore and survey the
relatively unfrequented area between Tahiti and Timor.
Before, during and after the voyage, the Admiralty's attentions

were concentrated elsewhere. Their attitude to the venture is probably expressed most clearly in the parsimonious way they allocated the necessary resources for it to be undertaken, which contributed considerably to the eventual disastrous outcome.

The *Bounty* mutiny has become the most famous mutiny in history. Whereas most people would be unable to remember the names of the leaders of the Spithead and Nore mutinies of 1797, which involved over one hundred ships and thousands of seamen during the war with France and the Netherlands, or that of the captain of the *Hermione* whose style more closely resembled that of the Hollywood version of Bligh, it is unlikely that one in a hundred would be unable to identify the captain of the *Bounty* and the man who led the mutiny. The cinema (and now television) certainly helped to popularize the characters in the *Bounty* story but the question must still be posed: why dramatize this particular mutiny when there are others to choose from, and many of them would not require the scriptwriter to imagine 'Bligh atrocities' (which never took place) in order to create dramatic tension?

One reason for the *Bounty's* fame must be the romance of the early Pitcairn Island refuge of Fletcher Christian and the eight hard-core mutineers. Another must be Bligh's epic boat voyage across 3,900 miles of the Pacific with a starving and often acrimonious crew. And above all there is the sudden and final confrontation between Bligh and his friend, Christian. It is in the theatre of that clash of personalities and wills that the fascination of the *Bounty* mutiny lies. And, fortunately for the story, there is not just one scene to play through. All that happened afterwards, by the accidents of history, have given that scene and its setting innumerable facets of far greater complexity than a mere recital of the lines spoken by each of the players. To see what I mean by this consider for a moment what would be left to the *Bounty* story *if* certain events had *not* been consequential on Christian's mutiny.

If Bligh's boat party had been massacred at Tofoa, as they nearly were, or had been swamped in the ocean, as was constantly threatened, what would the world know of Bligh's story? Probably as little as it does of Captain Pigot's of the *Hermione*. *If* the *Bounty* had been retaken by the *Pandora* at Tahiti (as the *Hermione* was by Captain Hamilton in a cutting-out expedition), almost everybody would have been executed and forgotten (as the unfortunate *Hermiones* were and are). There would have been no Pitcairn Island and its dreadful tales of massacre and evidence of moral redemption. *If* Bligh had dropped into obscurity after his return to Britain, instead of going on to a career full of controversial events that made their mark on history, what meaning would the events on the *Bounty* have for the early history of Australia, where Bligh was Governor in 1806–10? Moreover, in what condition would the archival records of Bligh and the *Bounty* be if the Australians had not spent so much time and money on accumulating them? The very existence of so much documentary material about the insignificant *Bounty* rests on the fact that Bligh's subsequent career gave it an importance which it would probably not otherwise have had. Without that importance the *Bounty* would be as topical as other backwater events in the history of the Royal Navy.

For these reasons the *Bounty* story is of great interest to a wide audience and because of this interest some of the important documents relating to the mutiny have been made available from time to time. The material in this collection covers the core literature of the subject and has a particular relevance because it is the work of two of the main protagonists in the first round of the debate, William Bligh and Edward Christian, Fletcher's brother and a Professor of Law.

Bligh's *Narrative* was written after he had returned to Britain in 1790 and it details events, of the mutiny and the open boat voyage, until his arrival at the Cape of Good Hope. When the *Voyage* (1792) appeared it contained an expanded section of the *Narrative* on occurrences from Timor to Europe and the publisher agreed to supply the additional parts to subscribers who had already bought the 1790 *Narrative*. While Bligh definitely was the author of the *Narrative* (his name appears on the title page) it is certain that he was not the sole author of the *Voyage* (which has no author's name credited to it). Du Rietz (1962) has shown that Bligh's Log was written up with additions (and some deletions) by [Rear-Admiral] James Burney and Sir Joseph Banks while Bligh was away on the second breadfruit voyage in the *Providence* (1791–3).

Bligh has been accused of falsifying his *Narrative*, official Log, reports and letters, in respect of the events in the *Bounty*. Admiral W. H. Smyth was among the first of his accusers

(1829, 1831), but much of his criticism is fanciful when investi-gated. More recent critics (McKee, 1961; Du Rietz, 1965) have made a stronger case, echoing the views expressed in Morrison's manuscript *Journal* (1792). One contention con-cerns the 'relative strengths of the parties'. Bligh adds up those who went with him in the boat (eighteen plus himself) and those who remained in the *Bounty* ('in all twenty-five hands, and the most able men of the ship's company'). Far too much is made of this in my view. Bligh had no need to show that the mutineers were stronger *numerically*. He only had to show they were armed and ready to use their weapons. His Log and letters, often quoted to show his 'shabby numbers game', were written under the most appalling conditions immediately after he had brought a party of starving survivors in an open boat to comparative safety. One would hardly expect that he would be feeling impartial towards those left in the *Bounty* and that he would judicially divide them into the innocent and the guilty. It was not his job to decide the fate of the 'pirates' or to make a case for those who were kept on board against their will. He listed those he thought were innocent and left the rest to defend themselves, if apprehended.

Mackaness refuted the charge of falsification eloquently:

'. . . after examining carefully all the entries of any import-ance in his private as well as his published journals, we are compelled to conclude that, while he is certainly not guilty of deliberately falsifying his narrative, he *is* guilty of suppressing important passages—some few of which, read in the cold atmosphere of a naval tribunal, he thought might be open to adverse criticism—concerning the delinquencies of his officers and crew. These would have done something to exculpate him from the charges of harsh conduct, and to reveal not only the trials he had to endure from his officers' inefficiency, but also how he forgave even Purcell (the carpenter) time and again. (1931, pp. 175–6)

Knowing now that Bligh had his Log edited by his friends Burney and Banks for the *Voyage* (1792) and that they used his public Log (PRO Adm 55/151) and not the private one (Mitchell Library Safe 1/46), it is possible he "suppressed' some highly critical remarks about some officers (written, we must note, *before* the mutiny) even from them. But whatever the case, whatever items Bligh left out, or Burney and Banks took out for him, the fact remains that his exclusions in the published accounts were to the advantage of the mutineers and not himself.

The Minutes of the Court Martial included here were prepared by Stephen Barney who was employed by William Muspratt at the trial. Muspratt got his money's worth because Barney spotted a legal loophole through which Muspratt—undeniably a mutineer—was able to get a pardon. Muspratt was unable by court procedures to call Byrne and Norman as his defence witnesses because the court was trying them for mutiny even though they had been cleared in writing by Bligh. When sentence was passed he immediately appealed on this legal technicality and eventually was freed on the advice of the legal authorities. The Minutes only cover the evidence for the prosecution; for the defence see Rutter (1931). [The date of the trial on the original title page should read 'September 12' not 'August 12'.]

Edward Christian used the publication of Barney's minutes to add an *Appendix*. It was a brilliant ploy. It purports to be a statement of the 'evidence' heard by 'several respectable gentlemen' of the 'true causes and circumstances which have hitherto been concealed or misrepresented of one of the most remarkable events in the annals of the navy'. What is not stated in the *Appendix* is the nature of the informal court of inquiry set up by Edward Christian. Unable to get a naval court-martial to discuss or take evidence on the causes of the mutiny (because under the Articles of War there was no justifiable cause for a mutiny whatsoever and if found guilty a mutineer received a mandatory death sentence) and with his brother still at large somewhere in the Pacific and liable to capture, Edward felt it necessary to make public what, in his view, were the real causes of the mutiny and by so doing discredit Bligh in the hope of making Fletcher's conviction, if he were caught, a little less certain.

The 'respectable gentlemen' were all connected with, and under friendly obligation to, the Christian family. This is not mentioned in the text. Mr Antrobus was from Cockermouth (home of Fletcher Christian) and had attended St John's College, Cambridge. Dr Frewen had been tutor at St John's to William Wordsworth (Fletcher's friend) and was a friend of Edward, a fellow at St John's. Mr Cookson was Words-

worth's uncle.   John Wordsworth was another relative of
William's and was also related by marriage to Fletcher's aunt,
Isabella Curwen (of whom Fletcher was fond enough to call
his Tahitian wife 'Isabella' at Pitcairn).   John Wordsworth
was employed by the East India Company, in which Dr Fisher
was a major influence.   Fisher became Rector of Nether
Stowey where the Wordsworths and Coleridge were to spend
time together.   James Losh was a friend of the Christian
family (deeply sympathetic to the French Revolution); so was
Samuel Romilly who became an honorary member of the
Convention.   No doubt parallels were struck between the
Bounty mutiny of 1789 and the events in France of that year.
Mr Gilpin and Mr Atkinson were neighbours of the Christians
and Wordsworths.   Only Edward Christian was present at all
the 'meetings' of the panel—the attendance of the other
members varied from once to several times.   This makes it
impossible to sort out who heard what from whom.   The
Appendix rarely credits individual *Bounty* witnesses with
particular statements, hence we cannot deploy knowledge of
their characters to judge the veracity of their statements.

Edward Christian intended to provoke Bligh into a libel
suit.   He said, in his *Reply*, 1795 (not included in this collection), that 'many gentlemen, besides myself, suppose that if
any answer could be given, it would be attempted in a court of
justice in some judicial proceeding'.   With a professor of law
('that sixpenny professor' Bligh called him), several distinguished and litigous lawyers, and men of the Church as
defendants, Bligh would have been sucked into a confused and
expensive case which, even if he emerged victorious, would have
ruined him unless he got exceptional damages.   And whom
would he sue?   The panel, the witnesses, or just Christian?
Bligh chose to reply with his *Answer to Certain Assertions*
(1795).   It is not really a proper answer—it presents material
which could form the basis for an answer.   The fifteen items
he presents are germane to the *Appendix* but are presented
without comment.   The reader is expected to understand their
relevance.   Whereas the *Appendix* is a brilliant polemic, the
Answer is a skeleton legal brief (which may have been its
original purpose), less than adequate to destroy the credibility
of the *Appendix* in the public's mind.

Christian's *Reply* continues the polemics of the *Appendix*
and rebuts some of Bligh's answers.   Among Bligh's papers

in the Mitchell Library, Sydney, there is a manuscript in draft which would have been a more powerful answer than the one he published. These are in letter form, addressed to Sir Joseph Banks and date from December 1792, indicating that Edward Christian was lobbying against Bligh from around that date. Bligh makes some good points in these notes. Of Heywood's role he writes: 'That Peter Heywood the Mutineer would write to Mr Christian a favourable account of His Brother, cannot be doubted; for by endeavouring to prove the Ringleader of the Mutiny not guilty; the rest of the party must in case he succeeded be surely free of any blame.' On the statements attributed to Fryer and Purcell (both with Bligh in the open boat) he writes: 'As all the Men & Officers who came home with Captain Bligh declare, that four Men were deserving of Mercy, & as such were recommended & acquitted; can a Mind open to conviction be more perfectly satisfied that it was their opinion that all else who remained on board were guilty.' Purcell, Fryer and Peckover knew of his displeasure with their conduct (he had Purcell court-martialled, refused a reference for Fryer and turned down Peckover's request to join him in the *Providence*) and because none of them made any statements to the authorities about him while he was in the country Bligh suggested that Christian had tampered with them.

Bligh remarks: 'The Mutineers, Heywood, Morrison & Musprat [sic] who were condemned & afterwards pardoned are now turned out upon the World & to paliate [sic] their own conduct they may think it the most effective way to plead their temptations arose from having been ill used.' Of the three, Morrison and Heywood were the main protagonists of the subsequent rounds of debate about Bligh's character. James Morrison wrote two manuscripts during the court-martial and in the weeks immediately following, giving his views on Bligh as a commander. The first and shortest was written in September–October 1792 on board HMS *Hector* (*Memorandums and Particulars* . . .) and the second from November 1792 to about January 1793 (known as the *Journal*). Morrison makes numerous accusations, many of a trivial and vexatious nature. But not all were trivial; some are very serious, if true. It was Morrison who accused Bligh of stealing two cheeses while the *Bounty* was fitting out at Deptford and then blaming the crew for their loss, and of falsifying account books at the Cape of Good Hope. Both offences could have cost Bligh his commission. Morrison had intended to have his manuscript published but for some reason this did not happen in his lifetime, except for some extracts relating to his descriptions of the people and customs of Tahiti which appeared anonymously in 1799. His charges against Bligh did not appear until 1825, under Peter Heywood's entry in Marshall's *Naval Biography*. Bligh only saw Morrison's first manuscript (*Memorandums*) and his draft replies are in the Mitchell Library (*Remarks on Morrison's Journal*, Safe 1/43).

Peter Heywood collaborated with Edward Christian in preparing the *Appendix* in 1792–3 but then appears to have left the whole subject alone until his biographical entry in Marshall in 1825. It may be that he was advised not to get embroiled in a public quarrel with Captain Bligh in view of his Royal Pardon for mutiny, particularly if he wished to continue his naval career.

Bligh died in 1817. Lord Byron's epic poem, *The Island, or Christian and his Comrades*, appeared in 1823 and was generally 'pro-Bligh'. Ships were visiting Pitcairn and their reports discussed the famous mutiny. In 1831, Captain Beechey published his *Voyage to the Pacific* which included the most detailed statement from John Adams, the only surviving mutineer, that he made on the mutiny. Parts of that statement contradicted some views of Heywood. Sir John Barrow, Second Secretary at the Admiralty, published his classic *The Eventful History of the Mutiny and Piratical Seizure of the Bounty* in late 1831. Admiral Smyth, writing (anonymously) in *the United Service Journal*, was outrageously hostile to Bligh. The *Bounty* mutiny was by now receiving the attention of the reading public, an attention which continues to this day.

In the 1930s there was a considerable amount of material published on the *Bounty* which made available many of the primary sources. Bligh's Logs, Morrison's manuscript *Journal*, Fryer's *Narrative*, and a great deal of the related correspondence appeared either verbatim or with commentary in the numerous books of the period. Foremost among these books was, as we have noted, the major biographical work of George Mackaness. The ironical aspect of this activity was that as the historical records were published, giving a more generous view of the career of William Bligh than was common in the latter part of the nineteenth century, the popular cinema was

presenting an entirely different characterization. Now while
it is not necessarily a matter of concern to scholars what
rubbish is playing at the local theatre or what travesty of the
facts is fed to the ordinary citizen on the television, they
would be only being human if they felt a trifle dismayed at
the stony ground the fruits of their labours were falling upon.
The community of scholars is not a self sufficient economy. In
the main it is paid for by the productive exertions of others.
This gives them some responsibility to the wider world. There
is no doubt that scholars like George Mackaness not only
accepted that precept but acted on it as far as was possible
within the limits of time and resources. Hence, much of the
work of writers on the *Bounty* mutiny since the Second World
War has been concerned with disseminating the results
achieved by scholars who researched the subject in the 1930s.

But no subject stands still. Research continues and earlier
conjectures about events are tested by those currently working
in the field. It is a credit to Mackaness that having made so
large a contribution to *Bounty* scholarship in the thirties he
should also make a lasting contribution of some considerable
significance towards the end of his life. I refer to his publication of the Bligh–Bond correspondence in 1949 and 1953.
The Swedish scholar, Rolf Du Rietz, has been one of the few
contributors to *Bounty* research who has consistently insisted
on the historical significance of this material. There is no
space here to raise some of the issues implied by Du Rietz's
conclusion that 'when it comes to the end, Prof. Christian was
right, and Mr Bligh was wrong, in the famous controversy
between them in 1794–5' and that Christian 'had discovered
that Mr Bligh had not been quite truthful in his version of the
mutiny, and therefore he thought it a duty, not only to his
family and to society, but also to the memory of his unfortunate
and defenceless brother, to reveal the truth'. (Du Rietz,
1965, I, pp. 32–3.) For Du Rietz, then, the Bond letters
serve to remove any doubts about the 'problem' of the *Bounty*
mutiny, i.e., 'who caused Christian to mutiny?' In Du
Rietz's view the answer is absolutely certain: Captain Bligh
caused the mutiny by his treatment of Fletcher Christian.
This is, of course, an entirely different question to that of
whether Fletcher Christian was *justifi*ed in leading the mutiny
in the *moral* not the legal sense (there can be no *legal* justification of mutiny).

Mackaness considered Bond's letter to his brother (written from St Helena in December 1792 when Bond was serving as First Lieutenant of the *Providence* on the voyage immediately following that of the *Bounty* mutiny), to be 'one of the most illuminating ever written concerning the character of Bligh'. The following is an extract from it covering the most relevant points (the original letter is in the National Maritime Museum, Greenwich):

To say a southern voyage is quite delectable is also to say you have every domestic comfort; but on this score I must be silent, for at present I mean to say but little of our Major Domo [i.e., Bligh]. I assure you it is no small disappointment to my hopes that I have not gained as much information as expected;—an insurmountable bar has always lain in my way, since my pride will not allow me to receive magisterial tuition, nor bow with servile flattery. Is it the fashion to begin or end a miscellaneous epistle with our own grievances? It is evident mine commences in that style, but my intention is to have no obstruction in the end; and to go on with my journal ad libitim. Before this enigma is cleared up let me enjoin the strictest secrecy [sic] and insist on your not acquainting even your good wife, my mother, nor my dear sister with the circumstance . . . Yes, Tom, our relation had the credit of being a tyrant in his last expedition, where his misfortunes and good fortunes have elevated him to a situation he is incapable of supporting with decent modesty. The very high opinion he has of himself makes him hold every one of our profession with contempt, perhaps envy. Nay, the Navy is but [a] sphere for fops and lubbers to swarm in, without one gem to vie in brilliancy with himself. I don't mean to depreciate his extensive knowledge as a seaman and nautical astronomer, but condemn that want of modesty, in self-estimation. To be less prolix I will inform you that he has treated me (nay, all on board) with the insolence and arrogance of a *Jacobs*: and not withstanding his passion is partly to be attributed to a nervous fever, with which he has been attacked most of the voyage, the chief part of his conduct must have arisen from the fury of an ungovernable temper. Soon after leaving England I wished to receive instruction from this imperious master, until I found he publically exposed any deficiency on my part in the Nautical Art, &c. A series of this conduct determined me to trust to myself, which I hope will in some measure repay me for the trouble of a disagreeable voyage—in itself pleasant but made otherwise by being worried at every opportunity. His maxims are the of that nature that at once pronounce him an enemy to lovers of Natural Philosophy; for to make use of his own words, 'No person can do the duty of a 1st Lieut. who does more than write the day's work of his publick Journal!' This is so inimical to the sentiments I always hope to retain that I find the utmost difficulty in keeping on tolerable terms with him. The general orders which have been given me are to that purport—I am constantly to keep on my legs from 8 o'th'morning to 12, or noon, altho' I keep the usual watch. The Officer of the morning watch attends to the cleaning of the Decks; yet I am also to be present, not only to get it done, but be even menially active on those, and all other occasions. He expects me to be acquainted with every transaction on board, notwithstanding he himself will give the necessary orders to the Warrant Officers, before I can put it in execution. Every dogma of power and consequence has been taken from the Lieutenants, to establish, as he thinks, his own reputation—what imbecility for a post Capn! The inferior Warrants have had orders from the beginning of the expedition, not to issue the least article to a Lieut. without his orders; so that a cleat, fathom of log line, or indeed a hand swab, must have the commander's sanction. One of the last and most *beneficent* commands was, that the Carpenter's Crew should not drive a nail for me without I would first ask his permission—but my heart is filled with the proper materials always to disdain this humiliation. Among many circumstances of envy and jealousy, he used to deride my keeping a private journal, and would often ironically say he supposed I meant to publish. My messmates have remarked he never spoke of my possessing one virtue—tho' by the bye he never dared to say I have none. Every officer who has nautical information, a knowledge of natural History, a taste for drawing, or anything to constitute him proper for circumnavigating, becomes odious; for great as he is in his own good opinion, he must have entertained fears some of the ship's company meant to submit a spurious Narrative to the judgement and perusal of the publick. Among the many misunderstandings that have taken place, that of my *Observing* has given most offence, for since I have not made the least application to him for information on that head, he has at all times found illiberal means of abusing my pursuit; saying at the same time, what I absolutely knew was from him. Tired heartily of my present situation, and even the subject I am treating of, I will conclude it by inserting the most recent illegal order. Every Officer is expected to deliver in their private Logs ere we anchor at St. Helena. As our expedition has not been on discoveries, should suppose this an arbitrary command, altho the words *King's request; Good of the Country; Orders of the Admiralty*, &c, &c, &c, are frequently in his mouth—but unparrelled [sic] pride is the principal ingredients of his composition. The future will determine whether promotion will be the reward for this voyage: I still flatter myself it will, notwithstanding what I have said. Consistent with self-respect, I still remain tolerably passive; and if nothing takes place very contrary to my feelings, all may end well; but this will totally depend on circumstances; one of which is the secrecy requested of you concerning the tenor of this letter.—My time is so effectually taken up by Duty, that to keep peace I neglect all kind of study; yet the company of a set of well informed Messmates make my moments pass very agreeably, so that I am by no means in purgatory. (Lieut. F. G. Bond to his brother, Thomas, undated, St Helena: Mackaness, 1953; Du Rietz, 1965.)

The significance of the letter lies in the fact that Francis Bond was at this time occupying roughly the same post, directly responsible to Bligh, that Fletcher Christian did on the *Bounty*. The argument goes: that if Bligh almost drove Bond to extremes of irritation, knowing the consequence when he had behaved similarly on the *Bounty* towards Christian, then the material evidence of the *Appendix* gains in credibility and this affirms that Bligh did *cause* the mutiny. The last two sentences hold a poignant significance when considering Fletcher's fate: he was unable to 'remain tolerably passive' because something took place 'contrary to (his) feelings' (Bligh's abuse over the theft of the coconuts?) and he did not have 'well informed messmates' but younger men with little experience of the world (Heywood, Stewart, and the thirteen-year-old Tinkler) whose company did not make his 'moments pass very agreeably'. Indeed, if Christian was as attached to his Tahitian 'Isabella' as is likely, the circumstances of his lack of 'well informed messmates', an irascible Bligh, with his 'ungovernable temper', and the final straw of Bligh impugning his honour, fully explain Christian's mutiny.

As always there are two sides to the argument, but it is not the purpose of this introduction to open up a debate. Having made this clear, however, it would still be somewhat unfair (and also uncharacteristic) if I did not make a couple of points for the reader to ponder in respect of the extract from Bond's letter. First, if the correspondence reproduced by Mackaness is taken as a whole it will be noticed that a large part of it consists of letters between Bligh and Bond about Bligh's efforts to get Bond promoted after the voyage of the *Providence* in 1793. Bligh was under a shadow at the time but he was soon out of it. Whatever else can be said about Bligh he was certainly persistent in trying to forward the interests of Bond, obviously completely unaware of how Bond saw their relationship. The second point to note is that Bond did get the promotion he desired. Lord Spenser promoted him to Commander in December 1800 and he achieved Post Captain's rank in 1802 but, for some reason, moved sideways from the floating service to the Sea Fencibles in 1803. He never commanded afloat after that but reached retired Rear-Admiral's rank in 1837 in a general promotion. In other words, was he really suited for the sea service and how much of his discomfort with Bligh in the *Province* was due to Bligh's discovery of this in the way Bond conducted himself as First Lieutenant? Bligh had the gift of the First Lieutenancy and he offered it to Bond. He did the same thing with Christian in the *Bounty* and, perhaps, found that this responsibility was a burden which neither could carry. Readers will know of all kinds of circumstances, in industry, commerce, the services, government, the universities and the local football team, where the 'top man's' right-hand man is expected to work the hardest, the longest and for the least credit. It is an inescapable part of career development today and we have no reason to assume it was any different in the eighteenth century navy. The difference between Christian and Bond is that Christian crumbled, perhaps because of his character, perhaps because of his circumstances (Isabella?), and Bond did not.

Bligh's pecularity of manner was well documented without the Bond letters. The evidence of the *Appendix*, such as it is, the minutes of the courts martial of Lieutenant Frazier in the *Warrior* (1805), of Short (1807), of Kent (1811) and Johnston (1811), fully describe Bligh's behaviour. He was given to abusive language. It was of a kind unacceptable in a Victorian drawing room and possibly unacceptable in our democratic age (I refer, of course, only to the parliamentary democracies) but was, it seems, only a colourful example of what was the norm in his own age.

It would, however, be inappropriate to allow only one officer of the *Providence* to have his say. We will hear from two others and then leave it to the reader to form a preliminary judgment before moving on to consult the items in this collection and, hopefully, to seek out and consider the literature mentioned in the bibliography.

The Third Lieutenant of the *Providence* was George Tobin, a talented artist whose sketches and water-colours of the voyage are in the Mitchell Library, Sydney. Tobin was related through marriage to Nelson's wife. He was promoted commander in 1798 and Post Captain in 1802. When news of Bligh's death reached him he wrote to Bond and made a perceptive summary of Bligh's character:

> So poor Bligh, for with all his infirmities, you and I cannot but think well of him has followed Portlock. He has had a long and turbulent journey of it—no one more so, and since the unfortunate Mutiny in the *Bounty*, has been rather in the shade. Yet perhaps was he not altogether understood,—I am sure, my dear Friend that in the *Providence* there was no settled System of Tyranny exercised by him likely to produce disatisfaction. It was in those violent Tornados of temper when he lost himself, yet, when all, in his opinion, *went right*, when could a man be more placid and interesting. For myself I feel that I am indebted to him. It was the first ship in which I ever sailed as an Officer—I joined full of apprehension,—I soon thought he was not disatisfied with me—it gave me

encouragement and on the whole we journeyed smoothly on. Once or twice I felt the *Unbridled* license *of* his *power of speech*, yet never without soon receiving something like an emollient plaister to heal the wound. Let our old Captain's frailties be forgotten and view him as a man of Science and excellent practical Seaman. He had suffered much and ever in difficulty by labour and perseverance extricated himself. But his great quality was Foresight. In this I think, Bond, you will accord with me. I have seen many men in his profession with more resources, but never one with so much precaution—I mean chiefly as a Navigator. (Tobin to Bond, 15 December 1817; Mackaness, 1949, pp. 32–3.)

Another witness from the *Providence* can also be called upon to give an insight into the complex personality of William Bligh. Matthew Flinders joined the *Providence* as a midshipman, largely under the advice of Captain Pasley, Peter Heywood's uncle. He became Australia's most famous maritime explorer. The extract is from his *Memoirs* (n.d.) and concerns Flinders' assessment of the nautical surveying Bligh reported from his open boat voyage, off the north east coast of Australia in 1789, compared to the work of Captain Cook and himself when both had the advantage of the use of fully equipped ships. Flinders writes:

It has been to me a cause of much surprise, that under such distress of hunger and fatigue, and an anxiety still greater than these and whilst running before a strong breeze in an open boat, captain Bligh should have been able to gather material for a chart; but that this chart should possess a considerable share of accuracy, is a subject for admiration. On the other hand that such errors should exist in any chart by captain Cook is equally wonderful. He has been highly and universally praised, not only for his perseverance [sic], ability and uncommon success, but also for the accuracy of his charts; and I have myself witnessed in so many instances how well he deserved this character, that I have always held his works to be sacred; and pride myself, not a little in being, in some sort his disciple; my first acquirements in nautical science having been made under one who mostly gained his from that great master himself; untoward circum-

stances shall not prevent me repeating the name of Bligh
at this moment." (State Library of Victoria, Melbourne.)

While, of course, it does not follow that because William
Bligh was a brilliant navigator he was necessarily right and
Christian necessarily wrong in the fateful hours preceeding the
mutiny, it must count for something when we weigh up the
contributions each made to their age and the respective strong
points and weaknesses of each. Christian's mutiny, for whatever reason it occurred, led directly to the deaths of many of
his shipmates and the deaths of many more Polynesian
islanders. This consequence is not unimportant, especially
when we consider the other crimes the mutineers committed
against innocent islanders which include rape, violence, theft,
destruction and kidnapping. Again this does not make Bligh
right but it does throw an enormous responsibility onto
Christian. It was *his* 'principled mind' which broke through,
perhaps, *his* indulgence in an over haughty sense of personal
honour. What sense of honour is worth the misery it inflicts
on those around it?

It remains once again to acknowledge the debt all those who
are interested in the *Bounty* affair owe to the Trustees, Librarian
and Staff of the Mitchell Library, Sydney, for their preservation
of the many items of 'Bountyana' in their collection. Nobody
who has ever had the good fortune to call upon the Mitchell's
resources will disagree with these sincere sentiments. All
sides of the continuing debate have much to thank the Mitchell
for, because without its carefully preserved collections, what
would there be left to argue over?

                                            Gavin Kennedy
Edinburgh, 1980

SELECT BIBLIOGRAPHY

The following is a highly selective bibliography of the important items of *Bounty* literature not published in this volume. It is a 'rock-bottom' guide and has no claims to being comprehensive. Necessarily, some items will be very difficult to obtain except by bona fide scholars in the main libraries. If access is not possible by a reader who genuinely wishes to read more material at, say, the Public Record Office, Kew, England, or the Mitchell Library, Macquarie Street, Sydney, NSW, Australia, then both these institutions may be approached with a view to acquiring a microfilm of the relevant documents, providing the purpose is exclusively for private research and providing they are satisfied that this is the case. This service is charged at cost and while expensive it is cheaper than the limited edition facsimiles in the commercial market and some of the auction-room prices of recent years. A preliminary letter is advised.

Manuscript Sources

Bligh, William: *Log of the 'Bounty'*, Public Record Office (PRO) Adm 55/151; Mitchell Library, (ML) Safe 1/46–47; *see* Rutter, Owen, *The Log of the 'Bounty'* . . . , Golden Cockerel Press, London, 2 vols, 1937: limited edition; *The Log of HMS 'Bounty'*, Genesis Publications, Guildford, 1976, facsimile limited edition; Bowker, R. M.: *Mutiny !! Aboard HM 'Bounty' in 1789*, Bowker & Bertram, 1979, popular edition.

Bligh, William: 'Remarks on Morrison's Journal', ML Safe 1/43.

Fryer, John: *Narrative*, United Service Institute, London; *see* Rutter, Owen: *The Voyage of the 'Bounty's Launch . . . and the Journal of John Fryer*, Golden Cockerel Press, 1934; also in facsimile by Genesis Publications, Guildford, 1979.

Heywood, Peter (and George Stewart): Extracts from *Journals* in Captain Edward Edwards' Papers, Admiralty Library, Fulham, London.

Morrison, James: *Memorandums and Particulars Respecting the*

'Bounty' and her Crew, ML Safe 1/33, Ms Journal, ML Safe
1/42; see Rutter, Owen, ed: The Journal of James Morrison
Boatswain's Mate of the 'Bounty', Golden Cockerel Press,
1935, limited edition. (A facsimile edition of the Journal,
Memorandums . . . , and Bligh's Remarks . . . , is to be
published by Genesis Press, Guildford in a limited edition.)
Peard, G.: MS Journal kept on HMS 'Blossom', Captain
Beechey, in 1825, British Museum Add. MSS 35141.

Minutes of the Courts-Martial of Frazier and Bligh, HMS
Warrior, are in the Public Record Office at Adm 1/5367; of
Captain Short at Mitchell Library, ML MS A85-5 Bank's Papers,
Brabourne Collection; Lieutenant Kent's court-martial is
reported in Naval Chronicle, Vol. 25, 1811 and Marshall's
Royal Naval Biography, Vol. 4, Part 1, 1825; and Lieutenant
Colonel Johnston in Bartrum, Mr: Proceedings of A General
Court-Martial . . . of Lieut. Col. Geo. Johnston . . . for deposing
William Bligh, London, 1811.

BOOKS AND ARTICLES

[Barrow, John]; The Eventful History of the Mutiny and
    Piratical Seizure of HMS 'Bounty': Its Cause and Conse-
    quences, London, 1831. (See under Kennedy.)
Beaglehole, John C.: Captain Cook and Captain Bligh, D. E.
    Collins Lecture, University of Wellington, N.Z., 1967.
Belcher, Lady [Diana]: The Mutineers of the 'Bounty' and their
    Descendants in Pitcairn and Norfolk Islands, London, 1870
    (N.Y., 1871).
Beechey, Captain F. W.: Narrative of a Voyage to the Pacific . . .
    Performed in HMS 'Blossom', London, 1831.
Bligh, William: 'Miscellaneous Letters' in Historical Records of
    New South Wales, Vols 6 and 7, Sydney, 1898–1901. (A
    facsimile was published in 1979 by Lansdown Slattery, NSW.)
Darby, Madge: Who Caused the Mutiny on the 'Bounty'?,
    Sydney, 1965.
Danielsson, Bengt: What Happened on the 'Bounty', London, 1962.
David, Andrew C. F.: The Surveyors of the 'Bounty': a prelim-
    inary study of the hydrographic Surveys of William Bligh,
    Thomas Hayward, and Peter Heywood and the charts published
    from them, Taunton, 1976.
—— 'Broughton's Schooner and the Bounty Mutineers',
    Mariner's Mirror, Vol. 63, pp. 207–13, 1977.

Dawson, Warren R., ed.: *The Banks Letters . . . correspondence of Sir Joseph Banks . . .* , London, 1958.

Du Rietz, Rolf: 'Three Letters from James Burney to Sir Joseph Banks: a contribution to the history of William Bligh's "A Voyage to the South Sea"', *Ethnos*, XXVII, pp. 115–25, 1962.

—— *The Causes of the 'Bounty' Mutiny: some comments on a book by Madge Darby*, (*Studia Bountyana Vol. 1*), Uppsala, 1965; see also *The Causes of the 'Bounty' Mutiny: a short reply to Mr Rolf du Rietz's comments*, by Madge Darby, (*Studia Bountyana, Vol. 2*), Uppsala, 1966 (both limited editions).

—— *Thoughts on the Present State of Bligh Scholarship*, (*Banksia 1*), Dahlia Books, Uppsala, 1979.

Ellis, M. H.: *John Macarthur*, Sydney, 1955.

Evatt, H. V.: *Rum Rebellion: a study of the overthrow of Governor Bligh by John Macarthur and the New South Wales Corps*, Sydney (1938), 1978.

Fletcher, W.: 'Fletcher Christian and the mutineers of the *Bounty*', *Transactions of the Cumberland Association for the Advancement of Literature and Science*, Part II, Carlisle, 1876–7.

Houston, Neal, B.: 'Fletcher Christian and the *Rime of the Ancient Mariner*, *The Dalhousie Review*', Vol. 45, no. 55, Winter, pp. 431–46, 1965–6.

Kennedy, Gavin: *Bligh*, London, 1978. (Includes extensive bibliography.)

—— *The Death of Captain Cook*, London, 1978.

—— 'Bligh and the Defiance Mutiny', *Mariner's Mirror*, Vol. 65, pp. 65–8, 1979.

—— edited and introduced: *Barrow's Mutiny on the Bounty*, Boston, 1980. (Illustrated.)

Knight, C.: 'HM Armed Vessel *Bounty*', *Mariner's Mirror*, Vol. 22, pp. 183–99, 1936.

Ledward, Thomas D.: 'Letters to his Family', *Notes and Queries*, 9th Series, Vol. XII, December, pp. 501–2, 1903.

Mackaness, George: *The Life of Vice-Admiral William Bligh*, RN, FRS, 2 vols, Sydney (1931); rev. ed., 1951.

—— *Captain William Bligh's Discoveries and Observations in Van Diemen's Land*, Sydney (limited edition), 1943. New ed. in *Australian Historical Monographs Series*, Vol. X (new series), Review Publications, 1976.

—— *Some Correspondence of Captain William Bligh RN with John and Francis Godolphin Bond*, Sydney (limited edition), 1949.

—— *Fresh Light on Bligh being Some Unpublished Correspon-*

dence . . . , Sydney (limited edition), 1953.   New edition in
Australian Historical Monographs Series, Vol. V (new series),
Review Publications, 1976 (bound with previous item).

—— 'Extracts from a Log-book of HMS *Providence* kept by
Lieut. Francis Godolphin Bond . . . ', *Journal and Proceedings
of the Royal Australian Historical Society* XLVI, pp. 24–66,
1960.

McKee, Alexander: *The Truth about the Mutiny on the 'Bounty'*,
London, 1961.

Marshall, John: *Royal Naval Biography* . . . , London, Vol. II,
Part II, 1925.

Maude, H. E.: 'In Search of a Home: from the Mutiny to
Pitcairn Island (1789–1790)', *The Journal of the Polynesian
Society*, Vol. 67, no. 2, June, pp. 106–16, 1958.

Montgomerie, H. S.: *William Bligh of the 'Bounty', in Fact and
Fable*, London, 1937.

Murray, Thomas Boyles: *Pitcairn: the Island, the People, the
Pastor, with a short account of the Mutiny of the 'Bounty'*,
London, 1853.

Pope, Dudley: *The Black Ship*, London, 1963.

Rutter, Owen: *The Court Martial of the 'Bounty' Mutineers*,
London, 1931.

—— *Turbulent Journey: a life of William Bligh, Vice-Admiral
of the Blue*, London, 1936.

Silverman, David: *Pitcairn Island*, Cleveland, Ohio, 1967.

Shapiro, H. L.: *The Heritage of the 'Bounty': the story of Pitcairn
through six generations*, London, 1936.

Smith, D. Bonner: 'Some Remarks about the Mutiny of the
Bounty', *Mariner's Mirror*, Vol. 22, pp. 200–37, 1936; see
also his 'More Light on Bligh and the *Bounty*', *Mariner's
Mirror*, Vol. 23, pp. 210–28, 1937.

[Smyth, W. H.]: 'Letter' (signed 'XYZ') *United Service Journal*,
II, pp. 366–7, 1829; 'Sketch of the Career of the Late Capt.
Peter Heywood', *United Service Journal*, I, pp. 468–81, 1831;
'The *Bounty* Again!', *United Service Journal*, III, pp. 305–14,
1831.

Tagart, E.: *A Memoir of the Late Captain Peter Heywood*, RN,
with extracts from his diaries and correspondence, London,
1832.

Wilkinson, C. S.: *The Wake of the 'Bounty'*, London, 1953.

Young, Rosalind Amelia: *Mutiny of the 'Bounty' and Story of
Pitcairn Island 1790–1894*, Oakland, California, 1894.

CONTENTS

A VOYAGE TO THE SOUTH SEA,

UNDERTAKEN BY COMMAND OF

HIS MAJESTY,

FOR THE PURPOSE OF

CONVEYING THE BREAD-FRUIT TREE TO THE WEST INDIES,

IN HIS MAJESTY's SHIP THE BOUNTY,

COMMANDED BY

LIEUTENANT *WILLIAM BLIGH.*

INCLUDING AN ACCOUNT OF THE

MUTINY ON BOARD THE SAID SHIP,

AND THE

SUBSEQUENT VOYAGE of Part of the CREW, in the SHIP's BOAT,

From TOFOA, one of the FRIENDLY ISLANDS,

To TIMOR, a DUTCH SETTLEMENT in the East Indies.

THE WHOLE ILLUSTRATED WITH CHARTS, &c.

———————

PUBLISHED BY PERMISSION OF THE

LORDS COMMISSIONERS OF THE ADMIRALTY.

———————

LONDON:

PRINTED FOR GEORGE NICOL, BOOKSELLER TO HIS MAJESTY, PALL-MALL.

M.DCC.XCII.

ADVERTISEMENT

AT the time I published the *Narrative of the Mutiny on Board the 'Bounty'* it was my intention that the preceding part of the voyage should be contained in a separate account. This method I have since been induced to alter. The reason of the narrative appearing first was for the purpose of communicating early information concerning an event which had attracted the public notice: and being drawn up in a hasty manner, it required many corrections. Some circumstances likewise were omitted; and the notation of time used in the *Narrative*, being according to sea reckoning, in which the days begin and end at noon, must have produced a degree of obscurity and confusion to readers accustomed only to the civil mode. And this would have increased, as the remainder of the voyage, on account of the numerous shore occurrences at Otaheite and elsewhere, could not with clearness and propriety have been related in any other than the usual manner of reckoning.

Besides remedying these inconveniencies, I have thought a fuller account of our passage from Timor to Europe than that contained in the *Narrative* would not be unacceptable. These reasons, with the manifest convenience of comprising the whole voyage in one continued narrative, in preference to letting it appear in disjointed accounts, will, it is hoped, be allowed a sufficient excuse for having varied from the original intention. Nevertheless, for the accommodation of the purchasers of the *Narrative* already published, those who desire it will be supplied with the other parts of the voyage separate; i.e. the part previous to the mutiny, and the additional account after leaving Timor.

(WILLIAM BLIGH)

A VOYAGE TO THE SOUTH SEA, ETC.

CHAPTER I

Plan of the expedition.—Outfit, and occurrences to the time of leaving England.—Description of the bread-fruit.

THE king having been graciously pleased to comply with a request from the merchants and planters interested in His Majesty's West India possessions, that the bread-fruit tree might be introduced into those islands, a vessel, proper for the undertaking, was bought and taken into dock at Deptford, to be provided with the necessary fixtures and preparations for executing the object of the voyage. These were completed according to a plan of my much honoured friend, Sir Joseph Banks, which, in the event, proved the most advantageous that could have been adopted for the intended purpose.

The ship was named the *Bounty*: I was appointed to command her on the 16th of August 1787. Her burthen was nearly two hundred and fifteen tons; her extreme length of deck, ninety feet ten inches; extreme breadth, twenty-four feet three inches; and height in the hold under the beams, at the main hatchway, ten feet three inches. In the cockpit were the cabins of the surgeon, gunner, botanist, and clerk, with a steward-room and storerooms. The between decks was divided in the following manner: the great cabin was appropriated for the preservation of the plants, and extended as far forward as the after hatchway. It had two large skylights, and on each side three scuttles for air, and was fitted with a false floor cut full of holes to contain the garden-pots, in which the plants were to be brought home. The deck was covered with lead, and at the foremost corners of the cabin were fixed pipes to carry off the water that drained from the plants, into tubs placed below to save it for future use. I had a small cabin on one side to sleep in, adjoining to the great cabin, and a place near the middle of the ship to eat in. The bulkhead of this apartment was at the after-part of the main hatchway, and on each side of it were the berths of the mates and midshipmen; between these berths the arm's-chest was placed. The cabin of the master, in which was always kept

3

the key of the arms, was opposite to mine. This particular
description of the interior parts of the ship is rendered necessary
by the event of the expedition.

The ship was masted according to the proportion of the Navy;
but, on my application, the masts were shortened, as I thought
them too much for her considering the nature of the voyage.

On the 3rd of September the ship came out of dock, but the
carpenters and joiners remained on board much longer, as they
had a great deal of work to finish.

The next material alteration made in the fitting out was
lessening the quantity of iron and other ballast. I gave directions that only nineteen tons of iron should be taken on board
instead of the customary proportion, which was forty-five tons.
The stores and provisions I judged would be fully sufficient to
answer the purpose of the remainder, for I am of opinion that
many of the misfortunes which attend ships in heavy storms
of wind are occasioned by too much dead weight in their
bottoms.

The establishment of men and officers for the ship were as
follows:

1	lieutenant to command
1	master
1	boatswain
1	gunner
1	carpenter
1	surgeon
2	master's mates
2	midshipmen
2	quartermasters
1	quartermaster's mate
1	boatswain's mate
1	gunner's mate
1	carpenter's mate
1	carpenter's crew
1	sailmaker
1	armourer
1	corporal
1	clerk and steward
23	able seamen
44	

Two skilful and careful men were appointed, at Sir Joseph Banks's recommendation, to have the management of the plants intended to be brought home: the one, David Nelson, who had been on similar employment in Captain Cook's last voyage; the other, William Brown, as an assistant to him. With these two our whole number amounted to forty-six.

It was proposed that our route to the Society Islands should be round Cape Horn, and the greatest dispatch became necessary, as the season was already far advanced; but the shipwrights not being able to complete their work by the time the ship was ready in other respects, our sailing was unavoidably retarded. However, by the 4th of October the pilot came on board to take us down the river; on the 9th we fell down to Long Reach, where we received our gunner's stores and guns, four four-pounders and ten swivels.

The ship was stored and victualled for eighteen months. In addition to the customary allowance of provisions, we were supplied with four krout, portable soup, essence of malt, dried malt, and a proportion of barley and wheat in lieu of oatmeal. I was likewise furnished with a quantity of ironwork and trinkets, to serve in our intercourse with the natives in the South Seas; and from the Board of Longitude I received a time-keeper, made by Mr Kendal.

On the 15th I received orders to proceed to Spithead, but the winds and weather were so unfavourable that we did not arrive there till the 4th of November. On the 24th I received from Lord Hood, who commanded at Spithead, my final orders. The wind, which for several days before had been favourable, was now turned directly against us. On the 28th the ship's company received two months' pay in advance, and on the following morning we worked out to St Helens, where we were obliged to anchor.

We made different unsuccessful attempts to get down Channel, but contrary winds and bad weather constantly forced us back to St Helens, or Spithead, until Sunday the 23rd of December, when we sailed with a fair wind.

During our stay at Spithead, the rate of the timepiece was several times examined by Mr Bailey's observations at the Portsmouth observatory. On the 19th of December, the last time of its being examined on shore, it was 1′ 52″, 5 too fast for mean time, and then losing at the rate of 1″, 1 per day; and at this rate I estimate its going when we sailed.

The object of all the former voyages to the South Seas under-taken by the command of his present majesty has been the advancement of science and the increase of knowledge. This voyage may be reckoned the first the intention of which has been to derive benefit from those distant discoveries. For the more fully comprehending the nature and plan of the expedition, and that the reader may be possessed of every information necessary for entering on the following sheets, I shall here lay before him a copy of the instructions I received from the Admiralty, and likewise a short description of the bread-fruit.

> *By the Commissioners for executing the office of Lord High Admiral of Great Britain and Ireland, etc.*

WHEREAS the king, upon a representation from the merchants and planters interested in His Majesty's West India possessions, that the introduction of the bread-fruit tree into the islands of those seas, to constitute an article of food, would be of very essential benefit to the inhabitants, hath, in order to promote the interests of so respectable a body of his subjects (especially in an instance which promises general advantage) thought fit that measures should be taken for the procuring some of those trees, and conveying them to the said West India islands: And whereas the vessel under your command hath, in consequence thereof, been stored and victualled for that service, and fitted with proper conveniences and necessaries for the preservation of as many of the said trees as, from her size, can be taken on board her; and you have been directed to receive on board her the two gardeners, David Nelson and William Brown, who, from their knowledge of trees and plants, have been hired for the purpose of selecting such as shall appear to be of a proper species and size:

You are, therefore, in pursuance of His Majesty's pleasure, signified to us by Lord Sydney, one of his principal secretaries of state, hereby required and directed to put to sea in the vessel you command, the first favourable opportunity of wind and weather, and proceed with her as expeditiously as possible round Cape Horn to the Society Islands, situate in the southern ocean, in the latitude of about eighteen degrees south, and longitude of about two hundred and ten degrees east from Greenwich, where, according to the accounts given by the late Capt. Cook, and persons who accompanied him during his

voyages, the bread-fruit tree is to be found in the most
luxuriant state.

Having arrived at the above-mentioned islands, and taken
on board as many trees and plants as may be thought necessary (the better to enable you to do which, you have already
been furnished with such articles of merchandize and trinkets
as it is supposed will be wanted to satisfy the natives), you are
to proceed from thence through Endeavour Straits (which
separate New Holland from New Guinea) to Prince's Island,
in the Straits of Sunda, or, if it should happen to be more
convenient, to pass on the eastern side of Java to some port on
the north side of that island, where any bread-fruit trees which
may have been injured, or have died, may be replaced by man-
gosteens, duriens, jacks, nancas, lansas, and other fine fruit-
trees of that quarter, as well as the rice plant which grows upon
dry land; all of which species (or such of them as shall be
judged most eligible) you are to purchase on the best terms
you can from the inhabitants of that island, with the ducats
with which you have also been furnished for that purpose;
taking care, however, if the rice plants above-mentioned cannot
be procured at Java, to touch at Prince's Island for them,
where they are regularly cultivated.

From Prince's Island, or the Island of Java, you are to proceed round the Cape of Good Hope to the West Indies (calling
on your way thither at any places which may be thought necessary) and deposit one-half of such of the above-mentioned trees
and plants as may be then alive at His Majesty's botanical
garden at St Vincent, for the benefit of the Windward
Islands, and then go on to Jamaica: and having delivered the
remainder to Mr East, or such person or persons as may be
authorized by the governor and council of that island to receive
them; refreshed your people, and received on board such provisions and stores as may be necessary for the voyage, make the
best of your way back to England; repairing to Spithead, and sending to our secretary an account of your arrival and proceedings.

And whereas you will receive herewith a copy of the instructions which have been given to the above-mentioned gardeners
for their guidance, as well in procuring the said trees and plants,
and the management of them after they shall be put on board,
as for bringing to England a small sample of each species, and
such others as may be prepared by the superintendent of the
botanical garden at St Vincent, and by the said Mr East, or

others, for His Majesty's garden at Kew; you are hereby
required and directed to afford, and to give directions to your
officers and company to afford, the said gardeners every possible
aid and assistance, not only in the collecting of the said trees
and plants at the places before-mentioned, but for their preservation during their conveyance to the places of their destination.

Given under our hands the 20th November 1787.

> HOWE,
> CHAS. BRETT,
> RD. HOPKINS,
> J. LEVESON GOWER.

*To Lieut. Wm Bligh, commanding His
Majesty's armed vessel the 'Bounty,'
at Spithead.*

> By command of their Lordships,
> P. STEPHENS.

In the foregoing orders it is to be observed that I was particularly directed to proceed round Cape Horn, but, as the
season was so far advanced, and we were so long detained by
contrary winds, I made application to the Admiralty for discretional orders on that point; to which I received the following
answer:

> *By the Commissioners for executing the
> office of Lord High Admiral of Great
> Britain and Ireland, etc.*

THE season of the year being now so far advanced as to render
it probable, that your arrival, with the vessel you command,
on the southern coast of America, will be too late for your
passing round Cape Horn without much difficulty and hazard;
you are, in that case, at liberty (notwithstanding former orders)
to proceed in her to Otaheite, round the Cape of Good Hope.

Given under our hands the 18th December 1787.

> HOWE,
> CHAS. BRETT,
> BAYHAM.

*To Lieut. Wm Bligh, commanding His
Majesty's armed vessel the 'Bounty,'
at Spithead.*

> By command of their Lordships,
> P. STEPHENS.

The bread-fruit is so well known and described, that to attempt a new account of it would be unnecessary and useless. However, as it may contribute to the convenience of the reader, I have given the following extracts respecting it.

EXTRACT FROM THE ACCOUNT OF DAMPIER'S VOYAGE ROUND THE WORLD, PERFORMED IN 1688

'The bread-fruit (as we call it) grows on a large tree, as big and high as our largest apple trees. It hath a spreading head, full of branches and dark leaves. The fruit grows on the boughs like apples; it is as big as a penny-loaf when wheat is at five shillings the bushel; it is of a round shape, and hath a thick tough rind. When the fruit is ripe, it is yellow and soft, and the taste is sweet and pleasant. The natives of Guam use it for bread. They gather it when full-grown, while it is green and hard; then they bake it in an oven, which scorcheth the rind and makes it black; but they scrape off the outside black crust, and there remains a tender thin crust; and the inside is soft, tender, and white like the crumb of a penny-loaf. There is *neither seed nor stone* in the inside, but all is of a pure substance, like bread. It must be eaten new, for if it is kept above twenty-four hours it grows harsh and choky, but it is very pleasant before it is too stale. This fruit lasts in season *eight months* in the year, during which the natives eat *no other sort of food of bread kind*. I did never see of this fruit anywhere but here. The natives told us that there is plenty of this fruit growing on the rest of the Ladrone Islands; and I *did never hear of it anywhere else.*' [1]

EXTRACT FROM THE ACCOUNT OF LORD ANSON'S VOYAGE, PUBLISHED BY MR WALTER

'There was at Tinian a kind of fruit peculiar to these (Ladrone) islands, called by the Indians *rhymay*, but by us the *bread-fruit*; for it was constantly eaten by us, during our stay upon the island, [2] instead of bread, and so *universally preferred* that no ship's bread was expended in that whole interval. It grew upon a

[1] Vol. i, p. 296.
[2] About two months; viz. from the latter end of August to the latter end of October 1742.

tree which is somewhat lofty, and which towards the top divides into large and spreading branches. The leaves of this tree are of a remarkable deep green, are notched about the edges, and are generally from a foot to eighteen inches in length. The fruit itself is found indifferently on all parts of the branches. It is in shape rather elliptical than round; it is covered with a tough rind, and is usually seven or eight inches long; each of them grows singly, and not in clusters. This fruit is fittest to be used when it is full-grown, but still green; in which state, after it is properly prepared by being roasted in the embers, its taste has some distant resemblance to that of an artichoke's bottom, and its texture is not very different, for it is soft and spongy.'

EXTRACTS FROM THE ACCOUNT OF THE FIRST VOYAGE OF CAPTAIN COOK

In the Society Islands

'The bread-fruit grows on a tree that is about the size of a middling oak; its leaves are frequently a foot and a half long, of an oblong shape, deeply sinuated like those of the fig-tree, which they resemble in consistence and colour, and in the exuding of a white milky juice upon being broken. The fruit is about the size and shape of a child's head, and the surface is reticulated not much unlike a truffle; it is covered with a thin skin, and has a core about as big as the handle of a small knife. The eatable part lies between the skin and the core; it is as white as snow, and somewhat of the consistence of new bread: it must be roasted before it is eaten, being first divided into three or four parts. Its taste is insipid, with a slight sweetness somewhat resembling that of the crumb of wheaten bread mixed with a Jerusalem artichoke. [1]

'Of the many vegetables that have been mentioned already as serving them for food, the principal is the bread-fruit, to procure which costs them no trouble or labour but climbing a tree. The tree which produces it does not indeed shoot up spontaneously; but, if a man plants ten of them in his life-time, which he may do in about an hour, he will as completely fulfil his duty to his own and future generations as the native of our less temperate climate can do by ploughing in the cold

[1] *Hawkesworth's Voyages*, vol. ii, pp. 80–1.

winter, and reaping in the summer's heat, as often as these seasons return; even if, after he has procured bread for his present household, he should convert a surplus into money, and lay it up for his children.

'It is true, indeed, that the bread-fruit is not always in season; but coconuts, bananas, plantains, and a great variety of other fruits supply the deficiency.' [1]

EXTRACT FROM THE ACCOUNT OF CAPTAIN COOK'S LAST VOYAGE

In the Society Islands

'I (Captain Cook) have inquired very carefully into their manner of cultivating the bread-fruit tree at Otaheite, but was always answered that they never planted it. This, indeed, must be evident to every one who will examine the places where the young trees come up. It will be always observed that they spring from the roots of the old ones, which run along near the surface of the ground. So that the bread-fruit trees may be reckoned those that would naturally cover the plains, even supposing that the island was not inhabited, in the same manner that the white-barked trees, found at Van Diemen's Land, constitute the forests there. And from this we may observe, that the inhabitant of Otaheite, instead of being obliged to plant his bread, will *rather* be under the necessity of preventing its progress; which, I suppose, is sometimes done, to give room for trees of another sort, to afford him some variety in his food.' [2]

EXTRACTS FROM CAPTAIN KING'S NARRATIVE

In the Sandwich Islands

'The bread-fruit trees are planted, and flourish with great luxuriance, on rising grounds. . . . Where the hills rise almost perpendicularly in a great variety of peaked forms, their steep sides and the deep chasms between them are covered with trees, amongst which those of the bread-fruit were observed particularly to abound.' [3]

---

[1] Ibid. p. 197.   [2] Ibid. p. 145.
[3] Ibid. vol. iii, pp. 105, 114.

'The climate of the Sandwich Islands differs very little from that of the West India Islands, which lie *in the same latitude*. Upon the whole, perhaps, it may be rather more temperate.'[1]

'The bread-fruit trees thrive in these islands, not in such abundance, but produce double the quantity of fruit they do on the rich plains of Otaheite. The trees are nearly of the same height, but the branches begin to strike out from the trunk much lower, and with greater luxuriance.'[2]

CHAPTER II

Departure from England.—Arrival at Teneriffe.—Sail from thence. —Arrival off Cape Horn.—Severity of the weather.—Obliged to bear away for the Cape of Good Hope.

On Sunday morning the 23rd of December 1787 we sailed from Spithead, and, passing through the Needles, directed our course down channel, with a fresh gale of wind at east.   In the afternoon one of the seamen, in furling the main-top-gallant-sail, fell off the yard, and was so fortunate as to save himself by catching hold of the main-top-mast-stay in his fall.   At night the wind increased to a strong gale, with a heavy sea.   It moderated, however, on the 25th, and allowed us to keep our Christmas with cheerfulness; but the following day it blew a severe storm of wind from the eastward, which continued till the 29th, in the course of which we suffered greatly.   One sea broke away the spare yards and spars out of the starboard main chains.   Another heavy sea broke into the ship, and stove all the boats.   Several casks of beer that had been lashed upon deck were broke loose and washed overboard, and it was not without great difficulty and risk that we were able to secure the boats from being washed away entirely.   On the 29th we were in latitude 39° 35′ N. and longitude 14° 26′ W. when the gale abated, and the weather became fair.   Besides other mischief done to us by the storm, a large quantity of our bread was damaged and rendered useless, for the sea had stove in our stern and filled the cabin with water.   From this time to our

[1] Ibid. vol. iii, p. 115.   [2] Ibid. p. 120.

arrival at Teneriffe we had moderate weather, and winds mostly from the northward.

January the 4th. This forenoon we spoke a French ship, bound to the Mauritius. The next day, at nine in the forenoon, we saw the island of Teneriffe, bearing WSW½W., about twelve leagues distant. It was covered with a thick haze, except the north-westernmost part, which is a remarkable headland, resembling a horse's head, the ears very distinct. To the eastward of this head [1] lie two round rocks, the northern boundary of Teneriffe. I had a good observation at noon, by which I make the latitude of the two rocks 28° 44′ N., and their longitude by our timekeeper 16° 5′ W. To the southward of these, and near the shore, is a high needle rock; about four leagues farther to the southward the coast inclines towards the west to the road of Santa Cruz, where we anchored at half-past nine on Sunday morning, in twenty-five fathoms water, and moored along shore in the same depth, with the cupola tower of the church of St Francis bearing W½N., one mile, the east part of the road E. by N., the castle on the south point SW., and the west part of the Grand Canary SSE. A Spanish packet, bound to Corunna, an American brig, and several other vessels, were lying here.

As soon as the ship was anchored, I sent an officer (Mr Christian) to wait on the governor, and to acquaint him I had put in to obtain refreshments and to repair the damages we had sustained in bad weather. To this I had a very polite answer from the governor,[2] that I should be supplied with whatever the island afforded. I had also directed the officer to acquaint him that I would salute, provided an equal number of guns were to be returned; but as I received an extraordinary answer to this part of my message, purporting that his excellency did not return the same number but to persons equal in rank to himself, this ceremony was omitted.

During this interval I was visited by the port-master (Captain Adams) and shortly afterwards several officers came on board from his excellency, to compliment me on my arrival. As soon as the ship was moored I went on shore and paid my respects to him.

On Monday morning I began to forward the ship's business with the utmost dispatch, and gave the necessary directions to Messrs Collogan & Sons, the contractors, for the supplies I

[1] S. 82° E. by the compass.   [2] Marquis de Brancheforté.

wanted. I also got leave of the governor for Mr Nelson to
range the hills and examine the country in search of plants and
natural curiosities.

As there was a great surf on the shore I bargained for everything I wanted to be brought off by the shore boats, and
agreed to give five shillings per ton for water. Very good wine
was bought at ten pounds per pipe, the contract price; but the
superior quality was fifteen pounds, and some of this was not
much inferior to the best London Madeira. I found this was an
unfavourable season for other refreshments: Indian corn,
potatoes, pumpkins, and onions were all very scarce, and
double the price of what they are in summer. Beef also was
difficult to be procured, and exceedingly poor; the price nearly
sixpence farthing per pound. The corn was three current
dollars per fanega, which is full five shillings per bushel; and
biscuit at twenty-five shillings for the hundred pounds.
Poultry was so scarce that a good fowl cost three shillings. This
is, therefore, not a place for ships to expect refreshments at a
reasonable price at this time of the year, wine excepted; but
from March to November supplies are plentiful, particularly
fruit, of which at this time we could procure none, except a few
dried figs and some bad oranges.

During our stay here the weather was fair, with NE. winds
and calms, and small drizzling rain in the night. The thermometer from 66° to 69° at noon in the shade. I could make
no lunar observations for the longitude, but by the help of the
time-keeper I have computed the situation of the town of
Santa Cruz to be 28° 28′ N. latitude, and 16° 18′ W. longitude.
I observed the variation by two compasses to be 20° 1′ W.
This much exceeded what I could have imagined, for in 1776
I observed it only 14° 40′ W., a difference of above five degrees
in eleven years; and this makes me reflect on the uncertainty
of obtaining the exact deviation of the magnetic pole, and of
course its annual variation, which never can be accurately
ascertained, unless the observations are made always in one
spot, and with the same compass.

Teneriffe, though considerably without the tropic, is so nearly
within the limits of the trade wind that navigators generally
steer to it from the eastward. The road of Santa Cruz lies on
the east side of the island, at the end of a range of craggy hills,
barren and very lofty; along which you sail W. by S. by compass
into the road, with a sea unfathomable until near the shore.

The anchoring ground may be accounted from fifty fathoms to twenty, or even fifteen. The bank is very steep, and gives but little time to sound, for which reason it should be done effectually with a heavy lead, or a ship will be too near in before a stranger is aware of it. He will likewise too soon expect to find bottom, owing to the great deception of the adjacent high land. To obviate these difficulties, it is necessary to observe, that while a town which lies some distance to the southward of Santa Cruz is open with the castle on the south part of the road, though you may appear near to the shore there is no anchorage; but after it is shut entirely in you get on the bank. The church bearing W., or W. by S., and the south point of the road SW½S., to SW. by W., is a good situation for anchoring; the depth about twenty-five fathoms. The distance from the shore will be three-quarters of a mile, and the southernmost land that can be seen then will be a half or quarter point of the compass farther out than the south point of the road.

The bottom is black soft mud, with some patches of rocks; for which reason vessels that lie here any length of time buoy their cables. This precaution, besides being useful in that particular, they think makes them ride more easy when there is much sea setting into the road, which, with the wind any way to the southward of east, or at south-west, must be very considerable; it is therefore usual to moor with four anchors, though more than two are scarce ever of use. Mooring is, however, advisable if a ship is only to remain twenty-four hours, and the tighter the better, that the cables may keep clear of the ground.

The landing on the beach is generally impracticable with our own boats, at least without great risk; but there is a very fine pier, on which people may land without difficulty if there is not much swell in the road. To this pier the water is conveyed by pipes for the use of shipping, and for which all merchant ships pay.

There is a degree of wretchedness and want among the lower class of people, which is not anywhere so common as among the Spanish and Portuguese settlements. To alleviate these evils the present governor of Teneriffe has instituted a most charitable society, which he takes the trouble to superintend; and by considerable contributions a large airy dwelling, that contains one hundred and twenty poor girls, and as many men and boys, has been built, and endowed with a sufficiency of land round it, not only for all present purposes, but for enlarging the building for more objects of charity as their funds increase.

I had the honour to be shown by his excellency this asylum (Hospicio, they call it), where there appeared in every counte-nance the utmost cheerfulness and content. The decency and neatness of the dress of the young females, with the order in which they were arranged at their spinning-wheels and looms, in an extensive airy apartment, was admirable. A governess inspected and regulated all their works, which were the manu-facturing of ribbons of all colours, coarse linens, and tapes, all which were managed and brought to perfection by themselves from the silk and flax in their first state; even the dyeing of the colours is performed by them. These girls are received for five years, at the end of which they are at liberty to marry, and have for their portions their wheel and loom, with a sum of money proportioned to the state of the fund, which is assisted by the produce of their labour, and at this time was estimated at two thousand dollars per annum.

The men and boys are not less attended to. They are em-ployed in coarser work, blanketing and all kinds of common woollens; if they become infirm they spend the remainder of their days here comfortably, and under a watchful inspector, who attends them in the same manner as the governess does the girls. They are all visited every day by the governor, and a clergyman attends them every evening. By this humane institution a number of people are rendered useful and indus-trious, in a country where the poor, from the indulgence of the climate, are too apt to prefer a life of inactivity, though attended with wretchedness, to obtaining the comforts of life by industry and labour.

The number of inhabitants in the island, I was informed, were estimated at between eighty and one hundred thousand. Their annual export of wine is twenty thousand pipes, and of brandy half that quantity. Vessels are frequently here from St Eustatia, and from thence a great quantity of Teneriffe wine is carried to the different parts of the West Indies, under the name of Madeira.

Teneriffe is considered of more value than all the other Canaries; the inhabitants, however, in scarce seasons receive supplies from the Grand Canary; but their vineyards here are said to be greatly superior. Their produce of corn, though exceedingly good, is not sufficient for their consumption; and, owing to this, the Americans have an advantageous trade here for their flour and grain, and take wine in return.

The town of Santa Cruz is about half a mile in extent each way, built in a regular manner, and the houses in general large and airy, but the streets are very ill-paved. I am told that they are subject to few diseases, but if any epidemic distemper breaks out it is attended with the most fatal consequences, particularly the smallpox, the bad effects of which they now endeavour to counteract by inoculation. For this reason they are very circumspect in admitting ships to have communication with the shore without bills of health.

A sloop from London, called the *Chance*, William Meridith, master, bound to Barbadoes, out nineteen days from the Downs, came into the road the day before we sailed. She had suffered much by the bad weather; but, having brought no bill of health, the governor would not allow any person to come on shore, unless I could vouch for them, that no epidemic disease raged in England at the time they sailed, which I was able to do, it being nearly at the same time that I left the land; and by that means they had the governor's permission to receive the supplies they wanted, without being obliged to perform quarantine.

Having finished our business at Teneriffe, on Thursday the 10th we sailed with the wind at SE., our ship's company all in good health and spirits.

I now divided the people into three watches, and gave the charge of the third watch to Mr Fletcher Christian, one of the mates. I have always considered this as a desirable regulation, when circumstances will admit of it, on many accounts; and am persuaded that unbroken rest not only contributes much towards the health of a ship's company, but enables them more readily to exert themselves in cases of sudden emergency.

As it was my wish to proceed to Otaheite without stopping, I ordered everybody to be at two-thirds allowance of bread. I also directed the water for drinking to be filtered through dripstones that I had bought at Teneriffe for that purpose.

In the evening we passed the south end of Teneriffe, which is a round lump of land that, from the lowness of the contiguous land, has at a distance the appearance of a separate island. By our run from the bay of Santa Cruz, I make the latitude of the south end of Teneriffe to be 28° 6′ N.

We ran all night towards the SSW., having the wind at SE. The next morning we could see nothing of the land. I now made the ship's company acquainted with the intent of the voyage; and, having been permitted to hold out this encouragement to them, I gave assurances of the certainty of promotion to every one whose endeavours should merit it.

The winds for some days after leaving Teneriffe were mostly from the southward. Fishing-lines and tackle were distributed amongst the people, and some dolphins were caught.

On the 17th the wind came round to the NE., and continued steady in that quarter till the 25th, on which day, at noon, we were in 3° 54' N. As the cloudiness of the sky gave us reason to expect much rain, we prepared the awnings with hoses for the convenience of saving water, in which we were not disappointed. From this time to our meeting with the SE. trade wind we had much wet weather, the air close and sultry, with calms and light variable winds, generally from the southward.

On the 29th there was so heavy a fall of rain that we caught seven hundred gallons of water.

On the 31st, latitude at noon, 2° 5' N., found a current setting to the NE., at the rate of fourteen miles in the twenty-four hours. The thermometer was at 82° in the shade, and 81° ½ at the surface of the sea, so that the air and the water were within half a degree of the same temperature. At eight o'clock in the evening we observed a violent rippling in the sea, about half a mile to the NW. of us, which had very much the appearance of breakers. This I imagine to have been occasioned by a large school (or multitude) of fish, as it was exactly in the track the ship had passed, so that if any real shoal had been there, we must have seen it at the close of the evening, when a careful look-out was always kept. However, if it had appeared ahead of us, instead of astern, I should certainly have tacked to avoid it. To such appearances I attribute the accounts of many shoals within the tropics, which cannot be found anywhere but in maps. Our latitude at this time was 2° 8' N., and longitude 19° 43' W. The next day we had more of these appearances, from the number of schools of fish by which the ship was surrounded.

Saturday the 2nd. This morning we saw a sail to the NNW., but at too great a distance to distinguish what she was.

Monday the 4th. Had very heavy rain, during which we nearly filled all our empty water casks. So much wet weather, with the closeness of the air, covered everything with mildew. The ship was aired below with fires, and frequently sprinkled with vinegar; and every little interval of dry weather was taken advantage of to open all the hatchways and clean the ship, and to have all the people's wet things washed and dried.

With this weather, and light unsteady winds, we advanced but 2½ degrees in twelve days; at the end of which time we were relieved by the SE. trade wind, which we fell in with on the 6th at noon in latitude 1° 21′ N. and longitude 20° 42′ W.

The next afternoon we crossed the equinoctial line, in longitude 21° 50′ W. The weather became fine, and the SE. trade wind was fresh and steady, with which we kept a point free from the wind and got to the southward at a good rate.

The weather continuing dry, we put some of our bread in casks, properly prepared for its reception, to preserve it from vermin. This experiment, we afterwards found, answered exceedingly well.

On the 16th, at daylight, we saw a sail to the southward. The next day we came up with her, and found her to be the *British Queen*, Simon Paul, master, from London, bound to the Cape of Good Hope on the whale fishery. She sailed from Falmouth the 5th of December, eighteen days before I left Spithead. By this ship I wrote to England. At sunset she was almost out of sight astern.

Monday the 18th. In the course of this day's run the variation changed from west to east. According to our observations, the true and magnetic meridians coincided in latitude 20° 0′ S., and longitude 31° 15′ W. At noon we were in latitude 20° 44′ S., and longitude 31° 23′ W. In our advances towards the south the wind had gradually veered round to the east, and was at this time at ENE. The weather, after crossing the Line, had been fine and clear, but the air so sultry as to occasion great faintness, the quicksilver in the thermometer in the daytime standing at between 81 and 83 degrees, and one time at 85 degrees. In our passage through the northern tropic the air was temperate, the sun having then high south declination and the weather being generally fine till we lost the NE. trade wind, but such a thick haze surrounded the horizon that no object could be seen except at a very small distance. The haze commonly cleared away at sunset and gathered again at sunrise. Between the NE. and SE. trade winds, the calms and rains, if of long continuance, are very liable to produce sickness unless great attention is paid to keeping the ship clean and wholesome by giving all the air possible, drying between decks with fires, and drying and airing the people's clothes and bedding.

Besides these precautions, we frequently wetted with vinegar, and every evening the pumps were used as ventilators. With these endeavours to secure health, we passed the low latitudes without a single complaint.

The currents we met with were by no means regular, nor have I ever found them so in the middle of the ocean. However, from the Channel to the southward, as far as Madeira, there is generally a current setting to the SSE.

On the evening of the 21st a ship was seen in the NE., but at too great a distance to distinguish of what country. The next day the wind came round to the N. and NW., so that we could no longer consider ourselves in the trade wind. Our latitude at noon was 25° 55′ S., longitude 36° 29′ W. Variation of the compass three degrees east.

Saturday the 23rd. Towards night the wind died away and we had some heavy showers of rain, of which we profited by saving a ton of good water. The next day we caught a shark and five dolphins.

Tuesday the 26th. We bent new sails and made other necessary preparations for encountering the weather that was to be expected in a high latitude. Our latitude at noon was 29° 38′ S., longitude 41° 44′ W. Variation 7° 13′ E. In the afternoon, the wind being westerly and blowing strong in squalls, some butterflies and other insects, like what we call horse-flies, were blown on board of us. No birds were seen except sheerwaters. Our distance from the coast of Brazil at this time was above a hundred leagues.

Sunday the 2nd. In the forenoon, after seeing that every person was clean, divine service was performed, according to my usual custom on this day. I gave to Mr Fletcher Christian, whom I had before directed to take charge of the third watch, a written order to act as lieutenant.

Saturday the 8th. We were at noon in latitude 36° 50′ S. and longitude 52° 53′ W. The last four days we several times tried for soundings, without finding bottom, though considerably to the westward of Captain Wallis's track, who had soundings at fifty-four fathoms depth, in latitude 35° 40′ S. and longitude 49° 54′ W. This day we tried with two hundred and forty fathoms of line, but did not find bottom; at the same time, observing a rippling in the water, we tried the current by mooring a keg with one hundred fathoms of line, by which it appeared to run to the NNW., at the rate of a mile and a half

per hour. By the noon observation, however, we were eighteen
miles to the southward of our reckoning. In the afternoon we
saw a turtle floating, and, not having much wind, hoisted a
boat out and sent after it; but it was found to be in a putrid
state, with a number of crabs feeding upon it.

The change of temperature began now to be sensibly felt,
there being a variation in the thermometer since yesterday of
eight degrees. That the people might not suffer by their own
negligence, I gave orders for their light tropical clothing to be
put by, and made them dress in a manner more suited to a cold
climate. I had provided for this before I left England by
giving directions for such clothes to be purchased as were
necessary.

Monday the 10th. In the forenoon we struck soundings at
eighty-three fathoms depth, our latitude 40° 8′ S. and longitude
55° 40′ W. This I conclude to have been near the edge of
the bank, for the wind being at SSW. we stood towards the
SE., and, after running fourteen miles in that direction, we
could find no bottom with one hundred and sixty fathoms of
line. In the night we stood towards the WSW., with a southerly
wind, and got again into soundings. The next day we saw a
great number of whales of an immense size, that had two spout-
holes on the back of the head. Upon a complaint made to me
by the master, I found it necessary to punish Matthew Quintal,
one of the seamen, with two dozen lashes, for insolence and
mutinous behaviour. Before this I had not had occasion to
punish any person on board.

On the 12th we caught a porpoise by striking it with the
grains. Every one eat heartily of it, and it was so well liked
that no part was wasted.

On the 14th, in the afternoon, we saw a land-bird like a lark,
and passed part of a dead whale that had been left by some
whalers after they had taken the blubber off. Saw, likewise,
two strange sail. The next day, at noon, our latitude was
43° 6′ S. and longitude 58° 42′ W. Had soundings at seventy-
five fathoms, the bottom a fine greenish sand. Saw two hawks.

On the 16th another ship was seen to the WNW., standing
to the northward. Latitude at noon 43° 34′ S. We continued
running to the southward, keeping in soundings.

On the 19th, at noon by my account, we were within twenty
leagues of Port Desire, but the wind blowing fresh from the
NW. with thick foggy weather, I did not attempt to make the

land. We passed a good deal of rock-weed, and saw many whales and albatrosses and other sea-birds.

On the 20th, at noon, our latitude was 50° 24′ S. and longitude 65° 50′ W. In the afternoon, the wind, which had for some time past been northerly, suddenly shifted to the WSW., and blew hard. We steered to the SSE., and on the 23rd, at two o'clock in the morning, we discovered the coast of Terra del Fuego bearing SE. At nine in the forenoon we were off Cape St Diego, the eastern part of Terra del Fuego. Observed the variation here to be 21° 23′ E. The wind being unfavourable, I thought it more advisable to go round to the eastward of Staten Land than to attempt passing through Straits le Maire. The two opposite coasts of the straits exhibited very different appearances. The land of Terra del Fuego hereabouts, though the interior parts are mountainous, yet near the coast is of a moderate height, and at the distance we were from it had not an unpromising appearance. The coast of Staten Land, near the straits, is mountainous and craggy, and remarkable for its high-peaked hills. Straits le Maire is a fair opening, which cannot well be mistaken; but if any doubt could remain, the different appearances of the opposite shores would sufficiently make the straits known.

I did not sail within less than six leagues of the coast, that we might have the wind more regular and avoid being exposed to the heavy squalls that came off from the land. At noon Cape St Anthony bore S., and the westernmost of New Year's Isles SE¼S., five or six leagues. Latitude observed 54° 28′ S., longitude 64° 4′ W.

The sight of New Year's harbour almost tempted me to put in, but the lateness of the season, and the people being in good health, determined me to lay aside all thoughts of refreshment until we should reach Otaheite. At two o'clock in the afternoon the easternmost of New Year's Isles, where Captain Cook observed the latitude to be 55° 40′ S., bore from us south four leagues. We saw the entrance isles of New Year's harbour, at the back of which the land is very craggy and mountainous. This must be a very convenient port to touch at, as the access to it is safe and easy. The harbour lies SSE., by compass, from the NE. part of the easternmost of the New Year's Islands.

About two leagues to the westward of Cape St John I observed the separation of the mountains that Captain Cook has taken notice of, which has the appearance of Staten Land, being there divided into two islands.

At sunset Cape St John bore SSE. five or six leagues. The land hereabouts is of less height and not so rugged as near New Year's Harbour. The night coming on, I could get no good view of the coast near the Cape, and at daylight next morning we were at too great a distance.

Monday the 24th. We had stood to the southward all night, with the wind at WSW. and SW. At eight in the morning Cape St John bore NW., ten leagues distant. Soon after we lost sight of the land.

From the result of my lunar observations, assisted by the time-keeper, I make the longitude of the west side of Straits le Maire to be 64° 48' W.; the easternmost of the New Year's Isles 63° 52' W.; and the longitude of Cape St John 63° 19' W.

In our run from the latitude of 12° S. to 48° S., the ship was set 2° 30' to the eastward by currents, and from the latitude of 48° S. to Staten Land the currents set us to the westward 2° 43', which I imagine to have been occasioned by an indraught into the Straits of Magellan.

From the time we lost sight of the land to the end of the month we were struggling with bad weather and contrary winds, but on the morning of the 31st the wind came to the NNE. and made us entertain great hopes that we should be able to accomplish our passage round the Cape without much difficulty. At noon we were in latitude 60° 1' S. and in 71° 45' W. longitude, which is 8° 26' W. of the meridian of Cape St John. This flattering appearance was not of long continuance; in the night the wind became variable, and next day settled again in the W. and NW., with very bad weather.

On the 2nd, in the morning, the wind, which had blown fresh all night from the NW., came round to the SW. and increased to a heavy gale. At six in the morning the storm exceeded what I had ever met with before, and the sea, from the frequent shifting of the wind, running in contrary directions, broke exceeding high. Our ship, however, lay to very well, under a main and fore-stay sail. The gale continued, with severe squalls of hail and sleet, the remainder of this and all the next day. On the 4th the wind was less violent, but far from moderate. With so much bad weather I found it necessary to keep a constant fire, night and day, and one of the watch always attended to dry the people's wet clothes; and this,

I have no doubt, contributed as much to their health as to their comfort.

Our companions in this inhospitable region were albatrosses and two beautiful kinds of birds, the small blue petrel and pintada. A great many of these were frequently about the wake of the ship, which induced the people to float a line, with hooks baited, to endeavour to catch them, and their attempts were successful. The method they used was to fasten the bait a foot or two before the hook, and, by giving the line a sudden jerk when the bird was at the bait, it was hooked in the feet or body.

On the 6th the weather was moderate, and continued so till the 9th, with the wind veering between the NW. and SW., of which we were able to take advantage.

On the 7th, observed the variation 27° 9′ E., our latitude 60° 24′ S. and longitude 75° 54′ W. On the 9th, at noon, we were in latitude 59° 31′ S. and our longitude 76° 58′ W., which is farther to the west than we had yet been. The weather was now unfavourable again, blowing strong from the westward, with a high sea.

On the 10th we saw some fish, which appeared spotted, and about the size of bonetos; these were the only fish we had seen in this high latitude.

Saturday the 12th. The stormy weather continued with a great sea. The ship now began to complain, and required to be pumped every hour, which was no more than we had reason to expect from such a continuance of gales of wind and high seas. The decks also became so leaky that I was obliged to allot the great cabin, of which I made little use except in fine weather, to those people who had wet berths to hang their hammocks in, and by this means the between-decks was less crowded.

Every morning all the hammocks were taken down from where they hung, and when the weather was too bad to keep them upon deck they were put in the cabin, so that the between-decks were cleaned daily and aired with fires if the hatchways could not be opened. With all this bad weather we had the additional mortification to find, at the end of every day, that we were losing ground; for notwithstanding our utmost exertions, and keeping on the most advantageous tacks (which, if the weather had been at all moderate, would have sufficiently answered our purpose), yet the greater part of the time we were doing little better than drifting before the wind.

Sunday the 13th. Birds as usual were about the ship, and some of them caught; and, for the first time since we left Staten Land, we saw some whales. This morning, owing to the violent motion of the ship, the cook fell and broke one of his ribs, and another man, by a fall, dislocated his shoulder. The gunner, who had the charge of the watch, was laid up with the rheumatism: and this was the first sick list that appeared on board the ship. The time of full moon, which was approaching, made me entertain hopes that after that period we should experience some change of wind or weather in our favour; but the event did not at all answer our expectations. The latitude, at noon this day, was 58° 9′ S. and longitude 76° 1′ W.

As we caught a good many birds, but which were all lean and tasted fishy, we tried an experiment upon them, which succeeded admirably. By keeping them cooped up, and cramming them with ground corn, they improved wonderfully in a short time, so that the pintada birds became as fine as ducks and the albatrosses were as fat and not inferior in taste to fine geese. Some of the latter birds were caught that measured seven feet between the extremities of the wings when spread. This unexpected supply came very opportunely for none of our live stock remained except hogs, the sheep and poultry not being hardy enough to stand the severity of the weather.

Sunday the 20th. This morning the wind died away, and we had a calm for a few hours, which gave us hopes that the next would be a more favourable wind. A hog was killed for the ship's company, which gave them an excellent meal. Towards noon to our great disappointment the wind sprung up again from the westward, and in the afternoon blew strong, with snow and hail storms.

Monday the 21st. This was the second day after the full moon, but, as I have remarked before, it had no influence on the weather. At noon our latitude was 58° 31′ S. and longitude 70° 7′ W., which is near seven degrees to the eastward of our situation on the morning of the 9th instant, when we had advanced the farthest in our power to the westward, being then in 76° 58′ W., three degrees to the west of Cape Deseada, the west part of the Straits of Magellan; and at this time we were 3° 52′ to the east of it and hourly losing ground.

It was with much concern I saw how hopeless, and even unjustifiable it was, to persist any longer in attempting a passage this way to the Society Islands. We had been thirty days in this tempestuous ocean. At one time we had advanced so far to the westward as to have a fair prospect of making our passage round; but from that period hard gales of westerly wind had continued without intermission, a few hours excepted, which, to borrow an expression in Lord Anson's *Voyage*, were 'like the elements drawing breath to return upon us with redoubled violence.' The season was now too far advanced for us to expect more favourable winds or weather, and we had sufficiently experienced the impossibility of beating round against the wind, or of advancing at all without the help of a fair wind, for which there was little reason to hope. Another consideration which had great weight with me was that if I persisted in my attempt this way and should, after all, fail to get round, it would occasion such a loss of time, that our arrival at Otaheite, soon enough to return in the proper season by the East Indies, would be rendered precarious. On the other hand, the prevalence of the westerly winds in high southern latitudes left me no reason to doubt of making a quick passage to the Cape of Good Hope, and thence to the eastward round New Holland. Having maturely considered all circumstances I determined to bear away for the Cape of Good Hope, and at five o'clock on the evening of the 22nd, the wind then blowing strong at west, I ordered the helm to be put a-weather, to the great joy of every person on board. Our sick list at this time had increased to eight, mostly with rheumatic complaints. In other respects the people were in good health, though exceedingly jaded.

The passage round Cape Horn into the South Seas during the summer months has seldom been attended with difficulty, and is to be preferred in the moderate seasons to the more distant route to the eastward, round the Cape of Good Hope and New Holland. If we had been one month earlier, or perhaps less, I doubt not but we should have effected our passage.

The soundings that are met with off the coast of America, from the latitude of 36° S. to the southward, are very convenient to enable ships to judge of their distance from the land, as thick fogs are very frequent near that coast. If the winds are favourable, to go through Straits le Maire must considerably shorten the passage round Cape Horn, as all the distance saved is so much gained to the westward. I am informed that several harbours have been lately discovered by the South Sea whalers on the north side of Staten Island that afford safe anchorage, with supplies of wood and water.

While we were off Cape Horn I did not observe that our situation was at all affected by currents.

CHAPTER III

Passage towards the Cape of Good Hope, and search after Tristan da Cunha.—Arrival at False Bay.—Occurrences there.—Reports concerning the 'Grosvenor's' people.—Departure from the Cape.

THE westerly winds and stormy weather continuing, gave me no reason to repent of my determination. On the 25th, at noon, we were in latitude 54° 16′ S. and longitude 57° 4′ W. The nearest of the Falkland Islands, by my reckoning, then bore N. 13° W., distance twenty-three leagues. Our stock of water being sufficient to serve us to the Cape of Good Hope, I did not think it worth while to stop at these islands, as the refreshment we might obtain there would scarce repay us for the expense of time. We therefore continued our course towards the NE. and ENE.

On the 9th of May, at eight o'clock in the evening, we were near the situation of Tristan da Cunha, our latitude being 37° 7′ S. and longitude 15° 26′ W. All the afternoon the weather had been clear enough for land of a moderate height to be seen at least seven leagues; I therefore concluded that we had not yet passed the meridian of the island, for the most western position given to it from any authority is 15° 0′ W.

As I wished to make this island we kept our wind on different tacks during the night, that we might be nearly in the same place at daylight in the morning, as on the preceding evening. In the morning, no land being in sight, we continued to steer to the eastward.

We ran on all day, having clear weather, but without feeling anything to indicate our being near land. At noon our latitude observed was 37° 27′ S., which being more to the southward than we had reason to expect, I altered the course to the northward, and steered NE. all the afternoon. At six o'clock in the evening we were in latitude 37° 0′ S. and longitude 12° 42′ W., having a clear horizon, but not the least sign of being in the neighbourhood of land. With the night came thick rainy weather, and we were now to the eastward of the situation ascribed to Tristan da Cunha; I therefore determined to give over the search and to resume our course towards the Cape of Good Hope.

The island of Tristan da Cunha, by Robertson's *Elements*,

is laid down in 37° 12′ S. latitude and 13° 23′ W. longitude.
In Captain Cook's general map, prefixed to his last voyage, it is
placed in the same latitude, but in 15° W. longitude. From
our track, and the clearness of the weather, I am convinced,
if the latitude ascribed to it as above is correct, that it is not
to be found between the meridians of 16° 30′ W. and 12° 30′ W.
On the 13th I had a number of lunar observations for the longitude, the mean of which agreed exactly with the time-keeper.[1]

In this passage the weather was generally so cloudy that
I had few opportunities to make observations of any kind,
except for the noon latitudes. I could not determine when
we crossed the line of no variation. The two nearest observations to it were the first in 39° 51′ S. latitude and 26° 11′ W.
longitude, where the variation of the compass was found to
be 3° 17′ E.; and the other in latitude 35° 30′ S. and longitude 5° 21′ W., where I observed the variation 11° 35′ W.;
between these we had no intermediate observation for the
variation.

Thursday the 22nd. At two in the afternoon we saw the Table
Mountain of the Cape of Good Hope. As it is reckoned unsafe
riding in Table Bay at this time of the year, I steered for False
Bay. The next evening we anchored in the outer part, and on
the forenoon of the 24th got the ship secured in Simon's Bay,
which is in the inner part of False Bay. When moored, Noah's
Ark bore S. 35° E. three-quarters of a mile and the hospital
S. 72° W. We found lying here one outward bound Dutch
Indiaman, five other Dutch ships, and a French ship.

After saluting the fort, which was returned by an equal
number of guns, I went on shore, and dispatches were sent
away to Cape Town to acquaint the governor of our arrival.
A Dutch ship at this time lying in Table Bay, bound for Europe,
I sent letters by her to the Admiralty. It is very unusual for
ships to be in Table Bay so late in the year, on account of the
strong NW. winds. April is the time limited.

I gave the necessary directions for getting our wants supplied.
The ship required to be caulked in every part, for she was
become so leaky that we had been obliged to pump every hour
in our passage from Cape Horn. This we immediately set about,

---

[1] In Mr Dalrymple's collection of plans, which I had not with me, the
northernmost of the Islands of Tristan d'Acunha is placed in latitude
37° 22′ S. and longitude 13° 17′ W. I think it probable we missed them
by being too much to the northward.

as well as repairing our sails and rigging. The severe weather we had met with, and the leakiness of the ship, made it necessary to examine into the state of all the stores and provisions. Of the latter, a good deal was found damaged, particularly the bread. The time-keeper I took on shore to ascertain its rate, and other instruments, to make the necessary astronomical observations. Fresh meat, with soft bread and plenty of vegetables, were issued daily to the ship's company the whole time we remained here. A few days after our arrival I went over to Cape Town and waited on his excellency M. Van der Graaf, the governor, who obligingly arranged matters so much to our advantage that we scarcely felt the inconvenience of being at a distance from the Cape Town, whence we received all our supplies.

The Cape Town is considerably increased within the last eight years. Its respectability, with regard to strength, has kept pace with its other enlargements, and rendered it very secure against any attempt which is not made with considerable force. Great attention is paid to military order and discipline, and monthly signals are established to communicate with their shipping as they arrive near the coast, that they may not run unawares into the hands of an enemy. I found everything much dearer than when I was here in 1780. Sheep cost four Spanish dollars each, and were so small that it answered better to purchase the mutton, for the ship's daily use, at four-pence per pound.

During our stay here I took care to procure seeds and plants that would be valuable at Otaheite and the different places we might touch at in our way thither. In this I was greatly assisted by Colonel Gordon, the commander of the troops. In company with this gentleman, the loss of the *Grosvenor* East Indiaman was mentioned. On this subject Colonel Gordon expressed great concern, that from anything he had said hopes were still entertained to flatter the affectionate wishes of the surviving friends of those unfortunate people. He said that in his travels into the Kafir country he had met with a native who described to him that there was a white woman among his countrymen, who had a child, and that she frequently embraced the child and cried most violently. This was all he (the colonel) could understand, and being then on his return home, with his health much impaired by fatigue, the only thing that he could do was to make a friend of the native, by presents and promises of reward, on condition that he would take a letter to this woman and bring him back an answer. Accordingly he wrote letters in English, French, and Dutch, desiring that some sign or mark might be returned, either by writing with a burnt stick or by any means she should be able to devise, to satisfy him that she was there; and that on receiving such token from her, every effort should be made to ensure her safety and escape. But the Kafir, although apparently delighted with the commission which he had undertaken, never returned, nor has the colonel ever heard anything more of him, though he had been instructed in methods of conveying information through the Hottentot country.

To this account, that I may not again have occasion to introduce so melancholy a subject, I shall add the little information I received respecting it, when I revisited the Cape, in my return towards Europe. A reputable farmer of the name of Holhousen, who lives at Swellendam, eight days' journey from the Cape, had information from some Kafir Hottentots that at a kraal, or village, in their country there were white men and women. On this intelligence Mr Holhousen asked permission of the governor to make an expedition, with some of the farmers, into the country, requiring a thousand rix-dollars to bear his expenses. The governor referred him to Mr Wocke, the Landros of Graverennet, a new colony, in his way. But from the place where Mr Holhousen lives to the Landros, Mr Wocke's residence, is a month's journey, which he did not choose to undertake at an uncertainty, as Mr Wocke might have disapproved of the enterprise. It was in October last that Mr Holhousen offered to go on this service. He was one of the party who went along the sea-coast in search of these unfortunate people, when a few of them first made their appearance at the Cape. I am, however, informed that the Dutch farmers are fond of making expeditions into the country, that they may have opportunities of taking away cattle; and this, I apprehend, to be one of the chief reasons why undertakings of this kind are not encouraged.

On the 13th of June the Dublin East Indiaman arrived from England, on board of which ship was a party of the 77th Regiment under the command of Colonel Balfour.

The result of my lunar observations gave for the longitude of Simon's Bay 18° 48′ 34″ E., the latitude 34° 11′ 34″ S. The time-keeper likewise made the longitude 18° 47′ E. The

longitude, as established by former observations, is 18° 33′ E.
The variation of the compass on shore was 24° 4′ W., but on
board of the ship it was only 22° 28′ W. The time of high
water was three-quarters-past two on the full and change, and
it then flowed six feet.

With respect to the Cape Promontory, it lies about three
miles east of the meridian of Simon's Town. All the tables of
latitude and longitude place the Cape in 34° 29′ S. latitude, but
from many observations off it, with good instruments, I make
it to lie in 34° 23′ S., which agrees with its situation as laid
down in Major Rennel's map. The part which I call the Cape
is the southernmost point of the land between Table Bay and
False Bay, but the Dutch consider the westernmost part of the
coast to be the Cape.

On the 29th, being ready for sea, I took the time-keeper and
instruments on board. The error of the time-keeper was 3′ 33″,
2 too slow for the mean time at Greenwich, and its rate of
going 3″ per day, losing. The thermometer, during our stay
here, was from 51 to 66 degrees.

Tuesday the 1st. We had been thirty-eight days at this place,
and my people had received all the advantage that could be
derived from the refreshments of every kind that are here to
be met with. We sailed at four o'clock this afternoon, and
saluted the platform with thirteen guns as we ran out of the
bay, which were returned.

CHAPTER IV

*Passage towards Van Dieman's Land.—Make the Island of
St Paul.—Arrival in Adventure Bay.—Natives seen.—Sail
from Van Diemen's Land.*

WE lost sight of the land the day after leaving False Bay and
steered towards the ESE., having variable winds the first week,
with much thunder, lightning, and rain. The remainder of
this passage the winds were mostly between the S. and W.,
blowing strong. There were almost every day great numbers
of pintada, albatrosses, blue petrels, and other oceanic birds
about us; but it was observed that if the wind came from the
northward, only for a few hours, the birds generally left us, and
their presence again was the forerunner of a southerly wind.

Sunday the 13th. The variation of the compass was 30° 34′ W., which was the greatest variation we found in this track. Our latitude 36° 28′ S. and longitude 39° 0′ E.

Sunday the 20th. The latitude at noon was 40° 30′ S. and longitude 60° 7′ E. We were at this time scudding under the fore-sail and close-reefed main-top-sail, the wind blowing strong from the west. An hour after noon the gale increased, and blew with so much violence that the ship was almost driven forecastle under before we could get the sails clewed up. As soon as the sails were taken in we brought the ship to the wind, lowered the lower yards, and got the top-gallant-masts upon deck, which eased the ship very much. We remained lying to till eight the next morning, when we bore away under a reefed fore-sail. In the afternoon the sea ran so high that it became very unsafe to stand on; we therefore brought to the wind again, and remained lying to all night, without accident, excepting that the man at the steerage was thrown over the wheel, and much bruised.

Tuesday the 22nd. Towards noon the violence of the storm abated, and we again bore away under the reefed fore-sail. Our latitude, at noon, 38° 49′ S.; in the afternoon saw some whales.

We continued running to the eastward in this parallel, it being my intention to make the island St Paul. On Monday the 28th, at six in the morning, we saw the island, bearing E. by N., twelve leagues distant; between 10 and 11 o'clock we ran along the south side, at about a league distant from the shore. There was a verdure that covered the higher parts of the land, but I believe it was nothing more than moss, which is commonly found on the tops of most rocky islands in these latitudes. We saw several whales near the shore. The extent of this island is five miles from E. to W. and about two or three from N. to S. As we passed the east end we saw a remarkable high sugar-loaf rock, abreast of which, I have been informed, is good anchorage in twenty-three fathoms, the east point bearing SW. by S., by true compass. I had this information from the captain of a Dutch packet, in which I returned to Europe. He likewise said there was good fresh water on the island, and a hot spring, which boiled fish in as great perfection as on a fire. By his account the latitude, which he observed in the road, is 38° 39′ S.; and from the anchoring place the Island of Amsterdam was in sight to the northward. We had fair weather all the forenoon, but just at noon a squall came on, which was unfavourable for our observation. I had, however, two sets of double altitudes, and a good altitude exactly at noon, according to the time-keeper. The result of these give for the latitude of the centre of St Paul, 38° 47′ S. The longitude I make 77° 39′ E. The variation of the compass, taking the mean of what it was observed to be the day before we saw the island, and the day after, is 19° 30′ W.

At noon we were three leagues past the island. We kept on towards the ESE., and for several days continued to see rock-weed, which is remarked to be generally the case after ships pass St Paul's; but to the westward of it very seldom any is seen.

Wednesday the 13th. In latitude 44° 16′ S., longitude 122° 7′ E., I observed the variation of the compass to be 6° 23′ W. I had no opportunity to observe it again till in the latitude of 43° 56′ S., longitude 133° 16′ E., when it was 1° 38′ E., so that we had passed the line of no variation. In 1780, on board the *Resolution*, in latitude 44° 23′ S., longitude 131° 28′ E., the variation was observed 6° 0′ W., which is a remarkable difference. We had much bad weather, with snow and hail, and in our approach to Van Diemen's Land nothing was seen to indicate the nearness of the coast, except a seal, when we were within the distance of twenty leagues.

Tuesday the 19th. At two o'clock this afternoon we saw the rock named the Mewstone that lies near the SW. cape of Van Diemen's Land, bearing NE. about six leagues. The wind blew strong from the NW. As soon as we had passed the Mewstone we were sheltered from a very heavy sea, which ran from the westward. At eight o'clock at night we were abreast of the south cape, when the wind became light and variable. Saw several fires inland.

The Mewstone is a high bold rock that lies five leagues to the SE. of the SW. cape, and is the part that all ships bound this way should endeavour to make. Its latitude is 43° 46′ or 47′. Several islands lie to the northward, between that and the main, among which, bearing N. by W. from the Mewstone, is a high rock much resembling it; and NNE. from the Mewstone, on the mainland, is a remarkable high mountain, which in this direction appears notched like a cock's comb, but as viewed from the eastward seems round.

All the 20th we were endeavouring to get into Adventure Bay, but were prevented by variable winds. The next morning, at five o'clock, we anchored in the outer part, and at sunrise weighed again: at noon we anchored well in the bay, and moored the ship, Penguin Island bearing N. 57° ½ E., about two miles distant; Cape Frederick Henry N. 23° E.; and the mouth of the lagoon S. 16° E.

In our passage from the Cape of Good Hope the winds were mostly from the westward, with very boisterous weather; but one great advantage that this season of the year has over the summer months is in being free from fogs. I have already remarked that the approach of strong southerly winds is announced by many kinds of birds of the albatross or petrel tribe, and the abatement of the gale, or a shift of wind to the northward, by their keeping away. The thermometer also very quickly shows when a change of these winds may be expected, by varying sometimes six and seven degrees in its height. I have reason to believe that after we passed the island of St Paul there was a weatherly current, the ship being every day to the westward of the reckoning, which in the whole, from St Paul to Van Diemen's Land, made a difference of four degrees between the longitude by the reckoning and the true longitude.

Thursday the 21st. The ship being moored, I went in a boat to look out for the most convenient place to wood and water at, which I found to be at the west end of the beach, for the surf, though considerable, was less there than at any other part of the bay. The water was in a gully about sixty yards from the beach. It was perfectly good, but being only a collection from the rains, the place is always dry in the summer months, for we found no water in it when I was here with Captain Cook in January 1777. We had very little success in hauling the seine; about twenty small flounders and flat-headed fish, called foxes, were all that were taken.

I found no signs of the natives having lately frequented this bay, or of any European vessels having been here since the *Resolution* and *Discovery* in 1777. From some of the old trunks of trees, then cut down, I saw shoots about twenty-five feet high and fourteen inches in circumference.

In the evening I returned on board. The next morning, the 22nd, at daylight, a party was sent on shore for wooding and watering, under the command of Mr Christian and the gunner, and I directed that one man should be constantly employed in washing the people's clothes. There was so much surf that the wood was obliged to be rafted off in bundles to the boat. Mr Nelson informed me that in his walks to-day he saw a tree, in a very healthy state, which he measured and found to be thirty-three feet and a half in girth; its height was proportioned to its bulk.

Saturday the 23rd. The surf was rather greater than yesterday, which very much interrupted our wooding and watering. Nelson to-day picked up a male opossum that had been recently killed, or had died, for we could not perceive any wound, unless it had received a blow on the back, where there was a bare place about the size of a shilling. It measured fourteen inches from the ears to the beginning of the tail, which was exactly the same length.

Most of the forest trees were at this time shedding their bark. There are three kinds, which are distinguished from each other by their leaves, though the wood appears to be the same. Many of them are full one hundred and fifty feet high; but most of those that we cut down were decayed at the heart. There are, besides the forest trees, several other kinds that are firm good wood, and may be cut for most purposes, except masts; neither are the forest trees good for masts, on account of their weight and the difficulty of finding them thoroughly sound. Mr Nelson asserted that they shed their bark every year, and that they increase more from the seed than by suckers.

I found the tide made a difference of full two feet in the height of the water in the lake at the back of the beach. At high water it was very brackish, but at low tide it was perfectly fresh to the taste, and soap showed no sign of its being the least impregnated. We had better success in fishing on board the ship than by hauling the seine on shore, for with hooks and lines a number of fine rock cod were caught. I saw to-day several eagles, some beautiful blue-plumaged herons, and a great variety of paroquets. A few oyster-catchers and gulls were generally about the beach, and in the lake a few wild ducks.

Monday the 25th. Being in want of plank, I directed a saw-pit to be dug, and employed some of the people to saw trees into plank. The greater part of this week the winds were moderate, with unsettled weather. On Friday it blew strong from the SW., with rain, thunder, and lightning. We continued to catch fish in sufficient quantities for everybody, and had better success with the seine. We were fortunate, also, in angling in the lake, where we caught some very fine tench. Some of the people felt a sickness from eating mussels that were gathered from the rocks, but I believe it was occasioned by eating too many. We found some spider-crabs, most of them not good, being the female sort, and out of season. The males were tolerably good, and were known by the smallness of their two fore-claws, or feeders. We saw the trunk of a dead tree, on which had been cut 'A.D. 1773.' The figures were very distinct; even the slips made with the knife were discernible. This must have been done by some of Captain Furneaux's people, in March 1773, fifteen years before. The marks of the knife remaining so unaltered, I imagine the tree must have been dead when it was cut; but it serves to show the durability of the wood, for it was perfectly sound at this time. I shot two gannets. These birds were of the same size as those in England; their colour is a beautiful white, with the wings and tail tipped with jet black, and the top and back of the head of a very fine yellow. Their feet were black, with four claws, on each of which was a yellow line the whole length of the foot. The bill was four inches long, without nostrils, and very tapered and sharp-pointed.

The east side of the bay being not so thick of wood as the other parts, and the soil being good, I fixed on it, at Nelson's recommendation, as the most proper situation for planting some of the fruit trees which I had brought from the Cape of Good Hope. A circumstance much against anything succeeding here, is that in the dry season the fires made by the natives are apt to communicate to the dried grass and underwood and to spread in such a manner as to endanger everything that cannot bear a severe scorching. We, however, chose what we thought the safest situations, and planted three fine young apple trees, nine vines, six plantain trees, a number of orange and lemon seed, cherry stones, plum, peach, and apricot stones, pumpkins, also two sorts of Indian corn, and apple and pear kernels. The ground is well adapted for the trees, being of a rich loamy nature. The spot where we made our plantation was clear of underwood, and we marked the trees that stood nearest to the different things which were planted. Nelson followed the circuit of the bay, planting in such places as appeared most eligible. I have great hopes that some of these articles will succeed. The particular situations I had described in my survey of this place, but I was unfortunately prevented from bringing it home. Near the watering-place, likewise, we planted on a flat, which appeared a favourable situation, some onions, cabbage roots, and potatoes.

For some days past a number of whales were seen in the bay.

They were of the same kind as those we had generally met with before, having two blow-holes on the back of the head.

On the night of the 1st of September we observed, for the first time, signs of the natives being in the neighbourhood. Fires were seen on the low land, near Cape Frederick Henry, and at daylight we saw the natives with our glasses. As I expected they would come round to us, I remained all the forenoon near the wooding and watering parties, making observations, the morning being very favourable for that purpose. I was, however, disappointed in my conjecture, for the natives did not appear, and there was too great a surf for a boat to land on the part where we had seen them.

Tuesday the 2nd. The natives not coming near us, I determined to go after them, and we set out in a boat towards Cape Frederick Henry, where we arrived about eleven o'clock. I found landing impracticable, and therefore came to a grapnel, in hopes of their coming to us, for we had passed several fires. After waiting near an hour I was surprised to see Nelson's assistant come out of the wood; he had wandered thus far in search of plants, and told me that he had met with some of the natives. Soon after we heard their voices like the cackling of geese, and twenty persons came out of the wood, twelve of whom went round to some rocks, where the boat could get nearer to the shore than we then were. Those who remained behind were women.

We approached within twenty yards of them, but there was no possibility of landing, and I could only throw to the shore, tied up in paper, the presents which I intended for them. I showed the different articles as I tied them up, but they would not untie the paper till I made an appearance of leaving them. They then opened the parcels, and as they took the articles out, placed them on their heads. On seeing this I returned towards them, when they instantly put everything out of their hands, and would not appear to take notice of anything that we had given them. After throwing a few more beads and nails on shore, I made signs for them to go to the ship, and they, likewise, made signs for me to land; but as this could not be effected, I left them, in hopes of a nearer interview at the watering-place.

When they first came in sight they made a prodigious clattering in their speech, and held their arms over their heads. They spoke so quick that I could not catch one single word they uttered. We recollected one man, whom we had formerly seen among the party of the natives that came to us in 1777, and who is particularized in the account of Captain Cook's last voyage for his humour and deformity. Some of them had a small stick, two or three feet long, in their hands, but no other weapon.

Their colour, as Captain Cook remarks, is a dull black; their skin is scarified about their shoulders and breast. They were of a middle stature, or rather below it. One of them was distinguished by his body being coloured with red ochre, but all the others were painted black, with a kind of soot, which was laid on so thick over their faces and shoulders that it is difficult to say what they were like.

They ran very nimbly over the rocks, had a very quick sight, and caught the small beads and nails which I threw to them with great dexterity. They talked to us sitting on their heels, with their knees close into their armpits, and were perfectly naked.

In my return towards the ship I landed at the point of the harbour near Penguin Island, and from the hills saw the water on the other side of the low isthmus of Cape Frederick Henry, which forms the bay of that name. It is very extensive, and in or near the middle of the bay there is a low island. From this spot it has the appearance of being a very good and convenient harbour.

The account which I had from Brown, the botanist's assistant, was that in his search for plants he had met an old man, a young woman, and two or three children. The old man at first appeared alarmed, but became familiar on being presented with a knife. He nevertheless sent away the young woman, who went very reluctantly. He saw some miserable wigwams, in which were nothing but a few kangaroo skins spread on the ground and a basket made of rushes.

Among the wood that we cut here we found many scorpions and centipedes, with numerous black ants that were an inch long. We saw no mosquitoes, though in the summer months they are very troublesome.

What is called the New Zealand tea-plant grew here in great abundance, so that it was not only gathered and dried to use as tea, but made excellent brooms. It bears a small pointed leaf of a pleasant smell, and its seed is contained in a berry, about the size of a pea, notched into five equal parts on the top. The soil on the west and south sides of the bay is black mould, with a mixture of fine white sand, and is very rich. The trees are lofty and large, and the underwood grows so close together that in many places it is impassable. The east side of the bay is a rich loamy soil, but near the tops of the hills is very much encumbered with stones and rocks; the underwood thinly placed and small. The trees on the S., SE., and SW. sides of the hills grow to a larger size than those that are exposed to the opposite points, for the sides of the trees open or exposed to the north winds are naked, with few branches, while the other sides are in a flourishing state. From this I do not infer that the equatorial are more hurtful than the polar winds, but that the trees, by their situation, were more sheltered from the one than from the other.

Wednesday the 3rd. A calm prevented our sailing to-day. The friendly interview which we had had with the natives made me expect that they would have paid us a visit, but we saw nothing more of them, except fires in the night upon the low land to the northward.

The result of the observations which I made here, reduced to Penguin Island, place it in 43° 21′ 11″ S. latitude and in longitude 147° 33′ 29″ E., which scarcely differs from the observations made in 1777. The variation of the compass, observed on shore, was 8° 38′ E., and on board the ship 8° 29′ E. It was high water at the change of the moon, at forty-nine minutes past six in the morning. The rise was two feet eight inches. Southerly winds, if of any continuance, make a considerable difference in the height of the tides.

Thursday the 4th. This forenoon, having a pleasant breeze at NW., we weighed anchor and sailed out of Adventure Bay. At noon the southernmost part of Maria's Isles bore N. 52° E., about five leagues distant; Penguin Island S. 86° W.; and Cape Frederick Henry N. 65° W. In this position we had soundings at fifty-seven fathoms, a sandy bottom. Latitude observed 43° 22′ S.

The southern part of Maria's Islands lie in latitude 43° 16′ S. The country is not in general woody, but in some of the interior parts there appeared great abundance. Among these islands I have no doubt of there being many convenient places for shipping. On the east side, in latitude 42° 42′ S. and longitude 148° 24′ E., in July 1789 Captain Cox of the *Mercury* found a convenient and secure harbour from all winds, which he named Oyster Bay. Here he found wood, water, and fish in great abundance. It has two outlets, and lies north, a little easterly, distant thirty-four miles from the south-easternmost island or point seen from Adventure Bay.

Adventure Bay is a convenient and safe place for any number of ships to take in wood and water during the summer months, but in the winter, when the southerly winds are strong, the surf on all parts of the shore makes the landing exceedingly troublesome. The bay of Frederick Henry may perhaps be found preferable, as it appears to be equally easy of access. The soundings in Adventure Bay are very regular; near the west shore are some patches of weed, but no shoal or danger, the depth on them being from five to nine fathoms.

CHAPTER V

Rocky islands discovered.—See the island Maitea and arrive at Otaheite.—Ship crowded by the natives.

BEING clear of the land we steered towards the ESE., it being my intention to pass to the southward of New Zealand, as I expected in that route to meet with constant westerly winds; in which, however, I was disappointed, for they proved variable, and frequently from the eastward blowing strong, with thick misty weather. The thermometer varied from 41 to 46 degrees.

On the 14th, at noon, we were in 49° 24′ S. latitude and in 168° 3′ E. longitude, which is on the same meridian with the south end of New Zealand. We altered our course, steering to the northward of east, and frequently saw rock-weed, which I supposed to have drifted from New Zealand. The sea now became rougher, from our being exposed to a long swell which came from the NE.

On the 19th, at daylight, we discovered a cluster of small rocky islands, bearing east by north four leagues distant from us. We had seen no birds or anything to indicate the nearness of land, except patches of rock-weed, for which the vicinity of New Zealand sufficiently accounted. The wind being at NE. prevented our near approach to these isles, so that we were not less than three leagues distant in passing to the southward of them. The weather was too thick to see distinctly; their extent was only three and a half miles from east to west, and about half a league from north to south; their number, including the smaller ones, was thirteen.   I could not observe any verdure on any of them; there were white spots like patches of snow, but, as Captain Cook in describing the land of New Zealand near Cape South says, in many places there are patches like white marble, it is probable that what we saw might be of the same kind as what he had observed.   The westernmost of these islands is the largest; they are of sufficient height to be seen at the distance of seven leagues from a ship's deck.   When the easternmost bore north I tried for soundings, being then ten miles distant from the nearest of them, and found bottom at seventy-five fathoms, a fine white sand, and again at noon, having run six leagues more to the ESE., we had soundings at 104 fathoms, a fine brimstone-coloured sand.   The latitude of these islands is 47° 44′ S., their longitude 179° 7′ E., which is about 145 leagues to the east of the Traps, near the south end of New Zealand.   Variation of the compass here 17° E.   While in sight of the islands we saw some penguins and a white kind of gull with a forked tail.   Captain Cook's track in 1773 was near this spot, but he did not see the islands; he saw seals and penguins hereabouts, but considered New Zealand to be the nearest land.   I have named them after the ship, the Bounty Isles.

Sunday the 21st.   This day we saw a seal, some rock-weed, and a great many albatrosses.   I tried for soundings, but found no bottom at 230 fathoms depth.   Our latitude 47° 32′ S., longitude 182° 36′ E.

Thursday the 2nd.   Were in 40° 27′ S. latitude and 214° 4′ E. longitude.   It being calm, and a number of small blubbers about the ship, I took up some in a bucket, but I saw no difference between them and the common blubbers in the West Indies.   We frequently, in the night-time, observed the sea to be covered with luminous spots, caused by prodigious quantities of small blubbers, that from the strings which extend from them emit a light like the blaze of a candle, while the body continues perfectly dark.

The 3rd, in the morning, we saw a seal.   Captain Cook has remarked seeing seaweed when nearly in the same place.   Our latitude 40° 21′ S., longitude 215° E.   Variation of the compass 7° 45′ E.   Being now well to the eastward of the Society Islands I steered more to the northward.

We continued to have the southern oceanic birds accompany us and a few whales.   The people caught albatrosses and fattened them in the same manner which they had done when off

Cape Horn. Some of these measured near eight feet between the tips of the wings when spread.

On Thursday the 9th we had the misfortune to lose one of our seamen, James Valentine, who died in the night of an asthmatic complaint. This poor man had been one of the most robust people on board until our arrival at Adventure Bay, where he first complained of some slight indisposition, for which he was bled and got better. Some time afterwards the arm in which he had been bled became painful and inflamed; the inflammation increased, with a hollow cough and extreme difficulty of breathing, to his death.

The 13th, in the afternoon, we saw two land birds, like what are called sand-larks. Our latitude at this time was 28° 3' S. and longitude 223° 26' E. The next morning we saw a tropic bird and some fish. The winds were light and variable with calms from this time to the 19th, when a breeze sprung up from the NE., which gradually came round to the eastward and proved to be the trade wind. Our latitude on the 19th, at noon, was 24° 13' S., longitude 222° 17' E. Variation of the compass 5° 19' E.

On the 25th, at half-past seven in the morning, we saw the island Maitea, called Osnaburg by Captain Wallis, who first discovered it. At noon it bore SW. by W¼W., six miles distant. Our latitude 17° 50' S. and longitude 212° 24' E. Variation five degrees east. As Captain Wallis and Captain Cook had both passed near the south side I ran along the north side, which is remarkably steep. The island is high and round, and not more than three miles in its greatest extent. The south side, where the declivity from the hills is more gradual, is the chief place of residence of the natives; but the north side, from the very summit down to the sea, is so steep that it can afford no support to the inhabitants. We steered pretty close in to the northward of the east end, where we saw but few habitations. A very neat house on a small eminence, delightfully situated in a grove of coconut trees, particularly attracted our notice. About twenty of the natives followed us along shore, waving and showing large pieces of cloth but the surf on the shore was too high to think of having any communication with them. I observed a great number of coconut trees, but did not see one plantain tree. There were other trees, but of what kind we could not distinguish. Near the east end are two remarkable rocks, and a reef runs off to the eastward about half a league.

The latitude of Maitea is 17° 53′ S., and by our time-keeper its longitude is 1° 24′ E. from Point Venus. Variation of the compass 5° 36′ E.

We continued our course to the westward and at six in the evening saw Otaheite bearing W¾S., the island Maitea, then in sight, bearing E½S. eight leagues distant. As there was great probability that we should remain a considerable time at Otaheite, it could not be expected that the intercourse of my people with the natives should be of a very reserved nature. I therefore ordered that every person should be examined by the surgeon, and had the satisfaction to learn, from his report, that they were all perfectly free from any venereal complaint.

On the 26th, at four o'clock in the morning, having run twenty-five leagues from Maitea, we brought to till daylight, when we saw Point Venus bearing SW. by W., distant about four leagues. As we drew near a great number of canoes came off to us. Their first inquiries were if we were *tyos*, which signifies friends, and whether we came from *Pretanie* (their pronunciation of Britain) or from Lima. They were no sooner satisfied in this than they crowded on board in vast numbers, notwithstanding our endeavours to prevent it, as we were working the ship, and in less than ten minutes the deck was so full that I could scarce find my own people. At nine in the forenoon we were obliged to anchor in the outer part of Matavai Bay, in thirteen fathoms, being prevented by light variable winds from placing the ship in a proper berth. In this station the west part of One-tree Hill bore S. by E½E. one mile distant.

This passage of fifty-two days from Van Dieman's Land may be rated as moderate sailing. We passed New Zealand with the spring equinox, and the winds, though strong, were at no time violent. To the southward of 40° 0′ S. they were variable; between the latitudes of 40° and 33° S. the wind kept in the NW. quarter; afterwards, till we got into the trade, the winds were variable, mostly from the eastward, but light and inclinable to calms. The ship was 3° 22′ in longitude to the eastward of the dead reckoning, which the time-keeper almost invariably proved to be owing to a current giving us more easting than the log. Our track was as distant from any course of former ships as I could conveniently make it, and though we made no new discoveries, except the small cluster of islands near New Zealand, yet in other parts of the track, as has been noticed, we met with signs of being in the neighbourhood of land.

It may not be unworthy of remark that the whole distance which the ship had run by the log, in direct and contrary courses, from leaving England to our anchoring at Otaheite, was twenty-seven thousand and eighty-six miles, which, on an average, is at the rate of a hundred and eight miles each twenty-four hours.

CHAPTER VI

Account of an English ship lately sailed from Otaheite.—Death of Omai.—Captain Cook's picture sent on board.—Otoo visits the ship.—His visit returned.—Natives well disposed towards us.—Account of the cattle left by Captain Cook.—Bread-fruit plants promised.—Visit to the Earee Rahie.—Presents made to the Arreoys.

Sunday the 26th. The ship being anchored our number of visitors continued to increase, but as yet we saw no person that we could recollect to have been of much consequence. Some inferior chiefs made me presents of a few hogs and I made them presents in return. We were supplied with coconuts in great abundance, but bread-fruit was scarce.

Many inquiries were made after Captain Cook, Sir Joseph Banks, and many of their former friends. They said a ship had been here from which they had learnt that Captain Cook was dead, but the circumstances of his death they did not appear to be acquainted with, and I had given particular directions to my officers and ship's company that they should not be mentioned. The ship spoken of, they informed me, stayed at Otaheite one month and had been gone four months by some of their accounts; according to others, only three months. The captain they called Tonah. I understood likewise from them that Lieutenant Watts was in the ship, who, having been here in the *Resolution* with Captain Cook, was well known to them. One of my first inquiries, as will naturally be imagined, was after our friend Omai, and it was a sensible mortification and disappointment to me to hear that not only Omai, but both the New Zealand boys who had been left with him were dead. Every one agreed in their information that they died a natural death. Otoo, who was the chief of Matavai when Captain Cook was here the last time, was absent at another part of the island. They told me messengers were sent to inform him of our arrival and that he was expected to return soon. There appeared among the natives in general great good-will towards us, and they seemed to be much rejoiced at our arrival. This whole day we experienced no instance of dishonesty. We were so much crowded that I could not undertake to remove to a more proper station without danger of disobliging our visitors by desiring them to leave the ship. This business was therefore deferred till the next morning.

Early in the morning, before the natives began to flock off to us, we weighed anchor, to work farther into the bay, and moored at about a quarter of a mile distance from the shore: Point Venus bearing N. 16° E.; the west part of One-tree Hill SW. by S.; and the point of the reef N. 37° W.; the ship lying in seven fathoms of water.

Several chiefs now came on board and expressed great pleasure at seeing me. Among these were Otow, the father of Otoo, and Oreepyah, his brother; also another chief of Matavai, called Poeeno, and to these men I made presents. Two messengers likewise arrived from Otoo to acquaint me of his being on his way to the ship, each of whom brought me, as a present from Otoo, a small pig and a young plaintain tree as a token of friendship. The ship was now plentifully supplied with provisions, every person having as much as he could consume.

As soon as the ship was secured I went on shore with the chief Poeeno and accompanied by a multitude of the natives. He conducted me to the place where we had fixed our tents in 1777 and desired that I would now appropriate the spot to the same use. We then went across the beach and through a walk delightfully shaded with bread-fruit trees to his own house. Here we found two women at work staining a piece of cloth red. These I found were his wife and her sister. They desired me to sit down on a mat, which was spread for the purpose, and with great kindness offered me refreshments. I received the congratulations of several strangers who came to us and behaved with great decorum and attention. The people, however, thronged about the house in such numbers that I was much incommoded by the heat, which being observed they immediately drew back. Among the crowd I saw a man who had lost his arm just above the elbow; the stump was well covered and the cure seemed as perfect as could be expected from the greatest professional skill.

I made inquiries about the cattle that had been left here by Captain Cook, but the accounts I received were very unfavourable and so various that for the present I shall forbear speaking of them. After staying about an hour I got up to take leave, when the women, in a very obliging manner, came to me with a mat and a piece of their finest cloth, which they put on me after the Otaheite fashion. When I was thus dressed they each of them took one of my hands and accompanied me to the water-side, and at parting promised that they would soon return my visit.

In this walk I had the satisfaction to see that the island had received some benefit from our former visits. Two shaddocks were brought to me, a fruit which they had not till we introduced it. And among the articles which they brought off to the ship and offered for sale were capsicums, pumpkins, and two young goats.

On my return to the ship I found that a small disturbance had been occasioned by one of the natives making an attempt to steal a tin pot, which on being known to Oreepyah he flew into a violent rage, and it was with some difficulty that the thief escaped with his life. He drove all his countrymen out of the ship, and when he saw me he desired if at any time I found a thief that I would order him to be tied up and punished with a severe flogging.

This forenoon a man came on board with Captain Cook's picture, which had been drawn by Mr Webber in 1777 and left with Otoo. It was brought to me to be repaired. The frame was broken but the picture no way damaged, except a little in the background. They called it *Toote* (which has always been their manner of pronouncing Captain Cook's name) *Earee no Otaheite*, chief of Otaheite. They said Toote had desired Otoo, whenever any English ship came, to show the picture, and it would be acknowledged as a token of friendship. The youngest brother of Otoo, named Whydooah, visited me this afternoon. He appeared stupefied with drinking *ava*. At sunset all our male visitors left the ship.

The next morning early I received a message from Otoo to inform me of his arrival and requesting that I would send a boat for him, which I immediately did with an officer (Mr Christian) to conduct him on board. He came with numerous attendants and expressed much satisfaction at our meeting. After introducing his wife to me we joined noses, the customary manner of saluting, and to perpetuate our friendship he desired we should exchange names. I was surprised to find that instead of Otoo, the name by which he formerly went, he was now called Tinah. The name of Otoo, with the title of *Earee Rahie*, I was informed, had devolved to his eldest son, who was yet a minor, as is the custom of the country. The name of Tinah's wife was Iddeah. With her was a woman dressed with a large quantity of cloth in the form of a hoop, which was taken off and presented to me, with a large hog and some bread-fruit. I then took my visitors into the cabin and after a short time produced my presents in return. The present I made to Tinah (by which name I shall hereafter call him) consisted of hatchets, small adzes, files, gimlets, saws, looking-glasses, red feathers, and two shirts. To Iddeah I gave earrings, necklaces, and beads, but she expressed a desire also for iron and therefore I made the same assortment for her as I had for her husband. Much conversation took place among them on the value of the different articles and they appeared extremely satisfied so that they determined to spend the day with me, and requested I would show them all over the ship and particularly the cabin where I slept. This, though I was not fond of doing, I indulged them in, and the consequence was, as I had apprehended, that they took a fancy to so many things that they got from me nearly as much more as I had before given them. Afterwards Tinah desired me to fire some of the great guns. This I likewise complied with and as the shot fell into the sea at a great distance all the natives expressed their surprise by loud shouts and acclamations.

I had a large company at dinner, for besides Tinah and his wife there was Otow, the father of Tinah, Oreepyah and Whydooah, two of his brothers, Poeeno, and several other chiefs. Tinah is a very large man, much above the common stature, being not less than six feet four inches in height and proportionably stout, his age about thirty-five. His wife (Ideeah) I judged to be about twenty-four years of age; she is likewise much above the common size of the women at Otaheite and has a very animated and intelligent countenance. Whydooah, the younger brother of Tinah, was highly spoken of as a warrior, but had the character of being the greatest drunkard in the country, and indeed, to judge from the withered appearance of his skin, he must have used the pernicious drink called *ava* to great excess. Tinah was fed by one of his attendants, who sat by him for that purpose, this being a particular custom among some of the superior chiefs, and I must do him the justice to say he kept his attendant constantly employed. There was indeed little reason to complain of want of appetite in any of my guests. As the women are not allowed to eat in presence of the men, Iddeah dined with some of her companions about an hour afterwards in private, except that her husband Tinah favoured them with his company and seemed to have entirely forgotten that he had already dined.

Provisions were brought off to the ship in the greatest plenty, and to prevent as much as possible anything which might occasion disputes, I desired Mr Peckover, the gunner, to undertake the management of our traffic with the natives. Some of the hogs brought to-day weighed 200 lb. and we purchased several for salting. Goats were likewise brought off for sale and I bought a she-goat and kid for less than would have purchased a small hog. Our friends here expressed much disappointment that there was no portrait-painter on board; Tinah in particular, who wished to have had pictures of his father and family.

An intimacy between the natives and our people was already so general that there was scarce a man in the ship who had not his *tyo* or friend. Tinah continued with me the whole afternoon, in the course of which he eat four times of roast pork, besides his dinner. When he left the ship he requested I would keep for him all the presents I had given to him, as he had not at Matavai a place sufficiently safe to secure them from being stolen. I therefore showed him a locker in my cabin for his use and gave him a key to it. This is perhaps not so much a proof of his want of power as of the estimation in which they hold European commodities, and which makes more than the common means of security requisite to prevent theft.

I had sent Nelson and his assistant to look for plants and it was no small pleasure to me to find, by their report, that according to appearances the object of my mission would probably be accomplished with ease. I had given directions to every one on board not to make known to the islanders the purpose of our coming, lest it might enhance the value of the bread-fruit plants or occasion other difficulties. Perhaps so much caution was not necessary, but at all events I wished to reserve to myself the time and manner of communication. Nelson met with two fine shaddock trees which he had planted in 1777; they were full of fruit, but not ripe.

In the morning I returned Tinah's visit, for I found he expected it. He was in a small shed about a quarter of a mile to the eastward of Matavai Point, with his wife and three children, not their own, but who they said were relations. In my walk I had picked up a numerous attendance, for every one I met followed me, so that I had collected such a crowd that the heat was scarce bearable, every one endeavouring to get a look to satisfy their curiosity. They, however, carefully avoided pressing against me, and welcomed me with cheerful countenances and great good nature.

I made Tinah understand that my visit was particularly to him, and gave him a second present, equal to the first, which he received with great pleasure; and to the people of conse-quence that were about him I also presented some article or other. There were great numbers of children, and as I took notice of the little ones that were in arms and gave them beads, both small and great, but with much drollery and good humour, endeavoured to benefit by the occasion. Boys of ten and twelve years old were caught up in arms and brought to me which created much laughter, so that in a short time I got rid of all I had brought on shore.

In my return I called on Poeeno and an elderly chief, a relation of his called Moannah, the principal men of this district, and with whom I judged it my interest to be on good terms. I gave them several valuable articles, and as the situation here was eligible for a garden I planted melon, cucumber, and salad seeds. I told them many other things should be sown for their use, and they appeared much pleased when they understood I intended to plant such things as would grow to be trees and produce fruit. I saw large patches of tobacco growing without culture and many pumpkin vines. The bread-fruit trees and coconut trees at this time were full of fruit.

I went on board to dinner and Moannah accompanied me. In the afternoon I returned to Poeeno's with some additional seeds to improve the little garden I had began to make in the forenoon. While I was giving directions I received a message from Tinah inviting me to come to him at his brother Oreepyah's house, which was near the beach. At this place I found a great number of people collected, who on my appearance immediately made way for me to sit down by Tinah. The crowd being ordered to draw back, a piece of cloth about two yards wide and forty-one yards in length was spread on the ground, and another piece of cloth was brought by Oreepyah, which he put over my shoulders and round my waist in the manner the chiefs are clothed. Two large hogs, weighing each above two hundred pounds, and a quantity of baked bread-fruit and coconuts, were then laid before me as a present, and I was desired to walk from one end of the cloth spread on the ground to the other, in the course of which *tyo* and *ehoah* [1] were repeated with loud acclamations. This ceremony being ended Tinah desired I would send the things on board, which completely loaded the boat. We therefore waited till she came back, and then I took them on board with me, for I knew they expected some return. The present which I made on this occasion was equal to any that I had made before, but I discovered that Tinah was not the sole proprietor of what he had given to me, for the present I gave was divided among those who, I guessed, had contributed to support his dignity, among whom were Moannah, Poeeno, and Oreepyah. Tinah, however, kept the greatest part of what I had given, and every one seemed satisfied with the proportion he allotted them.

The Otaheite breed of hogs seems to be supplanted by the European. Originally they were of the China sort, short and very thick-necked, but the superior size of the European have made them encourage our breed.

Thursday the 30th. At break of day Tinah and his wife came again to the ship, and as their attendants were numerous I provided a breakfast for them of broiled and roasted pork, which they preferred to tea. Our arrival being known all over the island we had this day a great number of strangers on board, who came from the most remote parts, and in the forenoon some hooks and thimbles were cut out from the blocks. This induced me to order all the natives out of the ship, except the chiefs and their attendants. In executing these orders a daring fellow attacked the sentinel, but escaped among the crowd. Every one knew the consequence of offending the sentinel and were exceedingly alarmed at the appearance of anger I thought necessary to assume.

Among those who visited us to-day were two chiefs of great consequence, Marremarre and his son Poohaitaiah Otee, *earees* of the districts of Itteeah and Attahooroo. Otee was fed at

---

[1] *Tyo* and *ehoah* are words of the same signification, i.e. a friend.

dinner in the same manner as Tinah. It was evident that the
attention which I showed to these chiefs seemed to give uneasiness to Tinah. At sunset my visitors took leave and were
carried on shore by one of the ship's boats, which has always
been regarded as a mark of distinction and on that account
preferred by them to going in their own canoes. At their
request a race was rowed between our five-oared cutter and one
of their double canoes with four paddles. Great exertions were
used on both sides, but the cutter first reached the shore. In
their return to the ship Oreepyah stopped them till a large
piece of cloth that he had sent for was brought, which he tied
to the boat-hook and desired should be carried off as a trophy
of their victory.

The next morning, at sunrise, Moannah came on board with
a message from Tinah to acquaint me that he was *mattow*
(afraid to see me) till he had recovered some things that had
been stolen from the ship and which he had sent after. I knew
there was something wrong, as no canoes came off to us, and on
looking about we found the buoy of the best bower anchor had
been taken away, I imagine, for the sake of some iron hoops
that were on it. That this might not create any coolness I
sent a boat to Tinah to invite him and his friends to come on
board, which they immediately did and were no longer under
any apprehensions. I had made an appointment with Oreepyah
for him to go with me to Oparre this morning; but the accident
just mentioned caused him to break his engagement, he having
gone, as I was informed, in search of what had been stolen.

Oparre is the district next to the westward of Matavai. One
of my reasons for going to Oparre was to see if Nelson would
be able to procure plants there; but I gave the credit of my
visit to young Otoo, the son of Tinah, who was the Earee Rahie,
and lived with the rest of Tinah's children at Oparre. I prepared a magnificent present for this youth, who was represented
to me as the person of the greatest consequence, or rather of the
highest rank in the island. At noon I left the ship, accompanied
by Tinah, his wife Iddeah, and Poeeno. Moannah was to have
been of the party, but he insisted on remaining in the ship to
prevent his countrymen from attempting to steal anything.

After half an hour's sailing we arrived at Oparre. During
this time Tinah gave me a more circumstantial account of the
cattle and sheep that had been left with him. He related that
after five years from the time of Captain Cook's departure

(counting sixty-three moons) the people of the island Eimeo
joined with those of Attahooroo, a district of Otaheite, and
made a descent on Oparre; that after some resistance, by which
many men were killed, Tinah and his people fled to the mountains, leaving all their property to the mercy of the victorious
party, who destroyed almost everything which they found not
convenient to take away with them. Some of the cattle were
killed and eaten but the greater part were taken to Eimeo.
The cows, he said, had produced eight calves and the ewes ten
young ones. The ducks, among which they classed the geese, had
greatly increased, but the turkeys and peacocks, whatever was
the cause, had not bred. It seemed to give Tinah great pleasure
to observe how much I was concerned for the destruction of so
many useful animals, but the cause of his satisfaction, I found,
did not proceed from any expectation that I should replace
them, but from the belief that I would take vengeance on the
people who had deprived him of them; for with respect to the
loss of the cattle he appeared so unconcerned and indifferent
that I was very angry with him. There is, however, sufficient
excuse for his resentment against the people of Eimeo, for the
large extensive houses which we had seen in this part of Otaheite in the year 1777 were all destroyed, and at present they
had no other habitations than light sheds, which might be taken
by the four corners and removed by four men; and of the many
large canoes which they then had not more than three remained.
Tinah, understanding from my conversation that I intended
visiting some of the other islands in this neighbourhood, very
earnestly desired I would not think of leaving Matavai. 'Here,'
said he, 'you shall be supplied plentifully with everything you
want. All here are your friends and friends of King George;
if you go to the other islands you will have everything stolen
from you.' I replied that on account of their good will, and
from a desire to serve him and his country, King George had
sent out those valuable presents to him; 'and will not you,
Tinah, send something to King George in return?' 'Yes,' he
said, 'I will send him anything I have'; and then began to
enumerate the different articles in his power, among which he
mentioned the bread-fruit. This was the exact point to which
I wished to bring the conversation, and seizing an opportunity
which had every appearance of being undesigned and acci-
dental, I told him the bread-fruit trees were what King George
would like; upon which he promised me a great many should

be put on board, and seemed much delighted to find it so easily in his power to send anything that would be well received by King George.

On landing at Oparre an immense crowd of natives, as usual, immediately thronged about us. I inquired for Oreepyah, whom I expected to have met me here, but he was not yet returned from his search after the thieves. We therefore went under a shed of his to wait for him and in about a quarter of an hour he joined us, bringing with him an iron scraper and one of the hoops of the buoy. I thanked him for the trouble which he had taken, and assured him that I was perfectly satisfied, for he still seemed apprehensive of my displeasure.

We took leave for a short time of Oreepyah, and I proceeded with Tinah to make my visit to the young Otoo, the Earee Rahie. When we had walked about five minutes Tinah stopped and informed me that no person could be permitted to see his son who was covered above the shoulders. He then took off his upper garments and requested I would do the same. I replied that I had no objection to go as I would to my own king, who was the greatest in all the world, and, pulling off my hat, he threw a piece of cloth round my shoulders and we went on. About a quarter of a mile farther towards the hills, through a delightful shade of bread-fruit trees, we stopped at the side of a small serpentine river. Here I was in view of a house on the other side, at about fifty yards distance. From this house the young king was brought out on a man's shoulders, clothed in a piece of fine white cloth, and I was desired by Tinah to salute him by the name of Too Earee Rahie. The present which I had prepared was divided into three parts, and two other children made their appearance in the same manner. The first present I gave to a messenger who attended for that purpose, and I was instructed by Tinah to say that it was for the Earee Rahie; that I was his friend; that I hated thieves; and that I came from Britannie. The second present was sent in the same manner with a similar message to one of the other children; and likewise the third.

As I could not see the Earee Rahie distinctly I desired to be permitted to go over the river to him; but this, it seems, could not be complied with. Therefore, after seeing the presents delivered, I returned with Tinah towards Oreepyah's house. I was informed that Tinah had four children by his wife Iddeah. Otoo, or Too, the Earee Rahie, appeared to be about six years old; the second is a girl named Terrenah Oroah; the third a boy, Terreetappanooai; and a fourth, an infant girl, whom I did not see, named Tahamydooah.

When we came to the place where we had first stopped Tinah took the cloth from my shoulders and desired me to put my hat on. I expressed a desire to see more of the place and he took me back by a different way. On passing a trunk of a tree, rudely carved, I was desired again to pull my hat off and all uncovered their shoulders. This I discovered to be nothing more than the boundary of the king's land, on which whoever set their feet uncovered themselves out of respect.

We stopped at a house belonging to Tinah, where I was treated with a concert of one drum and three flutes, with singing by four men. I made some presents to the performers, and we removed to Oreepyah's house, where, after paying my compliments to him, which I found was expected, Tinah made me a present of a large hog and some coconuts. He then introduced an uncle of his called Mowworoah, a very old man, much tattooed and almost blind. To this chief I made a present, and soon after I embarked with Tinah, Oreepyah, their wives, and Poeeno. A vast number of people were collected on the beach to see us depart, and as soon as the boat had put off Tinah desired me to fire my pocket pistol, the *poopooe ete ete*, as he called it. The report seemed to electrify the whole crowd, but finding no harm done they gave great shouts of approbation.

Nelson, who accompanied me in this expedition, had but little opportunity to search after plants, the natives having crowded so much about him. He saw enough, however, to assure him that they were to be procured here as plentifully as at Matavai.

In our passage to the ship, which we rowed in one hour, nothing but Britannie was inquired after, and of the number of ships and guns. When I told them we had ships of a hundred guns they could not believe it till I drew one on paper. They then asked me if it was not as big as Tarrah, which is a high projecting head-land half-way between Matavai and Oparre, called by us One-tree Hill. Tinah much wished that one of these large ships should be sent to Otaheite and that myself should come in her and bring him a number of things that he wanted, among which he particularly desired beds and high-backed elbow chairs might not be forgotten, a request perfectly according with the indolent character of Tinah.

Saturday the 1st. As we had occasion to fix a tent on Point

Venus, this morning we moved the ship nearer to it and moored again in six fathoms, the point bearing NNE.

Tinah and several other chiefs dined on board with me. After dinner I went on shore with Tinah and made a visit to his father, Otow. I likewise went to the garden which I had made near Poeeno's house and found everything had been taken care of. After this I was invited to an entertainment called *heiva*, which Tinah had ordered and which consisted of singing and dancing by three men and a young girl. When this performance was finished I returned to the ship.

Sunday the 2nd. At daylight I sent Mr Christian with a party to erect our tent, and soon after followed myself with Tinah, Moannah, and Poeeno. With their consent I fixed a boundary within which the natives were not to enter without leave, and the chiefs cautioned them against it.

The principal use of the tents on shore was for a lodgement for the plants, and I had now, instead of appearing to receive a favour, brought the chiefs to believe that I was doing them a kindness in carrying the plants as a present from them to the Earee Rahie no Britanee. The party at the tent consisted of nine persons, including Nelson and his assistant.

Tinah dined with me on board and was to-day my only visitor. Nevertheless, the ceremony of being fed he so scrupulously observed, that even after all the attendants were sent away and we were left by ourselves, I was obliged to lift the wine to his mouth. The wives of the *earees* are sometimes subject to this restriction after the birth of a child, but are released after a certain time on performing a ceremony called *oammo*.

After dinner Tinah invited me to accompany him with a present of provisions to a party of the *arreoys*, a society described in the accounts of the former voyages; in this ceremony he made me the principal person. Our way to the place where the offering was to be made was by the side of a river, along the banks of which I had always walked before this time; but on the present occasion a canoe was provided for me and dragged by eight men. On arriving at the landing-place I saw a large quantity of bread-fruit, with some hogs ready dressed and a quantity of cloth. At about forty yards distant sat a man, who I was informed was a principal *arreoy*. A lane being made by the crowd he was addressed by one of Tinah's people, standing on the canoe, in a speech composed of short sentences which lasted about a quarter of an hour. During this a piece of cloth was produced, one end of which I was desired to hold, and five men, one with a sucking pig and the others having each a basket of bread-fruit, prepared to follow me. In this order we advanced to the *arreoy* and laid the whole down before him. I then spoke several sentences dictated to me by Tinah, the meaning of which I did not understand, and my pronunciation not being very exact, caused a great deal of mirth. This speech being finished I was shown another *arreoy* who had come from Ulitea, and to him likewise I was required to deliver an oration. Tinah understanding from me that I had children in my own country, he desired me to make one more offering on their account. There still remained three baskets of bread-fruit, a small pig, and another piece of cloth. With these, assisted as before, I made the offering in favour of my children to the man whom I had first addressed. He made no reply to all my fine speeches, but sat with great gravity and received everything as a matter of right and not of courtesy.

All that I could make out of this strange ceremony was that the *arreoys* are highly respected, and that the society is chiefly composed of men distinguished by their valour or some other merit, and that great trust and confidence is reposed in them; but I could not comprehend what this had to do with my children or why it should be imagined that an offering made on their account to a society of men who destroy all their children should be propitious. I learnt from Tinah, in talking about his children, that his first-born child was killed as soon as it came into the world, he being then an *arreoy*; but before his second child was born he quitted the society. The *arreoys* are allowed great latitude in their amours, except in times of danger. Then, as they are almost all fighting men (*tata toa*) they are restricted, that they may not weaken or enervate themselves.

These ceremonies being ended I returned to the ship.

Such of the natives as I conversed with about the institution of so extraordinary a society as the *arreoy* asserted that it was necessary to prevent an over-population. 'Worrow worrow no te mydidde, worrow worrow te tata.' We have too many children and too many men was their constant excuse. Yet it does not appear that they are apprehensive of too great an increase of the lower class of people, none of them being ever admitted into the *arreoy* society. The most remarkable instance related to me of the barbarity of this institution was of Teppahoo, the *earee* of the district of Tettaha, and his wife, Tetteehowdeeah, who is sister to Otow, and considered as a person of the first consequence. I was told that they have had eight children, every one of which was destroyed as soon as born. That any human beings were ever so devoid of natural affection as not to wish to preserve alive one of so many children is not credible. It is more reasonable to conclude that the death of these infants was not an act of choice in the parents, but that they were sacrificed in compliance with some barbarous superstition with which we are unacquainted. What strengthens this conjecture is that they have adopted a nephew as their heir, of whom they are excessively fond.

In countries so limited as the islands in the South Seas, the natives of which before they were discovered by European navigators probably had not an idea of the existence of other lands, it is not unnatural that an increasing population should occasion apprehensions of universal distress. Orders of celibacy, which have proved so prejudicial in other countries, might perhaps in this have been beneficial, so far at least as to have answered their purpose by means not criminal. The number of inhabitants at Otaheite have been estimated at above one hundred thousand. The island, however, is not cultivated to the greatest advantage; yet, were they continually to improve in husbandry, their improvement could not for a length of time keep pace with an unlimited population.

An idea here presents itself, which, however fanciful it may appear at first sight, seems to merit some attention: While we see among these islands so great a waste of the human species that numbers are born only to die, and at the same time a large continent so near to them as New Holland, in which there is so great a waste of land uncultivated and almost destitute of inhabitants, it naturally occurs how greatly the two countries might be made to benefit each other, and gives occasion to regret that the islanders are not instructed in the means of emigrating to New Holland, which seems as if designed by nature to serve as an asylum for the superflux of inhabitants in the islands. Such a plan of emigration, if rendered practicable to them, might not only be the means of abolishing the horrid custom of destroying children as it would remove the plea of necessity, but might lead to other important purposes. A great continent would be converted from a desert to a populous country; a number of our fellow-creatures would be saved; the inhabitants of the islands would become more civilized;

and it is not improbable but that our colonies in New Holland would derive so much benefit as to more than repay any trouble or expense that might be incurred in endeavouring to promote so humane a plan.

The latter, however, is a remote consideration, for the inter-tropical parts of New Holland are those most suited to the habits and manner of living of the islanders, and likewise the soil and climate are the best adapted to their modes of agriculture. Man placed by his Creator in the warm climates perhaps would never emigrate into the colder unless under the tyrannous influence of necessity; and ages might elapse before the new inhabitants would spread to our settlers, though they are but barely within the limits of frost, that great cause of nine-tenths of the necessities of Europeans. Nevertheless, besides forwarding the purposes of humanity and general convenience in bringing a people without land to a land without people, the benefit of a mutual intercourse with a neighbouring and friendly colony would in itself be no inconsiderable advantage.

Among people so free from ostentation as the Otaheiteans, and whose manners are so simple and natural, the strictness with which the punctilios of rank are observed is surprising. I know not if any action, however meritorious, can elevate a man above the class in which he was born, unless he were to acquire sufficient power to confer dignity on himself. If any woman of the inferior classes has a child by an *earee* it is not suffered to live. Perhaps the offspring of Teppahoo and Tettee-howdeeah were destined to satisfy some cruel adjustment of rank and precedency.

CHAPTER VII

A theft committed.—Deception of the painted head.—Conversation with a priest.—A wrestling match.—Reports of the natives concerning other islands.—Some account of Omai.

Monday the 3rd. The trade for provisions I directed to be carried on at the tent by Mr Peckover, the gunner. Moannah likewise resided there as a guard over his countrymen, but though it appeared to be the wish of all the chiefs that we should remain unmolested it was not possible entirely to prevent them from pilfering.

My table at dinner was generally crowded. Tinah, Oreepyah, Poeeno, and Moannah were my regular guests, and I was seldom without some chiefs from other districts. Almost every individual of any consequence has several names, which makes it frequently perplexing when the same person is spoken of to know who is meant. Every chief has perhaps a dozen or more names in the course of thirty years, so that the person who has been spoken of by one visitor will not perhaps be known to another unless other circumstances lead to a discovery. The father of Tinah, at this time called Otow, was known in 1769 by the name of Whappai.

I showed Tinah the preparations I was making to take on board the bread-fruit plants, which pleased him exceedingly, but he did not forget to remind me that when the next ship came out he hoped King George would send him large axes, files, saws, cloth of all kinds, hats, chairs, and bedsteads, with arms, ammunition, and, in short, everything he could think of mentioning.

This afternoon the gudgeon of the rudder belonging to the large cutter was drawn out and stolen without being perceived by the man that was stationed to take care of her. Several petty thefts having been committed by the natives, mostly owing to the negligence of our own people, and as these kind of accidents generally created alarm and had a tendency to interrupt the good terms on which we were with the chiefs, I thought it would have a good effect to punish the boat-keeper in their presence, many of them happening to be then on board, and accordingly I ordered him a dozen lashes. Tinah, with several of the chiefs, attended the punishment and interceded very earnestly to get it mitigated; the women showed great sympathy and that degree of feeling which characterizes the amiable part of their sex.

The natives brought off to-day two different kinds of roots that grow like yams: one they call *ettee*, which is a sweet root, common also to the Friendly Islands, and may be eaten as a sweetmeat; the other they call *appay*, a root like the *tyah* of *eddie* in the West Indies. A fruit called *ayyah*, which is the *jambo* of Batavia, was likewise brought off to us; they are as large as middle-sized apples, very juicy and refreshing, and may be eaten in large quantities. Also some *avees*, which are the real Otaheite apple, but they were not yet in season. These are a delicious high-flavoured fruit, and before they are ripe answer the culinary purposes of our apples.

Tuesday the 4th. A chief called Tootaha, who came from the island Ulietea, was introduced to me to-day by Tinah as one of his particular friends. I was told that he was a priest and a person of great knowledge. I desired Tinah to take what he thought proper as a present for him, and I must do Tinah the justice to say he was more sparing than I should have been. I likewise received a visit to-day from Oedidee, the man who had been at sea with Captain Cook in 1773 and 1774, as related in the account of that voyage. He still retained some of the English words which he had learnt in that expedition.

Wednesday the 5th. The weather variable, with lightning, and frequent showers of rain. Wind ENE.

This was the first day of our beginning to take up plants. We had much pleasure in collecting them, for the natives offered their assistance and perfectly understood the method of taking them up and pruning them.

The crowd of natives was not so great as hitherto it had been. The curiosity of strangers was satisfied, and as the weather began to be unsettled and rainy they had almost all returned to their homes, so that only the people of Matavai and Oparre remained with us, except a few chiefs from other islands. Our supplies, however, were abundant, and what I considered as no small addition to our comforts, we ceased to be incommoded when on shore by the natives following us, and could take our walks almost unnoticed. In any house that we wished to enter we always experienced a kind reception, and without officiousness. The Otaheiteans have the most perfect easiness of manners, equally free from forwardness and formality. They offer refreshments; if they are not accepted they do not think of offering them the second time, for they have not the least idea of that ceremonious kind of refusal which expects a second invitation. In like manner, at taking leave we were never troubled with solicitations to prolong our visit, but went without ceremony, except making use of a farewell expression at parting. Another advantage seldom found in warm countries was in this part of Otaheite being free from mosquitoes, though at particular times of the year the inhabitants are pestered with great numbers of flies.

Moannah continued our constant friend at the tent, and, with Tinah and all his friends, dined with me every day.

The ship's barber had brought with him from London a painted head, such as the hairdressers have in their shops to

show the different fashions of dressing hair; and it being made
with regular features and well coloured I desired him to dress
it, which he did with much neatness, and with a stick and a
quantity of cloth he formed a body. It was then reported to
the natives that we had an English woman on board, and the
quarter-deck was cleared of the crowd that she might make her
appearance. Being handed up the ladder and carried to the
after-part of the deck there was a general shout of 'Huaheine
no Britanee myty.' *Huaheine* signifies woman and *myty*,
good. Many of them thought it was living and asked if it
was my wife. One old woman ran with presents of cloth and
bread-fruit and laid them at her feet. At last they found out
the cheat, but continued all delighted with it, except the old
lady who felt herself mortified and took back her presents, for
which she was laughed at exceedingly. Tinah and all the
chiefs enjoyed the joke, and after making many inquiries about
the British women they strictly enjoined me when I came again
to bring a ship full of them.

Some very fine sugar-cane was brought to me; each of the
pieces was six inches round. I had before told Tinah that our
sugar was made of it, and he was very desirous to discover the
means, for they were so fond of our loaf sugar that a present
to any chief would have been incomplete without a piece of it.
Another article in great estimation, and likewise expected to
make part of a present, was scissors, which they made use of
to keep their beards in order.

By this time Nelson had, with assistance from the ship, completed a large garden near the tents, in which were sown seeds
of different kinds that we had collected at the Cape of Good
Hope. I likewise distributed fruit-stones and almonds for
planting, among the chiefs, who I hope will endeavour to make
them succeed, and, as they are very fond of sweet-smelling
flowers with which the women delight to ornament themselves,
I gave them some rose-seed.

Thursday the 6th. We had very variable weather, much rain
and some westerly winds, so that a considerable swell ran into
the bay, and a number of spotted white and black porpoises
made their appearance.

I had the mortification to see that our garden-ground had
been much trod over, and, what was worse, the chiefs appeared
but little concerned at it. To this kind of carelessness and
indifference I attribute the miscarriage of many of the plants

left here by Captain Cook. I had now in a flourishing state two orange plants, some vines, a fig tree, and two pineapple plants, which I gave to Poeeno, whose residence is a place favourable for their growth.

We got on successfully with our plants, having a hundred potted at the tent and in a fair way of doing well. The cabin also was completed and ready to receive them on board.

I have before remarked that my friend Tinah was rather of a selfish disposition, and this afternoon he showed a stronger instance of it than I was witness to at any time before or after. His brother Oreepyah sent on board to me a present of a large hog and a quantity of bread-fruit, but these kind of presents are much more expensive than purchasing at the market. Soon after Oreepyah himself came on board. Tinah was with me at the time and whispered me to tell Oreepyah not to bring any more hogs or fruit and to take those back which he had sent. This advice, as may be supposed, did not produce the effect intended. Oreepyah appears to be a man of great spirit and is highly respected by his countrymen. Among other visitors to-day was one of the men who had been to Lima in 1776.

Saturday the 8th. Our plants had now increased to 252. As they were all kept on shore at the tent I augmented the guard there, though from the general conduct of the natives there did not appear the least occasion for so much caution.

While I was at dinner Tinah desired I would permit a man to come down into the cabin whom he called his *taowah*, or priest, for I was obliged to keep a sentinel at the hatchway to prevent being incommoded at my meals with too much company; a restriction which pleased the chiefs, who always asked leave for any particular person to be admitted of whom they wished me to take notice. The company of the priest brought on a religious conversation. He said their great god was called Oro, and that they had many others of less consequence. He asked me if I had a god, if he had a son, and who was his wife. I told them He had a son, but no wife. Who was His father and mother? was the next question. I said He never had father or mother; at this they laughed exceedingly. You have a god, then, who never had a father or mother, and has a child without a wife! Many other questions were asked which my little knowledge of the language did not enable me to answer.

The weather was now fine again and a great number of people

were come from other parts of the island. Tinah informed me
that there was to be a *heiva* and a wrestling match on shore,
and that the performers waited for our attendance. We therefore set off with several of our friends, and about a quarter of
a mile from the tents we found a great concourse of people
formed into a ring. As soon as we were seated a dancing *heiva*
began, which was performed by two girls and four men. This
lasted half an hour, and consisted of wanton gestures and
motions, such as have been described in the account of former
voyages. When the dance ended Tinah ordered a long piece
of cloth to be brought. His wife Iddeah and myself were desired
to hold the two first corners, and the remaining part being supported by many others we carried it to the performers and gave
it them. Several other chiefs made a like present or payment. The performers were strollers that travelled about the
country as in Europe.

After this the wrestling began, and the place soon became a
scene of riot and confusion. A party of the *arreoys* also began
to exercise a privilege, which it seems they are allowed, of
taking from the women such of their clothes as they thought
worth it, so that some of them were left little better than
naked. One young woman who was attacked opposed them
with all her strength and held fast her cloth, though they
almost dragged her along the ground. Observing that I took
notice of her, she held out her hand and begged my assistance;
and at my request she escaped being pillaged.

Soon after a ring was again made, but the wrestlers were so
numerous within it that it was impossible to restore order. In
the challenges they lay one hand upon their breast, and, on the
bending of the arm at the elbow, with the other hand they
strike a very smart blow, which, as the hand is kept hollow,
creates a sound that may be heard at a considerable distance;
and this they do so frequently and with such force that the flesh
becomes exceedingly bruised, and the skin breaking, bleeds
considerably. At this time the sound from so many resembled
that of a number of people in a wood felling trees. This is the
general challenge, but when any two combatants agree to a
trial, they present their hands forward, joining them only by
the extremities of the fingers. They begin by watching to take
an advantage; at length they close, seize each other by the hair,
and are most commonly parted before either receives a fall.
Only one couple performed anything like the part of good

wrestlers, and as they were an equal match this conflict lasted longer than any of the others; but they also were parted.

Ideeah was the general umpire, and she managed with so much address as to prevent any quarrelling, and there was no murmuring at her decisions. As her person was large, she was very conspicuous in the circle. Tinah took no part in the management. Upon the whole, this performance gave me a better opinion of their strength than of their skill or dexterity.

Tuesday the 11th. For some time past Tinah had talked of going to the island of Tethuroa, which lies eight or ten leagues north from Otaheite, to fetch his mother, but I found I had only half understood him, for this morning he inquired when we were to sail there in the ship. However, he seemed to feel no great disappointment at my not complying with his wish. Tethuroa, he informed me, is the property of his family. He likewise spoke to me about an island called Roo-opow, the situation of which he described to be to the eastward of Otaheite four or five days' sail, and that there were large animals upon it with eight legs. The truth of this account he very strenuously insisted upon, and wished me to go thither with him. I was at a loss to know whether or not Tinah himself gave credit to this whimsical and fabulous account; for though they have credulity sufficient to believe anything, however improbable, they are at the same time so much addicted to that species of wit which we call humbug that it is frequently difficult to discover whether they are in jest or earnest. Their ideas of geography are very simple; they believe the world to be a fixed plane of great extent, and that the sun, moon, and stars are all in motion round it. I have been frequently asked by them if I have not been as far as the sun and moon, for they think we are such great travellers that scarce any undertaking is beyond our ability.

Another island, called Tappuhoi, situated likewise to the eastward, was described to me by Tinah, the inhabitants of which were said to be all warriors and that the people of Otaheite did not dare to go there. He told me that very lately a canoe from Tappuhoi was at the island Maitea; that as soon as they landed they began to fight with the people of Maitea, who killed them all, except a young lad and a woman, who have since been at Otaheite. I saw the boy, but could get no information from him. It is most probable that this unfortunate visit of the canoe from Tappuhoi was not designed, but occasioned by adverse winds which forced them so far from their own island, and that the people of Maitea began the attack, taking advantage of their superior numbers, on account of some former quarrel.

Thursday the 13th. I had a large company to dine with me to-day. Some of my constant visitors had observed that we always drank His Majesty's health as soon as the cloth was removed; but they were by this time become so fond of wine that they would frequently remind me of the health in the middle of dinner by calling out: 'King George Earee no Britanee'; and would banter me if the glass was not filled to the brim. Nothing could exceed the mirth and jollity of these people when they met on board.

I was assured by Oediddee and several others that the vines planted at the island Huaheine by Captain Cook had succeeded and bore fruit, and that some of the other plants, both at Huaheine and at Oaitepeha, a district on the SE. part of Otaheite, had been preserved and were in a thriving state. I was likewise informed that there was a bull and a cow alive at Otaheite, but on different parts of the island; the former at a place called Itteah, the latter at the district of Tettaha. All the rest were taken away or destroyed by the people of Eimeo. As Tettaha was at no great distance, I determined to go thither myself the first opportunity and make inquiries, in hopes that the breed might still be preserved.

I had much discourse with my guests about Omai. They confirmed to me that he died about thirty months after Captain Cook left the islands. Soon after Captain Cook's departure from Huaheine there were some disputes between the people of that island and those of Ulietea, in which also the natives of Bolabola took part. Omai, who was become of consequence from the possessing three or four muskets and some ammunition, was consulted on the occasion. Such was his opinion and assurances of success that a war was determined on, and took place immediately. Victory soon followed, through the means of those few arms, and many of the Ulietea and Bolabola men were killed. In this contest their flints proved bad, or probably the locks of the muskets had got out of order. This they remedied by a lighted stick, one man presenting the musket and another with the burnt stick setting fire to the priming, without which contrivance their arms would have proved useless. This expedition, it seems, consumed all their ammunition. Peace was soon after established, but I did not understand that

Omai had increased his possessions or his rank. Nevertheless, I have reason to conclude that he was in some degree of favour with his countrymen, from the general good character which they give of him. It appears that he always remembered England with kindness, for his accounts to his countrymen have been such as to give them not only a great idea of our power and consequence, but of our friendship and goodwill towards him.

Tyvarooah, the eldest of the New Zealand boys that were left with him, died a short time after Omai. About Coah, the youngest, I had always doubtful accounts till I came to Huaheine, where I learnt that he likewise was dead.

CHAPTER VIII

Expedition to Tettaha after a heifer.—Extraordinary domestic arrangements.—Tinah's mother visits the ship.—A sheep brought from Ulietea.—Heavy storm.—Death of the surgeon.—Taowne and Toahroah harbours examined.

AFTER dinner I went on shore, and while I was at the tents, from having exposed myself too much in the sun, I was taken ill, and continued in much pain for near an hour. This was soon known among the natives, and I was exceedingly surprised to see Tinah and all the principal people, both men and women, collecting round me and offering their assistance. For this short illness I was made ample amends by the pleasure I received from the attention and appearance of affection in these kind people.

Friday the 14th. This morning I had numberless inquiries after my health. The weather being fine I invited Tinah, Oreepyah, and Poeeno to accompany me to Tettaha, in order to inquire after the cow, and soon after sunrise we set off in the launch. Tettaha is nearly four leagues from Point Venus. On our arrival Tinah sent a man to give notice of our visit. The chief of the district, whose name was Teppahoo, did not appear, but sent a messenger to demand if I came only to see the cow or to take it away with me. In answer to this I sent assurances that I only desired to see it, and the chiefs who were with me spoke to the same effect. I was then desired to proceed in the boat farther along shore to the westward. In our way Tinah made me stop among some fishing canoes to purchase fish for him, which he eat raw, with salt water for sauce. When we arrived at the landing-place a great number of people had collected, and soon after Teppahoo arrived. Oreepyah and I went with him about a quarter of a mile, when I was shown one of the most beautiful heifers I ever saw. I asked if they had any more, but they all said there was no other than a bull at Itteah, as before mentioned. I could not refrain from expressing my displeasure at the destruction and the foolish separation of these fine animals. I had shared with Captain Cook in the trouble of this business and had been equally anxious for the success.

The district of Tettaha is not so luxuriant and fruitful as the country about Matavai. As I saw nothing of consequence to detain me I made a present to Teppahoo, and after inviting him to visit me on board the ship, which he promised to do, I took leave. Tinah had remained all this time in the boat. I observed that no respect was shown to him at this place, nor was he able to procure a coconut or a bread-fruit otherwise than by purchasing it. The heifer being here is a proof of this district not having been friendly to the people of Matavai and Oparre.

In our way back, having to row against the wind, we stopped to refresh at Oparre, and it was eight o'clock by the time we arrived at the ship. I kept my fellow-travellers on board to supper, and they did not fail to remind me of the king's health.

Monday the 17th. Our collection of bread-fruit plants at the tents continued increasing. This morning I sent twelve on board, in pots, to discover where they would thrive the best, the air being more temperate on board the ship than on shore. While I was absent from the ship, Teppahoo had been on board and left a hog as a present for me.

After dinner to-day Tinah, who was my constant visitor, left the table sooner than usual. When he was gone, Oreepyah, his brother, and Oedidde told me a piece of scandal which had been before hinted to me, but which till now I had not heard of with certainty: this was that Iddeah, Tinah's wife, kept a gallant, who was a *towtow*, or servant, and the very person who always fed Tinah at dinner; and this was so far from being without Tinah's knowledge or consent that they said it was by his desire. They added many other circumstances, and as I appeared to doubt they took several opportunities in the course of the day of mentioning it to other people, who all declared it was true.

Tuesday the 18th. This afternoon I saw Teppahoo and invited him on board; before we parted I bargained with him for the heifer, which he promised to bring in five days. My intention was that if I got the heifer I would endeavour to purchase the bull at Itteah, but if that could not be done, then I could send the heifer as a present to the possessor of the bull, which might equally well answer my purpose.

It has been mentioned that Tinah had a place in my cabin to keep those things which I gave him, as being more secure on board than on shore. I had remarked lately that his hoard seemed to diminish the more I endeavoured to increase it. At length I discovered that Iddeah kept another hoard in the master's cabin, which she regularly enriched from her husband's whenever I made him a present, apprehending that I should cease giving when I saw Tinah's locker full. At his request I set the carpenters to work to make him a chest large enough for himself and wife to sleep on. Captain Cook had formerly given him such a chest, but it had been taken from him by the Eimeo people.

Friday the 21st. This forenoon I received a message from Teppahoo to acquaint me the heifer was brought to Matavai. I immediately went on shore, and found that he had been as good as his word. The purchase money was paid, which consisted of a shirt, a hatchet, a spike nail, a knife, a pair of scissors, a gimlet, and file; to which was added a small quantity of loaf-sugar. Teppahoo appeared well pleased with his bargain, and I sent the heifer to Poeeno's residence, near which was plenty of grass.

In the afternoon I was invited to a *heiva*, the most extraordinary part of which was an oration, with some ceremonies in compliment to us. Twelve men were divided into four ranks, with two women in the front; behind them all stood a priest, who made a speech which lasted ten minutes and which was listened to with some attention. During this the picture of Captain Cook, which had been brought for that purpose, was placed by my side. When the priest left off speaking, a piece of white cloth was wrapped round the picture, and another piece round me. The priest then spoke again for a short time, and an old man placed a piece of plaited coconut leaf at my feet; the same was done to Tinah, and one piece was put under the picture. After this the dancing began, which was in the same style that we had already seen.

The head of the ship was the figure of a woman, and not ill carved. As we were painting the ship's upper works, I directed this figure to be painted in colours, with which the islanders were much pleased. Not only the men, but the women, desired me to bring English women when I came again. To-day Oedidde, thinking I was not convinced of the truth of what he had told me about Iddeah, mentioned the affair to the lady herself in my hearing, at which she laughed, but said he did ill to tell me of it. However, it was evident she was not much offended, for they were both very much diverted in discoursing upon the subject.

I find it is not at all uncommon for brothers to have connection with the wives of each other, particularly elder brothers with the wives of their younger brothers, which is generally allowed, and no offence taken; but if any person not belonging to the family endeavours at the same intimacy, it is resented as an injury. Inclination seems to be the only binding law of marriage at Otaheite.

As I purposed to get instruments on shore at Point Venus to make observations, I desired Tinah to order a house to be brought there for me; which was done and fixed in half an hour, being only a light shed supported by posts.

Monday the 24th. To-day I bought a turtle that was caught on the reefs. As Tinah was going to leave me for a few days I had it dressed for his dinner. He told me that his mother, Oberree-roah, was arrived from the island Tethuroa, and begged that I would send for her in the morning, and take care of her till he returned; which I willingly promised.

Tuesday the 25th. This morning I sent a boat to Oparre, which returned in the afternoon with Oberree-roah and two women, her servants. As she was old and corpulent, it was with difficulty that we helped her up the ship's side. As soon as she was in the ship she sat down on the gangway, and, clasping my knees in her arms, expressed her pleasure at seeing me by a flood of tears. Her servants then produced three pieces of cloth, which, with a large hog, some bread-fruit, plantains, and coconuts she had brought as a present. As she was fatigued by her journey, she wished to remain on board all night; and I directed accommodations to be prepared, which was done with little trouble, as nothing more was necessary than a mat and some cloth spread on the deck. She had with her a favourite cat, bred from one that had been given her by Captain Cook. She told me all the misfortunes that had befallen her son and friends since Captain Cook left Otaheite. All the accounts agree in some of the cattle being now alive at the island Eimeo: in the number they differ, but that there are eight is the least account.

Wednesday the 26th. In the morning Oberree-roah being desirous to go on shore, I made her a present of several things, which she did not care to take with her then, but requested that I would keep them safe for her. Only Moannah and Poeeno dined with me to-day. They told me that Tinah and his brother Oreepyah were not on good terms together, and it was imagined that they would fight as soon as the ship was gone. I had observed a coolness between them, and had at times endeavoured to make them more cordial, but with very little effect. Their quarrel had arisen from a disagreement between their wives.

In the afternoon a canoe from Ulietea arrived, in which was an *earee*, or chief, of that island, who is a nephew to Oberree-roah. He brought a sheep with him; the poor animal was infected with the mange and in very poor condition. The climate had not, as far as I could judge, altered the quality of the wool, with which she was well covered, except a part about the shoulders. I imagine this animal to be the English ewe left by Captain Cook. The owner assured me that there were ten sheep at Huaheine, the truth of which I much doubted. I was surprised and rather mortified to find that he set so little value on this, as to let me have it, at the first word, for a small adze. I sent it to be kept at Poeeno's with the heifer.

Friday the 28th. Tinah and his wife returned to Matavai, and, from appearances which I have no reason to mistrust, were sincerely glad to see me again after their short absence. They brought, as usual, a present of a hog and fruit. This morning there was an eclipse of the sun, but the weather was so cloudy that I had only an opportunity of observing the end of the eclipse, which was at 19h. 43′ 53″.

Saturday the 29th. I sent a man to shear the ewe, by which a remedy could more easily be applied to cure the disease with which it was infected. The garden made near the tents was not in a prosperous condition: most of the melons and cucumbers were destroyed by insects, and the soil, being sandy, was not favourable to the other seeds. I therefore chose another spot of ground, farther from the seaside, and had an assortment of seeds sown.

December the 1st. In the night the rudder of one of the boats was stolen from the tents. On landing in the morning neither Tinah nor any of his family came near me, being, I was informed, afraid of my displeasure. As the loss was not great I immediately sent to assure them that I had no anger, except against the person who committed the theft. In consequence of this message Tinah and some of the other chiefs came to the tents and promised that they would exert themselves to discover the thief and get the rudder restored. This was the first theft of any consequence that had been committed since the tents were on shore, and my suspicions fell chiefly on the people who were here from some of the other islands. Tinah had just begun to build a house for himself, and I promised that our carpenters should assist him. Whydooah, the youngest brother of Tinah, had lately been one of my constant visitors and seemed to have left off his former custom of getting drunk with the *ava*. He was esteemed one of their best warriors, and I was told that in the quarrel with the people of Eimeo he killed Maheine, the chief of that island.

Friday the 5th. The weather for some time past had been very unsettled. This afternoon the wind blew fresh from the NW., which occasioned the sea to break very high across the Dolphin bank; and in the night such a heavy broken sea came into the bay that we were obliged to batten all the hatchways down and to keep everybody upon deck all night, though the rain came down in torrents. The ship rolled in a most violent manner. In the morning the wind increasing, and there being no possibility of putting to sea, we struck yards and topmasts, and trusted to our anchors. The river swelled so much with the rain that the point of land on which the tents stood became an island; and, to preserve the bread-fruit plants from being endangered, the people were obliged to cut a passage for the river through a part of the beach, at a distance from the tents. The sea broke very high on the beach; nevertheless a canoe put off, and to my surprise Tinah, his wife, and Moannah made their way good through the surf and came on board to see me. There was no other person in the canoe, for the weather did not admit of useless passengers; each of them had a paddle, which they managed with great activity and skill. These kind people embraced me with many tears and expressed their apprehensions for the safety of the ship. Towards noon, however, the sea abated considerably, but the wind continued to blow strong from the NW. At sunset Iddeah went on shore, but Tinah would remain with me the whole night.

Sunday the 7th. The wind continued between the north and north-west, but had so much moderated that I no longer considered our situation to be alarming. At noon Iddeah returned to the ship, with a large hog and a supply of bread-fruit and coconuts, and soon after she and Tinah left the ship, having exacted a promise from me that if the weather was moderate I would go on shore in the morning and visit their parents and sister, who, they told me, had been much alarmed on our account. I received a visit likewise from Poeeno and his wife. This woman had always shown great regard for us, and now, on our meeting, before I could be aware of it, she began beating her head violently with a shark's tooth, so that her face was covered with blood in an instant. I put a stop to this as soon as I could, and with the drying up of the blood her agitation subsided. This ceremony is frequently performed upon occasions either of joy or grief. Her husband said that if any accident happened to the ship I should live with him, and that they would cut down trees and build me another ship.

From this sample of the weather, and the information of the natives, I was convinced it would not be safe to continue in Matavai Bay much longer, and I determined to get everything ready for sailing as speedily as I could.

The night proved moderate, and in the morning I went on shore, where I was received by Oberree-roah and several other friends with great affection.

The plants received no injury from the bad weather, having been carefully covered from the spray of the sea: some were in a dormant state and others were striking out young shoots. Nelson thought that it was better to refrain a few days from taking them on board; I therefore consented to defer it. He was of opinion that the plants could be propagated from the roots only, and I directed some boxes to be filled, as we could stow them where no others could be placed.

Tuesday the 9th. This afternoon, in hauling the launch on shore to be repaired, many of the natives assisting, one of them, a fine boy about ten years old, was thrown down and a roller which was placed under the boat went over him. The surgeon being ill I sent off for his assistant. Fortunately no limb was broken, nor did he receive any material injury. The surgeon had been a long time ill, the effect of intemperance and indolence. He had latterly scarce ever stirred out of his cabin, but was not apprehended to be in a dangerous state; nevertheless, this evening he appeared to be so much worse than usual that it was thought necessary to remove him to some place where he could have more air; but to no effect, for he died in an hour afterwards. This unfortunate man drank very hard, and was so averse to exercise that he never would be prevailed on to take half a dozen turns upon deck at a time in the whole course of the voyage.

Wednesday the 10*th.* As I wished to bury the surgeon on shore I mentioned it to Tinah, who said there would be no objection, but that it would be necessary to ask his father's consent first, which he undertook to do and immediately left me for that purpose. By this circumstance it appears that though the eldest son of an *earee* succeeds to the title and honours of the father as soon as he is born, yet a considerable portion of authority remains with the father even after the son is of age. When Tinah returned I went with him to the spot intended for the burial-place, taking with us two men to dig the grave, but on our arrival I found the natives had already begun it. Tinah asked me if they were doing right? 'There,' says he, 'the sun rises and there it sets.' The idea that the grave should be east and west, I imagine they learnt from the Spaniards, as the captain of one of their ships was buried at Oetepeha in 1774. Certain it is they had not the information from anybody belonging to our ship, for I believe we should not have thought of it. The grave, however, was marked out very exactly. At four in the afternoon the body was interred: the chiefs, and many of the natives, came to see the ceremony, and showed great attention during the service. Some of the chiefs were very inquisitive about what was to be done with the surgeon's cabin, on account of apparitions. They said, when a man died in Otaheite, and was carried to the *tupapow*, that as soon as night came he was surrounded by spirits, and if any person went there by himself they would devour him; therefore they said that not less than two people together should go into the surgeon's cabin for some time. I did not endeavour to dissuade them from this belief, otherwise than by laughing and letting them know that we had no such apprehensions.

In the afternoon the effects of the deceased were disposed of, and I appointed Mr Thomas Denman Ledward, the surgeon's mate, to do duty as surgeon.

Friday the 12th. I went in a boat to examine the harbours about Oparre, and found two formed by the reefs. The western-most is the most convenient for sailing in or out, but is not well sheltered from a NW. wind or sea. This harbour is called by the natives Taowne: it is about a league and a half distant from Point Venus, and may be known by a remarkable moun-tain, called by the natives Wawry, which bears SSE. from the entrance.

The easternmost harbour is called Toahroah. It is small, but as secure as a reef harbour can well be. It is about three miles distant from Point Venus. The chief objection to this harbour is the difficulty of getting out with the common trade wind, the entrance being on the east side, not more than one hundred yards wide, and the depth without inconvenient for warping. On the south side of the entrance is a *morai*: the reef side is to be kept on board and a look-out to be kept from aloft, whence the shoal water is better discerned than from the deck.

Sunday the 14th. This forenoon we performed divine service. Many of the principal natives attended and behaved with great decency. Some of the women at one time betrayed an inclina-tion to laugh at our general responses; but, on my looking at them, they appeared much ashamed. After the service I was asked if no offering was to be made for the *eatua* to eat.

The weather had been fair all the last week, and at this time appeared quite settled, so that I was under no apprehensions of danger from continuing a little longer in Matavai Bay.

CHAPTER IX

Wednesday the 17th. This morning I took a walk into the country,
accompanied by Nelson and my old friend Moannah. The
breadth of the border of low land, before we arrived at the foot
of the hills, was near three miles. This part of our journey
was through a delightful country, well covered with bread-fruit
and coconut trees, and strewed with houses in which were
swarms of children. We then proceeded along a valley, still
among houses, with plantations of yams, tarro, the cloth-plant,
and their favourite root the *ava*; there were bread-fruit trees
on the sides of the hills, which were dwarfs in comparison of
those on the low land. Our walk was very much interrupted
by a river, the course of which was so serpentine that we had to
cross it several times, being carried over on men's shoulders.

On arriving at a *morai* I saw a number of the natives collected,
and was informed that the priests were performing their devo-
tions. Sixteen men were sitting on their heels; in the front was
a pole covered with a plaited coconut branch, and before each
of the men there was a number of small pieces of the same leaf
plaited, which they call *hahyree,* and each had likewise a piece
round his wrist. One, who appeared to be the chief priest,
prayed aloud, and was answered by all the rest together: after
a few short sentences and responses they rose, and each carried
an *hahyree,* which they placed at the foot of the pole, and
returned to prayer: this was repeated till all the *hahyree* were
delivered, and then the ceremony ended. I must not forget to
mention that they had placed near the pole an offering of plantains and bread-fruit, which they left for the *eatua.* They very
kindly asked us to partake of a roasted hog that had been prepared for them whilst they were praying, but as I wished to
make the most of the morning, before the sun was too high,
I declined their offer, and Moannah bespoke refreshments to be
ready for us when we returned.

We continued our walk up the valley, which became very narrow, and had advanced a considerable way beyond all the houses and plantations when we were suddenly stopped by a cascade that fell into the river from a height of above two hundred feet: the fáll at this time was not great, but in the heavy rains must be considerable. The natives look upon this as the most wonderful sight in the island. The fall of water is the least curious part: the cliff over which it comes is perpendicular, forming an appearance as if supported by square pillars of stone, and with a regularity that is surprising. Underneath is a pool eight or nine feet deep, into which the water falls; and in this place all the natives make a point of bathing once in their lives, probably from some religious idea.

The hills here approach each other within a few yards, and are well covered with wood. As the road appeared difficult, I did not care to proceed towards the mountain. I cannot with certainty say how far this curious precipice is from the bay, but think, in the road by which we went, it cannot be less than seven miles. It is called Peeah Roah.

In our return we found a young pig prepared for us, and we made a hearty meal. We dined in the house of an old acquaintance of Nelson's, for whom he had in 1777 planted the two shaddock plants formerly mentioned, which he had brought from the Friendly Islands. These we had the satisfaction to see were grown to fine trees, and full of fruit.

In their plantations they do not take much pains, except with the *ava* and the cloth-plant, both of which they are careful to keep clear of weeds. Many of the plantations of the cloth-plant were fenced with stone and surrounded with a ditch. The yams and plantains are mostly on the higher grounds. As soon as we had finished our dinner we returned towards the ship. I was much delighted in this walk with the number of children that I saw in every part of the country: they are very handsome and sprightly and full of antic tricks. They have many diversions that are common with the boys in England; such as flying kites, cats' cradle, swinging, dancing or jumping in a rope, walking upon stilts, and wrestling.

Friday the 19th. The wind to-day blew fresh, but continued regular from the E. and ESE. We had likewise much rain, and a long swell set into the bay. I had not yet determined whether on leaving Matavai Bay I would go to the island Eimeo or to the harbour of Toahroah near Oparre. This uncertainty made Tinah and the rest of my friends very anxious, and they appeared much distressed on my desiring them, this afternoon, to send on board all the things which they wished to have repaired by the forge, without delay, that what they wanted might be done before the ship left Matavai, which I told them would be in a few days. They very earnestly entreated I would stay one month longer. I represented this as impossible, and asked Tinah if he would not go with me to Eimeo; but he said that notwithstanding my protection, he was certain that Eimeo people would watch for an opportunity to kill him. He remained on board with me all night, but his wife went on shore, and returned early in the morning, bringing with her some axes and other things that were in need of repair.

Saturday the 20th. When I went on shore I found Otow, Oberree-roah, Moannah, and several others in great tribulation at the thoughts that we were so soon to leave them. All the people of Matavai, I saw, were much concerned at my intention of going to Eimeo, and took every opportunity to prejudice me against the people of that island; to which I paid very little attention, as their motive was obvious. Their expressions of friendship and affection for me, however, I could not disregard, as I had no doubt of their being genuine and unaffected; and I felt my unwillingness to leave these kind people so much increased that the next day I sent the master in the launch to re-examine the depth of water between this bay and Toahroah harbour. He returned in the evening, and acquainted me that he found a good bottom, with not less than sixteen fathoms depth all the way. The harbour of Toahroah appearing every way safe, I determined to get the ship there as speedily as possible, and I immediately made my intention public, which occasioned great rejoicing.

Wednesday the 24th. This day we took the plants on board being 774 pots, all in a healthy state; for whenever any plant had an unfavourable appearance it was replaced by another. The number of those rejected was 302, of which not one in ten but was found to be growing at the root.

The natives reckon eight kinds of the bread-fruit tree, each of which they distinguish by a different name : (1) *patteah;* (2) *eroroo ;* (3) *awanna ;* (4) *mi-re ;* (5) *oree ;* (6) *powerro ;* (7) *appeere ;* (8) *rowdeeah.* In the first, fourth, and eighth class the leaf differs from the rest; the fourth is more sinuated; the eighth has a large broad leaf, not at all sinuated. The

difference of the fruit is principally in the first and eighth
class. In the first the fruit is rather larger and more of an
oblong form; in the eighth it is round and not above half the
size of the others. I inquired if plants could be produced from
the seed, and was told they could not, but that they must be
taken from the root. The plants are best collected after wet
weather, at which time the earth balls round the roots, and
they are not liable to suffer by being moved.

The most common method of dividing time at Otaheite is
by moons; but they likewise make a division of the year into
six parts, each of which is distinguished by the name of the
kind of bread-fruit then in season. In this division they keep
a small interval called *tawa*, in which they do not use the bread-
fruit. This is about the end of February, when the fruit is not
in perfection; but there is no part of the year in which the
trees are entirely bare.

Thursday the 25th. At daylight we unmoored, and I sent the
tents in the launch to Oparre, with directions that after landing
them the launch should meet the ship in the entrance of Toahroah harbour, to show the safest part of the channel. At
half-past ten we got the ship under sail, and ran down under topsails; when we were near the launch it fell calm and the ship
shot past her. We immediately let the anchor go, but to our
great surprise we found the ship was aground forwards. She
had run on so easy that we had not perceived it at the time.
This accident occasioned us much trouble, as we were obliged
to send anchors out astern to get the ship afloat. In doing this
one of the cables swept a rock, and was not got clear again
without much difficulty. When the ship was moored, Point
Venus bore N. 46° E. The east point of the harbour N. 65° E.
quarter of a mile. Our distance from the shore half a cable's
length; depth of water eight and a half fathoms.

The next morning, on my landing, I was welcomed by all
the principal people; I may say by the whole crowd, and
congratulated on the safety of the ship. Tinah showed me
a house near the water-side, abreast the ship, which he desired
I would make use of, and which was large enough for all
our purposes. He and his brother Oreepyah then desired
I would stay and receive a formal address and present, which
they called *otee.* To this I assented, and a stool was brought
for me to sit on. They then left me with Moannah, and in a
short time I saw Tinah returning with about twenty men, who

all made a stop at some distance, and a priest said a short prayer to the *eatua*, to which the rest made reply. A man was then sent to me three several times, at each time bringing me a small pig and the stem of a plantain leaf. The first they told me was for the God of Britanee, the next for King George, and the last for myself. Moannah then got up, and without being dictated to made an oration for me; the purport of which I understood to be, that I received their offering with thanks; that we were good people and friends; and therefore he exhorted them to commit no thefts. He told them to bring their pigs, coconuts, and bread-fruit, and they would receive good things in return; that we took nothing without their consent; and finally, that every man was to quit the place (the house we occupied) at night, for if they made any visit in the dark they would be killed. With this speech the ceremony ended.

I found this a delightful situation and in every respect convenient. The ship was perfectly sheltered by the reefs in smooth water, and close to a fine beach without the least surf. A small river, with very good water, runs into the sea about the middle of the harbour. I gave directions for the plants to be landed, and the same party to be with them as at Matavai. Tinah fixed his dwelling close to our station.

Monday the 29th. Some of the natives took advantage of the butcher's negligence and stole his cleaver. I complained of this to the chiefs who were on board, and they promised that they would endeavour to recover it; but an article so valuable as this was to the natives I had no great expectation of seeing restored.

The ship continued to be supplied by the natives as usual. Coconuts were in such plenty that I believe not a pint of water was drank on board the ship in the twenty-four hours. Bread-fruit began to be scarce, though we purchased without difficulty a sufficient quantity for our consumption: there was, however, another harvest approaching, which they expected would be fit for use in five or six weeks. The better kind of plantains also were become scarce, but a kind which they call *vayhee* were in great plenty. This fruit does not hang on the trees like the other kinds, but grows upon an upright stalk of considerable strength and substance. Though this plantain is inferior in quality to most of the others, it affords great subsistence to the natives. We received almost every day presents of fish, chiefly dolphin and albacore, and a few small rock fish. Their fishing is mostly in the night, when they make strong lights on the reefs, which attract the fish to them. Sometimes in fine weather the canoes are out in such numbers that the whole sea appears illuminated. In the canoes they fish with hook and line, and on the reefs they strike the fish with a spear. Some likewise carry out small nets, which are managed by two men. In the daytime their fishing canoes go without the reefs, sometimes to a considerable distance, where they fish with rods and lines, and catch bonetas and other fish. Whenever there is a show of fish a fleet of canoes immediately proceeds to sea. Their hooks, being bright, are used without bait, in the manner of our artificial flies. Their rods are made of bamboo; but when there are any very large fish they make use of an outrigger over the fore part of the canoe, about twenty-five feet in length, which has two prongs at the extremity, to each of which is fastened a hook and line; and when a fish takes the hook it is raised by ropes managed by two men in the stern of the canoe.

Thursday the 1st. Contrary to my expectation, Tinah this afternoon brought on board the cleaver that had been stolen. The thief had taken it to Attahooroo, and Tinah told me, which I could easily believe, that it was given up with great reluctance. The next morning I offered Tinah a present of axes and other things; but as he suspected this was meant by way of return for getting the cleaver restored, he would not be prevailed with to accept a single article.

I had constantly the company of Tinah, his wife, and some of his relations; but the royal children, though so near us, never came in sight of the ship. The river separated them from the place occupied by our people on shore, and for fear of giving alarm or offence, I gave strict orders that no one should attempt to go near their place of residence.

Monday the 5th. At the relief of the watch, at four o'clock this morning, the small cutter was missing. I was immediately informed of it, and mustered the ship's company, when it appeared that three men were absent: Charles Churchill, the ship's corporal, and two of the seamen, William Muspratt and John Millward, the latter of whom had been sentinel from twelve to two in the morning. They had taken with them eight stand of arms and ammunition, but what their plan was, or which way they had gone, no one on board seemed to have the least knowledge. I went on shore to the chiefs, and soon received information that the boat was at Matavai, and that the deserters had departed in a sailing canoe for the island Tethuroa. On this intelligence I sent the master to Matavai to search for the small cutter, and one of the chiefs went with him; but before they had got half-way they met the boat with five of the natives, who were bringing her back to the ship. This service rendered me by the people of Matavai pleased me much, and I rewarded the men accordingly.

I told Tinah and the other chiefs that I expected they would get the deserters brought back, for that I was determined not to leave Otaheite without them. They assured me that they would do everything in their power to have them taken, and it was agreed that Oreepyah and Moannah should depart the next morning for Tethuroa. Oreepyah inquired if they had pocket pistols, 'for,' said he, 'though we may surprise and seize them before they can make use of their muskets, yet if they have pistols they may do mischief even while they are held.' I quieted these apprehensions by assuring them that the deserters had no pistols with them.

Tuesday the 6th. At daylight, Oreepyah and Moannah set off in two canoes for Tethuroa, but the weather became so boisterous that they were obliged to return in the forenoon, and I was happy to see them get safe in, as the sea ran very high without the harbour. From the first of this month the weather and winds had been much unsettled, with a great deal of rain. Our former station at Matavai appeared not at all safe, the sea at times breaking high over the Dolphin bank and making a great swell in the bay. Oreepyah and Moannah both promised me that they would sail again as soon as the weather should be fine.

Friday the 9th. The wind continued to blow strong at sea, though in the harbour we had at times but light breezes. Poeeno, from Matavai, came to see me to-day; he said he was apprehensive that I was displeased with him, on account of our deserters having been carried to Tethuroa by a canoe from Matavai. This, he declared, had been done before he heard of it, and that the only service in his power he had not neglected to do for me, which was the sending our boat back. As this was really an act of friendship I received him with great cordiality, and he assured me that there could be no doubt, from the directions Tinah had given, of the deserters being brought to the ship as soon as the weather would admit canoes to go after them.

Saturday the 10th. One of the officers this morning on shore inadvertently plucked a branch from a tree called *tutuee*, that bears the oil nut, which was growing at a *morai*. On entering with it into the house occupied by our people, all the natives, both men and women, immediately went away. When I went on shore I found this branch tied to one of the posts of the house, although the effect it had on the natives was known. I was much displeased at this piece of wantonness, and ordered the branch to be taken away; but the natives, notwithstanding, would not come near the place. They said the house was *taboo*, which I understand to signify interdicted, and that none of them might approach it till the *taboo* was taken off, which could only be done by Tinah. To take anything away from a *morai* is regarded as a kind of sacrilege, and, they believe, gives great offence to the *eatua*. At my request Tinah took off the *taboo*, but not before the afternoon. This was performed by an offering of a plantain leaf at the *morai*, and a prayer made to the *eatua*. After this ceremony the house was resorted to by the natives as usual.

I had not yet given up the hope of obtaining the bull from Itteah, though I had hitherto received no satisfactory answer to the messages which Tinah had sent at my desire. I therefore spoke to Poeeno, who undertook to negotiate this business, and I commissioned him to make very liberal offers. He left me after dinner to return to Matavai. In the evening a messenger arrived from him to acquaint me that in his absence the sheep which I had trusted to his care had been killed by a dog, and that he had sent the culprit, hoping that I would kill him for the offence he had committed. This poor sheep had been so much diseased that I could not help suspecting she died without the dog's assistance, and that the story of the dog was invented to prevent my attributing it to want of care. This doubt did not appear in my answer; as for the dog, I told the messenger to do with him what he pleased.

Tuesday the 13th. This morning, the weather being more moderate than it had been for some days past, Oreepyah sailed with two canoes for Tethuroa. Some business prevented Moannah from accompanying him, but he followed the next day with two other canoes. The wood that we had got at Matavai being expended, I applied to Tinah, who sent three trees down to the water-side before night, which when cut up made a good launch-load.

I saw two instances of jealousy to-day, one of which had

nearly produced fatal consequences. A man was detected with a married woman, by the husband, who stabbed him in the belly with a knife: fortunately the intestines escaped, and the wound did not prove dangerous. The other instance was a girl, who had constantly lived with my coxswain, beating another girl that she discovered to have been too intimate with him.

Friday the 16th. In walking to-day with Tinah near a *tupapow*, I was surprised by a sudden outcry of grief. As I expressed a desire to see the distressed person, Tinah took me to the place, where we found a number of women, one of whom was the mother of a young female child that lay dead. On seeing us their mourning not only immediately ceased, but to my astonishment they all burst into an immoderate fit of laughter, and, while we remained, appeared much diverted with our visit. I told Tinah the woman had no sorrow for her child, otherwise her grief would not have so easily subsided; on which he jocosely told her to cry again: they did not, however, resume their mourning in our presence. This strange behaviour would incline us to think them hard-hearted and unfeeling, did we not know that they are fond parents, and, in general, very affectionate. It is therefore to be ascribed to their extreme levity of disposition, and it is probable that death does not appear to them with so many terrors as it does to people of a more serious cast.

Sunday the 18th. I received a message from Poeeno to acquaint me that he had been successful in his negotiation for the bull, which he had driven part of the way by land, but could not get farther on account of the rivers and therefore desired a boat should be sent for him. I accordingly ordered the launch to be got ready, and at two o'clock the next morning Mr Fryer, the master, set off in her.

In the afternoon the launch returned with the bull and my friend Poeeno. For the night I directed that the bull should remain at Oparre, and the next day he was taken to the cow at Matavai.

Wednesday the 21st. To-day Poeeno brought to me the person from whom he had the bull, to receive the stipulated payment, which was one of every article of traffic that I had in my possession. This man, whose name was Oweevee, they told me was inspired by a divine spirit, and that in all matters of consequence he was consulted, for that he conversed with the *eatua*. It was, they said, the *eatua* that ordered him to demand the bull from Tinah, which not to have complied with would have been the height of impiety. I endeavoured to convince them of the roguery of this man, thinking I had a fair argument to prove it by his selling that which the *eatua* had ordered him to keep; but here I was easily defeated, for it seems the *eatua* told him to sell me the beast. This being the case, I said I would not give the animals to any person; that they were now mine, and that I would leave them under the protection of Poeeno and Tinah, who I hoped would take care of them for me till I returned. They both entered into my views and promised the animals should be attended to, and told me that while they were considered as my property no one would attempt to take them away.

Thursday the 22nd. This afternoon I received a message from Teppahoo to inform me that our deserters had passed this harbour and were at Tettaha, about five miles distant. I ordered the cutter to be got ready and a little before sunset left the ship, taking Oedidee with me. By his advice I landed at some distance from the place where the deserters were, but thinking it necessary to have the boat within call, and Oedidee assuring me that there was safe landing farther on, I directed the boat to proceed along shore whilst Oedidee and I walked along the beach. The night was very dark and windy, and the shore being rocky I soon lost sight of the boat. A few of the natives had joined us in our walk, and from their manner I had reason to suspect them of a design to close upon us, with an intention, no doubt, to plunder. I was provided with pocket-pistols, and on producing one they left us. Oedidee was so much alarmed that I could scarce prevail on him to proceed. When we arrived at Teppahoo's house we were very kindly received by him and his wife. The cutter was arrived, but there being a very high surf she could not come within a hundred yards of the shore.

The deserters, I was informed, were in a house close to us, and I imagined there would be no great difficulty in securing them with the assistance of the natives. They had, however, heard of my arrival, and when I was near the house they came out, without their arms, and delivered themselves up. I sent directions off to the boat for one of my people to come on shore and for the boat to return to the place where I had landed. My next business was to secure the arms, which I delivered to Teppahoo to take charge of for the night. One musket and two bayonets were missing, which they said were lost, by the canoe in which they came from Tethuroa having overset. I then took leave of Teppahoo, who presented us with a plentiful supply of provisions, and we proceeded with the deserters towards the boat; but as the wind had increased and it rained hard I determined to remain on shore till the morning, and having found shelter for the people we passed the remainder of the night without accident. At daylight I sent for the arms, and we returned to the ship.

I learnt from the deserters that at Tethuroa they had seen Oreepyah and Moannah, who had made an attempt to secure them. They said it was their intention to have returned to the ship, and it is probable that they were so much harassed by the natives watching for an opportunity to surprise them that they might wish to have the merit of returning of their own accord to avoid the disgrace of being seized and brought back. At the time they delivered themselves up to me it was not in their power to have made resistance, their ammunition having been spoiled by the wet.

In consequence of my having been kept all night from the ship by the tempestuous weather the time-keeper went down at 10h. 5′ 36″. Its rate previous to this was 1″, 7 losing in 24 hours, and its error from the mean time at Greenwich was 7′ 29″, 2 too slow. I set it going again by a common watch, corrected by observations, and endeavoured to make the error the same as if it had not stopped; but being over-cautious made me tedious in setting it in motion, and increased the error from mean time at Greenwich. The rate of going I did not find to have altered.

At dinner Tinah congratulated me on having recovered my men, but expressed some concern that they had not been brought by Oreepyah and Moannah, lest I should imagine they had not done everything in their power. To this I replied that I was perfectly satisfied of their good intentions to serve me, and that I considered myself under great obligations to them for the trouble they had been at on my account. I learnt afterwards that they had actually seized and bound the deserters, but had been prevailed upon by fair promises of their returning peaceably to the ship to let them loose. The deserters, however, finding an opportunity to get possession of their arms again, set the natives at defiance.

Friday the 30th. This afternoon I punished one of the seamen,

Isaac Martin, with nineteen lashes for striking an Indian. This was a transgression of so serious a nature, and such a direct violation of my orders, that I would on no account be prevailed on to forgive it, though great intercession was made by some of the chiefs.

Oreepyah and Moannah were not yet returned from Tethuroa. This place is resorted to by the principal people of this part of Otaheite at particular seasons, when fish are in great plenty there. It was described to me to be a group of small keys surrounded by a reef; their produce is chiefly coconuts and plantains. During the season bread-fruit and other provisions are daily carried over from Otaheite. Not less than a hundred sail of canoes were at Tethuroa when our deserters were there.

Teppahoo and his wife were become my constant visitors. He had for some time past been ill and had made Oparre his place of residence, for the benefit of our surgeon's advice and assistance. At this time he complained of a hoarseness and sore throat. Mr Ledward, on examining him, discovered there had been two holes in the roof of his mouth, which, though healed, had the appearance of having been large. The adjacent parts appeared sound, yet the surgeon was of opinion that they were cancerous and would in the end occasion his death.

Saturday the 31st. This morning I ordered all the chests to be taken on shore and the inside of the ship to be washed with boiling water to kill the cockroaches. We were constantly obliged to be at great pains to keep the ship clear of vermin on account of the plants. By the help of traps and good cats we were freed from rats and mice. When I was at Otaheite with Captain Cook there were great numbers of rats about all the houses, and so tame that they flocked round the people at their meals for the offals, which were commonly thrown to them; but at this time we scarce ever saw a rat, which must be attributed to the industry of a breed of cats left here by European ships.

After breakfast I walked with Tinah to Matavai to see the cattle and the gardens. Tinah had already taken so large a dose of the *ava* that he was perfectly stupefied. Iddeah, however, was with us, and she is one of the most intelligent persons I met with at Otaheite. We went first to Poeeno's house, and saw the bull and cow together in a very fine pasture. I was informed that the cow had taken the bull, so that if no untoward accident happens there is a fair chance of the breed being established. In the garden near Poeeno's house many things had failed. The Indian corn was in a fine state, and I have no doubt but they will cultivate it all over the country. A fig-tree was in a very thriving way, as were two vines, a pine-apple plant, and some slips of a shaddock-tree. From this place we walked to the garden at Point Venus, but I had the mortification to find almost everything there destroyed by the hogs. Some underground peas and Indian corn had escaped, and likewise the caliloo green and ocra of Jamaica.

We returned to the ship, and after dinner I was not a little surprised to hear Tinah seriously propose that he and his wife should go with me to England. He said he would only take two servants, that he much wished to see King George, who, he was sure, would be glad to see him. Tinah and many of his countrymen were become extremely eager to get a knowledge of other countries, and were continually inquiring about the situations of the islands which we told them of in these seas. To quiet his importunity I was obliged to promise that I would ask the king's permission to carry them to England if I came again, that then I should be in a larger ship and could have accommodations properly fitted up. I was sorry to find that Tinah was apprehensive he should be attacked by his enemies as soon as our ship left Otaheite, and that if they joined they would be too powerful for him. The illness of Teppahoo, with whom he was on good terms, gave him much uneasiness; Teppahoo's wife being a sister of Otow's and aunt to Tinah. They have no children, as has been before related, and if Teppahoo were to die he would be succeeded as *earee* of the district of Tettaha by his brother, who is an enemy to Tinah. I have on every occasion endeavoured to make the principal people believe that we should return again to Otaheite, and that we should revenge any injury done in our absence to the people of Matavai and Oparre.

The wife of Oedidee is likewise an aunt to Tinah and sister to Otow. His native place is Ulietea, where he has some property, but which, I imagine, is not of such consequence to him as the countenance of the chiefs with whom he is connected at Otaheite.

CHAPTER X

The ship's cable cut in the night.—Coolness with the chiefs on that account.—Visit to an old lady.—Disturbance at a heiva.—Tinah's hospitality.—A thief taken, and punished.—Preparations for sailing.

Tuesday the 3rd. I was present this afternoon at a wrestling match, where a young man by an unlucky fall put his arm out of joint at the elbow. Three stout men immediately took hold of him, and two of them fixing their feet against his ribs, replaced it. I had sent for our surgeon, but before he arrived all was well, except a small swelling of the muscles in consequence of the strain. I inquired what they would have done if the bone had been broken, and, to show me their practice, they got a number of sticks and placed round a man's arm, which they bound with cord. That they have considerable skill in surgery is not to be doubted. I have before mentioned an instance of an amputated arm being perfectly healed, and which had every appearance of having been treated with great propriety.

The part of the beach nearest the ship was become the general place of resort towards the close of the day. An hour before sunset the inhabitants began to collect, and here they amused themselves with exercising the lance, dancing, and various kinds of merriment till nearly dark, when they retired to their homes. Of this cheerful scene we were spectators and partakers every fine evening.

Friday the 6th. An occurrence happened to-day that gave me great concern, not only on account of the danger with which the ship had been threatened, but as it tended greatly to diminish the confidence and good understanding which had hitherto been constantly preserved between us and the natives. The wind had blown fresh in the night, and at daylight we discovered that the cable by which the ship rode had been cut near the water's edge, in such a manner that only one strand remained whole. While we were securing the ship Tinah came on board. I could not but believe he was perfectly innocent of the transaction, nevertheless, I spoke to him in a very peremptory manner and insisted upon his discovering and bringing to me the offender. I was wholly at a loss how to account for this malicious act. My suspicions fell chiefly, I may say wholly, on the strangers that came to us from other parts of the island, for we had on

every occasion received such unreserved and unaffected marks
of goodwill from the people of Matavai and Oparre that in my
own mind I entirely acquitted them. The anger which I expressed, however, created so much alarm that old Otow and
his wife (the father and mother of Tinah) immediately quitted
Oparre and retired to the mountains in the midst of heavy rain,
as did Teppahoo and his family. Tinah and Iddeah remained,
and expostulated with me on the unreasonableness of my anger
against them. He said that he would exert his utmost endeavours to discover the guilty person, but it might possibly
not be in his power to get him delivered up, which would be the
case if he was either of Tiarraboo, Attahooroo, or of the island
Eimeo. That the attempt might have been made as much out
of enmity to the people of Matavai and Oparre as to me, every
one knowing the regard I had for them and that I had declared
I would protect them against their enemies. All this I was
inclined to believe, but I did not think proper to appear perfectly satisfied, lest Tinah, who was naturally very indolent,
should be remiss in his endeavours to detect the offender. To
guard as much as possible against future attempts of this kind
I directed a stage to be built on the forecastle, so that the cables
should be more directly under the eye of the sentinel, and I
likewise gave orders that one of the midshipmen should keep
watch forward.

In the afternoon Oreepyah returned from Tethuroa. He
told me that Moannah and himself had narrowly escaped being
lost in the bad weather, and that Moannah had been obliged
to take shelter at Eimeo. Several canoes had been lost lately
in their passage to or from Tethuroa. The oversetting of their
canoes is not the only risk they have to encounter, but is productive of another danger more dreadful; for at such times
many become a prey to the sharks, which are very numerous
in these seas. I was informed likewise that they were
sometimes attacked by a fish, which by their description
I imagine to be the barracoota, as they attribute to it the
same propensity.

Saturday passed without my seeing anything of Tinah the
whole day. The next morning he and Iddeah came to me and
assured me that they had made the strictest inquiries concerning
the injury intended us, but had not been able to discover any
circumstance which could lead them to suspect who were concerned in it. This was not at all satisfactory, and I behaved

towards them with great coolness, at which they were much distressed, and Iddeah at length gave vent to her sorrow by tears. I could no longer keep up the appearance of mistrusting them, but I earnestly recommended to them, as they valued the King of England's friendship, that they would exert their utmost endeavours to find out the offenders, which they faithfully promised. Our reconciliation accordingly took place, and messengers were sent to acquaint Otow and Teppahoo and to invite them to return.

It has since occurred to me that this attempt to cut the ship adrift was most probably the act of some of our own people, whose purpose of remaining at Otaheite might have been effectually answered, without danger, if the ship had been driven on shore. At the time I entertained not the least thought of this kind, nor did the possibility of it enter into my ideas, having no suspicion that so general an inclination, or so strong an attachment to these islands, could prevail among my people as to induce them to abandon every prospect of returning to their native country.

A messenger came to me this afternoon from the Earee of Tiarrabou, the SE. division of Otaheite, with an invitation for me to visit him. I excused myself on account of the distance, and at Tinah's request sent back by the messenger a handsome present, which I hope Tinah will get the credit of. I observed with much satisfaction that a great part of what Tinah had received from me he had distributed; to some out of friendship and esteem, and to others from motives of political civility.

Tuesday the 10th. Teppahoo and his family left us to-day to go to Tettaha, where a grand *heiva* was to be performed at which their presence was required.

Wednesday the 11th. A small party of *heiva* people passed through Oparre this morning in their way to Tettaha, where they were going by appointment. They had the civility to send me word that if I chose they would stay to perform a short *heiva* before me, and I immediately attended. It began by a dance of two young girls to the music of drums and flutes, which lasted no long time. At the conclusion they suddenly dropped all their dress, which was left as a present for me, and went off without my seeing them any more. After this the men danced: their performance was more indecent than any I had before seen, but was not the less applauded on that account by the natives, who seemed much delighted.

After this entertainment I went with Tinah and Iddeah to pay a visit to an old lady named Wanow-oora, widow to Towah, the late Earee of Tettaha, who conducted the expedition against Eimeo when Captain Cook was here in 1777. The old lady had just landed, and we found her sitting on the beach by the head of her canoe. With Tinah was a priest and three men, who carried a young dog, a fowl, and two young plantain boughs: these were intended for the offering or present called *otee*. Tinah and his party seated themselves at about ten yards distant from Wanow-oora, and were addressed by her in short sentences for a few minutes, and received her *otee*, which was exactly the same as his. Tinah's priest in return made a short prayer, and his offering was presented to the old lady. Tinah then rose and went to her, and embraced her in a very affectionate manner; and she returned his kindness with tears and many expressions which I could not understand. Soon after he conducted her to a shed, and we remained with her till it was time to go on board to dinner. I invited her to be of the party, but she excused herself on account of age and infirmity. Tinah gave directions for her and her attendants to be supplied with whatever they had occasion for, and we went off to the ship.

Friday the 13th. This forenoon Tinah sent to inform me that many strangers were arrived from all parts, to be present at a grand *heiva* which he had prepared in compliment to me. I accordingly went on shore and found a great crowd of people collected together. A ring was made at a little distance from our post, and Tinah and several other chiefs came to meet me. When we were all seated the *heiva* began by women dancing, after which a present of cloth and a *tawme* or breast-plate was laid before me. This ceremony being over, the men began to wrestle, and regularity was no longer preserved. Old Otow came to me and desired I would help to put a stop to the wrestling, as the people came from different districts, some of which were ill disposed towards others. What Otow had apprehended was not without reason, for in an instant the whole was tumult: every man took to his arms, and as I found my single interference could be of no service, I retired to our post and ordered all my people there under arms. At the time the disturbance began Tinah and Iddeah were absent; their first care was for me, and Iddeah came to see if I was safe at the post. She had a double covering of cloth round her, and her waist was girded with a large rope. I desired her to stay under my protection. This she would not consent to, but said she would return as soon as all was over, and away she went.

I immediately gave orders for two guns to be fired from the ship without shot, which had a good effect; and as no chief was concerned in the tumult, but, on the contrary, all of them exerted their influence to prevent mischief, everything was soon quiet, and Tinah and Iddeah returned to let me know that all was settled. They went on board with some other chiefs and dined with me.

After dinner I went on shore with Tinah and his friends, and I found three large hogs dressed, and a quantity of bread-fruit, which he had ordered to be prepared before he went on board, and now desired I would present them to the different parties that had come to see the entertainment: one to the chief people of Attahooroo, one to the *arreoys*, and a third to the performers of the *heiva*. I presented them according to his directions, and they were received with thankfulness and pleasure. This I looked upon as very handsomely done on the part of Tinah, and I was glad to see that it was regarded in the same light by his guests. These instances of liberality make full amends for the little slips which I have formerly noticed in Tinah. At this time a day seldom passed that he did not give proofs of his hospitality, by entertaining the principal people that came from different parts of the island to visit him or to see the ship. Some of the chiefs he commonly invited to dine on board, and made provision for others on shore. Scarce any person of consequence went away without receiving some present from him. This I encouraged, and was glad it was in my power to assist him. But besides the political motives that I have alluded to, it would be unjust to Tinah not to acknowledge that his disposition seemed improved. He was more open and unreserved in his manners than formerly, and his hospitality was natural and without ostentation.

Monday the 16*th.* I was present this afternoon at a wrestling match by women. The manner of challenging, and method of attack, was exactly the same as among the men. The only difference that I could observe was not in favour of the softer sex, for in these contests they showed less temper and more animosity than I could have imagined them capable of. The women, I was told, not only wrestle with each other, but sometimes with the men. Of this I have never seen an instance and imagine it can happen but seldom, as the women in general are small and by no means masculine. Iddeah is said to be very famous at this exercise.

Tuesday the 17th. I walked with Tinah towards the hills to see his country residence, which was at a very neat house, pleasantly situated, and surrounded with plantations. From this place we saw the island Tethuroa. The next morning I went to Matavai to look after the Indian corn, which I judged would be full ripe for gathering, but on my arrival I found that the natives had been beforehand with me, the whole being taken away. This I was not at all sorry for, as it shows that they value it too much to neglect cultivating it.

Monday the 23rd. Iddeah sent on board for our dinners to-day a very fine tarro pudding, and Tinah brought a bunch of bananas that weighed 81 pounds on which were 286 fine fruit: 10 had broken off in the carriage. The tarro pudding is excellent eating, and easily made. I shall describe this piece of cookery, as the knowledge of it may be useful in the West Indies. The tarro, being cleared of the outside skin, is grated down and made up in rolls of about half a pound each, which they cover neatly with leaves and bake for near half an hour. An equal quantity of ripe coconut meat is likewise grated, from which, through a strainer, the rich milky juice is expressed. This juice is heated by putting smooth hot stones in the vessel that contains it, and the tarro is then mixed with it and kept constantly stirring to prevent burning, till it is ready, which is known by the coconut juice turning to a clear oil.

Wednesday the 25th. Iddeah was very uneasy to-day on account of her youngest child being ill. She would not accept of assistance from our surgeon, but said she had sent to Tettaha for a man who she expected would come and tell her what to do. These physical people are called *tata rapaow.*

Thursday the 26th. This morning a man died of a consumption about two miles from our post. I was informed of it by Mr Peckover, the gunner, who I had desired to look out for such a circumstance. I therefore went, accompanied by Iddeah, in hopes of seeing the funeral ceremony; but before we arrived the body was removed to the *toopapow.* It lay bare, except for a piece of cloth round the loins and another round the neck; the eyes were closed; the hands were placed one over the pit of the stomach and the other upon his breast. On a finger of each hand was a ring made of platted fibres of the coconut tree, with a small bunch of red feathers. Under the *toopapow* a hole was dug, in which at the end of a month the corpse was to be buried. The deceased was of the lower class; the *toopapow*, however, was neat, and offerings of coconuts and platted leaves lay on the ground.

The dead are sometimes brought to the *toopapow* in wooden coffins, which are not shaped like ours but are simply a long box. This custom, Iddeah informed me, they learnt from the Europeans, and is not very common as making plank is a work of great labour.

Monday the 2nd. When I landed this morning I found the inhabitants that lived near to us had left their houses and retired towards the mountains, and was informed that in the night a water cask, part of an azimuth compass, and Mr Peckover's bedding had been stolen from the post on shore; the knowledge of which had caused a general alarm. I sent a message to complain of this theft to Tinah, who did not come near me. About two hours elapsed, during which time I went on board to breakfast, and returned when I saw Tinah and Oreepyah with a number of people at a house at some distance, and soon after they all marched to the eastward, passing close by our post. Oedidee, who was with me, told me that they had intelligence of the thief and were gone in quest of him, and in less than an hour news was brought that they had taken him. Shortly after the whole party appeared, with the water-cask and compass. Tinah had hold of the thief by the arm, and, showing him to me, desired that I would kill him. The bedding, he said, he had not heard of, but would go in search of it. I applauded him for the pains he had taken in this business, and explained, with some success, the injustice of stealing from us; that if any of our people committed the least offence against them it did not pass unnoticed, and that friendship required on their part that those who injured us should not be protected by them. Tinah stopped me from saying more by embracing me, and the whole crowd cried out: 'Tyo mity' (i.e. 'good friend'). Tinah then left me to inquire after the bedding, and I sent the offender on board, whom I punished with a severe flogging. I was glad to find this man was not of Oparre or Matavai.

The fine fruit called *avee* was just coming into season; it was likewise in season at the time of our arrival in October. The bread-fruit trees, I have no doubt, bear all the year round: we have seen a scarcity of bread-fruit, but have never been wholly without it. Some fern-root was shown to me, which in scarce seasons is used by the natives as bread. It bears a long even-edged leaf, about an inch wide; the taste somewhat resembled that of a yam. I was informed by our people that in their walks they saw in many places patches of Indian corn just making their appearance through the ground. This convinces me that the corn taken from Matavai could not have been better disposed of.

Goats are frequently offered for sale, but I rather discouraged the buying of them for fear of injuring the breed. The natives will not eat them, neither will they taste the milk, and ask, with some appearance of disgust, why we do not milk the sows. I endeavoured to prevail on Tinah and Iddeah to eat the goats' milk by mixing it with fruit, but they would only try one spoonful.

We had begun to make preparations for sailing, and Tinah supplied us with a sufficient stock of wood by ordering trees to be brought down from the country. He had frequently expressed a wish that I would leave some fire-arms and ammunition with him, as he expected to be attacked after the ship sailed; and perhaps chiefly on account of our partiality to him. I therefore thought it but reasonable to attend to his request, and I was the more readily prevailed on as he said his intentions were to act only on the defensive. This indeed seems most suited to his disposition, which is neither active nor enterprising. If Tinah had spirit in proportion to his size and strength he would probably be the greatest warrior in Otaheite, but courage is not the most conspicuous of his virtues. When I promised to leave with him a pair of pistols, which they prefer to muskets, he told me that Iddeah would fight with one and Oedidee with the other. Iddeah has learnt to load and fire a musket with great dexterity, and Oedidee is an excellent marksman. It is not common for women in this country to go to war, but Iddeah is a very resolute woman, of a large make, and has great bodily strength.

Friday the 6th. I sent Mr Fryer, the master, to sound Taowne harbour. The knowledge that we intended shortly to sail having spread among the natives, a great many broken iron tools were brought from all parts of the island to be repaired at our forge, and this morning a messenger arrived from Waheatua, the Earee of Tiarraboo, with several pieces of Spanish iron, which he desired to have made into small adzes. This request was of course complied with.

CHAPTER XI

Arrival of an 'arreoy' woman from Tethuroa.—A present delivered by Tinah for His Majesty.—Other occurrences to the time of the ship's departure from Otaheite.

FROM the 5th to the 14th of this month the wind blew constantly from between the NW. and SW., with a great deal of rain. This was the longest continuance of westerly winds without interruption that we experienced. On the 13th several canoes arrived here and at Matavai from Tethuroa. In these were a large tribe of the *arreoys*, and among them Huheine Moyere, the wife of Oreepyah, who is an *arreoy* woman, and remained at Tethuroa after Oreepyah came away. On her arrival a ceremony was performed, called *hooepippee*, which seemed to be designed as a public visit to all their friends who are collected on the occasion. In this ceremony there was nothing remarkable: the *arreoy* men took their opportunity to plunder the women who were near them, and Iddeah made a present of some cloth to Huheine Moyere and a baked hog to the *arreoys*.

Friday the 13th. After this ceremony a present was produced from many of the principal people for young Otoo, the Earee Rahie, which was received by Iddeah, Tinah being absent. This present consisted of five hogs and forty-eight baskets filled with bread-fruit, coconuts, tarro, and different kinds of puddings. The baskets were decorated with slips of cloth, stained with variety of colours and carried by twenty-four men, each of whom had a pole on his shoulder at each end of which was a basket.

I have seldom spoken of Otoo, who was too young to have any share in the management of affairs and with whom we were not permitted to have any intercourse, except speaking to him now and then across a river, at which times I did not neglect to send the children some little presents, so that they always rejoiced to see me. I might have been admitted to a nearer acquaintance if I would have gone with my shoulders uncovered, as his parents did, but this I declined. The children do not all live under the same roof, the two sisters eating and sleeping in a separate house, though at other times they are generally together.

The island Tethuroa may very properly be compared to some of our watering-places in England, producing a similar effect upon those who visit it. Many who went there covered with scurf returned plump and fair, and scarce like the same people. This alteration for the better is in a great measure to be attributed to the discontinuance of the *ava*, which Tethuroa does not produce; the coconut trees, likewise, which supply them with their only beverage, growing on low sandy keys and having their roots below the level of the sea, may probably have qualities different from the coconuts of Otaheite, which, with a plenty of fish that at other times they are not accustomed to, must no doubt contribute to the amendment described.

Saturday the 14th. I was visited to-day by a very old man, an uncle to Tupia, the person who went from these islands in the *Endeavour* in the year 1769 and who died at Batavia. He appeared to be near seventy years old, and was treated with much respect by the natives. He made several inquiries concerning his nephew, and requested that when I came again I would bring his hair. At the time that Tinah mentioned to me his desire of visiting England, I asked what account I could give to his friends if he should not live to return; to which he replied that I must cut off his hair and carry it to them, and they would be perfectly satisfied.

On the 16th I was informed that a stop was put to the sale of hogs in the district of Tettaha. Teppahoo, the *earee* of that district, told me that they had very few hogs left there, and that it was necessary for a certain time to prohibit every person from killing or selling, that they might have time to breed. I did not think it reasonable to solicit any indulgence on this head. My friends at Matavai and Oparre promised to supply us as long as we remained here, though we had considerably thinned their stock. After our departure the same restriction was to take place in these districts, and it being delayed on our account certainly deserves to be regarded among their acts of friendship towards us.

As it was generally known that we were preparing to sail, a number of the natives from other parts of the island were constantly with us, and petty thefts were committed whenever the negligence of our people afforded an opportunity; but no attempt of any consequence was made.

Thursday the 19th. This evening Mr Samuel, my clerk, returned from an excursion to the mountains, having been two days absent. He described the hills to be well clothed with wood, except the tops of the higher mountains, which only produced bushes and fern. The birds he saw were blue paroquets and green doves, except one, which he found burrowing in the ground, and brought to me. This bird was about the size of a pigeon and proved to be a white-bellied petrel, of the same kind as those seen in high latitudes which are called sheerwaters. He likewise brought a branch of a plant, like the New Zealand tea-plant, and which at Van Diemen's Land we had made use of for brooms. From the hills he saw the islands Maitea and Huaheine, which are situated nearly in opposite directions from Otaheite, and are seventy leagues distant from each other.

Friday the 27th. For some days past Tinah had been busied in getting two *parais,* or mourning-dresses, made, which he intended as a present to King George. Being finished, they were this morning hung up in his house as a public exhibition, and a long prayer made on the occasion; the substance of which was that the King of England might for ever remain his friend and not forget him. When he presented the *parais* for me to take on board, he could not refrain from shedding tears. During the short remainder of our stay here there appeared among the natives an evident degree of sorrow that we were so soon to leave them, which they showed by unusual kindness and attention.

We began this afternoon to remove the plants to the ship. They were in excellent order; the roots had appeared through the bottom of the pots, and would have shot into the ground if care had not been taken to prevent it.

The weather was considerably altered for the better, and the trade wind appeared settled. The rainy and bad season of the year may be reckoned to begin towards the end of November and to continue till near the end of March. During this time the winds are variable, and often westerly, though we seldom found them to blow strong in that direction. We likewise experienced frequent intervals of fine weather, but during these months so open a road as Matavai bay is not a safe anchoring-place for ships that intend remaining any length of time at Otaheite.

Tuesday the 31st. To-day all the plants were on board, being in 774 pots, 39 tubs, and 24 boxes. The number of breadfruit plants were 1,015; besides which we had collected a number of other plants: the *avee*, which is one of the finest-flavoured fruits in the world; the *ayyah*, which is a fruit not so rich, but of a fine flavour and very refreshing; the *rattah*, not much unlike a chestnut, which grows on a large tree in great quantities. They are singly in large pods from one to two inches broad, and may be eaten raw or boiled in the same manner as Windsor beans, and so dressed are equally good; the *orai-ah*, which is a very superior kind of plantain. All these I was particularly recommended to collect by my worthy friend, Sir Joseph Banks. I had also taken on board some plants of the *ettow* and *matte*, with which the natives here make a beautiful red colour, and a root called *peeah*, of which they make an excellent pudding.

I now made my last presents to several of my friends with whom I had been most intimate, particularly to Teppahoo. Several people expressed great desire to go with us to England. Oedidee, who was always very much attached to us, said he considered it as his right, having formerly left his native place to sail with Captain Cook. Scarce any man belonging to the ship was without a *tyo*, who brought to him presents, chiefly of provisions for a sea store.

Friday the 3rd. Tinah and his wife, with his parents, brothers, and sister, dined with me to-day, and as I meant to sail early the next morning they all remained on board for the night. The ship was crowded the whole day with the natives, and we were loaded with coconuts, plantains, bread-fruit, hogs, and goats. In the evening there was no dancing or mirth on the beach, such as we had been accustomed to, but all was silent.

At daylight we unmoored. The stock of the best bower anchor was so much eaten by the worms that it broke in stowing the anchor; the small bower had an iron stock, and in these voyages it is very necessary that ships should be provided with iron anchor stocks. At half-past six, there being no wind, we weighed, and with our boats and two sweeps towed the ship out of the harbour. Soon after the sea breeze came, and we stood off towards the sea.

The outlet of Toahroah harbour being narrow, I could permit only a few of the natives to be on board. Many others, however, attended in canoes till the breeze came, when I was obliged to leave them. We stood off and on almost all the remainder of the day. Tinah and Iddeah pressed me very strongly to anchor in Matavai bay and stay one night longer, but as I had already taken leave of most of my friends, I thought it better to keep to my intention of sailing. After dinner I ordered the presents which I had reserved for Tinah and his wife to be put in one of the ship's boats, and as I had promised him fire-arms, I gave him two muskets, a pair of pistols, and a good stock of ammunition. I then represented to them the necessity of their going away, that the boat might return to the ship before it was dark; on which they took a most affectionate leave of me and went into the boat. One of their expressions at parting was 'Yourah no t' Eatua tee eveerah.' ('May the Eatua protect you, for ever and ever.')

All the time that we remained at Otaheite the picture of Captain Cook, at the desire of Tinah, was kept on board the ship. On delivering it to him I wrote on the back the time of the ship's arrival and departure, with an account of the number of plants on board.

Tinah had desired that I would salute him at his departure with the great guns, which I could not comply with for fear of disturbing the plants; but as a parting token of our regard we manned ship with all hands and gave him three cheers. At sunset the boat returned and we made sail, bidding farewell to Otaheite, where for twenty-three weeks we had been treated with the utmost affection and regard, and which seemed to increase in proportion to our stay. That we were not insensible to their kindness the events which followed more than suffi- ciently proves; for to the friendly and endearing behaviour of these people may be ascribed the motives for that event which effected the ruin of an expedition that there was every reason to hope would have been completed in the most fortunate manner.

To enter into a description of the island or its inhabitants I look upon as superfluous. From the accounts of former voyages, and the facts which I have related, the character of the people will appear in as true a light as by any description in my power to give. The length of time that we remained at Otaheite, with the advantage of having been there before, gave me opportunities of making perhaps a more perfect vocabulary of the language than has yet appeared; but I have chosen to defer it for the present, as there is a probability that I may hereafter be better qualified for such a talk.

We left Otaheite with only two patients in the venereal list, which shows that the disease has not gained ground. The natives say that it is of little consequence, and we saw several instances of people that had been infected, who after absenting

themselves for fifteen or twenty days, made their appearance
again without any visible symptom remaining of the disease.
Their method of cure I am unacquainted with, but their
customary diet and mode of living must contribute towards
it. We saw a great many people, however, with scrofulous
habits and bad sores; these they denied to be produced from
any venereal cause, and our surgeon was of the same
opinion.

The result of the mean of fifty sets of lunar observations,
taken by me on shore, gives for the longitude of Point Venus,
210° 33′ 57″ E.; Captain Cook in 1769 places it in 210° 27′ 30″;
in 1777, his last voyage, 210° 22′ 28″.

The tide in Toahroah harbour was very inconsiderable, and
not regular. The greatest rise that I observed was eleven inches,
but what was most singular, the time of high water did not
appear to be governed by the moon, it being at the highest
every day between noon and two o'clock. The variable winds
and weather at this time of the year has no doubt an influence
on the tides; on some days scarce any rise was perceptible.

CHAPTER XII

*At the island Huaheine.—A friend of Omai visits the ship.—
Leave the Society Islands.—A water-spout.—The island Wytootackee discovered.—Anchor in Annamooka Road.—Our parties
on shore robbed by the natives.—Sail from Annamooka.—The
chiefs detained on board.—Part friendly.*

Sunday the 5th. We steered towards the island Huaheine, which
we got sight of the next morning. At noon we brought to near
the entrance of Owharre harbour, it not being my intention to
anchor. We could see every part of the harbour distinctly,
but my attention was particularly directed to the spot where
Omai's house had stood, no part of which was now visible. It
was near three o'clock before any canoes came off to us, for the
people on shore imagined that the ship was coming into the
harbour. The first that arrived had three men in it, who
brought a few coconuts. I inquired about the chief, or Earee
Rahie, and one of the fellows with great gravity said he was
the Earee Rahie, and that he had come to desire I would bring

the ship into the harbour. I could not help laughing at his impudence; however, I gave him a few nails for his coconuts and he left us. Immediately after a double canoe in which were ten men came alongside; among them was a young man who recollected and called me by my name. Several other canoes arrived, with hogs, yams, and other provisions, which we purchased. My acquaintance told me that he had lived with our friend Omai. He confirmed the account that has already been given, and informed me that of all the animals which had been left with Omai, the mare only remained alive. He said that Omai and himself had often rode together, and I observed that many of the islanders who came on board had the representation of a man on horseback tattooed on their legs. After the death of Omai his house was broken to pieces and the materials stolen. The fire-arms were at Ulietea, but useless. I inquired after the seeds and plants, and was informed that they were all destroyed except one tree; but of what kind that was I could not make out from their description. I was much pressed to take the ship into the harbour, and Omai's companion requested me to let him go to England. When they found that I would not stop among them they seemed jealous of our going to Ulietea, and it appeared to give them some satisfaction when I told them that I should not go near that island.

The canoes had left us, and we were making sail when we discovered an Indian in the water, swimming towards the shore, which in all probability he would not have been able to reach. We took him up, and luckily, another canoe coming alongside, we put him in her. The people of the canoe said that the man was insane, but how he came to be swimming so far from the land we could not conjecture. At six o'clock we made sail and ran all night to the SW., and SW. by S., between the islands Huaheine and Ulietea. The next morning I altered the course, steering more to the westward, for the Friendly Islands.

On the 9th, at nine o'clock in the morning, the weather became squally, and a body of thick black clouds collected in the east. Soon after a water-spout was seen at no great distance from us, which appeared to great advantage from the darkness of the clouds behind it. As nearly as I could judge, it was about two feet diameter at the upper part and about eight inches at the lower. I had scarce made these remarks when I observed

that it was advancing rapidly towards the ship. We immediately altered our course, and took in all the sails except the
fore-sail; soon after which it passed within ten yards of our
stern, making a rustling noise, but without our feeling the least
effect from its being so near us. The rate at which it travelled
I judged to be about ten miles per hour, going towards the west
in the direction of the wind. In a quarter of an hour after
passing us it dispersed. I never was so near a water-spout
before. The connection between the column, which was higher
than our mast-heads, and the water below, was no otherwise
visible than by the sea being disturbed in a circular space of
about six yards in diameter, the centre of which, from the
whirling of the water round it, formed a hollow; and from the
outer parts of the circle the water was thrown up with much
force in a spiral direction, and could be traced to the height
of fifteen or twenty feet. At this elevation we lost sight of it,
and could see nothing of its junction with the column above.
It is impossible to say what injury we should have suffered if
it had passed directly over us. Masts, I imagine, might have
been carried away, but I do not apprehend it would have
endangered the loss of a ship.

As we sailed very near the track made in former voyages,
I had little reason to expect that we should at this time make
any new discovery; nevertheless, on the 11th, at daylight, land
was seen to the SSW., at about five leagues distance, which
appeared to be an island of a moderate height. On the north
part was a round hill; the NW. part was highest and steep,
the SE. part sloped off to a low point.

The wind had been westerly since the preceding noon, and
at the time we saw the land the ship was standing to the NW.
At six we tacked to the southward, and as we advanced in that
direction discovered a number of low keys of which at noon
we counted nine; they were all covered with trees. The large
island first seen had a most fruitful appearance, its shore being
bordered with flat land on which grew innumerable coconut
and other trees, and the higher grounds beautifully interspersed
with lawns. The wind being light and unfavourable, we endeavoured all day, but without success, to get near the land.
In the night we had a heavy squall, which obliged us to clew
up all our sails, and soon after it fell calm.

On the 12th the winds were light and variable all day, with
calms. At two in the afternoon we were within three miles of

the southernmost key, and could see a number of people within
the reefs. Shortly after a canoe in which were four men paddled
off to us and came alongside, without showing any signs of
apprehension or surprise. I gave them a few beads, and they
came into the ship. One man, who seemed to have an ascen-
dancy over the others, looked about the ship with some appearance
of curiosity, but none of them would venture to go below. They
asked for some boiled fresh pork, which they saw in a bowl
belonging to one of the seamen, and it was given them to eat,
with boiled plantains. Being told that I was the *earee* or chief
of the ship, the principal person came and joined noses with me,
and presented to me a large mother-of-pearl shell, which hung
with platted hair round his neck. This he fastened round my
neck with signs of great satisfaction.

They spoke the same language as at Otaheite, with very little
variation, as far as I could judge. In a small vocabulary that
I made whilst conversing with these men, only four words out
of twenty-four differed from the Otaheite. The name of the
large island, they told me, was Wytootackee, and the *earee* was
called Lomakkayah. They said that there were no hogs, dogs,
or goats upon the island, nor had they yams or tarro; but that
plantains, coconuts, fowls, bread-fruit, and *avees* were there in
great abundance. Notwithstanding they said that no hogs
were on the island, it was evident they had seen such animals,
for they called them by the same name as is given to them at
Otaheite, which made me suspect that they were deceiving me.
However, I ordered a young boar and sow to be put into their
canoe, with some yams and tarro, as we could afford to part
with some of these articles. I also gave to each of them a
knife, a small adze, some nails, beads, and a looking-glass.
The latter they examined with great curiosity; but with the ironwork they appeared to be acquainted, calling it *aouree*, which is
the common name for iron among the islands where it is known.

As they were preparing to leave us the chief of the canoe
took possession of everything that I had given to the others.
One of them showed some signs of dissatisfaction, but after a
little altercation they joined noses and were reconciled. I now
thought they were going to leave the ship, but only two of
them went into the canoe, the other two purposing to stay all
night with us and to have the canoe return for them in the
morning. I would have treated their confidence with the regard
it merited, but it was impossible to say how far the ship might

be driven from the island in the night. This I explained to them, and they reluctantly consented to leave us. They were very solicitous that somebody from the ship should go on shore with them; and just before they quitted us they gave me a wooden spear, which was the only thing, the paddles excepted, they had brought with them in the canoe. It was a common long staff, pointed with the *toa* wood.

The island of Wytootackee is about ten miles in circuit; its latitude from 18° 50′ to 18° 54′ S. and longitude 200° 19′ E. A group of small keys, eight in number, lie to the SE., four or five miles distant from Wytootackee, and a single one to the WSW.; the southernmost of the group is in latitude 18° 58′ S. Variation of the compass, 8° 14′ E.

The people that came off to us did not differ in appearance from the natives of Hervey's Islands, seen in Captain Cook's last voyage, though much more friendly and inoffensive in their manners. They were tattooed across the arms and legs, but not on the loins or posteriors like the people of Otaheite. From their knowledge of iron they have doubtless communication with Hervey's Islands, which are not more than eighteen leagues distant from them.

In the night a breeze sprung up from the south, and we continued our course to the westward.

On the 18th, at sunset, we saw Savage Island, and in the night passed by to the southward of it.

At eleven o'clock in the forenoon of the 21st we saw the island Caow from the mast-head, bearing NW. by W¾W. This island is a high mountain with a sharp-pointed top, and is the north-westernmost of all the Friendly Islands. At noon we saw it very distinctly from the deck, it being then nineteen leagues distant from us.

The wind being to the southward we could not fetch Anna-mooka, at which island I intended to stop, before the evening of the 23rd, when we anchored in the road, in twenty-three fathoms, the extremes of Annamooka bearing E. by N. and S. by E., our distance from the shore being half a league. In the middle of the day a canoe had come off to us from the island Mango, in which was a chief named Latoomy-lange, who dined with me. Immediately on our anchoring several canoes came alongside with yams and coconuts, but none of the natives offered to come on board without first asking permission. As yet I had seen no person with whom I could recollect to have been formerly acquainted. I made inquiries after some of our old friends, particularly the chiefs, but I found myself not sufficiently master of the language to obtain the information I wanted.

Friday the 24th. Our station being inconvenient for watering, at daylight we weighed and worked more to the eastward, where we anchored in twenty-one fathoms: the extremes of Annamooka bearing N. 85° E. and S. 33° W.; the Sandy bay S. 73° E.; our distance from the shore half a league. Sounded all round the ship, and found the ground to be a coarse coral bottom, but with even soundings.

By this time some large sailing canoes were arrived from different islands in the neighbourhood of Annamooka, and an old lame man named Tepa, whom I had known in 1777 and immediately recollected, came on board. Two other chiefs, whose names were Noocaboo and Kunocappo, were with him. Tepa having formerly been accustomed to our manner of speaking their language, I found I could converse with him tolerably well. He informed me that Poulaho, Feenow, and Tubow were alive, and at Tongataboo, and that they would come hither as soon as they heard of our arrival, of which he promised to send them immediate notice. He said that the cattle which we had left at Tongataboo had all bred, and that the old ones were yet living. He inquired after several people who were here with Captain Cook. Being desirous to see the ship, I took him and his companions below and showed them the bread-fruit and other plants, at seeing which they were greatly surprised. I made each of them a present, and when they had satisfied their curiosity I invited them to go on shore with me in the ship's boat.

I took Nelson with me to procure some bread-fruit plants, one of our stock being dead and two or three others a little sickly. When we landed there were about two hundred people on the beach, most of them women and children. Tepa showed me a large boat-house, which he told me we might make use of, thinking we should have a party on shore, as our ships had formerly. I went with him in search of water, but could find no better place than where Captain Cook had watered, which is a quarter of a mile inland from the east end of the beach. I next walked to the west point of the bay, where some plants and seeds had been sown by Captain Cook, and had the satisfaction to see in a plantation close by about twenty fine pineapple plants, but no fruit, this not being the proper season. They told me that they had eaten many of them, that they were fine and large, and that at Tongataboo there were great numbers.

When I returned to the landing-place I was desired to sit down, and a present was brought me which consisted of some bundles of coconuts only. This fell short of my expectations; however, I appeared satisfied, and distributed beads and trinkets to the women and children near me.

Numerous were the marks of mourning with which these people disfigure themselves, such as bloody temples, their heads deprived of most of the hair, and, what was worse, almost all of them with the loss of some of their fingers. Several fine boys, not above six years old, had lost both their little fingers, and some of the men, besides these, had parted with the middle finger of the right hand.

The chiefs went off with me to dinner, and I found a brisk trade carrying on at the ship for yams; some plantains and bread-fruit were likewise brought on board, but no hogs. In the afternoon more sailing canoes arrived, some of which contained no less than ninety passengers. We purchased eight hogs, some dogs, fowls, and shaddocks. Yams were in great abundance, very fine and large; one yam weighed above forty-five pounds. Among the people that came this afternoon were two of the name of Tubow, which is a family of the first distinction among the Friendly Islands; one of them was chief of the island Lefooga; with him and Tepa I went on shore to see the wooding place. I found a variety of sizeable trees, but the kind which I principally pitched upon was the Barringtonia, of Forster. I acquainted Tepa with my intention of sending people to cut wood, which meeting with his approbation, we parted.

On the 25th, at daylight, the wooding and watering parties went on shore. I had directed them not to cut the kind of tree,[1] which, when Captain Cook wooded here in 1777, blinded for a time many of the wood-cutters. They had not been an hour on shore before one man had an axe stolen from him and another an adze. Tepa was applied to, who got the axe restored, but the adze was not recovered. In the evening we completed wooding.

[1] *Excoecaria Agallocha Linn. Sp. Pl.*, called in the Malay language, Caju Mata Boota, which signifies, the tree that wounds the eyes.

Sunday the 26th. In the morning Nelson went on shore to get a few plants, but no principal chief being among the people, he was insulted and a spade taken from him. A boat's grapnel was likewise stolen from the watering party. Tepa recovered the spade for us, but the crowd of natives was become so great, by the number of canoes that had arrived from different islands, that it was impossible to do anything where there was such a multitude of people without a chief of sufficient authority to command the whole. I therefore ordered the watering party to go on board, and determined to sail, for I could not discover that any canoe had been sent to acquaint the chiefs of Tonga-taboo of our being here. For some time after the thefts were committed the chiefs kept away, but before noon they came on board.

At noon we unmoored, and at one o'clock got under sail. The two Tubows, Kunocappo, Latoomy-lange, and another chief were on board, and I acquainted them that unless the grapnel was returned they must remain in the ship. They were surprised, and not a little alarmed. Canoes were immediately dispatched after the grapnel, which, I was informed, could not possibly be brought to the ship before the next day, as those who had stolen it immediately sailed with their prize to another island. Nevertheless I detained them till sunset, when their uneasiness and impatience increased to such a degree that they began to beat themselves about the face and eyes, and some of them cried bitterly. As this distress was more than the grapnel was worth, and I had no reason to imagine that they were privy to, or in any manner concerned in the theft, I could not think of detaining them longer, and called their canoes alongside. I then told them they were at liberty to go, and made each of them a present of a hatchet, a saw, with some knives, gimblets, and nails. This unexpected present, and the sudden change in their situation, affected them not less with joy than they had before been with apprehension. They were unbounded in their acknowledgments, and I have little doubt but that we parted better friends than if the affair had never happened.

We stood to the northward all night, with light winds, and on the next day, the 27th, at noon were between the islands Tofoa and Kotoo. Latitude observed, 19° 18′ S.

Thus far the voyage had advanced in a course of uninterrupted prosperity, and had been attended with many circumstances equally pleasing and satisfactory. A very different scene was now to be experienced. A conspiracy had been formed which was to render all our past labour productive only of extreme misery and distress. The means had been concerted and prepared with so much secrecy and circumspection that no one circumstance appeared to occasion the smallest suspicion of the impending calamity.

A NARRATIVE OF THE MUTINY

CHAPTER XIII

A MUTINY IN THE SHIP

WE kept near the island Kotoo all the afternoon, in hopes that some canoes would come off to the ship, but in this I was disappointed. The wind being northerly, in the evening we steered to the westward, to pass to the south of Tofoa. I gave directions for this course to be continued during the night. The master had the first watch, the gunner the middle watch, and Mr Christian the morning watch. This was the turn of duty for the night.

Tuesday the 28th. Just before sunrising, while I was yet asleep, Mr Christian, with the master-at-arms, gunner's mate, and Thomas Burkett, seaman, came into my cabin, and seizing me tied my hands with a cord behind my back, threatening me with instant death if I spoke or made the least noise. I, however, called as loud as I could, in hopes of assistance; but they had already secured the officers who were not of their party by placing sentinels at their doors. There were three men at my cabin door, besides the four within; Christian had only a cutlass in his hand, the others had muskets and bayonets. I was hauled out of bed and forced on deck in my shirt, suffering great pain from the tightness with which they had tied my hands. I demanded the reason of such violence, but received no other answer than abuse for not holding my tongue. The master, the gunner, the surgeon, Mr Elphinstone, master's mate, and Nelson were kept confined below, and the fore hatchway was guarded by sentinels. The boatswain and carpenter, and also the clerk, Mr Samuel, were allowed to come upon deck, where they saw me standing abaft the mizen-mast with my hands tied behind my back, under a guard, with Christian at their head. The boatswain was ordered to hoist the launch out, with a threat if he did not do it instantly *to take care of himself.*

When the boat was out, Mr Hayward and Mr Hallet, two of the midshipmen, and Mr Samuel were ordered into it. I demanded what their intention was in giving this order, and endeavoured to persuade the people near me not to persist in such acts of violence; but it was to no effect. 'Hold your tongue, sir, or you are dead this instant,' was constantly repeated to me.

The master by this time had sent to request that he might come on deck, which was permitted; but he was soon ordered back again to his cabin.

I continued my endeavours to turn the tide of affairs, when Christian changed the cutlass which he had in his hand for a bayonet that was brought to him, and, holding me with a strong grip by the cord that tied my hands, he with many oaths threatened to kill me immediately if I would not be quiet; the villains round me had their pieces cocked and bayonets fixed. Particular people were called on to go into the boat, and were hurried over the side; whence I concluded that with these people I was to be set adrift. I therefore made another effort to bring about a change, but with no other effect than to be threatened with having my brains blown out.

The boatswain and seamen who were to go in the boat were allowed to collect twine, canvas, lines, sails, cordage, an eight and twenty gallon cask of water, and Mr Samuel got a hundred and fifty pounds of bread, with a small quantity of rum and wine, also a quadrant and compass; but he was forbidden on pain of death to touch either map, ephemeris, book of astronomical observations, sextant, time-keeper, or any of my surveys or drawings.

The mutineers having forced those of the seamen whom they meant to get rid of into the boat, Christian directed a dram to be served to each of his own crew. I then unhappily saw that nothing could be done to effect the recovery of the ship: there was no one to assist me, and every endeavour on my part was answered with threats of death.

The officers were next called upon deck and forced over the side into the boat, while I was kept apart from every one abaft the mizen-mast; Christian, armed with a bayonet, holding me by the bandage that secured my hands. The guard round me had their pieces cocked, but, on my daring the ungrateful wretches to fire, they uncocked them.

Isaac Martin, one of the guard over me, I saw had an inclination to assist me, and as he fed me with shaddock (my lips being quite parched), we explained our wishes to each other by our looks; but this being observed Martin was removed from me. He then attempted to leave the ship, for which purpose he got into the boat; but with many threats they obliged him to return.

The armourer, Joseph Coleman, and two of the carpenters, M'Intosh and Norman, were also kept contrary to their inclination; and they begged of me, after I was astern in the boat, to remember that they declared they had no hand in the transaction. Michael Byrne, I am told, likewise wanted to leave the ship.

It is of no moment for me to recount my endeavours to bring back the offenders to a sense of their duty. All I could do was by speaking to them in general; but it was to no purpose, for I was kept securely bound, and no one except the guard suffered to come near me.

To Mr Samuel I am indebted for securing my journals and commission, with some material ship papers. Without these I had nothing to certify what I had done, and my honour and character might have been suspected without my possessing a proper document to have defended them. All this he did with great resolution, though guarded and strictly watched. He attempted to save the time-keeper and a box with my surveys, drawings, and remarks for fifteen years past, which were numerous, when he was hurried away with, 'Damn your eyes, you are well off to get what you have.'

It appeared to me that Christian was some time in doubt whether he should keep the carpenter or his mates; at length he determined on the latter, and the carpenter was ordered into the boat. He was permitted, but not without some opposition, to take his tool-chest.

Much altercation took place among the mutinous crew during the whole business; some swore: 'I 'll be damned if he does not find his way home, if he gets anything with him' (meaning me); and, when the carpenter's chest was carrying away: 'Damn my eyes, he will have a vessel built in a month.' While others laughed at the helpless situation of the boat, being very deep, and so little room for those who were in her. As for Christian, he seemed as if meditating destruction on himself and every one else.

I asked for arms, but they laughed at me, and said I was well acquainted with the people among whom I was going, and therefore did not want them; four cutlasses, however, were thrown into the boat after we were veered astern.

The officers and men being in the boat, they only waited for me, of which the master-at-arms informed Christian, who then said: 'Come, Captain Bligh, your officers and men are now in the boat, and you must go with them; if you attempt to make the least resistance you will instantly be put to death'; and without further ceremony, with a tribe of armed ruffians about me, I was forced over the side, where they untied my hands. Being in the boat, we were veered astern by a rope. A few pieces of pork were thrown to us, and some clothes, also the cutlasses I have already mentioned; and it was then that the armourer and carpenters called out to me to remember that they had no hand in the transaction. After having undergone a great deal of ridicule, and been kept some time to make sport for these unfeeling wretches, we were at length cast adrift in the open ocean.

I had with me in the boat the following persons:

Names	Stations
JOHN FRYER	Master
THOMAS LEDWARD	Acting-surgeon
DAVID NELSON	Botanist
WILLIAM PECKOVER	Gunner
WILLIAM COLE	Boatswain
WILLIAM PURCELL	Carpenter
WILLIAM ELPHINSTONE	Master's mate
THOMAS HAYWARD	Midshipmen
JOHN HALLET	
JOHN NORTON	Quartermasters
PETER LINKLETTER	
LAWRENCE LEBOGUE	Sailmaker
JOHN SMITH	Cooks
THOMAS HALL	
GEORGE SIMPSON	Quartermaster's mate
ROBERT TINKLER	A boy
ROBERT LAMB	Butcher
MR SAMUEL	Clerk

There remained on board the *Bounty*:

Names	Stations
FLETCHER CHRISTIAN . .	Master's mate
PETER HEYWOOD . .	
EDWARD YOUNG . .	Midshipmen
GEORGE STEWART . .	
CHARLES CHURCHILL . .	Master-at-arms
JOHN MILLS . . .	Gunner's mate
JAMES MORRISON . .	Boatswain's mate
THOMAS BURKETT . .	Able seaman
MATTHEW QUINTAL . . .	,,
JOHN SUMNER . . .	,,
JOHN MILLWARD . . .	,,
WILLIAM M'KOY . . .	,,
HENRY HILLBRANT . .	,,
MICHAEL BYRNE . . .	,,
WILLIAM MUSPRATT . .	,,
ALEXANDER SMITH . .	,,
JOHN WILLIAMS . . .	,,
THOMAS ELLISON . . .	,,
ISAAC MARTIN . . .	,,
RICHARD SKINNER . .	,,
MATTHEW THOMPSON . .	,,
WILLIAM BROWN . . .	Gardener
JOSEPH COLEMAN . . .	Armourer
CHARLES NORMAN . .	Carpenter's mate
THOMAS M'INTOSH . .	Carpenter's crew

In all twenty-five hands, and the most able men of the
ship's company

Having little or no wind, we rowed pretty fast towards Tofoa,
which bore NE. about ten leagues from us. While the ship
was in sight she steered to the WNW., but I considered this
only as a feint, for when we were sent away, 'Huzza for Otaheite' was frequently heard among the mutineers.

Christian, the chief of the mutineers, is of a respectable
family in the north of England. This was the third voyage

he had made with me, and as I found it necessary to keep my ship's company at three watches, I had given him an order to take charge of the third, his abilities being thoroughly equal to the task; and by this means the master and gunner were not at watch and watch.

Heywood is also of a respectable family in the north of England, and a young man of abilities, as well as Christian. These two had been objects of my particular regard and attention, and I had taken great pains to instruct them, having entertained hopes that as professional men they would have become a credit to their country.

Young was well recommended, and had the look of an able stout seaman. He, however, fell short of what his appearance promised.

Stewart was a young man of creditable parents in the Orkneys, at which place, on the return of the *Resolution* from the South Seas in 1780, we received so many civilities, that on that account only I should gladly have taken him with me; but, independent of this recommendation, he was a seaman, and had always borne a good character.

Notwithstanding the roughness with which I was treated, the remembrance of past kindnesses produced some signs of remorse in Christian. When they were forcing me out of the ship I asked him if this treatment was a proper return for the many instances he had received of my friendship? He appeared disturbed at my question, and answered with much emotion: 'That—Captain Bligh—that is the thing. I am in hell—I am in hell.'

As soon as I had time to reflect, I felt an inward satisfaction which prevented any depression of my spirits. Conscious of my integrity and anxious solicitude for the good of the service in which I had been engaged, I found my mind wonderfully supported, and I began to conceive hopes, notwithstanding so heavy a calamity, that I should one day be able to account to my king and country for the misfortune. A few hours before my situation had been peculiarly flattering. I had a ship in the most perfect order and well stored with every necessary both for service and health. By early attention to those particulars I had, as much as lay in my power, provided against any accident in case I could not get through Endeavour Straits, as well as against what might befall me in them; add to this the plants had been successfully preserved in the most flourishing state; so that, upon the whole, the voyage was two-thirds completed, and the remaining part, to all appearance, in a very promising way; every person on board being in perfect health, to establish which was ever amongst the principal objects of my attention.

It will very naturally be asked, What could be the reason for such a revolt? in answer to which I can only conjecture that the mutineers had flattered themselves with the hopes of a more happy life among the Otaheiteans than they could possibly enjoy in England; and this, joined to some female connections, most probably occasioned the whole transaction.

The women at Otaheite are handsome, mild and cheerful in their manners and conversation, possessed of great sensibility, and have sufficient delicacy to make them admired and beloved. The chiefs were so much attached to our people that they rather encouraged their stay among them than otherwise, and even made them promises of large possessions. Under these, and many other attendant circumstances equally desirable, it is now perhaps not so much to be wondered at, though scarcely possible to have been foreseen, that a set of sailors, most of them void of connections, should be led away; especially when, in addition to such powerful inducements, they imagined it in their power to fix themselves in the midst of plenty on one of the finest islands in the world, where they need not labour and where the allurements of dissipation are beyond anything that can be conceived. The utmost, however, that any commander could have supposed to have happened is that some of the people would have been tempted to desert. But if it should be asserted that a commander is to guard against an act of mutiny and piracy in his own ship more than by the common rules of service, it is as much as to say that he must sleep locked up, and when awake be girded with pistols.

Desertions have happened, more or less, from most of the ships that have been at the Society Islands, but it has always been in the commander's power to make the chiefs return their people. The knowledge, therefore, that it was unsafe to desert, perhaps first led mine to consider with what ease so small a ship might be surprised, and that so favourable an opportunity would never offer to them again.

The secrecy of this mutiny is beyond all conception. Thirteen of the party who were with me had always lived forward among the seamen, yet neither they, nor the messmates of Christian,

Stewart, Heywood, and Young had ever observed any circumstance that made them in the least suspect what was going on. To such a close-planned act of villainy, my mind being entirely free from any suspicion, it is not wonderful that I fell a sacrifice. Perhaps if there had been marines on board, a sentinel at my cabin-door might have prevented it; for I slept with the door always open, that the officer of the watch might have access to me on all occasions, the possibility of such a conspiracy being ever the farthest from my thoughts. Had their mutiny been occasioned by any grievances, either real or imaginary, I must have discovered symptoms of their discontent, which would have put me on my guard; but the case was far otherwise. Christian, in particular, I was on the most friendly terms with. That very day he was engaged to have dined with me, and the preceding night he excused himself from supping with me, on pretence of being unwell; for which I felt concerned, having no suspicions of his integrity and honour.

CHAPTER XIV

Proceed in the launch to the island Tofoa.—Difficulty in obtaining supplies there.—Treacherous attack of the natives.—Escape to sea, and bear away for New Holland.

MY first determination was to seek a supply of bread-fruit and water at Tofoa, and afterwards to sail for Tongataboo, and there risk a solicitation to Poulaho, the king, to equip our boat and grant us a supply of water and provisions so as to enable us to reach the East Indies.

The quantity of provisions I found in the boat was 150 lb. of bread, 16 pieces of pork (each piece weighing 2 lb.), 6 quarts of rum, 6 bottles of wine, with 28 gallons of water, and 4 empty *barrecoes*.

Fortunately it was calm all the afternoon till about four o'clock, when we were so far to windward that with a moderate easterly breeze which sprung up we were able to sail. It was nevertheless dark when we got to Tofoa, where I expected to land; but the shore proved to be so steep and rocky that we were obliged to give up all thoughts of it and keep the boat under the lee of the island with two oars, for there was no anchorage. Having fixed on this mode of proceeding for the night, I served to every person half a pint of grog, and each took to his rest as well as our unhappy situation would allow.

In the morning, at dawn of day, we rowed along shore in search of a landing-place, and about ten o'clock we discovered a cove with a stony beach at the NW. part of the island, where I dropped the grapnel within twenty yards of the rocks. A great surf ran on the shore, but as I was unwilling to diminish our stock of provisions I landed Mr Samuel and some others, who climbed the cliffs and got into the country to search for supplies. The rest of us remained at the cove, not discovering any other way into the country than that by which Mr Samuel had proceeded. It was great consolation to me to find that the spirits of my people did not sink, notwithstanding our miserable and almost hopeless situation. Towards noon Mr Samuel returned with a few quarts of water which he had found in holes, but he had met with no spring or any prospect of a sufficient supply in that particular, and had seen only the signs of inhabitants. As it was uncertain what might be our future necessities, I only issued a morsel of bread and a glass of wine to each person for dinner.

I observed the latitude of this cove to be 19° 41′ S. This is the NW. part of Tofoa, the north-westernmost of the Friendly Islands.

The weather was fair, but the wind blew so strong from the ESE. that we could not venture to sea. Our detention made it absolutely necessary to endeavour to obtain something towards our support, for I determined if possible to keep our first stock entire. We therefore weighed, and rowed along shore to see if anything could be got, and at last discovered some coconut trees; but they were on the top of high precipices and the surf made it dangerous landing. Both one and the other we, however, got the better of. Some of the people with much difficulty climbed the cliffs and got about twenty coconuts, and others slung them to ropes, by which we hauled them through the surf into the boat. This was all that could be done here, and as I found no place so safe as the one we had left to spend the night at I returned to the cove, and having served a coconut to each person we went to rest again in the boat.

At daylight we attempted to put to sea, but the wind and weather proved so bad that I was glad to return to our former station; where, after issuing a morsel of bread and a spoonful of rum to each person we landed, and I went off with Mr Nelson,

Mr Samuel, and some others into the country, having hauled ourselves up the precipice by long vines which were fixed there by the natives for that purpose, this being the only way into the country.

We found a few deserted huts, and a small plantain walk but little taken care of, from which we could only collect three small bunches of plantains. After passing this place we came to a deep gully that led towards a mountain near a volcano, and as I conceived that in the rainy season very great torrents of water must pass through it, we hoped to find sufficient for our use remaining in some holes of the rocks, but after all our search the whole that we collected was only nine gallons. We advanced within two miles of the foot of the highest mountain in the island, on which is the volcano that is almost constantly burning. The country near it is covered with lava and has a most dreary appearance. As we had not been fortunate in our discoveries and saw nothing to alleviate our distresses except the plantains and water above - mentioned, we returned to the boat exceedingly fatigued and faint. When I came to the precipice whence we were to descend into the cove, I was seized with such a dizziness in my head that I thought it scarce possible to effect it. However, by the assistance of Nelson and others they at last got me down, in a weak condition. Every person being returned by noon, I gave about an ounce of pork and two plantains to each, with half a glass of wine. I again observed the latitude of this place 19° 41′ S. The people who remained by the boat I had directed to look for fish or what they could pick up about the rocks, but nothing eatable could be found, so that upon the whole we considered ourselves on as miserable a spot of land as could well be imagined.

I could not say positively, from the former knowledge I had of this island, whether it was inhabited or not; but I knew it was considered inferior to the other islands, and I was not certain but that the Indians only resorted to it at particular times. I was very anxious to ascertain this point, for in case there had been only a few people here, and those could have furnished us with but very moderate supplies, the remaining in this spot to have made preparations for our voyage would have been preferable to the risk of going amongst multitudes where perhaps we might lose everything. A party, therefore, sufficiently strong, I determined should go another route as soon as the sun became lower; and they cheerfully undertook it.

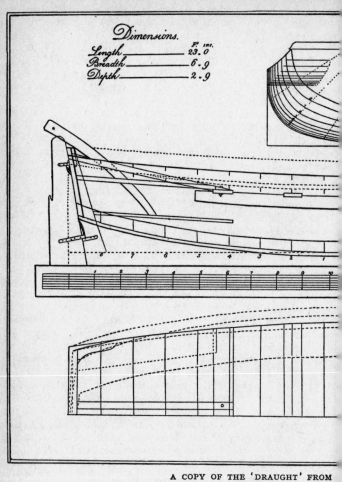

Dimensions.

	Ft. ins.
Length	23.0
Breadth	6.9
Depth	2.9

A COPY OF THE 'DRAUGHT' FROM

Reproduced from B

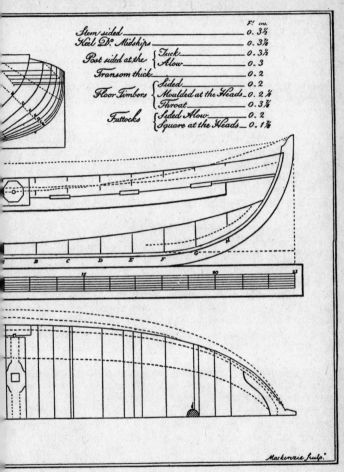

		F.t ins.
Stem sided		0. 3½
Keel D.º Midships		0. 3½
Post sided at the	Tuck	0. 3½
	Alow	0. 3
Transom thick		0. 2
Floor Timbers	Sided	0. 2
	Moulded at the Heads	0. 2¼
	Throat	0. 3½
Futtocks	Sided Alow	0. 2
	Square at the Heads	0. 1¾

Mackenzie sculp.

THE 'BOUNTY'S' LAUNCH WAS MADE

vage to the South Sea

About two o'clock in the afternoon the party set out, but after suffering much fatigue they returned in the evening, without any kind of success.

At the head of the cove, about a hundred and fifty yards from the water-side, there was a cave; the distance across the stony beach was about a hundred yards, and from the country in to the cove there was no other way than that which I have already described. The situation secured us from the danger of being surprised, and I determined to remain on shore for the night with a part of my people, that the others might have more room to rest in the boat, with the master, whom I directed to lie at a grapnel, and be watchful in case we should be attacked. I ordered one plantain for each person to be boiled, and having supped on this scanty allowance, with a quarter of a pint of grog, and fixed the watches for the night, those whose turn it was laid down to sleep in the cave, before which we kept up a good fire; yet notwithstanding we were much troubled with flies and mosquitoes.

Friday the 1st. At dawn of day the party set out again in a different route to see what they could find, in the course of which they suffered greatly for want of water. They, however, met with two men, a woman, and a child; the men came with them to the cove and brought two coconut shells of water. I endeavoured to make friends of these people, and sent them away for bread-fruit, plantains, and water. Soon after other natives came to us, and by noon there were thirty about us, from whom we obtained a small supply; but I could only afford one ounce of pork and a quarter of a bread-fruit to each man for dinner, with half a pint of water; for I was fixed in my resolution not to use any of the bread or water in the boat.

No particular chief was yet among the natives. They were, notwithstanding, tractable, and behaved honestly, exchanging the provisions they brought for a few buttons and beads. The party who had been out informed me of their having seen several neat plantations, so that it remained no longer a doubt of there being settled inhabitants on the island; for which reason I determined to get what I could, and to sail the first moment that the wind and weather would allow us to put to sea.

I was much puzzled in what manner to account to the natives for the loss of my ship. I knew they had too much sense to be amused with a story that the ship was to join me, when she was not in sight from the hills. I was at first doubtful whether

I should tell the real fact, or say that the ship had overset and sunk, and that we only were saved. The latter appeared to be the most proper and advantageous for us, and I accordingly instructed my people that we might all agree in one story. As I expected, inquiries were made about the ship, and they seemed readily satisfied with our account; but there did not appear the least symptom of joy or sorrow in their faces, although I fancied I discovered some marks of surprise. Some of the natives were coming and going the whole afternoon, and we got enough of bread-fruit, plantains, and coconuts for another day; but of water they only brought us about five pints. A canoe also came in with four men and brought a few coconuts and bread-fruit, which I bought as I had done the rest. Nails were much inquired after, but I would not suffer any to be shown, as they were wanted for the use of the boat.

Towards evening I had the satisfaction to find our stock of provisions somewhat increased, but the natives did not appear to have much to spare. What they brought was in such small quantities that I had no reason to hope we should be able to procure from them sufficient to stock us for our voyage. At sunset all the natives left us in quiet possession of the cove. I thought this a good sign, and made no doubt that they would come again the next day with a better supply of food and water, with which I hoped to sail without further delay; for if in attempting to get to Tongataboo we should be driven to lee-ward of the islands, there would be a larger quantity of provisions to support us against such a misfortune.

At night I served a quarter of a bread-fruit and a coconut to each person for supper, and a good fire being made, all but the watch went to sleep.

At daybreak the next morning I was pleased to find every one's spirits a little revived, and that they no longer regarded me with those anxious looks which had constantly been directed towards me since we lost sight of the ship; every countenance appeared to have a degree of cheerfulness, and they all seemed determined to do their best.

As there was no certainty of our being supplied with water by the natives, I sent a party among the gullies in the moun-tains, with empty shells, to see what could be found. In their absence the natives came about us, as I expected, and in greater numbers; two canoes also came in from round the north side of the island. In one of them was an elderly chief called Macca-ackavow. Soon after some of our foraging party returned, and with them came a good-looking chief called Egijeefow, or perhaps more properly Eefow, Egij or Eghee, signifying a chief. To each of these men I made a present of an old shirt and a knife, and I soon found they either had seen me, or had heard of my being at Annamooka. They knew I had been with Captain Cook, who they inquired after, and also Captain Clerk. They were very inquisitive to know in what manner I had lost my ship. During this conversation a young man named Nageete appeared, whom I remembered to have seen at Annamooka: he expressed much pleasure at our meeting. I inquired after Poulaho and Feenow, who, they said, were at Tongataboo, and Eefow agreed to accompany me thither if I would wait till the weather moderated. The readiness and affability of this man gave me much satisfaction.

This, however, was but of short duration, for the natives began to increase in number, and I observed some symptoms of a design against us. Soon after they attempted to haul the boat on shore, on which I brandished my cutlass in a threatening manner, and spoke to Eefow to desire them to desist; which they did, and everything became quiet again. My people who had been in the mountains now returned with about three gallons of water. I kept buying up the little bread-fruit that was brought to us, and likewise some spears to arm my men with, having only four cutlasses, two of which were in the boat. As we had no means of improving our situation, I told our people I would wait till sunset, by which time perhaps something might happen in our favour; for if we attempted to go at present we must fight our way through, which we could do more advantageously at night, and that in the meantime we would endeavour to get off to the boat what we had bought. The beach was lined with the natives, and we heard nothing but the knocking of stones together, which they had in each hand. I knew very well this was the sign of an attack. At noon I served a coconut and a bread-fruit to each person for dinner, and gave some to the chiefs, with whom I continued to appear intimate and friendly. They frequently importuned me to sit down, but I as constantly refused, for it occurred both to Nelson and myself that they intended to seize hold of me if I gave them such an opportunity. Keeping, therefore, constantly on our guard, we were suffered to eat our uncomfortable meal in some quietness.

After dinner we began by little and little to get our things into the boat, which was a troublesome business on account of the surf. I carefully watched the motions of the natives, who continued to increase in number, and found that instead of their intention being to leave us, fires were made, and places fixed on for their stay during the night. Consultations were also held among them, and everything assured me we should be attacked. I sent orders to the master that when he saw us coming down he should keep the boat close to the shore, that we might the more readily embark.

I had my journal on shore with me, writing the occurrences in the cave, and in sending it down to the boat it was nearly snatched away, but for the timely assistance of the gunner.

The sun was near setting when I gave the word, on which every person who was on shore with me boldly took up his proportion of things and carried them to the boat. The chiefs asked me if I would not stay with them all night. I said, 'No, I never sleep out of my boat; but in the morning we will again trade with you, and I shall remain till the weather is moderate, that we may go, as we have agreed, to see Poulaho at Tonga-taboo.' Macca-ackavow then got up and said, 'You will not sleep on shore? then *mattie*' (which directly signifies we will kill you), and he left me. The onset was now preparing. Every one, as I have described before, kept knocking stones together, and Eefow quitted me. All but two or three things were in the boat, when I took Nageete by the hand and we walked down the beach, every one in a silent kind of horror.

While I was seeing the people embark, Nageete wanted me to stay to speak to Eefow, but I found he was encouraging them to the attack, and it was my determination, if they had then began, to have killed him for his treacherous behaviour. I ordered the carpenter not to quit me till the other people were in the boat. Nageete, finding I would not stay, loosed himself from my hold and went off, and we all got into the boat except one man, who, while I was getting on board, quitted it, and ran up the beach to cast the stern fast off, notwithstanding the master and others called to him to return, while they were hauling me out of the water.

I was no sooner in the boat than the attack began by about two hundred men; the unfortunate poor man who had run up the beach was knocked down and the stones flew like a shower of shot. Many Indians got hold of the stern rope and were near hauling the boat on shore; which they would certainly have effected if I had not had a knife in my pocket with which I cut the rope. We then hauled off to the grapnel, every one being more or less hurt. At this time I saw five of the natives about the poor man they had killed, and two of them were beating him about the head with stones in their hands.

We had no time to reflect, for to my surprise they filled their canoes with stones, and twelve men came off after us to renew the attack, which they did so effectually as nearly to disable us all. Our grapnel was foul, but Providence here assisted us; the fluke broke, and we got to our oars and pulled to sea. They, however, could paddle round us, so that we were obliged to sustain the attack without being able to return it, except with such stones as lodged in the boat, and in this I found we were very inferior to them. We could not close, because our boat was lumbered and heavy, of which they well knew how to take advantage. I therefore adopted the expedient of throwing overboard some clothes, which, as I expected, they stopped to pick up, and as it was by this time almost dark, they gave over the attack and returned towards the shore, leaving us to reflect on our unhappy situation.

The poor man killed by the natives was John Norton. This was his second voyage with me as a quartermaster, and his worthy character made me lament his loss very much. He has left an aged parent, I am told, whom he supported.

I once before sustained an attack of a similar nature with a smaller number of Europeans against a multitude of Indians. It was after the death of Captain Cook, on the *morai* at Owhyhee, where I was left by Lieutenant King. Yet, notwithstanding this experience, I had not an idea that the power of a man's arm could throw stones, from two to eight pounds weight, with such force and exactness as these people did. Here unhappily we were without fire-arms, which the Indians knew; and it was a fortunate circumstance that they did not begin to attack us in the cave, for in that case our destruction must have been inevitable, and we should have had nothing left for it but to sell our lives as dearly as we could; in which I found every one cheerfully disposed to concur. This appearance of resolution deterred them, supposing that they could effect their purpose without risk after we were in the boat.

Taking this as a sample of the disposition of the natives, there was but little reason to expect much benefit by persevering in the intention of visiting Poulaho, for I considered their good behaviour formerly to have proceeded from a dread of our fire-arms, and which, therefore, was likely to cease as they knew we were now destitute of them; and, even supposing our lives not in danger, the boat and everything we had would most probably be taken from us, and thereby all hopes precluded of ever being able to return to our native country.

We set our sails and steered along shore by the west side of the island Tofoa, the wind blowing fresh from the eastward. My mind was employed in considering what was best to be done, when I was solicited by all hands to take them towards home; and when I told them that no hopes of relief for us remained (except what might be found at New Holland) till I came to Timor, a distance of full twelve hundred leagues, where there was a Dutch settlement, but in what part of the island I knew not, they all agreed to live on one ounce of bread and a quarter of a pint of water per day. Therefore, after examining our stock of provisions, and recommending to them in the most solemn manner not to depart from their promise, we bore away across a sea where the navigation is but little known in a small boat, twenty-three feet long from stem to stern, deep laden with eighteen men. I was happy, however, to see that every one seemed better satisfied with our situation than myself.

Our stock of provisions consisted of about one hundred and fifty pounds of bread, twenty-eight gallons of water, twenty pounds of pork, three bottles of wine, and five quarts of rum. The difference between this and the quantity we had on leaving the ship was principally owing to our loss in the bustle and confusion of the attack. A few coconuts were in the boat, and some bread-fruit, but the latter was trampled to pieces.

CHAPTER XV

*Passage towards New Holland.—Islands discovered in our route.—
Our great distresses.—See the reefs of New Holland, and find a
passage through them.*

IT was about eight o'clock at night when we bore away under
a reefed lug-foresail, and having divided the people into watches
and got the boat in a little order, we returned God thanks for
our miraculous preservation, and, fully confident of His gracious
support, I found my mind more at ease than it had been for
some time past.

At daybreak the gale increased, the sun rose very fiery and
red—a sure indication of a severe gale of wind. At eight
it blew a violent storm and the sea ran very high, so that
between the seas the sail was becalmed, and when on the
top of the sea it was too much to have set; but we could not
venture to take in the sail, for we were in very imminent danger
and distress, the sea curling over the stern of the boat, which
obliged us to bale with all our might. A situation more
distressing has perhaps seldom been experienced.

Our bread was in bags and in danger of being spoiled by the
wet: to be starved to death was inevitable if this could not be
prevented. I therefore began to examine what clothes there
were in the boat, and what other things could be spared; and
having determined that only two suits should be kept for each
person, the rest was thrown overboard, with some rope and
spare sails, which lightened the boat considerably, and we had
more room to bale the water out. Fortunately the carpenter
had a good chest in the boat, in which we secured the bread
the first favourable moment. His tool-chest also was cleared
and the tools stowed in the bottom of the boat, so that this
became a second convenience.

I served a teaspoonful of rum to each person (for we were
very wet and cold), with a quarter of a bread-fruit, which
was scarce eatable, for dinner. Our engagement was now strictly
to be carried into execution, and I was fully determined to make
our provisions last eight weeks, let the daily proportion be ever
so small.

At noon I considered our course and distance from Tofoa to
be WNW¼W. eighty-six miles, latitude 19° 27′ S. I directed

the course to the WNW., that we might get a sight of the
islands called Fiji, if they laid in the direction the natives had
pointed out to me.

The weather continued very severe, the wind veering from
NE. to ESE. The sea ran higher than in the forenoon, and
the fatigue of baling, to keep the boat from filling, was exceedingly
great. We could do nothing more than keep before the sea, in
the course of which the boat performed so well that I no longer
dreaded any danger in that respect. But among the hardships we were to undergo, that of being constantly wet was not
the least. The night was very cold, and at daylight our limbs
were so benumbed that we could scarce find the use of them.
At this time I served a teaspoonful of rum to each person, from
which we all found great benefit.

As I have mentioned before, I determined to keep to the
WNW. till I got more to the northward, for I not only expected
to have better weather, but to see the Fiji Islands, as I have
often understood from the natives of Annamooka that they lie
in that direction. Captain Cook likewise considered them to
be NW. by W. from Tongataboo. Just before noon we discovered a small flat island, of a moderate height, bearing WSW.
four or five leagues. I observed our latitude to be 18° 58′ S.;
our longitude was, by account, 3° 4′ W. from the island Tofoa,
having made a N. 72° W. course, distance ninety-five miles,
since yesterday noon. I divided five small coconuts for our
dinner, and every one was satisfied.

A little after noon other islands appeared, and at a quarter-
past three o'clock we could count eight, bearing from S. round
by the west to NW. by N.; those to the south, which were the
nearest, being four leagues distant from us.

I kept my course to the NW. by W., between the islands,
the gale having considerably abated. At six o'clock we discovered three other small islands to the NW., the westernmost
of them bore NW½W. seven leagues. I steered to the southward of these islands, a WNW. course for the night, under a
reefed sail.

Served a few broken pieces of bread-fruit for supper, and
performed prayers.

The night turned out fair, and having had tolerable rest,
every one seemed considerably better in the morning, and
contentedly breakfasted on a few pieces of yams that were
found in the boat. After breakfast we examined our bread,

a great deal of which was damaged and rotten; this, neverthe-less, we were glad to keep for use.

I had hitherto been scarcely able to keep any account of our run, but we now equipped ourselves a little better by getting a log-line marked, and having practised at counting seconds, several could do it with some degree of exactness.

The islands we had passed lie between the latitude of 19° 5′ S. and 18° 19′ S., and, according to my reckoning, from 3° 17′ to 3° 46′ W. longitude from the island Tofoa. The largest may be about six leagues in circuit, but it is impossible for me to be very correct. To show where they are to be found again is the most my situation enabled me to do. The sketch I have made will give a comparative view of their extent. I believe all the larger islands are inhabited, as they appeared very fertile.

At noon I observed, in latitude 18° 10′ S., and considered my course and distance from yesterday noon, NW. by W½W., 94 miles; longitude, by account, from Tofoa 4° 29′ W.

For dinner I served some of the damaged bread and a quarter of a pint of water.

About six o'clock in the afternoon we discovered two islands, one bearing W. by S. six leagues, and the other NW. by N. eight leagues. I kept to windward of the northernmost, and passing it by ten o'clock I resumed our course to the NW. and WNW. for the night.

Wednesday the 6th. The weather was fair and the wind moder-ate all day from the ENE. At daylight a number of other islands were in sight from SSE. to the W., and round to NE. by E.; between those in the NW. I determined to pass. At noon a small sandy island or key, two miles distant from me, bore from E. to S¾W. I had passed ten islands, the largest of which I judged to be six or eight leagues in circuit. Much larger lands appeared in the SW. and NNW., between which I directed my course. Latitude observed 17° 17′ S.; course since yesterday noon N. 50° W.; distance eighty-four miles; longitude made, by account, 5° 37′ W.

Our allowance for the day was a quarter of a pint of coco-nut milk, and the meat, which did not exceed two ounces to each person: it was received very contentedly, but we suffered great drought. I durst not venture to land, as we had no arms, and were less capable of defending ourselves than we were at Tofoa.

To keep an account of the boat's run was rendered difficult, from being constantly wet with the sea breaking over us; but as we advanced towards the land the sea became smoother, and I was enabled to form a sketch of the islands, which will serve to give a general knowledge of their extent and position. Those we were near appeared fruitful and hilly, some very mountainous, and all of a good height.

To our great joy we hooked a fish, but we were miserably disappointed by its being lost in trying to get it into the boat.

We continued steering to the NW., between the islands, which by the evening appeared of considerable extent, woody and mountainous. At sunset the southernmost bore from S. to SW. by W. and the northernmost from N. by W½W. to NE½E. At six o'clock we were nearly midway between them, and about six leagues distant from each shore, when we fell in with a coral bank on which we had only four feet water, without the least break on it or ruffle of the sea to give us warning. I could see that it extended about a mile on each side of us, but as it is probable that it may extend much farther, I have laid it down so in my sketch.

I directed the course W. by N. for the night, and served to each person an ounce of the damaged bread and a quarter of a pint of water for supper.

As our lodgings were very miserable and confined for want of room, I endeavoured to remedy the latter defect by putting ourselves at watch and watch; so that one-half always sat up while the other lay down on the boat's bottom, or upon a chest, with nothing to cover us but the heavens. Our limbs were dreadfully cramped, for we could not stretch them out; and the nights were so cold, and we so constantly wet, that after a few hours' sleep we could scarce move.

At dawn of day we again discovered land from WSW. to WNW., and another island NNW., the latter a high round lump of but little extent; the southern land that we had passed in the night was still in sight. Being very wet and cold, I served a spoonful of rum and a morsel of bread for breakfast.

The land in the west was distinguished by some extraordinary high rocks, which as we approached them assumed a variety of forms. The country appeared to be agreeably interspersed with high and low land, and in some places covered with wood. Off the NE. part lay some small rocky islands, between which and an island four leagues to the NE. I directed my course;

but a lee current very unexpectedly set us very near to the rocky isles, and we could only get clear of it by rowing, passing close to the reef that surrounded them. At this time we observed two large sailing canoes coming swiftly after us along shore, and being apprehensive of their intentions we rowed with some anxiety, fully sensible of our weak and defenceless state. At noon it was calm and the weather cloudy; my latitude is therefore doubtful to three or four miles. Our course since yesterday noon NW. by W., distance seventy-nine miles; latitude by account, 16° 29′ S., and longitude by account, from Tofoa, 6° 46′ W. Being constantly wet it was with the utmost difficulty I could open a book to write, and I am sensible that what I have done can only serve to point out where these lands are to be found again, and give an idea of their extent.

All the afternoon we had light winds at NNE.; the weather was very rainy, attended with thunder and lightning. Only one of the canoes gained upon us, which by three o'clock in the afternoon was not more than two miles off, when she gave over chase.

If I may judge from the sail of these vessels, they are of a similar construction with those at the Friendly Islands, which with the nearness of their situation gives reason to believe that they are the same kind of people. Whether these canoes had any hostile intention against us must remain a doubt. Perhaps we might have benefited by an intercourse with them, but in our defenceless situation to have made the experiment would have been risking too much.

I imagine these to be the islands called Fiji, as their extent, direction, and distance from the Friendly Islands answers to the description given of them by those islanders. Heavy rain came on at four o'clock, when every person did their utmost to catch some water, and we increased our stock to thirty-four gallons, besides quenching our thirst for the first time since we had been at sea; but an attendant consequence made us pass the night very miserably, for being extremely wet, and having no dry things to shift or cover us, we experienced cold and shiverings scarce to be conceived. Most fortunately for us the forenoon turned out fair, and we stripped and dried our clothes. The allowance I issued to-day was an ounce and a half of pork, a teaspoonful of rum, half a pint of coconut milk, and an ounce of bread. The rum, though so small in quantity, was of the greatest service. A fishing-line was generally towing from the stern of the boat, but though we saw great numbers of fish, we could never catch one.

At noon I observed in latitude 16° 4′ S., and found we had made a course from yesterday noon, N. 62° W., distance sixty-two miles; longitude, by account, from Tofoa, 7° 42′ W.

The land passed yesterday, and the day before, is a group of islands, fourteen or sixteen in number, lying between the latitude of 16° 26′ S. and 17° 57′ S., and in longitude, by my account, 4° 47′ to 7° 17′ W. from Tofoa. Three of these islands are very large, having from thirty to forty leagues of sea-coast.

In the afternoon we cleaned out the boat, and it employed us till sunset to get everything dry and in order. Hitherto I had issued the allowance by guess, but I now made a pair of scales with two coconut shells; and having accidentally some pistol-balls in the boat, twenty-five of which weighed one pound, or sixteen ounces, I adopted one,[1] as the proportion of weight that each person should receive of bread at the times I served it. I also amused all hands with describing the situation of New Guinea and New Holland, and gave them every information in my power, that in case any accident happened to me, those who survived might have some idea of what they were about, and be able to find their way to Timor, which at present they knew nothing of, more than the name, and some not even that. At night I served a quarter of a pint of water and half an ounce of bread for supper.

Saturday the 9th. In the morning, a quarter of a pint of coconut milk and some of the decayed bread was served for breakfast; and for dinner I divided the meat of four coconuts with the remainder of the rotten bread, which was only eatable by such distressed people.

At noon I observed the latitude to be 15° 47′ S.; course since yesterday N. 75° W., distance sixty-four miles; longitude made, by account, 8° 45′ W.

In the afternoon I fitted a pair of shrouds for each mast, and contrived a canvas weather-cloth round the boat, and raised the quarters about nine inches by nailing on the seats of the stern-sheets, which proved of great benefit to us.

The wind had been moderate all day, in the SE. quarter, with fine weather, but about nine o'clock in the evening the clouds began to gather, and we had a prodigious fall of rain, with

It weighed 272 grains.

severe thunder and lightning. By midnight we caught about twenty gallons of water. Being miserably wet and cold, I served to the people a teaspoonful of rum each, to enable them to bear with their distressed situation. The weather continued extremely bad, and the wind increased; we spent a very miserable night, without sleep, except such as could be got in the midst of rain. The day brought no relief but its light. The sea broke over us so much that two men were constantly baling, and we had no choice how to steer, being obliged to keep before the waves for fear of the boat filling.

The allowance now regularly served to each person was one-twenty-fifth of a pound of bread, and a quarter of a pint of water, at eight in the morning, at noon, and at sunset. To-day I gave about half an ounce of pork for dinner, which, though any moderate person would have considered only as a mouthful, was divided into three or four.

The rain abated towards noon, and I observed the latitude to be 15° 17′ S.; course N. 67° W., distance seventy-eight miles; longitude made 10° W.

The wind continued strong from SSE. to SE., with very squally weather and a high breaking sea, so that we were miserably wet, and suffered great cold in the night.

Monday the 11th. In the morning at daybreak I served to every person a teaspoonful of rum, our limbs being so cramped that we could scarce move them. Our situation was now extremely dangerous, the sea frequently running over our stern, which kept us baling with all our strength.

At noon the sun appeared, which gave us as much pleasure as in a winter's day in England. I issued the twenty-fifth of a pound of bread and a quarter of a pint of water, as yesterday. Latitude observed 14° 50′ S.; course N. 71° W., distance one hundred and two miles; and longitude, by account, 11° 39′ W. from Tofoa.

In the evening it rained hard, and we again experienced a dreadful night. At length the day came, and showed to me a miserable set of beings, full of wants, without anything to relieve them. Some complained of great pain in their bowels, and every one of having almost lost the use of his limbs. The little sleep we got was no ways refreshing, as we were covered with sea and rain. I served a spoonful of rum at day-dawn, and the usual allowance of bread and water for breakfast, dinner, and supper.

At noon it was almost calm, no sun to be seen, and some of us shivering with cold. Course since yesterday W. by N., distance eighty-nine miles; latitude, by account, 14° 33′ S.; longitude made 13° 9′ W. The direction of our course was to pass to the northward of the New Hebrides.

The wet weather continued, and in the afternoon the wind came from the southward, blowing fresh in squalls. As there was no prospect of getting our clothes dried, I recommended to every one to strip, and wring them through the salt water, by which means they received a warmth that while wet with rain they could not have.

This afternoon we saw a kind of fruit on the water which Nelson told me was the Barringtonia of Forster; and as I saw the same again in the morning, and some men-of-war birds, I was led to believe that we were not far from land.

We continued constantly shipping seas, and baling, and were very wet and cold in the night; but I could not afford the allowance of rum at daybreak.

Wednesday the 13th. At noon I had a sight of the sun, latitude 14° 17′ S.; course W. by N. seventy-nine miles; longitude made 14° 28′ W. All this day we were constantly shipping water, and suffered much cold and shiverings in the night.

Thursday the 14th. Fresh gales at SE., and gloomy weather, with rain and a high sea. At six in the morning we saw land, from SW. by S. eight leagues, to NW. by W¾W. six leagues, which soon after appeared to be four islands, one of them much larger than the others, and all of them high and remarkable. At noon we discovered a small island and some rocks, bearing NW. by N. four leagues, and another island W. eight leagues, so that the whole were six in number; the four I had first seen bearing from S½E. to SW. by S.; our distance three leagues from the nearest island. My latitude observed was 13° 29′ S., and longitude, by account, from Tofoa, 15° 49′ W.; course since yesterday noon N. 63° W., distance eighty-nine miles. At four in the afternoon we passed the westernmost island.

Friday the 15th. At one in the morning another island was discovered, bearing WNW., five leagues distance, and at eight o'clock we saw it for the last time, bearing NE. seven leagues. A number of gannets, boobies, and men-of-war birds were seen.

These islands lie between the latitude of 13° 16′ and 14° 10′ S.; their longitude, according to my reckoning, 15° 51′ to 17° 6′ W.

from the island Tofoa.[1]   The largest island I judged to be about twenty leagues in circuit, the others five or six.   The eastern-most is the smallest island, and most remarkable, having a high sugar-loaf hill.

The sight of these islands served only to increase the misery of our situation.   We were very little better than starving, with plenty in view; yet to attempt procuring any relief was attended with so much danger that prolonging of life, even in the midst of misery, was thought preferable while there remained hopes of being able to surmount our hardships.   For my own part, I con-sider the general run of cloudy and wet weather to be a blessing of Providence.   Hot weather would have caused us to have died with thirst, and probably being so constantly covered with rain or sea protected us from that dreadful calamity.

As I had nothing to assist my memory, I could not then determine whether these islands were a part of the New Hebrides or not.   I believed them to be a new discovery, which I have since found true; but though they were not seen either by Monsieur Bougainville or Captain Cook, they are so nearly in the neighbourhood of the New Hebrides that they must be considered as part of the same group.   They are fertile, and inhabited, as I saw smoke in several places.

The wind was at SE., with rainy weather all day.   The night was very dark, not a star could be seen to steer by, and the sea broke continually over us.   I found it necessary to counteract as much as possible the effect of the southerly winds, to prevent being driven too near New Guinea; for in general we were forced to keep so much before the sea, that if we had not at intervals of moderate weather steered a more southerly course, we should inevitably, from a continuance of the gales, have been thrown in sight of that coast; in which case there would most probably have been an end to our voyage.

Saturday the 16*th.*   In addition to our miserable allowance of one twenty-fifth of a pound of bread and a quarter of a pint of water, I issued for dinner about an ounce of salt pork to each person.   I was often solicited for this pork, but I con-sidered it more proper to issue it in small quantities than to suffer it to be all used at once or twice, which would have been done if I had allowed it.

---

[1] By making a proportional allowance for the error afterwards found in the dead reckoning, I estimate the longitude of these islands to be from 167° 17′ E. to 168° 34′ E. from Greenwich.

At noon I observed in 13° 33' S.; longitude made from Tofoa, 19° 27' W.; course N. 82° W., distance one hundred and one miles. The sun breaking out through the clouds gave us hopes of drying our wet clothes, but the sunshine was of short duration. We had strong breezes at SE. by S., and dark gloomy weather, with storms of thunder, lightning, and rain. The night was truly horrible, and not a star to be seen; so that our steerage was uncertain.

Sunday the 17th. At dawn of day I found every person complaining, and some of them solicited extra allowance; which I positively refused. Our situation was miserable; always wet, and suffering extreme cold in the night, without the least shelter from the weather. Being constantly obliged to bale, to keep the boat from filling, was perhaps not to be reckoned an evil, as it gave us exercise.

The little rum we had was of great service. When our nights were particularly distressing I generally served a teaspoonful or two to each person, and it was always joyful tidings when they heard of my intentions.

At noon a water-spout was very near on board of us. I issued an ounce of pork, in addition to the allowance of bread and water; but before we began to eat, every person stripped, and having wrung their clothes through the sea-water, found much warmth and refreshment. Course since yesterday noon WSW., distance one hundred miles; latitude, by account, 14° 11' S., and longitude made 21° 3' W.

The night was dark and dismal, the sea constantly breaking over us, and nothing but the wind and waves to direct our steerage. It was my intention, if possible, to make New Holland, to the southward of Endeavour Straits, being sensible that it was necessary to preserve such a situation as would make a southerly wind a fair one; that we might range along the reefs till an opening should be found into smooth water, and we the sooner be able to pick up some refreshments.

Monday the 18th. In the morning the rain abated, when we stripped and wrung our clothes through the sea-water as usual, which refreshed us greatly. Every person complained of violent pain in their bones; I was only surprised that no one was yet laid up. The customary allowance of one twenty-fifth of a pound of bread and a quarter of a pint of water was served at breakfast, dinner, and supper.

At noon I deduced my situation, by account, for we had no

glimpse of the sun, to be in latitude 14° 52′ S.; course since yesterday noon, WSW., one hundred and six miles; longitude made from Tofoa 22° 45′ W. Saw many boobies and noddies, a sign of being in the neighbourhood of land. In the night we had very severe lightning, with heavy rain, and were obliged to keep baling without intermission.

Tuesday the 19*th.* Very bad weather and constant rain. At noon, latitude, by account, 14° 37′ S.; course since yesterday, N. 81° W., distance one hundred miles; longitude made, 24° 30′ W. With the allowance of bread and water, served half an ounce of pork to each person for dinner.

Wednesday the 20*th.* Fresh breezes ENE. with constant rain; at times a deluge. Always baling.

At dawn of day some of my people seemed half dead; our appearances were horrible, and I could look no way but I caught the eye of someone in distress. Extreme hunger was now too evident, but no one suffered from thirst, nor had we much inclination to drink, that desire perhaps being satisfied through the skin. The little sleep we got was in the midst of water, and we constantly awoke with severe cramps and pains in our bones. This morning I served about two teaspoonfuls of rum to each person, and the allowance of bread and water as usual. At noon the sun broke out and revived every one. I found we were in latitude 14° 49′ S.; longitude made 25° 46′ W.; course S. 88° W., distance seventy-five miles.

All the afternoon we were so covered with rain and salt water that we could scarcely see. We suffered extreme cold, and every one dreaded the approach of night. Sleep, though we longed for it, afforded no comfort: for my own part I almost lived without it. About two o'clock in the morning we were over-whelmed with a deluge of rain. It fell so heavy that we were afraid it would fill the boat, and were obliged to bale with all our might. At dawn of day I served a larger allowance of rum. Towards noon the rain abated and the sun shone, but we were miserably cold and wet, the sea breaking constantly over us; so that notwithstanding the heavy rain, we had not been able to add to our stock of fresh water. Latitude, by observation, 14° 29′ S., and longitude made, by account, from Tofoa 27° 25′ W.; course, since yesterday noon, N. 78° W., ninety-nine miles. I now considered myself nearly on a meridian with the east part of New Guinea.

Friday the 22*nd.* Strong gales from ESE. to SSE., a high sea, and dark dismal night.

Our situation this day was extremely calamitous. We were obliged to take the course of the sea, running right before it, and watching with the utmost care, as the least error in the helm would in a moment have been our destruction.

At noon it blew very hard, and the foam of the sea kept running over our stern and quarters. I, however, got propped up, and made an observation of the latitude, in 14° 17′ S.; course N. 85° W., distance one hundred and thirty miles; longitude made 29° 38′ W.

The misery we suffered this night exceeded the preceding. The sea flew over us with great force, and kept us baling with horror and anxiety. At dawn of day I found every one in a most distressed condition, and I began to fear that another such night would put an end to the lives of several, who seemed no longer able to support their sufferings. I served an allowance of two teaspoonfuls of rum; after drinking which, having wrung our clothes and taken our breakfast of bread and water, we became a little refreshed.

Towards noon the weather became fair, but with very little abatement of the gale, and the sea remained equally high. With some difficulty I observed the latitude to be 13° 44′ S.; course since yesterday noon N. 74° W., distance one hundred and sixteen miles; longitude made 31° 32′ W. from Tofoa.

The wind moderated in the evening and the weather looked much better, which rejoiced all hands, so that they eat their scanty allowance with more satisfaction than for some time past. The night also was fair; but being always wet with the sea, we suffered much from the cold. A fine morning, I had the pleasure to see, produced some cheerful countenances, and the first time for fifteen days past we experienced comfort from the warmth of the sun. We stripped and hung our clothes up to dry, which were by this time become so threadbare that they would not keep out either wet or cold.

At noon I observed in latitude 13° 33′ S.; longitude, by account, from Tofoa, 33° 28′ W.; course N. 84° W., distance one hundred and fourteen miles. With the usual allowance of bread and water for dinner, I served an ounce of pork to each person. This afternoon we had many birds about us which are never seen far from land, such as boobies and noddies.

As the sea began to run fair and we shipped but little water, I took the opportunity to examine into the state of our bread, and found that according to the present mode of issuing there was a sufficient quantity remaining for twenty-nine days' allowance; by which time I hoped we should be able to reach Timor. But as this was very uncertain, and it was possible that after all we might be obliged to go to Java, I determined to proportion the allowance so as to make our stock hold out six weeks. I was apprehensive that this would be ill received, and that it would require my utmost resolution to enforce it; for small as the quantity was which I intended to take away for our future good, yet it might appear to my people like robbing them of life; and some, who were less patient than their companions, I expected would very ill brook it. However, on my representing the necessity of guarding against delays that might be occasioned in our voyage by contrary winds or other causes, and promising to enlarge upon the allowance as we got on, they cheerfully agreed to my proposal. It was accordingly settled that every person should receive one twenty-fifth of a pound of bread for breakfast, and the same quantity for dinner; so that by omitting the proportion for supper, we had forty-three days' allowance.

Monday the 25th. At noon some noddies came so near to us that one of them was caught by hand. This bird was about the size of a small pigeon. I divided it, with its entrails, into eighteen portions, and by a well-known method at sea, of 'Who shall have this?'[1] it was distributed, with the allowance of bread and water for dinner, and eat up bones and all, with salt water for sauce. I observed the latitude 13° 32′ S.; longitude made 35° 19′ W.; course N. 89° W., distance one hundred and eight miles.

In the evening several boobies flying very near to us, we had the good fortune to catch one of them. This bird is as large as a duck. Like the noddy, it has received its name from seamen, for suffering itself to be caught on the masts and yards of ships. They are the most presumptive proofs of being in the neighbourhood of land of any sea-fowl we are acquainted with. I directed the bird to be killed for supper, and the blood to be given to three of the people who were the most distressed for want of food. The body, with the entrails, beak, and feet, I divided into eighteen shares, and with an allowance of bread,

[1] One person turns his back on the object that is to be divided; another then points separately to the portions, at each of them asking aloud, 'Who shall have this?' to which the first answers by naming somebody. This impartial method of division gives every man an equal chance of the best share.

which I made a merit of granting, we made a good supper compared with our usual fare.

Tuesday the 26th. Fresh breezes from the SE., with fine weather. In the morning we caught another booby, so that Providence appeared to be relieving our wants in an extraordinary manner. Towards noon we passed a great many pieces of the branches of trees, some of which appeared to have been no long time in the water. I had a good observation for the latitude, and found our situation to be in 13° 41′ S.; longitude, by account, from Tofoa, 37° 13′ W.; course S. 85° W., one hundred and twelve miles. The people were overjoyed at the addition to their dinner, which was distributed in the same manner as on the preceding evening, giving the blood to those who were the most in want of food.

To make the bread a little savoury, most of the people frequently dipped it in salt water; but I generally broke mine into small pieces and eat it in my allowance of water, out of a coconut shell, with a spoon, economically avoiding to take too large a piece at a time, so that I was as long at dinner as if it had been a much more plentiful meal.

The weather was now serene, which nevertheless was not without its inconveniences, for we began to feel distress of a different kind from that which we had lately been accustomed to suffer. The heat of the sun was so powerful that several of the people were seized with a languor and faintness which made life indifferent. We were so fortunate as to catch two boobies in the evening. Their stomachs contained several flying fish and small cuttlefish, all of which I saved to be divided for dinner the next day.

Wednesday the 27th. A fresh breeze at ESE., with fair weather. We passed much driftwood this forenoon and saw many birds; I therefore did not hesitate to pronounce that we were near the reefs of New Holland. From my recollection of Captain Cook's survey of this coast, I considered the direction of it to be NW., and I was therefore satisfied that with the wind to the southward of E., I could always clear any dangers.

At noon I observed in latitude 13° 26′ S.; course since yesterday N. 82° W., distance one hundred and nine miles; longitude made 39° 4′ W. After writing my account I divided the two birds, with their entrails and the contents of their maws, into eighteen portions, and as the prize was a very valuable one it was divided as before, by calling out 'Who shall have this?'

So that to-day, with the allowance of a twenty-fifth of a pound of bread at breakfast and another at dinner, with the proportion of water, I was happy to see that every person thought he had feasted.

In the evening we saw a gannet, and the clouds remained so fixed in the west that I had little doubt of our being near the land. The people, after taking their allowance of water for supper, amused themselves with conversing on the probability of what we should find.

Thursday the 28th. At one in the morning the person at the helm heard the sound of breakers, and I no sooner lifted up my head than I saw them close under our lee, not more than a quarter of a mile distant from us. I immediately hauled on a wind to the NNE., and in ten minutes' time we could neither see nor hear them.

I have already mentioned my reason for making New Holland so far to the southward, for I never doubted of numerous openings in the reef through which I could have access to the shore, and knowing the inclination of the coast to be to the NW., and the wind mostly to the southward of E., I could with ease range such a barrier of reefs till I should find a passage, which now became absolutely necessary, without a moment's loss of time. The idea of getting into smooth water, and finding refreshments, kept my people's spirits up. Their joy was very great after we had got clear of the breakers, to which we had approached much nearer than I thought was possible without first discovering them.

In the morning, at daylight, we could see nothing of the land or of the reefs. We bore away again, and at nine o'clock saw the reefs. The sea broke furiously over every part, and we had no sooner got near to them than the wind came at E., so that we could only lie along the line of the breakers; within which we saw the water so smooth that every person already anticipated the heart-felt satisfaction he should receive as soon as we could get within them. I now found we were embayed, for we could not lie clear with the sails, the wind having backed against us, and the sea set in so heavy towards the reef that our situation was become unsafe. We could effect but little with the oars, having scarce strength to pull them, and I began to apprehend that we should be obliged to attempt pushing over the reef. Even this I did not despair of effecting with success, when happily we discovered a break in the reef about one mile from us, and at the same time an island of a moderate height within it, nearly in the same direction, bearing W½N. I entered the passage with a strong stream running to the westward, and found it about a quarter of a mile broad, with every appearance of deep water.

On the outside the reef inclined to the NE. for a few miles, and from thence to the NW. On the south side of the entrance it inclined to the SSW. as far as I could see it, and I conjecture that a similar passage to this which we now entered may be found near the breakers that I first discovered, which are twenty-three miles S. of this channel.

I did not recollect what latitude Providential Channel [1] lies in, but I considered it to be within a few miles of this, which is situate in 12° 51′ S. latitude.

Being now happily within the reefs, and in smooth water, I endeavoured to keep near them to try for fish, but the tide set us to the NW. I therefore bore away in that direction, and having promised to land on the first convenient spot we could find, all our past hardships seemed already to be forgotten.

At noon I had a good observation, by which our latitude was 12° 46′ S., whence the foregoing situations may be considered as determined with some exactness. The island first seen bore WSW. five leagues. This, which I have called the island Direction, will in fair weather always show the channel from which it bears due W., and may be seen as soon as the reefs from a ship's mast-head: it lies in the latitude of 12° 51′ S. These, however, are marks too small for a ship to hit, unless it can hereafter be ascertained that passages through the reef are numerous along the coast, which I am inclined to think they are, in which case there would be little risk, even if the wind was directly on the shore.

My longitude, made by dead reckoning, from the island Tofoa to our passage through the reef, is 40° 10′ W. Providential Channel, I imagine, must lie very nearly under the same meridian with our passage; by which it appears we had out-run our reckoning 1° 9′.

We now returned God thanks for His gracious protection, and with much content took our miserable allowance of a twenty-fifth of a pound of bread and a quarter of a pint of water for dinner.

[1] Providential Channel is laid down by Captain Cook in 12° 34′ S., longitude 143° 33′ E.

CHAPTER XVI

Progress to the northward, along the coast of New Holland.—Land on different islands in search of supplies.

As we advanced within the reefs the coast began to show itself very distinctly, in a variety of high and low land, some parts of which were covered with wood. In our way towards the shore we fell in with a point of a reef which is connected with that towards the sea, and here we came to a grapnel and tried to catch fish, but had no success. The island Direction at this time bore S. three or four leagues. Two islands lay about four miles to the W. by N., and appeared eligible for a resting-place, if for nothing more; but on our approach to the nearest island, it proved to be only a heap of stones, and its size too inconsiderable to shelter the boat. We therefore proceeded to the next, which was close to it and towards the main. On the NW. side of this I found a bay and a fine sandy point to land at. Our distance was about a quarter of a mile from a projecting part of the main, which bore from SW. by S., to NNW¾W. We landed to examine if there were any signs of the natives being near us. We saw some old fire-places, but nothing to make me apprehend that this would be an unsafe situation for the night. Every one was anxious to find something to eat, and it was soon discovered that there were oysters on the rocks, for the tide was out; but it was nearly dark, and only a few could be gathered. I determined therefore to wait till the morning, when I should better know how to proceed, and I directed that one-half of our company should sleep on shore and the other half in the boat. We would gladly have made a fire, but as we could not accomplish it we took our rest for the night, which happily was calm and undisturbed.

Friday the 29th. The dawn of day brought greater strength and spirits to us than I expected, for notwithstanding every one was very weak, there appeared strength sufficient remaining to make me conceive the most favourable hopes of our being able to surmount the difficulties we might yet have to encounter.

As there were no appearances to make me imagine that any of the natives were near us, I sent out parties in search of supplies, while others of the people were putting the boat in order, that we might be ready to go to sea in case any unfore-

seen cause should make it necessary. One of the gudgeons of
the rudder had come out in the course of the night, and was
lost. This, if it had happened at sea, might have been attended
with the most serious consequences, as the management of the
boat could not have been so nicely preserved as these very
heavy seas required. I had been apprehensive of this accident,
and had in some measure prepared for it by having grummets
fixed on each quarter of the boat for oars; but our utmost
readiness in using them would not probably have saved us.
It appears therefore a providential circumstance that it happened in a place of safety, and that it was in our power to
remedy the defect, for by great good luck we found a large
staple in the boat which answered the purpose.

The parties returned, highly rejoiced at having found plenty
of oysters and fresh water. I had also made a fire, by the help
of a small magnifying glass; and what was still more fortunate,
we found among the few things which had been thrown into
the boat and saved, a piece of brimstone and a tinder-box, so
that I secured fire for the future.

One of the people had been so provident as to bring away
with him from the ship a copper pot. By being in possession
of this article we were enabled to make a proper use of the
supply we now obtained, for with a mixture of bread and a little
pork we made a stew that might have been relished by people
of far more delicate appetites, and of which each person received
a full pint.

The general complaints of disease among us were a dizziness
in the head, great weakness of the joints, and violent tenesmus;
most of us having had no evacuation by stool since we left the
ship. I had constantly a severe pain at my stomach, but none
of our complaints were alarming. On the contrary, every one
retained marks of strength that, with a mind possessed of a
tolerable share of fortitude, seemed able to bear more fatigue
than I imagined we should have to undergo in our voyage to
Timor.

As I would not allow the people to expose themselves to
the heat of the sun, it being near noon, every one took his
allotment of earth where it was shaded by the bushes for a
short sleep.

The oysters which we found grew so fast to the rocks that
it was with difficulty they could be broken off, and at length
we discovered it to be the most expeditious way to open them

where they were fixed. They were of a good size and well tasted. To add to this happy circumstance, in the hollow of the land there grew some wire grass, which indicated a moist situation. On forcing a stick about three feet long into the ground we found water, and with little trouble dug a well, which produced as much as our occasions required. It was very good, but I could not determine if it was a spring or not. We were not obliged to make the well deep, for it flowed as fast as we emptied it; which, as the soil was apparently too loose to retain water from the rains, renders it probable to be a spring. On the south side of the island likewise we found a small run of good water.

Besides places where fires had been made, there were other signs of the natives sometimes resorting to this island. I saw two ill-constructed huts or wigwams, which had only one side loosely covered; and a pointed stick was found, about three feet long, with a slit in the end of it to sling stones with; the same as the natives of Van Diemen's Land use.

The track of some animal was very discernible, and Nelson agreed with me that it was the kangaroo; but whether these animals swim over from the mainland or are brought here by the natives to breed, it is impossible to determine. The latter is not improbable, as they may be taken with less difficulty in a confined spot like this, than on the continent.

The island is about a league in circuit. It is a high lump of rocks and stones covered with wood, but the trees are small, the soil, which is very indifferent and sandy, being barely sufficient to produce them. The trees that came within our knowledge were the manchineel and a species of purow; also some palm trees, the tops of which we cut down, and the soft interior part or heart of them was so palatable that it made a good addition to our mess. Nelson discovered some fern-roots, which I thought might be good roasted as a substitute for bread, but in this I was mistaken. It, however, was very serviceable in its natural state to allay thirst, and on that account I directed a quantity to be collected to take into the boat. Many pieces of coconut shells and husk were found about the shore, but we could find no coconut trees, neither did I see any on the main.

I had cautioned the people not to touch any kind of berry or fruit that they might find; yet they were no sooner out of my sight than they began to make free with three different kinds that grew all over the island, eating without any reserve. The symptoms of having eaten too much began at last to frighten some of them; but on questioning others, who had taken a more moderate allowance, their minds were a little quieted. The others, however, became equally alarmed in their turn, dreading that such symptoms would come on, and that they were all poisoned, so that they regarded each other with the strongest marks of apprehension, uncertain what would be the issue of their imprudence. Fortunately the fruit proved wholesome and good. One sort grew on a small delicate kind of vine. They were the size of a large gooseberry, and very like in substance, but had only a sweet taste; the skin was a pale red, streaked with yellow the long way of the fruit: it was pleasant and agreeable. Another kind grew on bushes, like that which is called the seaside grape in the West Indies; but the fruit was very different, being more like elderberries, and grew in clusters in the same manner. The third sort was a black berry; this was not in such plenty as the others, and resembled a bullace or large kind of sloe, both in size and taste. When I saw that these fruits were eaten by the birds, I no longer doubted of their being wholesome, and those who had already tried the experiment, not finding any bad effect, made it a certainty that we might eat of them without danger.

Wild pigeons, parrots, and other birds were about the summit of the island, but having no fire-arms relief of that kind was not to be expected, unless we should find some unfrequented spot where the birds were so tame that we might take them with our hands.

The shore of this island is very rocky, except the place at which we landed, and here I picked up many pieces of pumice-stone. On the part of the main nearest to us were several sandy bays, which at low-water became an extensive rocky flat. The country had rather a barren appearance, except in a few places where it was covered with wood. A remarkable range of rocks lay a few miles to the SW., and a high peaked hill seemed to terminate the coast towards the sea, with islands to the southward. A high fair cape showed the direction of the coast to the NW., about seven leagues distant, and two small isles lay three or four leagues to the northward of our present station.

I saw a few bees or wasps and several lizards; and the blackberry bushes were full of ants' nests, webbed like a spider's, but so close and compact as not to admit the rain. A trunk of a tree, about fifty feet long, lay on the beach; from which I conclude that a heavy sea sets in here with a northerly wind.

This day being the anniversary of the restoration of King Charles the Second, and the name not being inapplicable to our present situation (for we were restored to fresh life and strength), I named this Restoration Island, for I thought it probable that Captain Cook might not have taken notice of it. The other names which I have presumed to give the different parts of the coast are meant only to show my route more distinctly.

At noon I observed the latitude of the island to be 12° 39′ S.; our course having been N. 66° W., distance eighteen miles from yesterday noon. The wind was at ESE., with very fine weather.

In the afternoon I sent parties out again to gather oysters, with which and some of the inner part of the palm-top, we made another good stew for supper, each person receiving a full pint and a half; but I refused bread to this meal, for I considered that our wants might yet be very great, and was intent on saving our principal support whenever it was in my power. After supper we again divided, and those who were on shore slept by a good fire.

Saturday the 30th. In the morning I discovered a visible alteration in our company for the better, and I sent them away again to gather oysters. We had now only two pounds of pork left. This article, which I could not keep under lock and key as I did the bread, had been pilfered by some inconsiderate person, but every one denied having any knowledge of this act. I therefore resolved to put it out of their power for the future, by sharing what remained for our dinner. While the party was out picking up oysters I got the boat in readiness for sea, and filled all our water-vessels, which amounted to nearly sixty gallons.

The party being returned, dinner was soon ready, which was as plentiful a meal as the supper on the preceding evening, and with the pork I gave an allowance of bread. As it was not yet noon, I sent the people once more to gather oysters for a sea store, recommending to them to be as diligent as possible, for that I was determined to sail in the afternoon.

At noon I again observed the latitude 12° 39′ S.; it was then high-water, the tide had risen three feet, but I could not be certain from whence the flood came. I deduce the time of high-water at full and change to be ten minutes past seven in the morning.

Early in the afternoon the people returned with the few
oysters that they had collected, and everything was put into
the boat. I then examined the quantity of bread remaining,
and found thirty-eight days' allowance, according to the last
mode of issuing a twenty-fifth of a pound at breakfast and
at dinner.

Fair weather, and moderate breezes at ESE. and SE.

Being ready for sea I directed every person to attend prayers.
At four o'clock we were preparing to embark, when about
twenty of the natives appeared, running and hallooing to us,
on the opposite shore. They were each armed with a spear or
lance, and a short weapon which they carried in their left
hand; they made signs for us to come to them. On the top
of the hills we saw the heads of many more. Whether these
were their wives and children, or others who waited for our
landing, meaning not to show themselves, lest we might be
intimidated, I cannot say; but as I found we were discovered
to be on the coast, I thought it prudent to make the best of our
way, for fear of being pursued by canoes, though from the
accounts of Captain Cook, the chance was that there were very
few if any of consequence on any part of the coast. I passed
these people as near as I could with safety: they were naked,
and apparently black, and their hair or wool bushy and short.

I directed my course within two small islands that lie to the
north of Restoration Island, passing between them and the mainland, towards Fair Cape, with a strong tide in my favour, so
that I was abreast of it by eight o'clock. The coast we passed
was high and woody. As I could see no land without Fair Cape
I concluded that the coast inclined to the NW. and WNW.
I therefore steered more towards the W., but by eleven o'clock
at night we met with low land, which inclined to the NE., and
at three o'clock in the morning I found that we were embayed,
which obliged us to stand back for a short time to the southward.

Sunday the 31st. At daybreak I was exceedingly surprised to
find the appearance of the country entirely changed, as if in the
course of the night we had been transported to another part of
the world; for we had now a low sandy coast in view, with very
little verdure, or anything to indicate that it was at all habitable
to a human being, except a few patches of small trees or
brushwood.

Many small islands were in sight to the NE., about six miles
distant. The E. part of the main bore N. four miles, and Fair

Cape SSE. five or six leagues. I took the channel between the nearest island and the mainland, which were about one mile apart, leaving all the islands on the starboard side. Some of these were very pretty spots, covered with wood and well situated for fishing; large shoals of fish were about us, but we could not catch any. In passing this strait we saw another party of Indians, seven in number, running towards us, shouting and making signs for us to land. Some of them waved green branches of the bushes which were near them as a token of friendship, but some of their other motions were less friendly. A little farther off we saw a larger party, who likewise came towards us. I therefore determined not to land, though I much wished to have had some intercourse with these people. Nevertheless I laid the boat close to the rocks and beckoned to them to approach, but none of them would come within two hundred yards of us. They were armed in the same manner as the people we had seen from Restoration Island; they were stark naked, their colour black, with short bushy hair or wool, and in their appearance were similar to them in every respect. An island of a good height bore N$\frac{1}{2}$W., four miles from us, at which I resolved to land, and from thence to take a look at the coast. At this isle we arrived about eight o'clock in the morning. The shore was rocky, but the water was smooth, and we landed without difficulty. I sent two parties out, one to the northward and the other to the southward, to seek for supplies, and others I ordered to stay by the boat. On this occasion fatigue and weakness so far got the better of their sense of duty that some of the people expressed their discontent at having worked harder than their companions, and declared that they would rather be without their dinner than go in search of it. One person, in particular, went so far as to tell me, with a mutinous look, that he was as good a man as myself. It was not possible for me to judge where this might have an end if not stopped in time. Therefore to prevent such disputes in future I determined either to preserve my command or die in the attempt, and seizing a cutlass I ordered him to take hold of another and defend himself; on which he called out that I was going to kill him and immediately made concessions. I did not allow this to interfere further with the harmony of the boat's crew, and everything soon became quiet.

The parties continued collecting what they could find, which were some fine oysters and clams and a few small dog-fish that were caught in the holes of the rocks. We also found some rain-water in the hollow of the rocks on the north part of the island, so that of this essential article we were again so fortunate as to obtain a full supply.

After regulating the mode of proceeding I walked to the highest part of the island to consider our route for the night. To my surprise no more of the mainland could be seen here than from below, the northernmost part in sight, which was full of sand-hills, bearing W. by N., about three leagues. Except the isles to the ESE. and S. that we had passed, I could only discover a small key NW. by N. As this was considerably farther from the main than the spot on which we were at present, I judged it would be a more secure resting-place for the night; for here we were liable to an attack if the Indians had canoes, as they undoubtedly must have observed our landing. My mind being made up on this point, I returned, after taking a particular look at the island we were on, which I found only to produce a few bushes and some coarse grass, the extent of the whole not being two miles in circuit. On the north side, in a sandy bay, I saw an old canoe, about thirty-three feet long, lying bottom upwards and half buried in the beach. It was made of three pieces, the bottom entire, to which the sides were sewed in the common way. It had a sharp projecting prow rudely carved in resemblance of the head of a fish; the extreme breadth was about three feet, and I imagine it was capable of carrying twenty men. The discovery of so large a canoe confirmed me in the purpose of seeking a more retired place for our night's lodging.

At noon the parties were all returned, but had found much difficulty in gathering the oysters from their close adherence to the rocks, and the clams were scarce. I therefore saw that it would be of little use to remain longer in this place, as we should not be able to collect more than we could eat. I named this Sunday Island: it lies N. by W¾W. from Restoration Island; the latitude, by a good observation, 11° 58′ S.

We had a fresh breeze at SE. by S., with fair weather. At two o'clock in the afternoon we dined, each person having a full pint and a half of stewed oysters and clams, thickened with small beans, which Nelson informed me were a species of dolichos. Having eaten heartily, and completed our water, I waited to determine the time of high-water, which I found to be at three o'clock, and the rise of the tide about five feet.

According to this, it is high-water on the full and change at nineteen minutes past nine in the morning. I observed the flood to come from the southward, though at Restoration Island I thought it came from the northward. I think Captain Cook mentions that he found great irregularity in the set of the flood on this coast.

We steered for the key seen in the NW. by N., where we arrived just at dark, but found it so surrounded by a reef of rocks that I could not land without danger of staving the boat, and on that account we came to a grapnel for the night.

Monday the 1st. At dawn of day we got on shore and tracked the boat into shelter, for the wind blowing fresh without and the ground being rocky it was not safe to trust her at a grapnel, lest she should be blown to sea. I was therefore obliged to let her ground in the course of the ebb. From appearances I expected that if we remained till night we should meet with turtle, as we discovered recent tracks of them. Innumerable birds of the noddy kind made this island their resting-place, so that we had reason to flatter ourselves with hopes of getting supplies in greater abundance than it had hitherto been in our power. Our situation was at least four leagues distant from the main. We were on the north-westernmost of four small keys, which were surrounded by a reef of rocks connected by sand-banks, except between the two northernmost, and there likewise it was dry at low water; the whole forming a lagoon island into which the tide flowed. At this entrance I kept the boat.

As usual I sent parties away in search of supplies, but to our great disappointment we could only get a few clams and some dolichos. With these, and the oysters we had brought from Sunday Island, I made up a mess for dinner, with the addition of a small quantity of bread.

Towards noon Nelson and some others who had been to the easternmost key returned; but Nelson was in so weak a condition that he was obliged to be supported by two men. His complaint was a violent heat in his bowels, a loss of sight, much drought, and an inability to walk. This I found was occasioned by his being unable to support the heat of the sun, and that when he was fatigued and faint, instead of retiring into the shade to rest, he had continued to attempt more than his strength was equal to. I was glad to find that he had no fever, and it was now that the little wine, which I had so carefully saved, became of real use. I gave it in very small quantities, with some pieces of bread soaked in it, and he soon began to recover. The boatswain and carpenter also were ill, and complained of headache and sickness of the stomach. Others, who had not had any evacuation by stool, became shockingly distressed with the tenemus, so that there were but few without complaints. An idea prevailed that the sickness of the boatswain and carpenter was occasioned by eating the dolichos. Myself, however, and some others who had taken the same food felt no inconvenience; but the truth was that many of the people had eaten a large quantity of them raw, and Nelson informed me that they were constantly teasing him, whenever a berry was found, to know if it was good to eat; so that it would not have been surprising if many of them had been really poisoned.

Our dinner was not so well relished as at Sunday Island, because we had mixed the dolichos with our stew. The oysters and soup, however, were eaten by every one, except Nelson, whom I fed with a few small pieces of bread soaked in half a glass of wine, and he continued to mend.

In my walk round the island I found several coconut shells, the remains of an old wigwam, and the backs of two turtle, but no sign of any quadruped. One of the people found three sea-fowl's eggs.

As is common on such spots, the soil is little other than sand, yet it produced small toa-trees, and some others that we were not acquainted with. There were fish in the lagoon, but we could not catch any. Our wants, therefore, were not likely to be supplied here, not even with water for our daily expense; nevertheless, I determined to wait till the morning, that we might try our success in the night for turtle and birds. A quiet night's rest also, I conceived, would be of essential service to those who were unwell.

The wigwam and turtle shell were proofs that the natives at times visited this place, and that they had canoes; the remains of the large canoe that we saw at Sunday Island left no room to doubt; but I did not apprehend that we ran any risk by remaining here a short time. I directed our fire, however, to be made in the thicket, that we might not be discovered by its light.

At noon I observed the latitude of this island to be 11° 47' S. The mainland extended towards the NW. and was full of white sand-hills; another small island lay within us, bearing W. by N¼N., three leagues distant. Our situation being very low we could see nothing of the reef towards the sea.

The afternoon was advantageously spent in sleep. There were, however, a few not disposed to it, and those were employed in dressing some clams to take with us for the next day's dinner; others we cut up in slices to dry, which I knew was the most valuable supply we could find here, but they were very scarce.

Towards evening I cautioned every one against making too large a fire, or suffering it after dark to blaze up. Mr Samuel and Mr Peckover had the superintendence of this business, while I was strolling about the beach to observe if I thought it could be seen from the main. I was just satisfied that it could not, when on a sudden the island appeared all in a blaze that might have been discerned at a much more considerable distance. I ran to learn the cause, and found that it was occasioned by the imprudence and obstinacy of one of the party, who in my absence had insisted on having a fire to himself; in making which the flames caught the neighbouring grass and rapidly spread. This misconduct might have produced very serious consequences, by discovering our situation to the natives, for if they had attacked us we had neither arms nor strength to oppose an enemy. Thus the relief which I expected from a little sleep was totally lost, and I anxiously waited for the flowing of the tide, that we might proceed to sea.

It was high-water at half-past five this evening, whence I deduced the time, on the full and change of the moon, to be fifty-eight minutes past ten in the morning; the rise was nearly five feet. I could not observe the set of the flood, but imagined it to come from the southward, and that I was mistaken at Restoration Island, as I found the time of high-water gradually later the more we advanced to the northward.

At Restoration Island, high-water, full and change	7h.	10′
Sunday Island	9h.	19′
Here	10h.	58′

After eight o'clock Mr Samuel and Mr Peckover went out to watch for turtle, and three men went to the east key to endeavour to catch birds. All the others complaining of being sick took their rest, except Mr Hayward and Mr Elphinstone, whom I directed to keep watch. About midnight the bird party returned, with only twelve noddies, birds which I have already described to be about the size of pigeons; but if it had not been for the folly and obstinacy of one of the party, who separated from the other two and disturbed the birds, they might have caught a great number. I was so much provoked at my plans being thus defeated that I gave this offender [1] a good beating. I now went in search of the turtling party, who had taken great pains, but without success. This did not surprise me, as it was not to be expected that turtle would come near us after the noise which had been made at the beginning of the evening in extinguishing the fire. I therefore desired them to come back, but they requested to stay a little longer, as they still hoped to find some before daylight. However, they returned by three o'clock without any reward for their labour.

The birds we half dressed, that they might keep the better; and these, with a few clams, made the whole of the supply procured here. I tied a few gilt buttons and some pieces of iron to a tree, for any of the natives that might come after us, and finding my invalids much better for their night's rest, we embarked, and departed by dawn of day. Wind at SE.; course to the N. by W.

When we had ran two leagues to the northward the sea suddenly became rough, which not having before experienced since we were within the reefs, I concluded to be occasioned by an open channel to the ocean. Soon afterwards we met with a large shoal, on which were two sandy keys; between these and two others, four miles to the west, I passed on to the northward, the sea still continuing to be rough.

Towards noon I fell in with six other keys, most of which produced some small trees and brushwood. These formed a pleasing contrast with the mainland we had passed, which was full of sand-hills. The country continued hilly, and the northern-most land, the same we had seen from the lagoon island, appeared like downs, sloping towards the sea. Nearly abreast of us was a flat-topped hill, which on account of its shape I called Pudding Pan Hill, and a little to the northward were two other hills, which we called the Paps; and here was a small tract of country without sand, the eastern part of which forms a cape, whence the coast inclines to the NW. by N.

[1] Robert Lamb. This man, when he came to Java, acknowledged he had eaten nine birds raw, after he separated from his two companions.

At noon I observed in the latitude of 11° 18′ S. the cape bearing W., distant ten miles. Five small keys bore from NE. to SE., the nearest of them about two miles distant, and a low sandy key between us and the cape bore W., distant four miles. My course from the lagoon island had been N½W., distant thirty miles.

I am sorry it was not in my power to obtain a sufficient knowledge of the depth of water, but in our situation nothing could be undertaken that might have occasioned delay. It may, however, be understood, that to the best of my judgment, from appearances a ship may pass wherever I have omitted to represent danger.

I divided six birds, and issued one twenty-fifth of a pound of bread, with half a pint of water, to each person for dinner, and I gave half a glass of wine to Nelson, who was now so far recovered as to require no other indulgence.

The gunner when he left the ship brought his watch with him, by which we had regulated our time till to-day, when unfortunately it stopped; so that noon, sunrise, and sunset are the only parts of the twenty-four hours which from henceforward I can speak with certainty as to time.

The wind blew fresh from the SSE. and SE. all the afternoon, with fair weather. As we stood to the N. by W. we found more sea, which I attributed to our receiving less shelter from the reefs to the eastward. It is probable they do not extend so far north as this; at least, it may be concluded that there is not a continued barrier to prevent shipping having access to the shore. I observed that the stream set to the NW., which I considered to be the flood. In some places along the coast we saw patches of wood. At five o'clock, steering to the NW., we passed a large and fair inlet, into which I imagine there is a safe and commodious entrance; it lies in latitude 11° S. About three leagues to the northward of this is an island, at which we arrived about sunset, and took shelter for the night under a sandy point, which was the only part we could land at. This being rather a wild situation, I thought it best to sleep in the boat; nevertheless I sent a party away to see if anything could be got, but they returned without success. They saw a great number of turtle bones and shells, where the natives had been feasting, and their last visit seemed to be of late date. The island was covered with wood, but in other respects it was a lump of rocks.

Wednesday the 3rd. We lay at a grapnel till daylight, with a very fresh gale and cloudy weather. The main bore from SE. by S. to NNW ½ W., three leagues; and a mountainous island with a flat top, N. by W., four or five leagues; between which and the mainland were several other islands. The spot we were at, which I call Turtle Island, lies in latitude, by account, 10° 52′ S.; and forty-two miles W. from Restoration Island. Abreast of it the coast has the appearance of a sandy desert, but improves about three leagues farther to the northward, where it terminates in a point near to which are many small islands. I sailed between these islands, where I found no bottom at twelve fathoms; the high mountainous island with a flat top, and four rocks to the SE. of it, that I call the Brothers, being on my starboard hand. Soon after an extensive opening appeared in the mainland, in which were a number of high islands. I called this the Bay of Islands. We continued steering to the NW. Several islands and keys were in sight to the northward: the most northerly island was mountainous, having on it a very high round hill, and a smaller was remarkable for a single-peaked hill.

The coast to the northward and westward of the Bay of Islands is high and woody, and has a broken appearance, with many islands close to it; among which there are fine bays and convenient places for shipping. The northernmost of these islands I call Wednesday Island; to the NW. of this we fell in with a large reef, which I believe joins a number of keys that were in sight from the NW. to the ENE. We therefore stood to the SW. half a league, when it was noon, and I had a good observation of the latitude in 10° 31′ S. Wednesday Island bore E. by S. five miles; the westernmost land in sight SW. two or three leagues; the islands to the northward, from NW. by W. to NE., and the reef from W. to NE., distant one mile. I was now tolerably certain that we should be clear of New Holland in the afternoon.

I know not how far this reef extends. It may be a continuation, or a detached part of the range of shoals that surround the coast. I believe the mountainous islands to be separate from the shoals, and have no doubt that near them may be found good passages for ships. But I rather recommend to those who are to pass this strait from the eastward to take their direction from the coast of New Guinea; yet, I likewise think that a ship coming from the southward will find a fair strait in the latitude of 10° S. I much wished to have ascertained this point, but in our distressful situation, any increase of fatigue or loss of time might have been attended with the most fatal consequences. I therefore determined to pass on without delay.

As an addition to our dinner of bread and water, I served to each person six oysters.

At two o'clock in the afternoon, as we were steering to the SW. towards the westernmost part of the land in sight, we fell in with some large sand-banks that run off from the coast: I therefore called this Shoal Cape. We were obliged to steer to the northward again, till we got round the shoals, when I directed the course to the W.

At four o'clock the westernmost of the islands to the northward bore N. four leagues; Wednesday Island E. by N. five leagues; and Shoal Cape SE. by E. two leagues. A small island was seen bearing W., at which we arrived before dark, and found that it was only a rock where boobies resort, for which reason I called it Booby Island. Here terminated the rocks and shoals of the N. part of New Holland, for except Booby Island, no land was seen to the westward of S. after three o'clock this afternoon.

I find that Booby Island was seen by Captain Cook, and by a remarkable coincidence of ideas, received from him the same name; but I cannot with certainty reconcile the situation of some parts of the coast that I have seen to his survey. I ascribe this to the various forms in which land appears when seen from the different heights of a ship and a boat. The chart I have given is by no means meant to supersede that made by Captain Cook, who had better opportunities than I had, and was in every respect properly provided for surveying. The intention of mine is chiefly to render this narrative more intelligible, and to show in what manner the coast appeared to me from an open boat. I have little doubt but that the opening which I named the Bay of Islands is Endeavour Straits, and that our track was to the northward of Prince of Wales's Isles. Perhaps by those who shall hereafter navigate these seas more advantage may be derived from the possession of both our charts than from either of them singly.

CHAPTER XVII

Passage from New Holland to the island Timor.—Arrive at Coupang.—Reception there.

At eight o'clock in the evening we once more launched into the open ocean. Miserable as our situation was in every respect, I was secretly surprised to see that it did not appear to affect any one so strongly as myself. On the contrary, it seemed as if they had embarked on a voyage to Timor in a vessel sufficiently calculated for safety and convenience. So much confidence gave me great pleasure, and I may venture to assert that to this cause our preservation is chiefly to be attributed.

I encouraged every one with hopes that eight or ten days would bring us to a land of safety; and after praying to God for a continuance of his most gracious protection, I served an allowance of water for supper, and directed our course to the WSW., to counteract the southerly winds in case they should blow strong.

We had been just six days on the coast of New Holland, in the course of which we found oysters, a few clams, some birds, and water. But perhaps a benefit nearly equal to this we received, by having been relieved from the fatigue of being constantly in the boat, and enjoying good rest at night. These advantages certainly preserved our lives; and, small as the supply was, I am very sensible how much it alleviated our distresses. By this time nature must have sunk under the extremes of hunger and fatigue. Some would have ceased to struggle for a life that only promised wretchedness and misery, and others, though possessed of more bodily strength, must soon have followed their unfortunate companions. Even in our present situation we were most deplorable objects, but the hopes of a speedy relief kept up our spirits. For my part, incredible as it may appear, I felt neither extreme hunger nor thirst. My allowance contented me, knowing that I could have no more.

Thursday the 4th. I served one twenty-fifth of a pound of bread and an allowance of water for breakfast, and the same for dinner, with an addition of six oysters to each person. At noon, latitude observed 10° 48′ S.; course since yesterday noon

S. 81° W., distance one hundred and eleven miles; longitude, by account, from Shoal Cape, 1° 45′ W. A strong trade wind at ESE., with fair weather.

This day we saw a number of water-snakes that were ringed yellow and black, and towards noon we passed a great deal of rock-weed. Though the weather was fair we were constantly shipping water, which kept two men always employed to bale the boat.

Friday the 5th. At noon I observed in latitude 10° 45′ S.; our course since yesterday W¼N., one hundred and eight miles; longitude made 3° 35′ W. Six oysters were, as yesterday, served to each man, in addition to the usual allowance of bread and water.

In the evening a few boobies came about us, one of which I caught with my hand. The blood was divided among three of the men who were weakest, but the bird I ordered to be kept for our dinner the next day. Served a quarter of a pint of water for supper, and to some, who were most in need, half a pint. In the course of the night, being constantly wet with the sea, we suffered much cold and shiverings.

Saturday the 6th. At daylight I found that some of the clams, which had been hung up to dry for sea-store, were stolen; but every one solemnly denied having any knowledge of it. This forenoon we saw a gannet, a sand-lark, and some water-snakes, which in general were from two to three feet long.

The usual allowance of bread and water was served for breakfast, and the same for dinner, with the bird, which I distributed in the usual way of 'Who shall have this?' I proposed to make Timor about the latitude of 9° 30′ S., of 10° S. At noon I observed the latitude to be 10° 19′ S.; course N. 77° W., distance one hundred and seventeen miles; longitude made from the Shoal Cape, the north part of New Holland, 5° 31′ W.

In the afternoon I took an opportunity of examining our store of bread, and found remaining nineteen days' allowance, at the former rate of serving one twenty-fifth of a pound three times a day. Therefore, as I saw every prospect of a quick passage, I again ventured to grant an allowance for supper, agreeable to my promise at the time it was discontinued.

We passed the night miserably wet and cold, and in the morning I heard heavy complaints. The sea was high and breaking over us. I could only afford the allowance of bread and water for breakfast, but for dinner I gave out an ounce of dried clams to each person, which was all that remained.

At noon I altered the course to the WNW., to keep more from the sea, as the wind blew strong. Latitude observed 9° 31′ S.; course N. 57° W., distance eighty-eight miles; longitude made 6° 46′ W.

The sea ran very high all this day and we had frequent showers of rain, so that we were continually wet and suffered much cold in the night. Mr Ledward, the surgeon, and Lawrence Lebogue, an old hardy seaman, appeared to be giving way very fast. I could only assist them by a teaspoonful or two of wine, which I had carefully saved, expecting such a melancholy necessity.

Monday the 8th. Wind at SE. The weather was more moderate than it had been for some days past. A few gannets were seen. At noon I observed in 8° 45′ S.; course WNW¼W., one hundred and six miles; longitude made 8° 23′ W. The sea being smooth I steered W. by S.

At four in the afternoon we caught a small dolphin, which was the first relief of the kind that we obtained. I issued about two ounces to each person, including the offals, and saved the remainder for dinner the next day. Towards evening the wind freshened, and it blew strong all night, so that we shipped much water and suffered greatly from wet and cold.

Tuesday the 9th. At daylight, as usual, I heard much complaining, which my own feelings convinced me was too well founded. I gave the surgeon and Lebogue a little wine, but I could afford them no further relief, except encouraging them with hopes that a very few days longer, at our present fine rate of sailing, would bring us to Timor.

Gannets, boobies, men-of-war, and tropic birds, were constantly about us. Served the usual allowance of bread and water, and at noon we dined on the remains of the dolphin, which amounted to about an ounce per man. I observed the latitude to be 9° 9′ S.; longitude made 10° 8′ W.; course since yesterday noon S. 76° W.; distance one hundred and seven miles.

This afternoon I suffered great sickness from the nature of part of the stomach of the fish, which had fallen to my share at dinner. At sunset I served an allowance of bread and water for supper.

Wednesday the 10th. In the morning, after a very comfortless night, there was a visible alteration for the worse in many of the people, which gave me great apprehensions. An extreme weakness, swelled legs, hollow and ghastly countenances, a more than common inclination to sleep, with an apparent debility of understanding, seemed to me the melancholy presages of an approaching dissolution. The surgeon and Lebogue, in particular, were most miserable objects. I occasionally gave them a few teaspoonfuls of wine out of the little that remained, which greatly assisted them. The hopes of being able to accomplish the voyage was our principal support. The boatswain very innocently told me that he really thought I looked worse than any one in the boat. The simplicity with which he uttered such an opinion amused me, and I returned him a better compliment.

Our latitude at noon was 9° 16′ S. Longitude from the north part of New Holland, 12° 1′ W. Course since yesterday noon W½S., one hundred and eleven miles. Birds and rock-weed showed that we were not far from land; but I expected such signs here, as there are many islands between the east part of Timor and New Guinea. The night was more moderate than the last.

Thursday the 11*th.* Every one received the customary allowance of bread and water, and an extra allowance of water was given to those who were most in need. At noon I observed in latitude 9° 41′ S.; course S. 77° W., distance one hundred and nine miles; longitude made 13° 49′ W. I had little doubt of having now passed the meridian of the eastern part of Timor, which is laid down in 128° E. This diffused universal joy and satisfaction.

In the afternoon we saw gannets and many other birds, and at sunset we kept a very anxious look-out. In the evening we caught a booby, which I reserved for our dinner the next day.

Friday the 12*th.* At three in the morning, with an excess of joy, we discovered Timor bearing from WSW. to WNW., and I hauled on a wind to the NNE. till daylight, when the land bore from SW. by S. to NE. by N. Our distance from the shore, two leagues.

It is not possible for me to describe the pleasure which the blessing of the sight of this land diffused among us. It appeared scarce credible to ourselves, that in an open boat, and so poorly provided, we should have been able to reach the coast of Timor in forty-one days after leaving Tofoa, having in that time run, by our log, a distance of 3,618 miles; and that, notwithstanding our extreme distress, no one should have perished in the voyage.

I have already mentioned that I knew not where the Dutch settlement was situated, but I had a faint idea that it was at the SW. part of the island. I therefore, after daylight, bore away along shore to the SSW., which I was the more readily induced to do, as the wind would not suffer us to go towards the NE. without great loss of time.

The day gave us a most agreeable prospect of the land, which was interspersed with woods and lawns; the interior part mountainous, but the shore low. Towards noon the coast became higher, with some remarkable headlands. We were greatly delighted with the general look of the country, which exhibited many cultivated spots and beautiful situations; but we could only see a few small huts, whence I concluded that no European resided in this part of the island. Much sea ran on the shore, which made landing impracticable. At noon we were abreast of a high headland; the extremes of the land bore SW½W. and NNE½E.; our distance off shore being three miles; latitude, by observation, 9° 59′ S., and my longitude, by dead reckoning from the north part of New Holland, 15° 6′ W.

With the usual allowance of bread and water for dinner, I divided the bird we had caught the night before, and to the surgeon and Lebogue I gave a little wine.

The wind blew fresh at E., and ESE., with very hazy weather. During the afternoon we continued our course along a low shore, covered with innumerable palm-trees, called the fan palm from the leaf spreading like a fan; but here we saw no signs of cultivation, nor had the country so fine an appearance as to the eastward. This, however, was only a small tract, for by sunset it improved again, and I saw several great smokes where the inhabitants were clearing and cultivating their grounds. We had now run twenty-five miles to the WSW. since noon, and were W. five miles from a low point, which in the afternoon I imagined had been the southernmost land; and here the coast formed a deep bend, with low land in the bight that appeared like islands. The west shore was high, but from this part of the coast to the high cape which we were abreast of at noon the shore is low, and I believe shoal. I particularly remark this situation, because here the very high ridge of mountains that run from the east end of the island terminate, and the appearance of the country changes for the worse.

That we might not run past any settlement in the night, I determined to preserve my station till the morning, and

therefore brought to under a close-reefed foresail. We were
here in shoal water, our distance from the shore being half a
league, the westernmost land in sight bearing WSW½W. Served
bread and water for supper, and the boat lying-to very well,
all but the officer of the watch endeavoured to get a little
sleep.

Saturday the 13th. At two in the morning, we wore, and
stood in shore till daylight, when I found we had drifted during
the night about three leagues to the WSW., the southernmost
land in sight bearing W. On examining the coast, and not
seeing any sign of a settlement, we bore away to the westward,
having a strong gale, against a weather current, which occasioned much sea. The shore was high and covered with wood,
but we did not run far before low land again formed the coast,
the points of which opening at west, I once more fancied we
were on the south part of the island; but at ten o'clock we
found the coast again inclining towards the south, part of it
bearing WSW½W. At the same time, high land appeared in
SW.; but the weather was so hazy that it was doubtful whether
the two lands were separated, the opening only extending one
point of the compass. For this reason I stood towards the
outer land, and found it to be the island Roti.

I returned to the shore we had left and brought to a grapnel
in a sandy bay, that I might more conveniently calculate my
situation. In this place we saw several smokes, where the
natives were clearing their grounds. During the little time we
remained here the master and carpenter very much importuned
me to let them go in search of supplies; to which at length
I assented, but not finding any other person willing to be of
their party, they did not choose to quit the boat. I stopped
here no longer than for the purpose just mentioned, and we
continued steering along shore. We had a view of a beautiful-
looking country, as if formed by art into lawns and parks.
The coast is low and covered with woods, in which are innumerable fan palm-trees that look like coconut walks. The
interior part is high land, but very different from the more
eastern parts of the island, where it is exceedingly mountainous,
and to appearance the soil better.

At noon the island Roti bore SW. by W. seven leagues. I had
no observation for the latitude, but by account we were in
10° 12′ S., our course since yesterday noon being S. 77° W.,
fifty-four miles. The usual allowance of bread and water was

served for breakfast and dinner, and to the surgeon and Lebogue I continued to give wine.

We had a strong breeze at ESE., with hazy weather, all the afternoon. At two o'clock, having run through a very dangerous breaking sea, the cause of which I attributed to be a strong tide setting to windward, and shoal water, we discovered a spacious bay or sound, with a fair entrance about two or three miles wide. I now conceived hopes that our voyage was nearly at an end, as no place could appear more eligible for shipping or more likely to be chosen for an European settlement. I therefore came to a grapnel near the east side of the entrance in a small sandy bay, where we saw a hut, a dog, and some cattle; and I immediately sent the boatswain and gunner away to the hut to discover the inhabitants.

The SW. point of the entrance bore W$\frac{1}{2}$S. three miles; the SE. point S. by W. three-quarters of a mile; and the island Roti from S. by W$\frac{1}{4}$W. to SW$\frac{1}{4}$W., about five leagues.

While we lay here I found the ebb came from the northward, and before our departure the falling of the tide discovered to us a reef of rocks, about two cables' length from the shore; the whole being covered at high-water renders it dangerous. On the opposite shore also appeared very high breakers, but there is nevertheless plenty of room, and certainly a safe channel for a first-rate man-of-war.

The bay or sound within seemed to be of a considerable extent, the northern part being about five leagues distant. Here the land made in moderate risings joined by lower grounds. But the island Roti to the southward is the best mark by which to know this place.

I had just time to make these remarks when I saw the boatswain and gunner returning with some of the natives; I therefore no longer doubted of our success and that our expectations would be fully gratified. They brought five Indians and informed me that they had found two families, where the women treated them with European politeness. From these people I learned that the governor resided at a place called Coupang, which was some distance to the NE. I made signs for one of them to go in the boat and show us the way to Coupang, intimating that I would pay him for his trouble. The man readily complied and came into the boat.

These people were of a dark tawny colour, had long black hair, and chewed a great deal of betel. Their dress was a square piece of cloth round the hips, in the folds of which was stuck a large knife, a handkerchief wrapped round the head, and another hanging by the four corners from the shoulders, which served as a bag for their betel equipage. They brought us a few pieces of dried turtle and some ears of Indian corn. This last was the most welcome, for the turtle was so hard that it could not be eaten without being first soaked in hot water. They offered to bring us some other refreshments if I would wait, but as the pilot was willing I determined to push on. It was about half an hour past four when we sailed.

By direction of the pilot we kept close to the east shore under all our sail, but as night came on the wind died away and we were obliged to try at the oars, which I was surprised to see we could use with some effect. At ten o'clock, finding we advanced but slowly, I came to a grapnel, and for the first time I issued double allowance of bread and a little wine to each person.

Sunday the 14th. At one o'clock in the morning, after the most happy and sweet sleep that ever men enjoyed, we weighed and continued to keep the east shore on board, in very smooth water, when at last I found we were again open to the sea, the whole of the land to the westward that we had passed being an island, which the pilot called Pulo Samow. The northern entrance of this channel is about a mile and a half or two miles wide, and I had no ground at ten fathoms.

The report of two cannon that were fired gave new life to every one, and soon after we discovered two square-rigged vessels and a cutter at anchor to the eastward. We endeavoured to work to windward, but were obliged to take to our oars again, having lost ground on each tack. We kept close to the shore and continued rowing till four o'clock, when I brought to a grapnel and gave another allowance of bread and wine to all hands. As soon as we had rested a little we weighed again and rowed till near daylight, when we came to a grapnel off a small fort and town, which the pilot told me was Coupang.

Among the things which the boatswain had thrown into the boat before we left the ship was a bundle of signal flags that had been used by the boats to show the depth of water in sounding. With these we had in the course of the passage made a small jack, which I now hoisted in the main shrouds as a signal of distress, for I did not think proper to land without leave.

Soon after daybreak a soldier hailed us to land, which I immediately did, among a crowd of Indians, and was agreeably

surprised to meet with an English sailor who belonged to one
of the vessels in the road. His captain, he told me, was the
second person in the town. I therefore desired to be conducted to him, as I was informed the governor was ill and could
not then be spoken with.

Captain Spikerman received me with great humanity. I informed him of our distressed situation and requested that care
might be taken of those who were with me without delay. On
which he gave directions for their immediate reception at his
own house, and went himself to the governor, to know at what
time I could be permitted to see him; which was fixed to be at
eleven o'clock.

I now desired my people to come on shore, which was as
much as some of them could do, being scarce able to walk.
They, however, were helped to the house, and found tea with
bread and butter provided for their breakfast.

The abilities of a painter, perhaps, could seldom have been
displayed to more advantage than in the delineation of the two
groups of figures which at this time presented themselves to each
other. An indifferent spectator would have been at a loss
which most to admire; the eyes of famine sparkling at immediate relief, or the horror of their preservers at the sight of so
many spectres, whose ghastly countenances, if the cause had
been unknown, would rather have excited terror than pity.
Our bodies were nothing but skin and bones, our limbs were
full of sores, and we were clothed in rags. In this condition,
with the tears of joy and gratitude flowing down our cheeks,
the people of Timor beheld us with a mixture of horror,
surprise, and pity.

The governor, Mr William Adrian Van Este, notwithstanding
extreme ill health, became so anxious about us that I saw him
before the appointed time. He received me with great affection,
and gave me the fullest proofs that he was possessed of every
feeling of a humane and good man. Sorry as he was, he
said, that such a calamity could ever have happened to us, yet
he considered it as the greatest blessing of his life that we had
fallen under his protection; and though his infirmity was so
great that he could not do the office of a friend himself, he
would give such orders as I might be certain would procure us
every supply we wanted. A house should be immediately prepared for me, and with respect to my people, he said that I
might have room for them either at the hospital or on board of

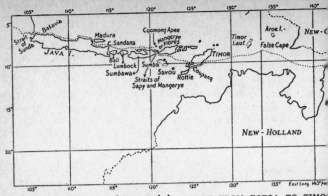

THE TRACK OF THE 'BOUNTY'S' LAUNCH FROM TOFOA TO TIMO

Captain Spikerman's ship, which lay in the road; and he expressed much uneasiness that Coupang could not afford them better accommodations, the house assigned to me being the only one uninhabited and the situation of the few families that lived at this place such that they could not conveniently receive strangers. For the present, till matters could be properly regulated, he gave directions that victuals for my people should be dressed at his own house.

On returning to Captain Spikerman's house I found that every kind relief had been given to my people. The surgeon had dressed their sores, and the cleaning of their persons had not been less attended to, several friendly gifts of apparel having been presented to them.

I desired to be shown to the house that was intended for me, which I found ready, with servants to attend. It consisted of a hall, with a room at each end and a loft overhead; and was surrounded by a piazza, with an outer apartment in one corner, and a communication from the back part of the house to the street. I therefore determined, instead of separating from my people, to lodge them all with me, and I divided the house as follows: One room I took to myself, the other I allotted to the master, surgeon, Mr Nelson, and the gunner; the loft to the other officers; and the outer apartment to the men. The hall was common to the officers, and the men had the back piazza. Of this disposition I informed the governor, and he sent down chairs, tables, and benches, with bedding and other necessaries for the use of every one.

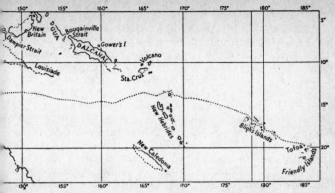

his map is copied from the map in Bligh's *Voyage to the South Sea*)

The governor, when I took my leave, had desired me to
acquaint him with everything of which I stood in need; but
it was only at particular times that he had a few moments of
ease or could attend to anything, being in a dying state with
an incurable disease. On this account I transacted whatever
business I had with Mr Timotheus Wanjon, the second of this
place, who was the governor's son-in-law, and who also contributed everything in his power to make our situation comfortable. I had been, therefore, misinformed by the seaman, who
told me that Captain Spikerman was the next person in command to the governor.

At noon a dinner was brought to the house, sufficiently good
to make persons more accustomed to plenty eat too much.
Yet I believe few in such a situation would have observed more
moderation than my people did. My greatest apprehension
was that they would eat too much fruit, of which there was
great variety in season at this time.

Having seen every one enjoy this meal of plenty, I dined
myself with Mr Wanjon, but I felt no extraordinary inclination
to eat or drink. Rest and quiet, I considered, as more necessary
to the re-establishment of my health, and therefore retired soon
to my room, which I found furnished with every convenience.
But instead of rest, my mind was disposed to reflect on our
late sufferings, and on the failure of the expedition; but, above
all, on the thanks due to Almighty God, who had given us power
to support and bear such heavy calamities, and had enabled me
at last to be the means of saving eighteen lives.

In times of difficulty there will generally arise circumstances that bear particularly hard on a commander. In our late situation it was not the least of my distresses to be constantly assailed with the melancholy demands of my people for an increase of allowance, which it grieved me to refuse. The necessity of observing the most rigid economy in the distribution of our provisions was so evident that I resisted their solicitations and never deviated from the agreement we made at setting out. The consequence of this care was that at our arrival we had still remaining sufficient for eleven days, at our scanty allowance, and if we had been so unfortunate as to have missed the Dutch settlement at Timor we could have proceeded to Java, where I was certain that every supply we wanted could be procured.

Another disagreeable circumstance to which my situation exposed me was the caprice of ignorant people. Had I been incapable of acting they would have carried the boat on shore as soon as we made the island of Timor, without considering that landing among the natives, at a distance from the European settlement, might have been as dangerous as among any other Indians.

The quantity of provisions with which we left the ship was not more than we should have consumed in five days had there been no necessity for husbanding our stock. The mutineers must naturally have concluded that we could have no other place of refuge than the Friendly Islands; for it was not likely they should imagine that so poorly equipped as we were in every respect there could have been a possibility of our attempting to return homewards, much less can they suspect that the account of their villainy has already reached their native country.

When I reflect how providentially our lives were saved at Tofoa, by the Indians delaying their attack; and that, with scarce anything to support life, we crossed a sea of more than twelve hundred leagues, without shelter from the inclemency of the weather; when I reflect that in an open boat, with so much stormy weather we escaped foundering, that not any of us were taken off by disease, that we had the great good fortune to pass the unfriendly natives of other countries without accident, and at last happily to meet with the most friendly and best of people to relieve our distresses; I say, when I reflect on all these wonderful escapes, the remembrance of such great

mercies enables me to bear with resignation and cheerfulness the
failure of an expedition the success of which I had so much at
heart, and which was frustrated at a time when I was congratu-
lating myself on the fairest prospect of being able to complete
it in a manner that would fully have answered the intention
of His Majesty and the humane promoters of so benevolent
a plan.

With respect to the preservation of our health, during a
course of sixteen days of heavy and almost continual rain, I
would recommend to every one in a similar situation the method
we practised, which is to dip their clothes in the salt-water and
wring them out as often as they became filled with rain.   It
was the only resource we had, and I believe was of the greatest
service to us, for it felt more like a change of dry clothes than
could well be imagined.   We had occasion to do this so often
that at length all our clothes were wrung to pieces, for except
the few days we passed on the coast of New Holland we were
continually wet either with rain or sea.

Thus, through the assistance of Divine Providence, we sur-
mounted the difficulties and distresses of a most perilous
voyage and arrived safe in an hospitable port, where every
necessary and comfort were administered to us with a most
liberal hand.

CHAPTER XVIII

AT COUPANG

FROM the great humanity and attention of the governor and
the gentlemen at Coupang, we received every kind of assistance,
and were not long without evident signs of returning health.
Shortly after our arrival I presented to the governor a formal
account of the loss of the *Bounty*, and a requisition in His
Majesty's name that instructions might be sent to all the
Dutch settlements to stop the ship if she made her appearance.
With this a complete descriptive list of the mutineers was
given.

I likewise requested in one of my first visits to the governor
that Nelson might have permission to walk about the country
in search of plants, which was readily granted, with an offer of

whatever assistance I should think necessary; and the governor assured me that the country was well worth examination, as it abounded with many curious and medicinal plants. From this indulgence I derived no benefit, for Nelson, who since we left New Holland had been but in a weak condition, about this time was taken ill in consequence of a cold caused by imprudently leaving off warm clothing.

To secure our arrival at Batavia before the October fleet sailed for Europe, I gave public notice of my intention to hire a vessel to carry us to Batavia. In consequence of this notice several offers were made, but none that I thought reasonable, which determined me to purchase a small schooner in the road, that was thirty-four feet long, for which I gave a thousand rix-dollars, and fitted her for sea under the name of His Majesty's schooner *Resource*. As the coast of Java is frequently infested with small piratical vessels, it was necessary that we should be provided with the proper means of defence. In this I was assisted by the friendship of Mr Wanjon, who supplied me with four brass swivels, fourteen stand of small arms and ammunition, which he obligingly let me have as a loan to be returned at Batavia.

On the 20th of July I had the misfortune to lose Mr David Nelson; he died of an inflammatory fever. The loss of this honest man I very much lamented. He had with great care and diligence attended to the object for which he was sent, and had always been ready to forward every plan that was proposed for the good of the service in which we were engaged. He was not less useful in our voyage hither, in the course of which he gave me great satisfaction by the patience and fortitude with which he conducted himself.

July 21st. This day I was employed attending the funeral of Mr Nelson. The corpse was carried by twelve soldiers dressed in black, preceded by the minister; next followed myself and the second governor; then ten gentlemen of the town and the officers of the ships in the harbour; and after them my own officers and people.

After reading our burial service the body was interred behind the chapel, in the burying-ground appropriated to the Europeans of the town. I was sorry I could get no tombstone to place over his remains.

This was the second voyage Mr Nelson had undertaken to the South Seas, having been sent out by Sir Joseph Banks to collect plants, seeds, etc., in Captain Cook's last voyage. And now, after surmounting so many difficulties, and in the midst of thankfulness for his deliverance, he was called upon to pay the debt of nature at a time least expected.

Our schooner being victualled and ready for sea, on the 20th of August I took an affectionate leave of the hospitable and friendly inhabitants of Coupang, and embarked. In the afternoon we sailed, having the launch, which had so much contributed to our preservation, in tow. We exchanged salutes with the fort and shipping as we ran out of the harbour.

The town of Coupang is situated in a great bay, which is an excellent road for shipping. The latitude of the town is 10° 12′ S. According to the Dutch charts it is in 121° 51′ E. longitude. Taking the mean between the longitude by my reckoning on our arrival at Coupang, and the longitude afterwards calculated from our run to Batavia, gives me for the longitude of Coupang 124° 41′ E.

This settlement was formed in the year 1630, and is the only one the Dutch have on the island Timor. They have residents in different parts of the country. On the north side of Timor there is a Portuguese settlement. The produce of the island is chiefly sandal-wood and bees-wax; the former article is now scarce. Wax they have in great plenty. The bees build their nests in bushes and in the boughs of trees, to which the natives cannot approach but with fire. The honey is put into jars, and the wax is run into blocks of three feet in length and from twelve to fifteen inches square. The natives, at least those who live in the neighbourhood of Coupang, are of a very indolent disposition, of which the Chinese have taken advantage; for though the Malays are very fond of traffic, most of their trade is carried on in small Chinese vessels of from ten to thirty tons burthen. There is a market at Coupang for the country people, in which, however, there is little business done. I have seen a man from the country come to market with two potatoes; and this is not unusual. These being sold for two doits (equal to a halfpenny English) serve to supply him with betel to chew and the remainder of the day is passed in lounging about the town. The inland people, who live at a distance from the Europeans, are strong and active; but their want of cleanliness subjects them to filthy diseases.

The chief of the natives, or king of the island, is by the Dutch stiled Keyser (Emperor). This prince lives at a place called Backennassy, about four miles distant from Coupang. His authority over the natives is not wholly undisputed, which is by the Dutch attributed to the intrigues of the Portuguese, who are on the north part of Timor. The island has lately suffered much by a competition between the present king and one of his nephews, which caused a civil war that lasted from the beginning of the year 1786 to 1788, when their differences were settled by a treaty, chiefly in favour of the king. The ravages committed in these disputes have occasioned a scarcity of provisions, that probably from the want of industry in the natives will not soon be remedied. I had an opportunity of making a visit to the king. His dwelling was a large house, which was divided into only three apartments and surrounded by a piazza; agreeably situated, but very dirty, as was all the furniture. The king, who is an elderly man, received me with much civility, and ordered refreshments to be set before me, which were tea, rice cakes, roasted Indian corn, and dried buffalo flesh, with about a pint of arrack, which I believe was all he had. His dress was a check wrapper girded round his waist with a silk and gold belt, a loose linen jacket, and a coarse handkerchief about his head. A few of his chiefs were with him, who partook of our repast; after which the king retired with three of them for a short time, and when he returned presented me with a round plate of metal, about four inches diameter, on which was stamped the figure of a star. As I had been informed that arrack would be an acceptable present, I was prepared to make a return, which was well received. They never dilute their liquor, and from habit are able to drink a large quantity of spirits at a time without being intoxicated.

When a king dies a large feast is made, to which all the inhabitants are invited. The body, after a few days, is put into a coffin, which is closed up and kept three years before it is interred.

The Dutch have been at some pains to establish Christianity among the natives, but it has not gained much ground, except in the neighbourhood of Coupang. The present king was christened by the name of Barnardus. His Indian name is Bacchee Bannock. The scriptures are translated into the Malay language and prayers are performed in the church at Coupang by a Malay clergyman in that language.

I met at Timor with most of the fruits that are described in

Captain Cook's first voyage, as natives of Batavia, except the mangostan. The bread-fruit tree, called by the Malays *soccoom*, likewise grows here with great luxuriance, and appears to be as much a native of this island as it is of Otaheite. The fruit is exactly of the same kind, but not so good. A bread-fruit of Timor weighs half as much more as one of equal size at Otaheite. It is not used here as bread, but generally eaten with milk and sugar. At Backennassy I saw about twenty of the trees, larger than any I have seen at Otaheite. Here is also a sort of bread-fruit tree that produces seeds, not unlike Windsor beans, and equally palatable, either boiled or roasted. No other part of the fruit is eatable, and though the tree, I am told, is to all appearance the same as the other, the fruits have but little resemblance, the fruit of this being covered with projecting points, nearly half an inch in length.

I received a present of some fine plants from the governor, which I was afterwards unfortunately obliged to leave at Batavia for want of proper room to take care of them in the packet by which I returned to Europe. Mr Wanjon likewise favoured me with some seeds for His Majesty's garden at Kew, which I had the good fortune to deliver safe on my return; and some of the mountain rice, cultivated at Timor, on the dry land, which was forwarded to His Majesty's botanic garden at St Vincent, and to other parts in the West Indies.

A resemblance of language between the people of the South Sea Islands and the inhabitants of many of the islands in the East Indies, has been remarked in Captain Cook's first voyage. Here the resemblance appeared stronger than has yet been noticed, particularly in their numerals. But besides the language I observed some customs among the people of Timor still more striking for their similarity. They practise the *tooge-tooge* [1] of the Friendly Islands, which they call *toombock*; and the *roomee* of Otaheite, which they call *ramas*. I likewise saw, placed on their graves, offerings of baskets with tobacco and betel.

I left the governor, Mr Van Este, at the point of death. To this gentleman our most grateful thanks are due for the humane and friendly treatment that we received from him. His ill state of health only prevented him from showing us more particular marks of attention. Unhappily it is to his memory

[1] The *tooge-tooge* is described in Captain Cook's last voyage, vol. i, p. 323; and the *roomee*, in the same voyage, vol. ii, p. 64.

only that I now pay this tribute. It was a fortunate circumstance for us that Mr Wanjon, the next in place to the governor, was equally humane and ready to relieve us. His attention was unremitting, and when there was a doubt about supplying me with money to enable me to purchase a vessel, he cheerfully took it upon himself, without which, it was evident, I should have been too late at Batavia to have sailed for Europe with the October fleet. I can only return such services by ever retaining a grateful remembrance of them.

Mr Max, the town surgeon, likewise behaved to us with the most disinterested humanity. He attended every one with the utmost care, for which I could not prevail on him to receive any payment, or to render me any account, or other answer, than that it was his duty.

CHAPTER XIX

FROM TIMOR TO BATAVIA

Thursday the 20th. From Coupang we steered NW. by W. having a moderate breeze at SE. with fair weather.

Saturday the 22nd. At daylight we saw the island Flores to the northward. At noon latitude observed 9° 27′ S. and longitude by account, from Coupang, 2° 10′ W. Our distance from the coast of Flores was about ten leagues, and two high-peaked mountains bore N½E. and NNW. These two mountains resemble each other in shape, and the westernmost is a volcano. The interior parts of Flores are mountainous and woody, but near the sea-coast is a fine open country. A Dutch map, with which I was provided, places the south part of Flores in 9° 3′ S., which I am of opinion is too far south. We steered along the south side of Flores, mostly with light winds and hazy weather, so that we did not constantly keep sight of the coast.

Tuesday the 25th. At noon we were off Toorns island, which bore NW. by N., three or four leagues distant. Our latitude observed was 8° 57′ S. and longitude made by dead reckoning from Coupang, 3° 27′ W. Toorns island is about four leagues in circuit and has a craggy and uneven appearance. There is a curious high peak on the SW. part; the land near the shore is low and woody.

On the 27th, at noon, we were near the entrance of the Straits of Mangaryn, which not appearing so open and clear as represented in the map I steered for the Straits of Sapi, intending to pass through; but was obliged to give up this plan by strong currents setting to the SE., which there was not sufficient wind to enable us to stem. I therefore again stood for the Straits of Mangaryn, which we ran through in the afternoon of the 29th, being favoured with a fresh breeze from the SSE. On our first entering the straits we got close to the Flores shore; our course through was N½E. We tried for soundings, but could not anywhere find bottom at twenty-five and thirty fathoms depth. On the Flores side there are many good harbours and bays, where vessels may anchor, but the country hereabouts appears burnt up and desolate.

I had no azimuth-compass, and consequently could not observe very accurately the variation, but I believe there is so little in Mangaryn Straits that no great error will be occasioned by considering the true and magnetic bearings to be the same.

When we had passed the straits we kept to the westward, running along the north side of the island Sumbawa, where there is a very high mountain near the coast, at the foot of which, I am informed, are many runs of good water conveniently situated for ships to supply themselves. The latitude of the north part of Sumbawa I make, by my observations and bearings, to be 8° 6′ S., which differs very little from the Dutch charts.

In the night of the 31st several prows were rowing about us, on which account we kept all night under arms.

Thursday the 3rd. This and the two following days we were sailing along the north side of the island Lombock, on which is a high mountain. Most of the islands in this route are distinguished by high mountains. Lombock appears to be well clothed with wood. In the nights we saw fires upon the high lands, at a distance from the coast.

Sunday the 6th. In the afternoon we saw the high land of Cape Sandana, which is the NE. part of Java.

The next day we were off Cape Sandana, which is a low cape, projecting from the high land already mentioned. This cape is placed by the Dutch maps in 7° 52′ S. But according to my observation, and our estimated distance from the land, I make it in 7° 46′ S. latitude. The longitude, by my dead reckoning, from Coupang to Cape Sandana, was 11° 33′ W.

We steered to the westward, along the coast of Java; and

on the 10th, at noon, we anchored off Passourwang, a Dutch settlement on the coast of Java, in two fathoms; distant from the shore half a league; the entrance of the river bearing SW. The coast hereabouts is so shoal that large ships are obliged to anchor three or four miles from the land. As soon as we were at anchor, I got in my boat and went on shore. The banks of the river, near the entrance, were mud, on which grew a few mangrove bushes. Among them we saw hogs running, and many were laying dead in the mud, which caused a most intolerable stench and made me heartily repent having come here; but after proceeding about a mile up the river, the course of which was serpentine, we found a very pleasant country, and landed at a small and well-constructed fort, where I was received in a friendly and polite manner by M. Adrian Van Rye, the commandant. By the return of the boat I sent on board a small bullock and other provisions. I likewise took a pilot to conduct us to Sourabya.

The houses at Passourwang are neatly built, and the country appears to be well cultivated. The produce of this settlement is rice, of which they export large quantities. There are but few Dutch here: the Javanese are numerous and their chief lives with considerable splendour. They have good roads and posts are established along the coast, and it appears to be a busy and well-regulated settlement. Latitude 7° 36′ S.; longitude 1° 44′ W. of Cape Sandana.

The next day, about noon, we sailed, and on the 12th, in the evening, anchored in Sourabya road in seven fathoms; the flagstaff bearing S¼W., distance from the shore one mile. We found riding here seven square-rigged and several smaller vessels.

It was too late when we anchored to send a boat on shore. The next morning, before daylight, three guard-boats stationed themselves near us, and I was informed that I must not land or send a boat on shore. This restriction, I learnt from the officer of the guard-boats, was in conformity to general orders concerning all strange vessels on their first arrival. At nine in the forenoon leave came off for us to land, and soon after the guard-boats quitted us.

I was received on shore with great civility and friendship by the governor, or *opperhooft*, M. Ant. Barkay, and the commandant of the troops, M. de Bose. By these gentlemen I was hospitably entertained and advised to remain till the 16th, when some vessels were to sail, with whom I might keep company, which they recommended on account of pirates.

Sourabya is one of the most pleasant places I ever saw. It is situated on the banks of a river, and is a mile and a half distant from the seashore, so that only the flag-staff can be seen from the road. The river is navigable up to the town for vessels of 100 tons burthen, and the bank on one side is made convenient for tracking. The Chinese carry on a considerable trade here, and have a town or camp on the side of the river opposite to Sourabya. The country near the town is flat and the soil light, so that they plough with a single bullock or buffalo (*karrabow*). The interior parts of the country, near the mountains, are infested with a breed of fierce tigers, which makes travelling inland very dangerous. They have here a breed of horses, which are small, but they are handsome and strong.

The Javanese in this neighbourhood are numerous. M. Barkay and M. de Bose took me with them to pay a visit to two of the principal natives, whom we found attended by a number of men armed with pikes, in great military order. We were entertained with a concert of music; the instruments were gongs, drums, and a fiddle with two strings. I hired a pilot here to carry us to Batavia. Our latitude observed in Sourabya road was 7° 11′ S. Longitude made from Cape Sandana 1° 52″ W.

On the 17th we sailed from Sourabya in company with three prows. At noon we anchored at Crissey, which is a town with a small fort, belonging to the Dutch. We remained here about two hours and then weighed. Latitude of Crissey 7° 9′ S.; longitude from Cape Sandana 1° 55′ W.

The navigation through the Straits of Madura is so intricate that with the little opportunity I had I am unable to undertake a description of it. The next day (18th September), having passed the straits, we bore away to the westward, along the coast of Java, in company with the prows before mentioned. We had regular soundings all the way to Samarang, off which place we anchored on the 22nd in the afternoon; the church bearing SE.; distance from the shore half a league; depth of water two fathoms. The shoalness of the coast here makes the road of Samarang very inconvenient, both on account of the great distance that large ships (of which there were several in the road) are obliged to lay from the shore, and of the landing, which is in a river that cannot be entered before half-flood.

This river resembles the one at Passourwang, the shores being low, with offensive dead animals laying about. I was met at the landing-place by the equipage-master, and he furnished me with a carriage to carry me to the governor, whose residence is about two miles from the town of Samarang. I requested and obtained leave to have our wants supplied, which were to recruit our provisions and to get a new main-mast, having sprung ours in the passage from Sourabya.

Samarang is a fortified town, surrounded by a wall and ditch, and is the most considerable settlement, next to Batavia, that the Dutch have in Java. Here is a very good hospital and a public school, chiefly for teaching the mathematics. They have likewise a theatre. Provisions are remarkably cheap here, beef being at ten doits per pound, and the price of a fowl twelve doits.

I experienced great civility from some of the gentlemen at Samarang, particularly from M. Le Baron de Bose, a merchant, brother to the M. de Bose, commandant of the troops at Sourabya; and from M. Abegg, the surgeon of the hospital, to whom we were indebted for advice and medicines, for which he would not consent to receive payment.

The latitude of Samarang is 6° 57′ S.; longitude, by my reckoning, from Cape Sandana 4° 7′ W.

On the 26th we sailed from Samarang, and with us a galley mounting six swivels, which the governor had directed to accompany us to Batavia.

On the 1st of October we anchored in Batavia road, where we found riding a Dutch ship-of-war and twenty sail of Dutch East India ships, besides many smaller vessels.

CHAPTER XX

OCCURRENCES AT BATAVIA AND PASSAGE THENCE TO ENGLAND

IN the afternoon at four o'clock I went on shore, and landed at a house by the river, where strangers first stop and give an account who they are, whence they came, etc. From this place a Malay gentleman took me in a carriage to the sabandar, Mr Englehard, whose house was in the environs of the city, on the side nearest the shipping. The sabandar is the officer with whom all strangers are obliged to transact their business; at least, the whole must go through his hands. With him I went to pay my respects to the governor-general, who received me with great civility. I acquainted his excellency with my situation, and requested my people might be taken care of, and that we should be allowed to take a passage to Europe in the first ship that sailed. I likewise desired permission to sell the schooner and launch. All this his excellency told me should be granted. I then took leave, and returned with the sabandar, who wrote down the particulars of my wants, in order to form from them a regular petition to be presented to the council the next day. I had brought from the governor of Coupang, directed for the governor-general at Batavia, the account of my voyage and misfortune, translated into Dutch from an account that I had given to Mr Van Este, so attentive had they been at Timor to everything that related to us.

There is a large hotel at Batavia, fitted up purposely for the accommodation of strangers, who are not allowed to reside at any other place. It is situated near the great river, in a part of the city that is reckoned the most airy and healthy. Nevertheless, I found the air hot and suffocating, and was taken ill in the night with a violent pain in my head. The next morning at nine the council sat, and I attended, accompanied by the sabandar, and was informed that the council had complied with all I had requested.

When I returned to the hotel my headache increased and a violent fever came on. I sent to acquaint the sabandar of my situation, and was soon after attended by the head surgeon of the town hospital, Mr Aansorp, by whose care and skill in less than twenty-four hours the fever considerably abated, but a severe headache continued. I had an invitation from the governor-general to dine with him, which of course I was obliged to decline.

I hired a carriage, which cost three dollars per day, for the benefit of taking an airing. My lodgings at the hotel were so close and hot that I desired the sabandar to apply to the governor-general for leave to hire a house in the country, which request his excellency not only immediately complied with, but gave directions for my being accommodated at the house of the physician or surgeon-general, Mr Sparling.

One of my people, Thomas Hall, being ill with a flux, I obtained leave for him to be sent to the country hospital, which is a convenient airy building.

Tuesday the 6th. This morning at sunrise I left the hotel

and was carried to Mr Sparling's house, about four miles distant
from the city and near the convalescent hospital, which at this
time had also sick men in it, the whole number of patients
amounting to eight hundred.   I found everything prepared for
my comfort and convenience.   Mr Sparling would suffer me to
take no medicine, though I had still considerable fever with
headache; but I found so much relief from the difference of the
air that in the evening I was able to accompany Mr Sparling on
a visit to the governor-general, at one of his country seats, where
we found many ladies, all dressed in the Malay fashion, some
of them richly ornamented with jewels.   I had invitations from
several gentlemen, and some very kindly pressed me to make
their country houses my abode till my health should be
re-established.

Thursday the 8th. My indisposition increasing, Mr Sparling
advised me to quit Batavia as speedily as possible, and represented the necessity of it to the governor-general.   I was
informed from his excellency that the homeward-bound ships
were so much crowded that there would be no possibility of
all my people going in one ship, and that they could be accommodated no other way than by dividing them into different
ships.   Seeing, therefore, that a separation was unavoidable,
I determined to follow the advice of the physician, and as a
packet was appointed to sail for Europe on the 16th instant,
I sent to request of the governor that I might be allowed to
take a passage in her for myself and as many of my people as
they were able to receive.   In answer to this, I was acquainted
that myself and two more could be accommodated in the
packet, she being too small to admit a greater number, but
that I might rest assured of passages being provided for those
that remained by the earliest opportunities.

Friday the 9th. This day anchored in the road the *General
Elliot*, an English ship, commanded by Captain Lloyd.   In the
Straits of Banca he had met with some boats belonging to the
East India Company's ship *Vansittart*, that was lost in the
Straits of Billaton by having struck on a rock that went through
her bottom.   Captain Wilson, who commanded the *Vansittart*,
I was informed had just finished a survey of those straits, and
was hoisting his boat in when the ship struck.   Immediately
on receiving the intelligence, Captain Lloyd in the *General
Elliot*, and another ship in company called the *Nonsuch*, sailed
for the wreck.   They found the ship had been burnt down to

the water's edge by the Malays. They, however, saved forty chests of treasure out of fifty-five, which were said to have been on board. Most of the ship's company were saved; one man only was lost in the ship, and five others in a small boat were missing, who were supposed to have taken some of the treasure. The greater part of the people went with Captain Wilson to China, and some were with Captain Lloyd.

Saturday the 10th. This morning the *Resource* was sold by public auction. The custom at Batavia is to begin high, and to lower the price till some person bids, and the first bidder is the buyer. She was accordingly put up at 2,000 rix-dollars, but to my great disappointment no one offered to purchase before the auctioneer had lowered the demand to 295 rix-dollars, for which price she was sold, the purchaser being an Englishman, Captain John Eddie, who commanded an English ship from Bengal. If no strangers had been present at the sale, I imagine they would have let her run down to 200 dollars, in which case I should have had no alternative.

The launch likewise was sold. The services she had rendered us made me feel great reluctance at parting with her, which I would not have done if I could have found a convenient opportunity of getting her conveyed to Europe.

Little as the schooner had sold for, I found I was in danger of having the sum lessened, for the sabandar informed me that by an order of the council there was a duty on the sale of all vessels. With this demand I would by no means comply, for I thought I had sufficiently suffered, in sustaining a loss of 705 rix-dollars out of 1,000 by the purchase and sale of the vessel, she having cost 1,000 rix-dollars.

This day Thomas Hall, whom I had sent to be taken care of at the hospital, died. He had been ill of a flux from the time of our arrival at Timor.

Monday the 12th. I agreed with the captain of the packet for a passage to Europe for myself, my clerk, and a servant. The sabandar informed me it was necessary that my officers and people should be examined before a notary respecting the loss of the *Bounty*, as otherwise the governor and council were not legally authorized to detain her if she should be found in any of the Dutch settlements. They were therefore at my desire examined, and afterwards made affidavit before the governor and council at the Stadthouse.

My officers complaining to me of the unreasonableness of

some tradesmen's bills, I spoke to the sabandar. A bill of fifty-one dollars for five hats he reduced to thirty dollars, and in other articles made proportionable deductions.

Paper money is the currency of Batavia, and is so understood in all bargains. At this time paper was at 28 per cent discount. There is likewise a difference in the value of the ducatoon, which at Batavia is 80 stivers, and in Holland only 63 stivers. This occasions a loss of $21\frac{1}{4}$ per cent on remittance of money. It therefore follows that if any person at Batavia remits money by bills of exchange to Europe, they lose by the discount and the exchange $49\frac{1}{4}$ per cent.

Those who have accounts to pay, and can give unexceptionable bills on Europe, will find a considerable saving by negotiating their bills with private people, who are glad to give for them a premium of 20 per cent at the least. This discovery I made somewhat too late to profit by.

One of the greatest difficulties that strangers have to encounter is their being obliged to live at the hotel. This hotel was formerly two houses, which by doors of communication have been made one. It is in the middle of a range of buildings, more calculated for a cold country than for such a climate as Batavia. There is no free circulation of air, and what is equally bad it is always very dirty, and there is great want of attendance. What they call cleaning the house is another nuisance, for they never use any water to cool it or to lay the dust, but sweep daily with brooms in such a manner that those in the house are almost suffocated by a cloud of dust.

The months of December and January are reckoned the most unhealthy of the year, the heavy rains being then set in. The account of the seasons, as given to me here, I believe may be relied on:

The middle of November, the west monsoon begins, and rain.

December and January. Continual rain with strong westerly wind.

February. Westerly wind. Towards the end of this month the rain begins to abate.

March. Intervals of fine weather. Wind westerly.

April. In this month the east monsoon begins. Weather generally fine, with showers of rain.

May. East monsoon fixed. Showery.

June and July. Clear weather. Strong east wind.

August and September. Wind more moderate.

October. In this month the wind begins to be variable, with showers of rain.

The current is said always to run with the wind. Nevertheless, I found the reverse in sailing from Timor to Java. Between the end of October and the beginning of the ensuing year, no Dutch ship bound for Europe is allowed to sail from Batavia, for fear of being near the Mauritius at the time of the hurricanes, which are frequent there in December and January.

My illness prevented me from gaining much knowledge of Batavia. Of their public buildings I saw nothing that gave me so much satisfaction as their country hospital for seamen. It is a large, commodious, and airy building, about four miles from the town, close to the side of the river, or rather in the river; for the ground on which it stands has by labour been made an island of and the sick are carried there in a boat; each ward is a separate dwelling and the different diseases are properly classed. They have sometimes one thousand four hundred patients in it; at this time there were eight hundred, but more than half of these were recovered and fit for service, of whom three hundred were destined for the fleet that was to sail for Europe. I went through most of the wards and there appeared great care and attention. The sheets, bedding, and linen of the sick were perfectly neat and clean. The house of the physician, Mr Sparling, who has the management of the hospital, is at one extremity of the building: and here it was that I resided. To the attention and care of this gentleman, for which he would receive no payment, I am probably indebted for my life.

The hospital in the town is well attended, but the situation is so ill chosen that it certainly would be the saving of many lives to build one in its stead up the river; which might be done with great advantage, as water carriage is so easy and convenient. A great neglect in some of the commanders of the shipping here was suffering their people to go dirty, and frequently without frock, shirt, or anything to cover their bodies, which besides being a public nuisance must probably be productive of ill health in the most robust constitution.

The governor-general gave me leave to lodge all my people at the country hospital, which I thought a great advantage, and with which they were perfectly satisfied. The officers, however, at their own request remained in the town.

The time fixed for the sailing of the packet approaching, I

settled my accounts with the sabandar, leaving open the victualling account, to be closed by Mr Fryer, the master, previous
to his departure; who I likewise authorized to supply the men
and officers left under his command with one month's pay, to
enable them to purchase clothing for their passage to England.

I had been at great pains to bring living plants from Timor
in six tubs, which contained jacks, nancas, karambolas, namnams, jambos, and three thriving bread-fruit plants.   These
I thought might be serviceable at the Cape of Good Hope, if
brought no farther; but I had the mortification of being obliged
to leave them all at Batavia.   I took these plants on board at
Coupang on the 20th of August; they had experienced a passage
of forty-two days to my arrival here.   The bread-fruit plants
died to the root and sprouted afresh from thence.   The karambolas, jacks, nancas, and namnams I had raised from the seed,
and they were in fine order.   No judgment can hence be formed
of the success of transporting plants, as in the present trial
they had many disadvantages.

Friday the 16*th.* This morning before sunrise I embarked on
board the *Vlydte* packet, commanded by Captain Peter Couvret,
bound for Middlesbrough.   With me likewise embarked Mr
John Samuel, clerk, and John Smith, seaman.   Those of our
company who stayed behind the governor promised me should
follow in the first ships, and be as little divided as possible.
At seven o'clock the packet weighed and sailed out of the road.

On the 18th we spoke the *Rambler,* an American brig belonging to Boston, bound to Batavia.   After passing the Straits
of Sunda we steered to the north of the Cocos Isles.   These
islands, Captain Couvret informed me, are full of coconut-trees;
there is no anchorage near them, but good landing for boats.
Their latitude 12° 0′ S.; longitude 96° 5′ E.

In the passage to the Cape of Good Hope there occurred
nothing worth remark.   I cannot, however, forbear noticing
the Dutch manner of navigating.   They steer by true compass,
or rather endeavour so to do, by means of a small movable
central card, which they set to the meridian; and whenever
they discover the variation has altered two and a half degrees
since the last adjustment they again correct the central card.
This is steering within a quarter of a point, without aiming at
greater exactness.   The officer of the watch likewise corrects
the course for leeway, by his own judgment, before it is marked
down in the log board.   They heave no log: I was told that the

company do not allow it. Their manner of computing their run is by means of a measured distance of forty feet, along the ship's side; they take notice of any remarkable patch of froth when it is abreast the foremost end of the measured distance, and count half-seconds till the mark of froth is abreast the after end. With the number of half-seconds thus obtained they divide the number forty-eight, taking the product for the rate of sailing in geographical miles in one hour, or the number of Dutch miles in four hours.

It is not usual to make any allowance to the sun's declination, on account of being on a different meridian from that for which the tables are calculated; they in general compute with the numbers just as they are found in the table. From all this, it is not difficult to conceive the reason why the Dutch are frequently above ten degrees out in their reckoning. Their passages likewise are considerably lengthened by not carrying a sufficient quantity of sail.

December the 16th, in the afternoon, we anchored in Table Bay. The next morning I went on shore and waited on his excellency M. Van der Graaf, who received me in the most polite and friendly manner. The *Guardian*, commanded by Lieutenant Riou, had left the Cape about eight days before with cattle and stores for Port Jackson. This day, anchored in Table Bay, the *Astrée*, a French frigate, commanded by the Count de St Rivel, from the Isle of France, on board of which ship was the late governor, the Chevalier d'Entrecasteaux. Other ships that arrived during my stay at the Cape were a French forty-gun frigate, an East India ship, and a brig of the same nation; likewise two other French ships, with slaves, from the coast of Mosambique, bound to the West Indies; a Dutch packet from Europe, after a four months' passage; and the *Harpy*, a South Sea whaler, with five hundred barrels of spermaceti, and four hundred of seal and other oils. There is a standing order from the Dutch East India Company that no person who takes a passage from Batavia for Europe in any of their ships shall be allowed to leave the ship before she arrives at her intended port. According to which regulation I must have gone to Holland in the packet. Of this I was not informed till I was taking leave of the governor-general at Batavia, when it was too late for him to give the captain an order to permit me to land in the Channel. He, however, desired I would make use of his name to Governor Van der Graaf, who readily complied with my request and gave the necessary orders to the captain of the packet, a copy of which his excellency gave to me; and at the same time recommendatory letters to people of consequence in Holland, in case I should be obliged to proceed so far.

I left a letter at the Cape of Good Hope to be forwarded to Governor Phillips, at Port Jackson, by the first opportunity, containing a short account of my voyage, with a descriptive list of the pirates; and from Batavia I had written to Lord Cornwallis, so that every part of India will be prepared to receive them.

Saturday the 2nd. We sailed from the Cape in company with the *Astrée* French frigate. The next morning neither ship nor land were in sight. On the 15th we passed in sight of the island St Helena. The 21st we saw the island Ascension. On the 10th of February, the wind being at NE., blowing fresh, our sails were covered with a fine orange-coloured dust. Fuego, the westernmost of the Cape de Verd Islands, and the nearest land to us, on that day at noon bore NE. by E½E., distance one hundred and forty leagues. When we had passed the latitude of the Western Islands a look out was kept for some rocks which Captain Couvret had been informed lay in latitude 44° 25′ N. and 2° 50′ E. longitude from the east end of St Michael. This information Captain Couvret had received from a person that he knew and who said he had seen them. On the 13th of March we saw the Bill of Portland, and on the evening of the next day, Sunday, March the 14th, I left the packet and was landed at Portsmouth by an Isle of Wight boat.

Those of my officers and people whom I left at Batavia were provided with passages in the earliest ships, and at the time we parted were apparently in good health. Nevertheless, they did not all live to quit Batavia. Mr Elphinstone, master's mate, and Peter Linkletter, seaman, died within a fortnight after my departure, the hardships they had experienced having rendered them unequal to cope with so unhealthy a climate as that of Batavia. The remainder embarked on board the Dutch fleet for Europe and arrived safe at this country, except Robert Lamb, who died on the passage, and Mr Ledward, the surgeon, who has not yet been heard of. Thus, of nineteen who were forced by the mutineers into the launch, it has pleased God that twelve should surmount the difficulties and dangers of the voyage and live to revisit their native country.

MINUTES

OF THE

PROCEEDINGS

OF THE

COURT MARTIAL held at PORTSMOUTH

12th AUGUST 1792

on

TEN PERSONS charged with MUTINY on board
His Majesty's Ship the BOUNTY

With an

APPENDIX

Containing

A full account of the real Causes and Circumstances of that
unhappy Transaction, the most material of which have
hitherto been withheld from the Public.

[by
Stephen Barney]

LONDON:

Printed for J. DEIGHTON, opposite GRAY'S-INN, HOLBORN

MDCCXCIV

ADVERTISEMENT

THE following minutes of the trial of the mutineers of the *Bounty* were taken by myself and my clerks, being employed to give assistance before the court martial, to William Muspratt, one of the prisoners. They were not continued beyond the evidence for the prosecution, nor do they comprise the whole of the evidence respecting the capture of all the different prisoners at Otaheite. They were not intended for publication. Repeated assurances have been given that an impartial state of all the circumstances attending that unhappy mutiny, as well as a complete trial of the prisoners, would be published. The anxious relations of the unfortunate parties in that mutiny, worn out with expectation of that publication, have repeatedly solicited my consent to publish my minutes, and as such publication may in some degree alleviate their distress, I cannot think myself justified in withholding such consent, and hope this will be a sufficient apology for my conduct.

I affirm, that as far as those minutes go, they contain a just state of the evidence given at the court martial.

STEPN. BARNEY.

PORTSMOUTH,
   1st May 1794.

THE TRIAL, &c.

At a Court Martial, assembled and holden on the twelfth day of August 1792, on board His Majesty's ship *Duke*, in Portsmouth Harbour.

BEFORE

The Right Honourable Lord Hood, } President.
Vice-Admiral of the Blue }

CAPTAINS

Sir And. Snape Hammond	John Thomas Duckworth
John Colepoys	Jno Nicholson Ingoldfield
George Montague	John Knight
Sir Roger Curtis	Richard Goodwin Keates
John Bazeley	and
Sir Andrew Douglas	Albemarle Bertie

On a charge of Mutiny on the 28th April 1789, on board His Majesty's ship *Bounty*, for running away with the ship and deserting His Majesty's Service;

AGAINST

Joseph Coleman	James Morrison	Thomas Ellison
Charles Norman	John Millward	and
Thomas M'Intosh	William Muspratt	Michael Byrne
Peter Heywood	Thomas Burkett	

The following letter from Captain Bligh to the Lords of the Admiralty was read, as containing the Charge of Mutiny and Desertion:

Coupang in Timor,
18th August 1789.

Sir,

I am now unfortunately to request of you to acquaint the Lords Commissioners of the Admiralty, that His Majesty's armed vessel *Bounty*, under my command, was taken from me by some of the inferior officers and men, on the 28th April 1789, in the following manner:

A little before sunrise, Fletcher Christian, who was mate of the ship and officer of the watch, with the ship's corporal, came into my cabin while I was asleep, and seizing me tied my hands with a cord, assisted by others who were also in the cabin, all armed with muskets and bayonets. I was now threatened with instant death if I spoke a word; I, however, called for assistance and awakened every one; but the officers who were in their cabins were secured by sentinels at their doors, so that no one could come to me. The arms were all secured, and I was forced on deck in my shirt with my hands tied, and secured by a guard abaft the mizzen-mast, during which the mutineers expressed much joy that they would soon see Otaheite. I now demanded of Christian the cause of such a violent act, but no other answer was given but 'Hold your tongue, sir; or you are dead this instant'; and holding me by the cord, which tied my hands, he as often threatened to stab me in the breast with a bayonet he held in his right hand. I, however, did my utmost to rally the disaffected villains to a sense of their duty, but to no effect. The boatswain was ordered to hoist the launch out, and while I was kept under a guard with Christian at their head abaft the mizzen-mast, the officers and men not concerned in the mutiny were ordered into the boat. This being done, I was told by Christian, 'Sir, your officers and men are now in the boat, and you must go with them'; and with the guard they carried me across the deck, with their bayonets presented on every side, when attempting to make another effort one villain said to the others, 'Blow his brains out.' I was at last forced into the boat, and we were then veered astern, in all, nineteen souls. I was at this time 10 leagues to the SW. of Tofoa, the north westernmost of the Friendly Islands, having left Otaheite the 4th of April with 1,015 fine bread-fruit plants and many fruit kind, in all 774 pots, 39 tubs, and 24 boxes. These plants were now in a very flourishing order. I anchored at Annamocha 24th April, and left it on the 26th. The boatswain and carpenter, with some others, while the boat was alongside, collected several necessary things and water, and with some difficulty a compass and quadrant were got, but arms of no kind, or any maps or drawings, of which I had many very valuable ones. The boat was very deep and much lumbered, and in this condition we were cast adrift, with about 28 gallons of water, 150 lb. of pork, 6 quarts of rum, and 6 bottles of wine. The day was calm, attended with light breezes, and I got to Tofoa by seven o'clock in the evening, but found no place to land, the land being so steep and rocky. On the 30th I found landing in a cove, on the north-west part of the island, and here I remained in search of supplies until the 2nd of May; when the natives discovered we had no fire-arms they made an attack on us with clubs and stones, in the course of which I had the misfortune to lose a very worthy man, John Norton, quartermaster, and most of us were hurt, more or less. But getting into our boat was no security, for they followed us in canoes loaded with stones, which they threw with much force and exactness; happily night saved the rest of us. I had determined to go to Amsterdam in search of Paulehow, the king; but taking this transaction as a real sample of their native dispositions, there was little hope to expect much from them; for I considered their good behaviour hitherto owing to a dread of our fire-arms, which now knowing us to have none would not be the case, and that supposing our lives were in safety, our boat and everything would be taken from us, and thereby I should never be able to return. I was also earnestly solicited by all hands to take them towards home, and when I told them no hopes of relief remained for us but what I might find in New Holland, until I came to Timor, a distance of 1,200 leagues, they all agreed to live on one ounce of bread per day and a gill of water. I therefore, after recommending this promise for ever to their memory, bore away for New Holland and Timor, across a sea but little known, and in a small boat deep loaded with eighteen souls, without a single map of any kind, and nothing but my own recollection and general knowledge of the situation of places to direct us. Unfortunately we lost part of our provision; our stock therefore only consisted of 20 lb. of pork, 3 bottles of wine, 5 quarts of rum, 150 lb. of bread, and 28 gallons of water. I steered to the WNW. with strong gales and bad weather, suffering every calamity and distress. I discovered many islands, and at last, on the 28th May, the coast of New Holland, and entered a break of the reef in latitude about 12° 50′ S. and longitude 145° 00′ E. I kept on in the direction of the coast to the northward, touching at such places as I found convenient, refreshing my people by the best means in my power. These refreshments consisted of oysters and a few clams; we were, however, greatly benefited by them and a few good nights' rest. On the 4th June I passed the north part of New Holland and steered for Timor, and made it on the 12th, which was a happy sight to every one, particularly several who perhaps could not have existed a week or a day longer.

I followed the direction of the south side of the island, and on the 14th in the afternoon saw the island Rotty and west part of Timor, round which I got that night, and took a Malay on board to show me Coupang, where he described to me the governor resided. On the next morning before day I anchored under the fort, and about eleven I saw the governor, who received me with great humanity and kindness. Necessary directions were instantly given for our support, and perhaps more miserable beings were never seen.

Thus happily ended, through the assistance of Divine Providence, without accident, a voyage of the most extraordinary nature that ever happened in the world, let it be taken either in its extent, duration, or so much want of the necessaries of life.

The people who came in the boat were:

John Fryer	. .	Master
William Cole	. .	Boatswain
William Peckover	.	Gunner
William Purcell	.	Carpenter
Thomas Ledward	.	Acting-Surgeon
William Elphinstone	.	Master's mate
Thomas Hayward	.	Midshipman
John Hallet	. .	Midshipman
John Samuel	.	Clerk
Peter Linkletter	.	Quartermaster
John Norton	.	Ditto, killed at Tofoa
George Simpson	.	Quartermaster
Lawrence Lebogue	.	Sail-maker
Robert Tinkler	.	Able Seaman
John Smith	.	Ab.
Thomas Hall	.	Able Seaman
Robert Lamb	.	Ab.
David Nelson	.	Botanist, since dead

Total: 18

The people who remained in the ship were:

Fletcher Christian	.	Master's mate
George Stewart .	.	Acting ditto
Peter Heywood .	.	Midshipman
Edward Young .	.	Ditto
Charles Churchill	.	Corporal
James Morrison .	.	Boatswain's mate
John Mills	.	Gunner's ditto
Charles Norman .	.	Carpenter's ditto
Thomas M'Intosh	.	Ditto crew
Joseph Coleman .	.	Armourer
Thomas Burkett .	.	Able seaman
John Sumner	.	Ab.
John Williams .	.	Ab.
Matthew Thompson	.	Ab.
Thomas Ellison .	.	Ab.
William M'Koy .	.	Ab.
John Millward .	.	Ab.
Richard Skinner .	.	Ab.
Matthew Quintal	.	Ab.
Michael Byrne .	.	Ab.
Henry Hillbrant .	.	Ab.
Isaac Martin	.	Ab.
Alexander Smith	.	Ab.
William Muspratt	.	Ab.
William Brown .	.	Botanist's assistant

(Charles Norman, Thomas M'Intosh, Joseph Coleman) detained against their consent

Total: 25

The secrecy of this mutiny was beyond all conception, so that I cannot discover that any who were with me had the least knowledge of it; and the comparative lists will show the strength of the pirates.

I found three vessels here bound to Batavia, but as their sailing would be late, I considered it to the advantage of His Majesty's service to purchase a vessel to take my people to Batavia, before the sailing of the fleet for Europe in October, as no one could be hired but at a price equal to a purchase;

I therefore gave public notice of my intent, and, assisted by the governor, I got a vessel for 1,000 rix-dollars, and called her the *Resource*.

We have not yet our health perfectly established. Four of my people are still ill, and I had the misfortune to lose Mr Nelson the botanist, whose good conduct in the course of the whole voyage, and manly fortitude in our late disastrous circumstances, deserve this tribute to his memory.

I have given a summary account of my proceedings to the governor, and have requested, in His Majesty's name, that necessary orders and directions may be given to their different settlements, to detain the ship wherever she may be found.

There is but little chance that their lordships can receive this before I arrive myself; I therefore have not been so particular as I shall be in my letters from Batavia.

I shall sail in the morning without fail, and use my utmost exertions to appear before their lordships and answer personally for the loss of His Majesty's ship.

I beg leave to acquaint their lordships, that the greatest kindness and attention have been shown to us while here by the second governor, Timotheus Wanjon, whose zeal to render services to His Majesty's subjects has been unremitting during the sickness of the governor William Adrian Van Este, who is now at the point of death.

The surgeon of the fort, a Mr Max, has also been ever attentive to my sick people, and has daily and hourly attended them with great care.

> I have the honour to be, sir,
> Your most obedient humble servant,
> WILLIAM BLIGH.

To Philip Stephens, Esq. [A copy.]

JOHN FRYER, Master of the *Bounty* [sworn]

I had the first watch on the 28th April 1789; Captain Bligh came on deck and gave orders for the night. I was relieved at twelve o'clock by William Peckover the gunner, and the gunner was relieved at four by Mr Christian; all was quiet at twelve when I was relieved. At dawn of day I was alarmed by a noise in the cabin, and as I went to jump up from my bed, Sumner and Quintal laid their hands on my breast, and desired me to lay down, adding, 'Sir, you are a prisoner.' I attempted to expostulate with them, but they told me to hold my tongue, or I was a dead man; if quiet, no man in the ship would hurt me. I then, by raising myself on the locker, saw Captain Bligh on the ladder going on the quarter-deck in his shirt, with his hands tied behind him, Christian holding him by the cord; Churchill came to my cabin and took a brace of pistols and a hanger, saying 'I'll take care of these, Mr Fryer.' When I saw Captain Bligh on the ladder, I asked what they were going to do with him, when Sumner answered, 'Damn his eyes, put him into the boat and let the bugger see if he can live upon three-quarters of a pound of yams per day.' I said, 'For God's sake for what?' Sumner and Quintal replied, 'Hold your tongue, Mr Christian is captain of the ship, and recollect, Mr Bligh brought all this upon himself.' I advised them to consider what they were about. Sumner replied they knew well what they were about or they would not persist. I then persuaded them to lay down their arms, and assured them nothing should happen for what they had done. They replied, 'Hold your tongue, it is too late now.' They said they would put Captain Bligh into the small cutter. I said her bottom was almost worn out. They said, 'Damn his eyes, the boat is too good for him.' I said I hoped he was not to be sent by himself. They said, 'No; Mr Samuel, Mr Heywood, and Mr Hallet are going with him.' I then requested to go on deck to Captain Bligh before he went into the boat; they refused to let me. I then prevailed on them to let me call to Christian on the deck to get permission; I did so and was permitted to go on deck. When I came on deck Captain Bligh was standing by the mizzen-mast with his hands tied behind him, Christian holding the cord with one hand and a bayonet in the other. I said to Christian, 'Consider what you are about.' Christian answered, 'Hold your tongue, sir; I've been in hell for weeks past. Captain Bligh has brought all this upon himself.' I said their not agreeing was no reason for taking the ship. Christian replied, 'Hold your tongue, sir, this instant.' I then said, 'You and I have been upon friendly terms during the voyage, give me leave to speak: let Captain Bligh go down to his cabin, I make no doubt all will be friends again in a short time.' Christian again said, 'Hold your tongue, sir; it is too late.' Being threatened by Christian, I said no more on that head. I then said, 'Mr Christian, pray give Captain Bligh a better boat than the cutter, the bottom is almost out; let him have a chance to get on shore.' Christian answered, 'No; that boat is good enough.' I whispered to Captain Bligh to keep up his spirits, 'for if I stay on board I may find means to follow you.' Captain Bligh said aloud, 'By all means stay, Mr Fryer'; and further said, 'Isaac Martin (then under arms) was a friend'; and likewise said several times, 'Knock Christian down.' Christian must have heard all this, but took no notice. Sumner and Quintal, who had followed me upon deck, were behind all the time with muskets and bayonets. I tried to pass Christian to speak to Martin, but could not. Christian, putting a bayonet to my breast, said, 'If you advance an inch further, I'll run you through,' and ordered me down to my cabin, and Sumner and Quintal conveyed me there. Going down the hatchway I saw Morrison fixing a tackle to the launch's stern. I said, 'Morrison, I hope you have no hand in this business.' He said, 'No, sir; I do not know a word about it.' I said in a low voice, 'If that is the case be on your guard; there may be an opportunity of rescueing the ship.' His answer was, 'Go down, sir, it is too late.' I was then confined to my cabin and Millward was put over me as a third sentinel. I then thought Millward friendly and winked at him to knock Sumner down, who stood next him. Millward immediately cocked his piece and dropped it, pointing to me, saying, 'Mr Fryer, be quiet, no one will hurt you.' I said, 'Millward, your piece is cocked; you had better uncock it, you may shoot some person.' Then, holding up his piece, said, 'Sir, there is no one means to hurt you.' Sumner said, 'No, that was our agreement not to commit murder.' Mr Peckover and Nelson continued in the cock-pit, and I persuaded the guards set over me to let me go to them. I found Mr Nelson and Mr Peckover in his cabin. Nelson said, 'Mr Fryer, what have we brought on ourselves?' and Mr Peckover said, 'What is best to be done?' I told them I had spoke to Captain Bligh to keep up his spirits, and if I stayed on board I hoped soon to be able to follow him, and that Captain Bligh had desired me to stay by all means. I then said to Mr Nelson and Mr Peckover, 'If you are ordered into the boat say you will stay on board and I flatter myself we shall restore the ship in a short time.' Mr Peckover said, 'If we stay we shall all be deemed pirates.' I said, 'No; I would be answerable for any one who would join me.' Whilst we were talking Hillbrant was in the bread-room getting bread to put in the boat. I think Hillbrant must have heard our conversation and went upon deck and told Christian, for I was immediately ordered up into the cabin. I then heard from the sentinels Sumner, Quintal, and Millward, that Christian had consented to give Captain Bligh the launch, but not for his sake, but for the safety of those that were going with him. I then asked if they knew who were going with him; they said no, but they believed a great many. Christian then ordered every man a dram that was under arms, and Smith, the captain's servant, served the drams out. I then hoped I should stay on board, that if the men got drunk I should be able to take the ship. Mr Nelson and Peckover were then ordered upon deck, and I soon afterwards. And Christian said to me, 'Mr Fryer, go into the boat.' I said, 'I will stay with you, sir, if you will give me leave,' but Christian said, 'No, sir, go directly.' Captain Bligh, being on the gangway without the rail, his hands at liberty, said, 'Mr Fryer, stay in the ship.' Christian said, 'No, by God, sir, go into the boat, or I will run you through,' pointing the bayonet at my breast. I then went outside the rail to Captain Bligh and asked Christian to let Mr Tinkler (my brother-in-law) go with me. Churchill said, 'No'; but after some time Christian permitted it, and upon request let me have his trunk, but ordered nothing else to be taken out of my cabin; I requested my log-book and quadrant, but they were denied, as Captain Bligh had a quadrant. I cannot say who went into the boat first, whether Captain Bligh or myself; we were both on the gangway together, and all the time bad language was used towards Captain Bligh by the people under arms. I begged for muskets, but Churchill refused, saying Captain Bligh was well acquainted where he was going. The boat was then ordered astern, and four cutlasses handed into her, by whom I know not; but the people all this time used very bad language towards the captain, adding, 'Shoot the bugger.' William Cole, the boatswain, said to Captain Bligh, 'We had better put off, or they will do us some mischief'; which Captain Bligh agreed to, and we rowed astern to get out of the way of the guns. Christian ordered the top-gallant sails to be loosened, and the ship steered the same course as Captain Bligh had ordered. From the confusion and great attention we were obliged to pay for our preservation, I had no means or opportunity to make any notes or memorandum until we arrived at Timor. I observed under arms: Christian, Churchill, and Burkett, that they were in the cabin securing the captain; Sumner, Quintal, and

Millward were sentinels over me; Martin was sentinel at the hen-coop, and the four persons following wished to go into the boat. Coleman, who called to the witness several times to recollect that he had no hand in the business; M'Intosh and Norman were leaning over the rail, and Byrne was alongside; all appeared to be crying. Byrne said if he went into Captain Bligh's boat the people would leave him when he got on shore, as he could not see to follow them. I did not perceive Heywood upon the deck the time the ship was seized.

Court. What number of men did you see on the deck at each time you went there?

A. Eight or ten.

Q. How long did you remain there each time?

A. Ten minutes or a quarter of an hour.

Q. What works were going on each time?

A. When I went first hoisting out the boats; the last time nothing particular except the sentinels over Captain Bligh and myself forcing us into the boat.

Q. Do you thing the boats could be hoisted out by eight or ten persons?

A. No.

Q. You have no reason to know who were under arms besides those you have named?

A. No.

Q. When you was on the quarter-deck or gangway, did you see either of the prisoners active in obeying orders given by Christian or Churchill?

A. Burkett and Millward were under arms as sentinels over Captain Bligh and myself on the gangway, which I suppose was by their orders.

Q. You say you saw Morrison, the boatswain's mate, helping to hoist out the boats; did you see any others of the prisoners employed so, or otherwise?

A. No; my attention was taken up with Captain Bligh. I did not.

Q. When the dram was served did you see any of the prisoners partake?

A. One—Millward.

Q. When the boat in which Captain Bligh and others were put had veered astern, did you observe any one of the prisoners use the bad language which you say passed on that occasion?

A. Not to the best of my recollection. I saw Millward on

the tafferel-rail with a musket; there was so much noise in the boat I could not hear one man from another.

Q. You say when the cutlasses were handed into the boat there was much bad language; did any one of the prisoners join on that occasion?

A. Not to my knowledge; it was a general thing.

Q. Did you see Ellison on the day of the mutiny?

A. No.

Q. Did you see Muspratt?

A. No.

Q. At the time you were ordered upon the deck after the conversation in the cockpit, how, and by whom, were these orders conveyed to you?

A. By the sentinels: Millward, Sumner, and Quintal.

Q. When you and Captain Bligh were ordered into the boat did any person assist Christian, or offer so to do?

A. Yes; Churchill, Sumner, and Quintal, and Burkett were under arms on the quarter-deck.

Q. You say when the boat was cast off you rowed astern to get out of the way of the guns; had you seen any preparations made for firing?

A. I meant the small arms they had in their hands when they said, 'Shoot the bugger.'

Q. When you heard Christian order the top-gallant sails to be hoisted, was you near enough to know any of the people that went on the yards?

A. I saw only Ellison.

Q. I ask you as master of His Majesty's ship *Bounty*, how many men it would require to hoist out the launch?

A. Ten.

Q. Was the remark of your not having seen Heywood on the deck on the 29th of April made at Timor, or since you knew he was apprehended by the *Pandora*?

A. Since. I frequently told the people in the boat that I had not seen the Youngsters on deck.

Q. How many men went up to loosen the topsails?

A. Only Ellison.

Q. What reason had you to imagine that Millward was friendly when he was sentinel over you?

A. He appeared very uneasy.

Q. You say you obtained permission for Tinkler to go with you. Had he been compelled to remain in the ship?

A. He had been told by Churchill that he was to stay on board as his servant; then came crying to me.

Q. Do you think that any of the people who remained in the *Bounty* were kept against their consent?

A. None but the four.

Q. In what part of the ship was the Youngster's berth?

A. Down the main hatchway on each side.

Q. Did you observe any sentinel over the main hatchway?

A. Yes; I omitted to mention Thompson, who was sitting on the arms chest. I wanted to go to my mess-place, but was stopped by Sumner and Quintal.

Q. Was Thompson armed?

A. I believe he was, with a cutlass.

Q. Did you consider him as a sentinel over the Youngsters' berth?

A. Yes; and a sentinel on the arms chest at the same time.

Q. Was any effort made by any person to rescue the ship?

A. Only by what I said to Mr Peckover and Morrison; Mr Cole the boatswain came down, and I whispered him to stay in the ship.

Q. What was the distance of time from the first alarm to the time of your being forced into the boat?

A. Two hours and a half, or three hours.

Q. What did you suppose Christian meant when he said he had been in hell for a fortnight?

A. His frequent quarrels with, and abuse received from, Captain Bligh.

Q. Had there been any recent quarrel?

A. The day before Captain Bligh had been challenging all the young gentlemen and people with stealing coconuts.

Q. When you went into the cockpit were any sentinels over Mr Peckover and Mr Nelson?

A. No; the same sentinels that confined me kept them below.

N.B.—Prisoners were now asked if they had any questions to ask the witness.

Coleman. None.

Heywood. None at present.

Q. per Byrne. Was you on the deck when the large cutter was hoisted out?

A. No.

Q. per Morrison. Do you recollect when you spoke to me

my particular answer; and are you positive it was I who said, 'Go down to your cabin'?

A. Yes, I am, 'Go down to your cabin, it is too late.'

Q. ditto. Do you recollect my saying, 'I will do my endeavours to raise a party and rescue the ship'?

A. No.

Q. ditto. Did you observe any part of my conduct on any part of that day that leads you to think I was one of the mutineers?

A. I never saw him only at that time, and his appearance gave me reason to speak to him. He appeared friendly, but his answer surprised me; I did not expect it from him. Whether he spoke from fear of the others I know not.

Court. Might not Morrison speaking to you, telling you to keep below, be from a laudable motive, supposing your assistance at that time might prevent a more advantageous effort?

A. Probably it might; if I had stayed in the ship he would have been one of the first I should have opened my mind to from his good behaviour.

Q. Did he speak to you in a threatening tone, or address you as advice?

A. As advice.

Q. Did you see any person that appeared to be forcing the prisoner Morrison to put the tackle to the launch?

A. No.

Q. Did you see Morrison employed in any other way than you have related from the time you was first confined, till the boat was cast loose from the ship.

A. No.

Q. Did you consider the hoisting out of that boat as assisting the mutineers, or as giving Captain Bligh a better chance for his life?

A. As assisting Captain Bligh and giving him a better chance for his life.

Norman. None.

M'Intosh. None.

Muspratt. None at present.

Q. per Burkett. If you did not see Captain Bligh before he was going up the ladder how could you see me seize him in the cabin?

A. I have not said I saw you assist in seizing him, but when Captain Bligh was on the ladder I saw you and Churchill come out of the cabin armed.

Q. Did you see or hear me swearing or giving any directions, or taking any charge when on the deck, or during the mutiny?

A. No.

Q. Did I not do my duty on the voyage as a seaman?

A. Yes.

Q. per Millward. Did you see me when you spoke to Morrison to rescue the ship?

A. No, you was ordered as an additional sentinel over me afterwards.

Q. Had I the arms I held at that time voluntarily, or by force?

A. I cannot tell.

Q. Do you recollect what I said when I came down to the cockpit?

A. Nothing but what I have said already.

WILLIAM COLE, Boatswain of the *Bounty* (deposed)

That Quintal, a seaman belonging to the *Bounty* but in what part of the ship he knows not, calling, to the carpenter (Purcell), said they had mutinied and taken the ship; that Christian had the command and the captain was a prisoner upon the quarter-deck; that the witness being thus awaked jumped out of the cabin and said to the carpenter, 'For God's sake I hope you know nothing of this.' He said he did not; that the sail-maker, Lawrence Lebogue, lying by witness's cabin witness asked him what he meant to do; Lebogue answered he did not know, but would do as the witness did; that witness went up the fore hatchway and looking aft saw Thompson sentinel at the main hatchway and Heywood leaning over his hammock in the larboard berth, and Mr Young in the starboard berth, Mr Elphinstone looking likewise over the side of the berth which was boarded up; that witness then went on deck, saw men under arms around the fore hatchway, Churchill, Brown, Alexander Smith, William M'Koy, and Williams; that Williams looked aft, saw the captain's hands tied behind him, and Mills, Martin, Ellison, and Burkett sentinels over him; that witness jumped down the fore hatchway, awaked Morrison, Millward, M'Intosh, and Simpson, all lying in the same tier. I informed them what happened and hoped to form a party; they denied all knowledge of the mutiny; that Millward said he was very sorry for it, and said he had a hand in the foolish piece of

business before, and was afraid they would make him take a
part in that; that Churchill then came forward and called out
to Millward to come on deck immediately, for he had a musket
for him, or to take a musket; that they all went up as they got
their clothes on; that witness did not see any of the rest at that
time have arms.   That witness went on deck and asked Christian
what he meant to do; that Christian then ordered this witness
to hoist out the boat, and threatening him with the bayonet if
he did not take care that the boat was hoisted out; and witness
asked liberty to go and speak with Mr Fryer, which was granted.
Witness went below and asked Mr Fryer what was best to do,
when Mr Fryer in a low voice told witness by all means to stay;
that one of the sentinels over Mr Fryer (Sumner, as witness
believes) said to Mr Fryer, 'You have a wife and family, but
all will be forgot in a little time'; that Mr Fryer came upon deck
and asked Christian what he was about, and told him if he
did not approve of the captain's behaviour, to put him under
arrest and proceed on the voyage; that Christian then said, 'If
that's all you have to say go down to your cabin, for I've been
in hell for weeks past'; that they were then intending to send
away the captain and Hayward, Hallet, and Samuel, with him;
that the small cutter being stove, they made interest with
Christian for the other cutter, which was fitted out; that
Christian still threatened the witness if he carried anything
away or sprung any yard; that witness then finding the captain was to be sent from the ship went aft and asked for
the long boat; that Hayward and Hallet were upon deck all
this time; that after asking Christian three or four times without
an answer, Captain Bligh said, 'For God's sake, Mr Cole, do
all in your power'; that the carpenter said, 'I've done nothing
I am ashamed or afraid of, I want to see my native country';
that the launch was then granted; that the carpenter and
armourer were employed in fitting her; that when the boat was
going over the side, Byrne was in the cutter alongside, but how
he came there witness don't know.   Witness says we were
employed in getting the launch out; that Christian ordered a
dram to be given to each of the men under arms; that Smith
brought some spirits and gave witness some in water; that
Christian was continually threatening witness with the bayonet
to take care not to carry anything away; that witness saw
Heywood standing there at the same time, lending a hand to
get the fore-stay sail along; that when the boat was hooked

Heywood said something to me, but what it was I do not know, Christian threatening witness at the time; that Heywood then went below and witness saw no more of him; that witness says they got the boat out and Norman, M'Intosh, Coleman, and Morrison, who did not go into the boat with others who did, were busy in getting necessary things into the launch; that Churchill and Quintal were walking about, saying, 'Damn them, they have enough'; that at this time witness saw William Muspratt with a musket in his hand, but don't remember seeing him before; that witness heard Churchill call out, 'Keep (some body) below,' but who he knows not; that Churchill and Quintal were forcing the people into the boat; that Coleman was handing a bag into the boat which appeared to contain iron, or it was in the boat before; that Christian ordered it to be stopped; that Norman and M'Intosh were then going into the boat and endeavouring to get in the carpenter's tool chest when Quintal said, 'If you will let them have these things they will build a vessel in a month'; that the chest was then handed in, some tools first being taken out; that the carpenter got his clothes chest in; that they were then forcing the people out that were going and not of their side; that witness went then into the boat, and that Peckover, Samuel, Hayward, and Hallet soon after were put or came into the boat; that Captain Bligh was then brought to the side and put into the boat, which was then veered astern; that Coleman and Norman were crying on the gangway from the time they were ordered not to go into the boat; that M'Intosh was standing by, not crying, but wished to come into the boat; that Byrne was in the cutter all the time crying; that when the launch was dropped astern some pork and other provisions and necessaries were handed over; that Burkett went and got some clothes from the gunner and threw into the boat; that Sumner demanded the boatswain's call of witness, and said it would be of no use to him where he was going; that witness asked him in the Indian tongue if he would give him anything for it, and sent it up, but got nothing for it; that Norton asked for his jacket, when Sumner said, 'If I had my will, you bugger, I would blow your brains out'; that witness then told Captain Bligh it would be best to cast off, as the witness thought they might fire upon the boat; that Captain Bligh then called and wished to speak to Christian, but he did not come aft; that Coleman called over and said he had no hand in it and desired if any of them reached England to remember him to Mr Green of Greenwich; that the boat then cast off, being at midships only seven or eight inches out of water; that the last person witness saw was Ellison, loosing the main-top-gallant sail, and they sailed directly.

Court. How many men did you see under arms?

A. Nine at first on the deck, viz. Churchill, Williams, Mills, Brown, M'Koy, Burkett, A. Smith, Martin, Ellison, and two or three at other parts; Thompson at the main hatchway; Quintal and Sumner over the master's cabin, and at the cockpit; Hillbrant about the deck; Skinner on the deck, but not at first; Muspratt on the deck abaft the fore-hatchway; it was at the latter part of the time I saw him. Millward was ordered to take a musket and had it on the deck; Churchill called out to him, 'Damn you, come up. Here 's a musket ready for you.'

Q. What number of men was helping you to hoist the launch out?

A. Fourteen or fifteen; those who had no arms helped out with the boat, but those who had did not quit their arms; the master-at-arms had a pistol. I was not put under any restraint, but often threatened by Christian.

Q. Did any of the prisoners assist you in getting the launch out?

A. Yes; Coleman, Norman, M'Intosh, and Morrison were forward, Heywood and Hallet aft, I believe.

Q. Had you any conversation with the prisoners respecting the mutiny?

A. No conversation about the mutiny, except with the men mentioned whom I awaked.

Q. What force was used to prevent the people getting into the boat who were not permitted to go?

A. Nothing but orders; the people stood round them with arms, but they did not attempt to break the order.

Q. Did you see any attempt by any one of the prisoners to prevent the mutiny?

A. None; I saw Heywood handle the forestay tackle fall.

Q. You say you saw Heywood handle the forestay tackle fall; was that voluntarily done?

A. Voluntarily. He was not forced.

Q. You say you saw no one of the prisoners make any attempt to stop the mutiny. Did you see any make any marks of disapprobation at what was going forward?

A. No.

Q. When the drams were ordered, did either of the prisoners partake?

A. Smith the servant served all in general. I did not observe who in particular.

Q. Did you hear any one threaten to shoot into the launch before you cast off?

A. Skinner.

Q. You have said that Coleman, M'Intosh, and Norman were detained against their will. Have you reason to believe that any other of the prisoners were so detained?

A. I believe Heywood. I thought he intended to come away; he had no arms.

Q. Have you any other reason to think that Heywood was detained against his will?

A. I heard Churchill call out to keep *them* below; who he meant I do not know, but I believe Heywood.

Q. You have said you did not see any of the prisoners show any marks of disapprobation of what was going on. What was the cause of Coleman, Norman, and Byrne crying, as you have represented?

A. Coleman and Norman wanted to come into the boat. Why Byrne cried I know not, but he was blind.

Q. What was Burkett's situation when on deck?

A. He was on the starboard side next the wheel; he had his musket shouldered and was standing there.

Q. When you awoke Morrison, Millward, M'Intosh, and Simpson, what did they do when first on the deck?

A. Millward was ordered to take a musket and went up; the other three were clearing the boat from yams.

Q. How long was it from the time Heywood quitted the tackle fall and went below before you was forced into the boat?

A. Twenty minutes, or half an hour.

Q. Did you see any of the prisoners forcing Captain Bligh into the boat, or any under arms at that particular time?

A. I was in the boat alongside and cannot tell who forced him.

Q. In consequence of Churchill calling to Millward to come upon deck and take a musket; did Millward make any objection?

A. Not to my knowledge.

Q. You say that Coleman, Norman, and M'Intosh assisted at the top tackle fall to get out the launch. Did you suppose that they meant to be of use to Captain Bligh and accompany him, or that they were well disposed towards the mutineers and wished to get quit of their captain?

A. I think they wished to go with him.

Q. Do you think Heywood assisted from the same motive?

A. I have no reason to think otherwise; we did not converse at all. I did not see him at the tackle fall until the boat went out.

Q. Where was Muspratt when under arms?

A. Abaft the hatchway.

Q. Did he appear to be sentinel over any place or person?

A. He did not.

Q. Who were the persons that forced Captain Bligh into the boat?

A. I do not remember. I was in the boat, they on the deck.

Q. per Byrne. When the large cutter was hoisted out, who was the person that threw the fall out of her to hook on the fore-stay tackle?

A. I do not remember.

Q. When the orders were given for hoisting her out, did you not look down the hatchway and see three or four people abreast in the starboard cable tier?

A. No; I saw Norton [since killed] get out of his hammock, and I believe the cook was there.

Q. Do you remember any one ordering some person to hook on the tackle to the boat?

A. Not in particular.

Q. Did you not call to people below to come up and hoist out the cutter?

A. I do not know that I did, but I might.

Q. When the cutter was out, did you not order me to stay in her; to keep her from thumping against the ship?

A. I do not remember I did, but I told you to haul her ahead when the launch was going over the side.

Q. When Purcell and you came out of the cockpit, on the first alarm, did you perceive any one sitting on the chest on the fore hatchway?

A. I do not remember.

Q. Did any one speak to you or Mr Purcell on the fore hatchway?

A. They may, but I do not know.

Q. When Mr Purcell and you came up did not I say to you, 'Sir, the people are in arms and Captain Bligh is a prisoner'?

A. I do not remember seeing you, but you might be there; but your being blind I should have taken but little notice of you in the confusion.

Q. per Morrison. Do you recollect when I came upon deck, after you called me out of my hammock, I came to you abaft the windlass and said, 'Mr Cole, what's to be done?' Your answer was, 'By God, James, I don't know, but go and help them out with the cutter.'

A. Yes, I do remember it.

Q. Do you remember in consequence of your order I went about clearing the cutter?

A. Yes.

Q. Do you remember I did haul a trawl or grapnel from the main hold, and put them into the boat?

A. I remember such things being in the boat; who put them in I know not.

Q. Do you remember calling me to assist in hoisting a cask of water from the hold, same time threatening Norton the quartermaster that he should not go in the boat if he was not more attentive in getting the things into her?

A. I remember telling Norton that, for he was frightened, and believe that Morrison was employed on that business.

Q. Do you recollect I came to you when you were getting your things (which were tied up in part of your bedding) into the boat, and telling you the boat was then overloaded, and that Captain Bligh had begged no more should go into her, and in consequence I would take my chance in the ship; that you took me by the hand and said, 'God bless you, my boy, I'll do you justice if ever I get to England'?

A. I remember shaking hands with you and your saying you would take your chance in the ship; I had no reason before but to think you meant to leave the ship.

Court. Do you remember saying, If you get to England you would do him justice.

A. I do not remember it, but I have no doubt but I did.

Q. per Morrison. Was my conduct on that day such, or during the voyage, as to give you reason to suppose I was concerned in the mutiny?

A. I had no reason to suppose so.

Court. Did you hear prisoner Morrison say that Captain

Bligh said that no other men could come into the boat, as she was deeply laden already?

A. I remember taking him by the hand, but the conversation I do not recollect.

Q. Did you at that time believe that prisoner Morrison would have gone with you into the boat if it had not been apprehended the boat was too deeply laden?

A. From his conduct and behaviour I had no reason but to think so; he did what I ordered him.

Q. What was Morrison doing when you desired him to clear the cutter?

A. To the best of my knowledge standing on the booms doing nothing, just come up.

Q. You said Morrison assisted in getting out the boat. Did you consider all those that assisted in getting out that boat to be of the captain's party?

A. No. Some were under arms.

Q. Did you consider these not under arms, at that time, to be of the captain's party?

A. I certainly did think they had no hand in the mutiny.

Q. Do you think all Mr Christian's party was entrusted with arms?

A. I do not know, for some came on deck with arms; afterwards Mr Young came upon deck with a musket, and Muspratt came afterwards, which was after the first boat was hoisted out.

Q. Did you on that day consider Morrison as a person that was awed by the people under arms, to assist in hoisting the boat out, or as one aiding and assisting them in their design?

A. I do not think he was in awe of the people, nor that he was aiding or assisting them in their design.

Q. Did Morrison express any desire to come into the boat, and was he prevented?

A. He did not make any express desire, nor was he prevented from so doing.

Q. per Ellison. Are you certain, when you came upon deck and looked round, whether it was me that was armed, or the man that stood before me, as I stood at the wheel?

A. To the best of my knowledge I think it was you under arms; there were four men then on the quarter-deck under arms: Ellison, Mills, Martin, and Burkett.

Q. Are you certain it was me? I was only a boy and scarcely able to lift a musket at that time?

A. You stood by Captain Bligh part of the time; he was upon deck with a musket and I believe a bayonet fixed.

Q. In what position did I stand?

A. I do not know, I cannot answer that question.

Q. per Burkett. When you came aft to get the compass out of the binnacle from the starboard-side of the quarter-deck did not Quintal come and say he would be damned if you should have it. You said, 'Quintal, it is very hard you will not let me have a compass when there is a plenty more in the store-room'; then you looked very hard at me and I said, 'Quintal, let Mr Cole have it, and anything else that will be of service'?

A. Quintal objected to the compass going, but I do not remember that you said what you mention. You might, you were standing there; I do not remember what conversation I passed, the confusion was so great.

Q. Did you hear me that morning, during the time you said I was under arms, give any orders or use any bad language?

A. I did not. But when Mr Peckover asked you for the clothes, you went and got them, and threw them into the boat.

Q. Do you remember my coming aft and looking over and asking the people in the boat if they wanted anything I could get for them? Mr Peckover told me to get his pocket-book out of his cabin and his clothes.

A. I do not remember your asking anybody if they wanted anything; I have said you brought Mr Peckover's clothes.

Q. per Millward. Can you positively say that I took the musket according to Churchill's orders?

A. I don't know if by Churchill's orders, but you had one.

Q. Do you recollect speaking to me as I stood by the windlass, when you came up the fore-hatchway, and asked me what I was doing. I told you, 'Nothing.' You told me to lend a hand and clear the large cutter?

A. No.

Court. Were all the people that were called on deck bound and put in the boat, or were they all at liberty?

A. They were not bound, but brought up by sentinels at different times and put into the boat.

Q. Were there no other arms in the ship but in the chest at the main hatchway?

A. Not to my knowledge.

Q. Was it Burkett's watch on deck the morning of the mutiny?

A. I think it was.

Q. Was it Muspratt's?

A. I do not know he watched at all; he assisted the cook.

Q. Was it Ellison's watch?

A. To the best of my knowledge it was.

Q. Was it Norman's?

A. I do not remember what watch he was in.

Q. Was it Byrne's?

A. I do not think it was.

Q. Was Byrne on deck when you first came up?

A. I do not remember.

Q. Was it Coleman's watch?

A. No.

Q. Was he on deck in the morning early?

A. I did not see him.

Q. What time did day break?

A. About a quarter before five o'clock.

Q. per Byrne. When you and all the people were in the boat did you not hear me speak to some of the people forward in the launch's bow, as I was in the large cutter's stern?

A. I do not remember; you may.

Q. Did you ever hear any of the people in the launch say I had so spoken to them.

A. Yes; Mr Purcell.

Q. Did you hear any one else?

A. I do not remember.

Q. Did you say yesterday you did not know how I came in the cutter?

A. I did not know if you was hoisted out in her or not.

Mr Peckover, the Gunner of the *Bounty* (sworn)

I was awaked from my sleep by a confused noise, and directly afterwards thought I heard the fixing of bayonets; I jumped up and at the door met Mr Nelson; he told me the ship was taken from us. I answered, 'We were a long way from land when I came off deck.' Mr Nelson said, 'It is by our own people, Christian at their head, or Christian has the command, but we know whose fault it is, or who is to blame.' I answered, 'Let us go forward and see what's to be done.' On going to the hatchway to get up we were stopped by Sumner and Quintal by a fixed bayonet down the hatchway, who said, 'Peckover, you can't come up; we have mutinied and taken the ship and Mr Christian is captain.' That in a short while Mr Samuel came down and said he was going away in the small cutter with Captain Bligh, Hayward, and Hallet. He advised with me what he should take with him. I advised him but a few things; he took away a few shirts and stockings in a bag. That Mr Fryer came down afterwards and asked me what I meant to do. I told him I wished to do for the best and to get home if I could, for staying behind we should be reckoned as pirates if taken. He said he would be answerable for that and something about Captain Bligh, but what I could not distinguish, as we were about this time ordered on the deck. I was a long while down before I was ordered on the deck; when I came up I saw Captain Bligh and Christian alongside of him with a naked bayonet. I saw Burkett in arms on the quarter-deck, with a cartouche box around him, but whether he had any arms I cannot say. I asked Christian to let me go down forward, to get my things out of my chest. Christian said, 'You have no things down aft.' I said, 'Only a few,' then stepped to the gangway and went over the side. There was a sentinel on the gangway, but who I cannot say. I saw Muspratt forward on the forecastle; he seemed to be doing something about wood; he was not under arms, nor was he splitting wood. I saw three or four more people, I don't recollect their names, nor who they were, under arms. I then went into the boat, and a sentinel saw me down; I believe there were then in the boat ten or twelve. The cutter was alongside with Byrne in it, and in about four or five minutes the remainder of the people who went with Captain Bligh came into the boat; and in a short time after we dropped or were veered astern. When lying astern Burkett asked me if I wanted anything; I told him I had nothing but what I stood in. He said if I would send the keys up he would get me some clothes. I said I had lost them. He made some answer which I do not remember. He told me he would go and get me some things, and being gone about ten minutes returned and threw a handkerchief full of different clothes into the boat. Another person, who I don't know, went and fetched me more clothes. Coleman called to me over the stern and begged I would call on his friend at Greenwich and acquaint him of the matter. I think he said he wished to come into the boat. Cole at different times asked Captain Bligh to cast off the boat, fearing the people would fire into the boat, soon after cast adrift.

Court. Was you upon deck any considerable time before you was put in the boat?

A. Two or three minutes.

Q. Was you carried on the quarter-deck?

A. No.

Q. What part of the ship did you remain in?

A. I believe on the after hatchway.

Q. Did you see Christian, and where was he?

A. Yes, on the starboard side of the quarter-deck.

Q. Could you discover every one on the quarter-deck from the combings of the hatchway on which you stood?

A. By looking round I could, except in the wake of the mizen-mast.

Q. Could you see any persons that were not below in any other part of the ship?

A. All, except where the pigs were stowed, on the larboard side of the deck.

Q. What hindered you from seeing the larboard side?

A. The main mast, I don't doubt; I looked round, but I saw nobody.

Q. Was any sentinel over you while you was upon deck?

A. I don't remember any. The two sentinels that were over us were at the bottom of the ladder.

Q. Were you placed there by sentinels, or were you at liberty to go to any part of the ship?

A. I was not at liberty to go to any part of the ship. Christian ordered me into the boat and told me the boat was alongside, and Captain Bligh was just going in.

Q. What number of men did you see under arms in any part of the ship?

A. Burkett, Mills with a cartouche box round him, but whether under arms I cannot say; Christian upon deck with a bayonet, and Sumner and Quintal below.

Q. Are you sure no more?

A. No more.

Q. Name them again.

A. Christian, Burkett, Sumner, Quintal, and Mills with a cartouche box.

Q. Where are the arms kept?

A. All in the chest upon the main grating.

Q. Was the arms chest usually kept locked?

A. Yes. And the keys in the master's cabin.

Q. How long was it from that time you first heard of the mutiny to the time you went into the boat?

A. Two hours, or two hours and a half.

Q. How many people did the *Bounty's* company consist of?

A. Only forty-three at that time.

Q. How many of the people did you consider were concerned in the mutiny?

A. Four or five.

Q. Was it your opinion that four people could take the ship from thirty-nine?

A. By no means.

Q. Give your reasons for thinking so.

A. There must have been more concerned. I saw no more under arms when I came on deck.

Q. What was your reason for submitting when you saw four only under arms?

A. I came naked on the quarter-deck, except my trousers. I saw Burkett with a musket and bayonet, Christian alongside Captain Bligh, and the sentinel on the gangway; who he was I do not know.

Q. Did you expostulate with Christian?

A. No.

Q. Did you with the sentinels over you?

A. I reasoned with those below, but to no purpose.

Q. Was any force used to put you into the boat?

A. The sentinel saw me up, and Burkett being on the quarter-deck as I mentioned, and Christian ordered me into the boat.

Q. Did you on that day see Coleman?

A. Yes.

Q. Did he appear under arms?

A. No.

Q. What was he doing?

A. Looking over the stern.

Q. Did you see Heywood that day?

A. No.

Q. Did you see Byrne?

A. Yes.

Q. At what time?

A. Near eight o'clock.

Q. Was he under arms?

A. No.

Q. What was he doing?

A. In the cutter alongside.

Q. Did you see Morrison?

A. No.

Q. Did you see Norman?

A. Yes.

Q. Was he under arms?

A. No.

Q. What was he doing?

A. Looking over the stern.

Q. Did you consider him as one of the mutineers?

A. No.

Q. Did you see Ellison?

A. No.

Q. Did you see M'Intosh?

A. Yes.

Q. What was he doing?

A. Looking over the stern.

Q. Did you consider him as one of the mutineers?

A. No.

Q. Did you see Muspratt?

A. Yes.

Q. Was he under arms, or what was he doing?

A. Upon the forecastle.

Q. Did he appear to be obeying the orders of Christian?

A. He was standing on the forecastle not doing anything.

Q. Did you see Millward?

A. Yes.

Q. Was he under arms?

A. Not to my knowledge.

Q. Did you consider him as a mutineer?

A. I cannot say; he was not under arms.

Q. Was he one that awed you to go into the boat?

A. No.

Q. You saw Coleman looking over the stern. Did you consider him as a mutineer?

A. No.

Q. You saw Byrne in the cutter. Did you consider him as a mutineer?

A. No.

Q. You said you was put into the boat by a sentinel. Do you know by whom?

A. No.

Q. Was any sentinel on the gangway as you went over the ship's side?

A. There was, but I cannot say what his name is. He must have been under arms at the same time, but I cannot upon my oath say whether he was or not.

Q. In what situation was Byrne in the cutter?

A. To the best of my knowledge standing.

Q. Did he seem to be sorrowful?

A. He did.

Q. Did Norman, when he looked over the stern, call to any one in the boat?

A. I don't recollect.

Q. What are your reasons for believing Coleman, Norman, M'Intosh, and Byrne were adverse to the mutiny?

A. I often heard Captain Bligh mention it in the launch.

Q. What are your observations?

A. It is impossible for me to say; they were upon the stern and appeared to wish to come into the boat; I was busy. I do recollect Coleman calling to me.

Q. In conversation with Nelson he said to you, 'You know who's fault it was.' Did you apprehend he alluded to any of the prisoners?

A. No; it was impossible to judge what he meant.

Q. Did either of the thirty-nine people, not of the mutineers or under arms, offer to relieve Captain Bligh?

A. No.

Q. Of these men who remained in the ship, did you believe them all to be of Christian's party except the four?

A. I had every reason to suppose so.

Q. Do you know if Burkett had the watch upon deck in the morning?

A. He had.

Q. Was Muspratt on that watch?

A. I believe he was not on any watch; he was in the galley.

Q. Was Ellison on that watch?

A. I cannot say.

Q. Was it your watch?

A. No.

Q. In what watch was Norman?

A. I believe in that watch; he was not in mine.

Q. Had Coleman and Byrne that watch?

A. I cannot remember.

Q. Where was Millward when you saw him?

A. Looking over the stern.

Q. In what watch was Heywood?

A. In the first with Mr Fryer.

Q. per Morrison. Do you recollect when you was in the boat astern I handed over cutlasses, pork, water, spunyarn, etc.

A. No.

Q. per ditto. Did you observe anything in my conduct that led you to believe I was concerned in the mutiny?

A. No.

Q. per Burkett. Did you see me when you came upon deck, or did I offer to force you or anybody else into the boat?   Did I use any bad expressions, or make any game at any one?

A. No farther than standing with musket and bayonet fixed.

Q. Did ever my conduct during the voyage, or the five months I was on shore with you at Otaheite, before the mutiny, give you reason to think I was ringleader in the mutiny?

A. Not in the least.

Observations per Court. You said it was concluded that each person left on board was concerned in the mutiny, now you say Morrison was not concerned.

Q. Who were Christian's messmates?

A. Elphinstone, Young, Hallet, Ledward, and Tinkler.

Q. When he relieved you at four in the morning did you observe anything particular in his conduct?

A. No.

Q. Were sentinels usually placed on board the *Bounty* when at sea in any part of the ship?

A. No.

WILLIAM PURCELL, Carpenter of the *Bounty* (sworn)

April the 28th, the morning of the mutiny, Quintal came to my cabin and awaked me, saying, 'You and Mr Cole may go on deck and do as you think proper, for we have mutinied and taken the ship; Mr Christian has the command, Captain Bligh is confined, resistance is in vain, and if you attempt it you are a dead man.'   I called Mr Cole and went up the hatchway, saw Thompson standing sentinel armed in the main hatchway, Heywood and Stewart were in their berths abreast of the main hatchway, on the larboard side, Mr Elphinstone on the other side.   John Williams came down the fore hatchway armed and accompanied us on deck. I saw Captain Bligh standing on the quarter-deck with his hands tied, Christian standing over him with a bayonet. The small cutter was alongside. I asked Alexander Smith what they meant to do. He answered, 'To put Captain Bligh, Hayward, Hallet, and Samuel into her, to put Captain Bligh on shore.' I then said to Christian, 'I hope you will not send anybody in that boat, the bottom is almost out, and she cannot swim to the shore.' An altercation then happened between Christian, Churchill, and others about another boat; that being determined, Christian ordered me to get the large cutter ready; I hesitated obeying him. He said, 'Sir, you'll get the boat ready directly'; Cole was gone below to turn those in their hammocks on deck. I called M'Intosh and Norman to go down to my storeroom and hand the gear of the cutter to get her ready for hoisting out. They did so, and we in the meantime were clearing the cutter of yams, coconuts, and lumber. When ready Christian ordered her to be hoisted out. I went to Christian and interceded for the launch and asked Christian if he meant to turn us adrift in the boat, to let us have the launch and not make a sacrifice of us. Christian then ordered out the launch, but told Cole and the boatswain to carry nothing away. The launch was hoisted out and I went down to my cabin to procure such things as I thought might be useful. I desired M'Intosh and Norman to fill a bucket of nails and hand a cross-cut saw out of the storeroom. I then got my chest upon deck and into the launch, and afterwards got sails and other articles, and asked Christian for my tool chest and a cross-cut saw. The latter he granted, and also my tool chest, after Churchill the master-at-arms had opposed my having the chest, and taken what he thought proper out of it. Prior to this I had been down to Fryer's cabin, when he desired me to ask Christian to let him come on deck. He came on deck and had some discourse with Captain Bligh, I could not hear what, Alexander Smith desiring me not to come aft. I then addressed Churchill on the quarter-deck, with Smith, Martin, Mills, Ellison, and Burkett, desiring them to lay down their arms, asking them what they were about, and advising if the captain had done anything wrong to confine him, when Churchill replied, 'You ought to have done that months ago,' and used other abusive language. Mr Fryer was then ordered down to his cabin, that Captain Bligh attempted to speak to Christian, who said, 'Hold your tongue and I'll not hurt you;

it is too late to consider now. I have been in hell for weeks past with you.' I then went forward to get what necessaries were handed on the deck into the boat, and then went into the boat and stowed my chest and other things. That Martin, one of the mutineers, came into the boat with a bag. I asked him what he did there; he said he was going into the boat. I told him, 'If ever we get to England I'll endeavour to hang you myself.' Quintal and Churchill hearing me presented their pistols and desired Martin to come out of the boat, which he did. Christian not being determined whether to keep me on board or not, several of the mutineers opposed my going into the boat, saying that I should be the last suffered to go out if they had their wills, adding they might as well give us the ship as to suffer me to have tools, for we should have another vessel in a month. I then went into the boat to receive a cask of water and other articles that were handing in. Several of the people were in the boat, the rest were then ordered in; we were then veered astern. After much abusive language to the captain they threatened to blow his brains out. Cole asked Captain Bligh if she should cast off as some of the people talked of firing. Captain Bligh consented and we quitted the ship, keeping right astern to prevent the guns from bearing on us. We were nineteen in number in the launch and about seven inches and a half out of water.

Court. Who were the people under arms?

A.

Christian	Churchill	Sumner
Quintal	Mills	Skinner
Martin	A. Smith	Williams
Thompson	M'Koy	Brown
Ellison	Burkett	Millward
Young	Hillbrant	

were under arms at different times.

N.B.—I forgot to mention a circumstance respecting Millward when Mr Cole turned the hands up. Millward came up to me and said, 'Mr Purcell, I assure you I know nothing of this business, but as I had a hand in the former foolish affair I suppose they will make me have a hand in this.'

Q. When you came on deck did you see any of the other prisoners?

A. I did.

Q. Did you see Heywood?

A. No.

Q. Had you any conversation with him?

A. Not at that time.

Q. Had you at any other?

A. Yes.

Q. Did you see Heywood standing at the booms?

A. Yes.

Q. Had he a cutlass in his hand?

A. Yes; leaning the flat part of his hand upon it on the booms. I instantly exclaimed, 'In the name of God, Peter, what do you do with that?' He instantly dropped it. One or two of the people previous to that had laid down their arms to assist in hoisting out the boats; one or two laid down their cutlasses, but not their pistols.

Q. Did Millward assist in hoisting out the boat?

A. Yes.

Q. What number of men did you see with pistols?

A. About four with pistols and cutlasses, the rest with muskets and bayonets fixed.

Q. Do you recollect seeing any other prisoners upon deck, and having any other conversation with them?

A. I saw all upon deck, but had no other conversation but what I have related.

Court. As you was upon deck during the mutiny, do you recollect what all the prisoners were doing at that time?

A. Coleman assisted in getting the boat ready, and handing things into it after it was hoisted out; he wanted to come in with us, but was prevented by the mutineers, and he desired me to notice that he had no hand in the conspiracy. Heywood, when I came on deck, was in his berth; I did not see him on deck until the launch was getting out. Then he was standing on the booms, resting his hand on a cutlass. I exclaimed, 'For God's sake, Peter, what do you do with that?' He dropped it, and assisted in hoisting out the launch and handing things into it, then went below. I heard Churchill call to Thompson to keep them below, but could not tell who he meant. I did not see Heywood after.

Q. Did Heywood hand any of his own things into the boat?

A. Not to my knowledge. Byrne was in the large cutter, keeping her off from the side, and remained there when we left the ship. He was crying and said if he went with us he could be of no service, being blind; he was not armed. Morrison I observed when Mr Cole went down to turn the hands up, who were in their hammocks, but I did not observe he was armed. He assisted in hoisting out the launch.

Q. Did you hear any conversation between him and Fryer?

A. I did not.

Q. Did he appear to you at that time to be in league with the mutineers?

A. No.   Norman I called out of his hammock, and ordered him to fetch tools and clothes, which he did; he gave me every assistance during the whole transaction, was crying when we came away, and desired me to take notice he had no hand in the conspiracy.   Ellison, when I came on the deck, was standing near the gangway, on the larboard side, armed with a musket and bayonet.   In that situation he was during the whole time to the best of my knowledge but in different parts of the ship; I had no conversation with him.

Court. Relate as to M'Intosh.

A. M'Intosh I called out of his hammock and desired him to go down with Morrison to the store-room to get the gear for the boat.   He did, and gave me every assistance, and desired me to take notice he had no hand in the mutiny.   Muspratt, I cannot charge my memory with any particular circumstances as to him. I do not remember seeing him in arms.

Q. What was he doing?

A. Walking about the ship, handing liquor to the ship's company, I think, and handing the captain's and Mr Fryer's things up.

Q. Was that when the dram was ordered?

A. Yes.   Burkett, when I came upon deck, was standing upon the windlass armed with a musket and bayonet.   Soon after he went aft on the quarter-deck, and I believe remained there during the whole transaction under arms.

Q. Did Burkett make an answer to the master when he desired him and the other men, for God's sake to lay down their arms?

A. Not that I heard.   Millward, when I came upon deck, was in his hammock.   Mr Cole turned him up, and when he came over the booms he said, 'I assure you, Mr Purcell, I know nothing of this business; but as I had a hand in the former foolish affair, I suppose they will force me to take a part in this.'   I saw Millward afterwards down the after-ladder by Mr Fryer's cabin armed with a musket, but do

not recollect he had a bayonet fixed, nor seeing him afterwards until we were in the boat; then I saw him look over the
tafferel, but cannot tell if he was armed then or not.

Q. When you all went into the boat was any sentry on the
gangway?

A. Yes; Quintal and Skinner.

Q. Were they armed?

A. I cannot say they were armed; they were placed as
sentinels.

Q. Were you forced in the boat suddenly, or did it take some
time?

A. I do not think it was above ten minutes before every one
was in the boat.

Q. Was it generally known about the ship that the boat was
going to put off?

A. I think it must; we were a long time collecting our things.

Q. Did you hear anybody say he wished to go in the boat
except those you have named already?

A. I cannot say I did.

Q. Did Norman and M'Intosh show any intention to regain
the ship?

A. They did not.

Q. Did you propose any such thing to them?

A. I did not.

Q. Did any of the prisoners show any such wish?

A. No.

Q. In what light did you look upon Mr Heywood at the time
you say he dropped the cutlass?

A. I looked upon him as a person confused.

Court. You must answer that question.

Witness. And that he did not know he had the weapon in his
hand; his hand being on it, it was not in his hand.

Q. What reason had you to suppose him so confused?

A. By his instantly dropping it and assisting in hoisting out
the boat convinced me in my own mind that he had no hand
in the conspiracy.

Q. Were any people armed near Heywood at that time?

A. I do not know there were.

Q. After the launch was hoisted out, you say Heywood went
below and you saw no more of him. Did he of your knowledge
go below of his own accord, or was he compelled to go by any
of the mutineers?

A. I think he went of his own accord, or to get some of the things to put in the boat.

Q. How long was it after the launch was hoisted out before she went from the ship?

A. Near two hours.

Q. Do you think then that Heywood was so long employed in collecting his things as you before supposed?

A. No. He was assisting me and the rest to get the things into the boat, which I suppose prevented him from collecting any things of his own until that time.

Q. You have said just now you saw no more of Heywood after he went below. Did he go below immediately after the boat was hoisted out?

A. No.

Q. How long did the launch remain alongside after Heywood went below?

A. I cannot be positive; ten minutes or a quarter of an hour was the outside.

Q. Were the booms of the *Bounty* above deck?

A. Yes; off the deck on chocks.

Q. When you represented Heywood leaning his hand upon the cutlass, was that cutlass leaning against, or supported by, anything else?

A. I cannot be positive.

Court. Describe the situation he was standing in with the cutlass. Was it leaning against the booms?

A. I cannot be positive; it might be supported by something.

Court. Describe, with your own hand, his hand as to the top and handle of the cutlass?

N.B.—The witness then described the cutlass perpendicular on the point and Mr Heywood's hand flat on it.

Court. Do you, upon the solemn oath you have taken, believe Heywood by being armed with a cutlass at the time you mentioned, by anything you could collect, either by gestures, speeches, or anything else, had any intention of opposing or assisting and joining others who might endeavour to stop the progress of the mutiny?

A. No.

Q. Except the cutlass upon which you saw Mr Heywood's hand, did you see any cutlass on the deck other than those in the mutineers' hands at any time during the mutiny?

A. I cannot say I did; I can't say I did at that time. One man laid one down by him and assisted in hoisting out the launch.

N.B.—The witness said, one man laid one down by him and took it up, but afterwards recalled his words, 'and took it up again,' and added while he assisted in hoisting out the launch.

Q. Do you know if any one of the mutineers took notice of Mr Heywood's having a cutlass?

A. No.

Q. Have you reason to believe that the cutlass you saw in the possession of Heywood was placed upon the booms accidentally, and that he did not furnish himself with it?

A. I have reason to think he did not furnish himself with it.

Q. What is your reason?

A. As Thompson was standing over the arms chest, and Heywood in his berth, had he meant to arm himself he certainly might have done it before he came on deck.

Q. Was the arms chest near Mr Heywood's berth?

A. It stood in the centre of the main hatchway, between the two berths at the after-part.

Q. Did you go on deck before or after Mr Heywood?

A. Before him; he was in his berth.

Q. Did you see him leave his berth and go upon deck?

A. No.

Q. Can you say that he might not have carried the cutlass on deck with him?

A. I have reason to think he did not.

Q. What reason?

A. As Thompson was sentry over the arms chest and knew Mr Cole and myself were not of the conspiracy, and knew Mr Heywood was in his berth, and did not attempt to arm himself before we went upon deck, he most certainly suspected Mr Heywood wanted to procure arms to assist us in retaking the ship.

Q. Do you suppose it possible that if Mr Heywood had been inclined to join the mutineers he would have armed himself before you and Cole?

A. I should suppose not, as he might have armed himself before we were called up, Thompson being sentinel over the arms chest and Mr Heywood in his berth when I went on deck.

Q. From the bulkhead forward, were there any other sentinels except Thompson?

A. There were two more when I went upon deck: Quintal,

the man who accompanied and called me up, and John Williams; both came to the foot of the lower deck ladder and followed us up.

Q. Did you see Mr Heywood as you and Mr Cole the boatswain were going on deck?

A. I saw him in his berth as I went up the cockpit ladder, whether sitting or leaning I'm not positive; the hammocks were hanging.

Q. Had you any conversation with him?

A. No.

Q. Do you know if at that time he knew of the mutiny?

A. I think he must, as the sentinel was upon the arms chest close to his berth.

Q. Was the sentinel over the arms chest or their berths?

A. I cannot say; he was between both berths.

Q. Did the sentinel, or any other person, prevent his going on the deck with you and Mr Cole had he been inclined so to do?

A. I cannot say.

Q. Did you see any oppose him?

A. I did not.

Q. When Mr Heywood dropped the cutlass, as you say, did it fall down from his quitting his hand from it, or did he lay it down?

A. I think it fell, for he did not lay it down.

Q. Do you think any of the mutineers noticed Mr Heywood having the cutlass in his hand?

A. I don't know. As I was busy in getting the boat out, I had no time to make any observation.

Q. Would they have permitted you, or any well-disposed person to the captain, to have touched a cutlass?

A. I cannot tell. As they had pistols I should imagine not.

Q. Did it appear to you, after they had got possession of the ship, that they were careless of their arms?

A. By no means, only in that instance in hoisting out the boat.

Q. In the time Heywood was assisting you to get things into the boat, did he, in any degree whatever, manifest a disposition to assist in the mutiny?

A. No.

Q. Was he during that time deliberate or frightened? In what manner did he behave himself?

A. I had not an opportunity to observe every action, being myself at that time engaged in getting things into the boat. I was apprehensive the mutineers might have stopped our so doing.

Q. Putting every circumstance together on your going into the boat, declare to the court, upon the oath you have taken, how you consider his behaviour; whether as a person joined in the mutiny, or wishing well to Captain Bligh?

A. I by no means considered him as a person concerned in the mutiny or conspiracy.

Q. At the time Mr Heywood was assisting you in getting things into the boat, did he know it was the intention of the mutineers to send the commander of the *Bounty*, with several of the officers and men, away in the boat?

A. I cannot say.

Q. Did he know that you was going out of the ship?

A. He certainly must think so, seeing me getting my chest and things into the boat.

Q. Did you know Captain Bligh was going in the boat?

A. Yes.

Q. Could it be possible but that every person must have known that Captain Bligh was going to be sent away?

A. I suppose not.

Q. Did Mr Heywood know what caused you to quit the ship?

A. Everybody must have known who was on deck at the time that I meant to follow my commander.

Q. Did Mr Heywood express any desire or inclination to follow his commander with you?

A. Not to me.

Q. Was Captain Bligh confined on the quarter-deck in such a situation as he must have been seen by Mr Heywood whilst he was upon deck with you, or when he was assisting in getting out the boats?

A. I think he was in such a situation that he must have been seen by every one upon deck.

Q. Was any bulkhead round Mr Heywood's berth?

A. No; it was half boarded, and half canvas.

Q. If the screen was drawn, how could you see Mr Heywood?

A. The screen was not drawn.

Q. When you saw Mr Heywood with the cutlass, might it not have been used with advantage?

A. By no means, there being fourteen on the deck armed, the

officers confined, and most of the mutineers having cutlasses
or pistols.

Q. Were any of the prisoners amongst those who opposed
your going into the boat?

A. No.

Q. You say Morrison did not seem to be leagued with the
mutineers. Did he express to you any desire to follow the fate
of the commander in the boat?

A. No.

Q. Do you know if M'Intosh was prevented leaving the
Bounty?

A. He desired me to take notice that he was prevented by
the mutineers from coming into the boat.

Q. Did you see him prevented?

A. I did not personally see it, but Christian had given orders
before that neither Coleman, Norman, or M'Intosh should quit
the ship.

Q. How do you know that?

A. I heard him.

Q. per Byrne. When you were first alarmed, and came from
below with Cole, did you observe any one sitting on the chest
on the fore hatchway?

A. I did not.

Q. When you was in the launch, receiving things from some
person on board, did I not speak to you from the stern of
the large cutter?

A. I don't recollect it, only your desiring every one to take
notice that by your being blind you could be of no service, and
crying.

Q. Before Captain Bligh, Mr Fryer, and other officers came
on the deck, was you not down in the launch?

A. I was several times in her, stowing the things.

Q. Do you recollect my saying, 'Mr Purcell, if you live to go
home, I hope you will go to my friends and tell them I know
nothing of this transaction, or had any hand in it'?

A. No.

Mr Hayward (sworn)

At four o'clock in the morning of the twenty-eighth day of
April 1789, Fletcher Christian relieved the watch as usual at
about five o'clock. After giving orders to prepare for washing

the decks he ordered me to look out, as being master's mate of the watch, whilst he went down to lash his hammock up; a few minutes after I was looking out at a shark which was at the stern of the ship, when, to my unutterable surprise, I saw Christian, Charles Churchill, Thomas Burkett, one of the prisoners, John Sumner, Matthew Quintal, William M'Koy, Isaac Martin, Henry Hillbrant, and Alexander Smith coming aft, armed with muskets and bayonets. Going forward to prevent their proceeding, to ask Christian the cause of such an act, he told me to hold my tongue instantly, and left James Martin a sentinel upon deck, and proceeded with the rest of his party below to Captain Bligh's cabin; some men standing with their heads above the deck, Mr Hallet, myself, Lamb (Ellison at the helm), and Mills being on the deck. Christian being gone below, I asked Mills if he knew anything of the mutiny? He said, 'No.' Ellison quitted the helm and armed himself with a bayonet. The ship's decks now began to throng with men: Young, Millward, Muspratt, Williams, Skinner, and Brown on the deck, armed with muskets and bayonets; Heywood, Stewart, and Morrison unarmed on the booms. Christian and his gang had not been down long before I heard the cry of murder from Captain Bligh, and, on the other hand, heard Churchill calling for the rope. It was now I found Mills was of the mutineers' party: contrary to all orders he cut the deep-sea line and carried a piece of it to Christian. Soon after I saw Captain Bligh brought upon the quarter-deck, with his hands bound behind him, surrounded by most of those who came last on deck. Some of the officers were permitted to come on deck, and Christian ordered us to hoist out the cutter; we remonstrated against it, being too small and unable to contain us. As soon as the launch was out Christian ordered Mr Samuel, Mr Hallet, and me into it; we requested time to collect some things; which was granted. I was going down, but was prevented by Thompson, who was armed with a cutlass, and sentinel over the arms chest; he stood aft a part of the main hatchway. He assented, and I went down and saw Heywood in his berth. I told him to go into the boat, but in my hurry I do not remember receiving an answer. Mr Hallet and I went down the main hatchway together. After getting a few clothes I went up and put them into the launch; then went to Christian and asked him for my instruments and chart, but was refused and hurried into the boat; not before I had seen Captain Bligh brought to the gangway, held by Christian and surrounded by Mills, Burkett, Quintal, Sumner, Millward, and M'Koy, armed. I do not recollect any more, but Ellison came up in a hurry with a bayonet in his hand, swearing, 'Damn him, I will be sentinel over him.' I then went over the gangway. When I was in the launch I saw Byrne in the cutter. I heard him say he was sorry he could not have leave to come with us. The officers and men being in the boat, Captain Bligh was then forced in and we were veered astern, the mutineers saying they would give us a tow towards land. In this situation we prayed much for arms, ammunition, and more provisions, and then (for a watch and boatswain's call) we got four cutlasses and a small addition of pork; a number of mutineers collecting themselves on the taffrail, amongst them were Skinner, Quintal, Millward, Hillbrant, Ellison, Smith, and Brown publicly insulting Captain Bligh. Skinner would have shot into the boat, but was prevented by others of the mutineers; Millward, jeering, said, 'Go and see if you can live upon a quarter of a pound of yams per day.' Just before casting off Coleman came to the taffrail and avowed his innocence and ignorance of the matter. After casting off I heard orders given for loosing the top-gallant sails, and saw Ellison going up the shrouds for that purpose.

Court. I think you were sent to apprehend the prisoners gone to Otaheite. Inform the court what you know.

A. Before anchoring in Mattavai Bay, in the *Pandora*, in the island of Otaheite, I saw Coleman coming off to the ship. Soon after we were at anchor Stewart and Heywood came on board, but I did not see them until they were in Captain Edwards's cabin. They made themselves known to Captain Edwards, saying they belonged to the *Bounty*, and were happy they were arrived. On my asking some questions concerning the *Bounty*, Captain Edwards said it was unnecessary to ask any questions. I asked how they came to go away with the *Bounty*, and received for answer from Stewart that when called upon he would answer all particulars. I was prevented from asking any more questions by Captain Edwards saying again it was unnecessary. The next day I was dispatched to Papara with a party in order to receive the mutineers who were supposed to be in the valley; as soon as I arrived at Papara I had intelligence that they were not far off, and with a guide marched to find them, but without success. The next morning about eleven o'clock I had intelligence of them coming down. I drew out my party to receive them. When they came within hearing I called to them to lay down their arms and go on one side, which they did, and I took them into custody and brought them on board. I wrote to Lieutenant Corner, who was coming to the valley, that I had taken them.

Court. I think you say, in the morning of the mutiny you saw eighteen under arms?

A. Yes.

Q. Do you know of any conversation between Captain Bligh and the officers about launching the cutter?

A. None, but a general clamour.

Q. What number of men was in the boat when you were ordered into it?

A. None. I was the first that was ordered into it.

Q. How long did the boat remain alongside after you was in it?

A. About a quarter of an hour.

Q. Were all the people that went into the boat ordered in, or did they go voluntarily?

A. I heard no one ordered but Mr Hallet, Mr Samuel, and myself.

Q. What number of men were on the deck at the time of hoisting out the boat?

A. I cannot say.

Q. Can you tell if there were any below at that time?

A. None, except those who guarded the officers' cabins in the after part of the ship.

Q. Look at all the prisoners, and relate all you know of them on that day.

A. Coleman, I saw nothing of him till he came to the taff-rail, and declared his innocence.

Heywood I saw on the booms, not doing anything, and afterwards in his berth below, when I spoke to him and told him to go into the boat.

Q. Did he make any answer?

A. I believe not.

Q. Did you at any time that day see Mr Heywood with arms in his hands?

A. I did not.

Q. Did you see him assist in hoisting out the boats?

A. No.

Byrne I saw in the cutter alongside the ship when I was in

the launch; I heard him say he was sorry he could not go with us.

Morrison I saw assisting in clearing the yams from the boat, but am doubtful whether he was under arms at first or not.

Q. Did you hear any conversation between him and any officer of the ship?

A. I do not remember any.

Q. Did he at all appear to you by his conduct to be assisting the mutineers, or in obedience to orders to get the boats out?

A. If I was to give it as my opinion, I should say he was assisting the mutineers, wishing us away as fast as possible.

Q. Did you at any time that day see him with arms in his hands?

A. I am doubtful if he was under arms at all.

Norman was on deck forward. I neither saw him under arms nor assisting the mutineers, but assisting in getting things into the boat.

Ellison I saw at the helm, and soon after the people had gone to Captain Bligh's cabin and quitted it, armed himself with a bayonet, and just before my going into the boat saw him as a sentinel, with a bayonet in his hand, over Captain Bligh, saying, 'Damn him, I'll be sentinel over him.'

M'Intosh I did not see under arms, nor did I suppose him one of the mutineers; he assisted to get out the boat.

Muspratt I saw on the larboard side with a musket in his hand, supposing him one of the mutineers.

Burkett I saw come aft, following Christian and Churchill, and saw him descend the after-ladder with them armed with a bayonet.

Millward, I don't recollect seeing him at first, but after Captain Bligh was brought on deck, saw him armed as a sentinel. After the boat was astern saw him on the taffrail jeering us, and saying, 'Go and see if you can live upon a quarter of a pound of yams per day,' or something to that purpose.

Q. Was you present when Norman, Morrison, and Ellison were taken?

A. No. They had been left there by Lieutenant Corner, under the charge of Mr Saville.

Q. When you fell in with M'Intosh, Burkett, Muspratt, and Millward, did they make any resistance?

A. None.

Q. They surrendered themselves upon your demanding them to lay down their arms?

A. They did.

Q. When you went down the main hatchway, who were between decks besides Thompson?

A. Mr Heywood. Mr Hallet went with me and Mr Elphinstone.

Q. Was Thompson sentinel?

A. Thompson was the only sentinel; but there were armed men round the hatchways on the boom.

Q. Of the ten prisoners, six of whom you describe under arms, do you know of any effort made by those not under arms, or any of them, to restore the ship?

A. No.

Q. Did Norman express any desire to you of going into the boat?

A. To me, none.

Q. Did you hear him to any other person?

A. No.

Q. Did M'Intosh?

A. No.

Q. Or any disapprobation of the mutineers' conduct?

A. No.

Q. How long after the mutiny began that you saw Muspratt under arms?

A. I beg leave to remind the court that they did not come up together; it might be about ten minutes.

Q. At the time the mutineers went into the cabin, was Burkett one of them that remained on the hatchway?

A. No.

Q. Have you reason to know that Mr Heywood would have been prevented from going into the boat at the time you did, after you desired him?

A. No.

Q. How long before your going down in the boat, before you spoke to him?

A. About two or three minutes.

Q. You say if you were to give your opinion, it is that Morrison was assisting the mutineers by getting out the boats and wished to get you away from the ship. You have likewise said that M'Intosh was assisting in getting out the boats, and you did not look upon him in that light. I wish to know the reason of that difference.

A. The difference in the countenances of people may be ill-grounded. One looked rejoiced, the other depressed.

Q. You said Norman was employed in putting a tool-chest into the boat. Do you know why he did not accompany you?

A. No.

Q. When you spoke to Mr Heywood in his berth and admonished him to go into the boat, was he under any restraint as to going on deck?

A. No.

Q. What was he employed about at that time?

A. Nothing but sitting with his arms folded.

Q. Did you by his behaviour consider him as attached to his duty, or to a part of the mutineers?

A. I rather suppose, after telling him to go into the boat and not joining us, he was on the part of the mutineers; but that must be only stated as an opinion, as he was not employed during the acting part of it.

Q. Did you observe joy or sorrow in his behaviour?

A. Sorrow.

Q. You have said that M'Intosh was unfriendly to the mutineers; you mean he was not attached to them, because he was depressed in his countenance. Might not the sorrow in Mr Heywood arise from the same cause?

A. It might.

Q. per Morrison. You give it from your opinion that I was one of the mutineers. Can you declare before God and this court that such evidence is not the result of a private pique?

A. It is not. It is an opinion I formed after quitting the ship, from his not coming with us when he had as good an opportunity as the rest, there being more boats than one.

Q. Are you certain we might have had the large cutter to have accompanied you?

A. My not being present at any conversation with you, I cannot say, but perhaps you might.

Q. Can you deny you were present when Captain Bligh begged that the long boat might not be overloaded, and said he would do justice to those who remained?

A. I was present when Captain Bligh did make such declaration, but I understood it respected clothes and other heavy articles, with which the boat was already too full.

Q. Do you recollect in consequence of such declaration, I told you I would take my chance in the ship?

A. I do not.

Q. Do you remember when you handed your bag up the main hatchway, and with it your fusee, that I was the person that received them from you, and Quintal came and seized the fusee and swore, 'Damn his eyes, if you should have it'?

A. I do not remember the person who took the bag and fusee; it might have been you, but I remember Quintal swearing I should not have it, but from whose hands he took it I cannot say.

Q. Do you remember on any time that day calling on me to assist you in any point of duty, or to give any assistance to retake His Majesty's ship?

A. I have a faint remembrance of a circumstance of that nature.

Court. Relate it.

A. It is so very faint I can hardly remember it, or who it was.

Court. Relate it.

A. On seeing Churchill on the booms, I thought if I had a Friendly Island club, of which there were many on board, had I not been observed I could have gone forward and knocked him down at the time of handing the bag out, and you might have been the person I called to my assistance.

Q. per Morrison. What answer did I give you?

A. I do not know.

Q. Did I not say, 'Go it, I 'll back you; there are tools enough in the ship'?

A. I cannot remember.

Q. Did you ever observe anything in my conduct during the voyage, or on that day, to give cause of complaint?

A. None. But on that day I thought he was pleased in preparing the boat for our departure; but, as I said before, I do not know his real intention.

Q. Are you sure that there was a continual smile and appearance of joy upon my countenance all the time you observed me, or at the time only when you called upon me for assistance?

A. I cannot say.

Q. per Muspratt. In answer to a question just asked by Morrison, you allow Captain Bligh used these words, 'Don't let the boat be overloaded, my lads, I 'll do you justice'; which, you say, alluded to the clothes and other heavy articles. Do you mean to understand the latter words of 'My lads, I 'll do you justice,' to apply to clothes or men who he apprehended might go in the boat?

A. If Captain Bligh made use of the words 'my lads,' it was to the people already in the boat, and not to those in the ship.

Court. To whom do you think Captain Bligh alluded when he said he would do them justice? Was it your opinion to the men in the boat with him, or to any person remaining in the ship?

A. To persons remaining in the ship.

Q. Are you of opinion that he meant he would do them justice on account of remaining in the ship, or that he would cause satisfaction to be given them for anything they might lose.

A. I rather think it was the few who Captain Bligh knew to be of his party that were detained contrary to their inclination, that he would do them such justice that should throw aside all doubts of their being true to the service of their country.

Q. Do you know if any were detained contrary to their wish?

A. Coleman and Byrne, which, from the latter's answers, I suppose to be the case.

Q. What authority have you for saying Coleman was detained contrary to his inclination?

A. From hearing amongst the mutineers their intention to detain him, as well as the acting surgeon, who they afterwards let go, saying they would have little occasion for doctors.

MR HALLET'S evidence

On the 28th day of April 1789, at daybreak, I had the watch upon deck; I saw Christian, the officer of the watch, come up the fore hatchway armed, and several armed men following him: Burkett, Churchill, Sumner, and Martin, no more. At first I attempted to go down the fore hatchway, but was prevented by two fixed bayonets thrust up, and I was ordered to stay where I was; who they were I cannot say. I was then going aft, but before I got to the quarter-deck I heard Captain Bligh sing out 'Murder.' He was soon after brought on deck in his shirt, with his hands tied behind him, and Christian holding the cord that tied him and a bayonet in the other hand, and kept in that situation with the guard round him.

Court. Name the guard.

A. I do not know any more than I before mentioned. The cutter was ordered by Christian to be hoisted out and Mr Samuel and myself ordered into it; but upon the boatswain's and carpenter's coming aft and telling Christian they would prefer going in the boat with the captain than staying in the ship, desired to have the launch instead of the cutter. He granted it, and said he did not wish them or any other to stay against their inclinations, or to go; they then asked for various articles that would be of use; and Mr Heywood, Mr Samuel, and myself then went into the boat and were veered astern, Christian saying he would hove us in near the land. We then got a few more things from the ship and were cast loose.

Q. Did you hear any conversation between Christian and the officers of the *Bounty*, about the launch or cutter?

A. The boatswain and carpenter came aft, as I said before, and spoke to Christian about them.

Q. What number of men were in the boat when you went into it?

A. By Christian's order, I was the first in the boat.

Q. How long did the boat remain alongside after you was in it?

A. Ten minutes, or a quarter of an hour.

Q. Were all the people ordered in, or did they go voluntarily?

A. I believe the most part went voluntarily.

Q. What number of men assisted in hoisting out the launch?

A. About twenty.

Q. Were all unarmed?

A. One or two gave their arms to others and assisted, and as soon as done resumed their arms.

Q. What number of men did you see under arms that morning?

A. Ellison, Morrison, Millward, Burkett, Hillbrant, Sumner, Skinner, Christian, Young, Churchill, Thompson, Alexander Smith, Mills, M'Koy, Williams, Brown, Martin, and Quintal.

Q. What time did you make that memorandum?

A. Lately.

Q. Had you any conversation with the officers or men that morning, respecting retaking the ship?

A. Seeing so many armed men, and no possibility of our procuring any arms ourselves, I believe it was deemed impracticable.

Q. When the mutineers gave their arms to others whilst they hoisted out the boats, did they give them to their own party?

A. Entirely so.

Q. Did you see Coleman?

A. Yes.

Court. Relate his conduct that day.

A. Coleman assisted in getting things into the boat, and when astern called to the gunner, 'Remember, Mr Peckover, if ever you arrive in England, I had no hand in this.'

Q. Did you see Mr Heywood?

A. I saw him once.

Q. Where?

A. Upon the platform on the larboard side of the deck.

Q. What was he doing?

A. Standing still, looking attentively on Captain Bligh.

Q. Had he any arms at that time?

A. I did not see him under arms at all.

Q. Had you any conversation with him?

A. I do not recollect having spoken to him.

Q. Was he or not prevented from going into the boat?

A. I do not know that he offered to go into it.

Q. Did any person propose to him so to do?

A. I do not know.

Q. Do you know any other particulars of him that day.

A. When he was standing as before related, Captain Bligh said something to him, but what I did not hear; upon which he laughed, turned round, and went away.

Q. Did he appear at liberty, or at any time confined?

A. At liberty.

Q. Byrne—relate what you know of Byrne that day.

A. I remember to have seen him once, keeping the cutter alongside.

Q. Morrison—relate his conduct that day.

A. When I first saw him, he and Millward were talking together unarmed, but he shortly afterwards appeared with a musket.

Q. What part of the ship did you see him in with a musket?

A. I did not see him under arms till the boat veered astern, then he looked over the taffrail, and, jeering, said, 'If my friends inquire after me, tell them I am somewhere in the South Seas.'

Q. How was he employed at any time, and until you put off?

A. I have related all to the best of my recollection.

Q. Norman—relate all you know of him that day.

A. Norman was employed in getting things out of the carpenter's store-room. Just before we came away he cried and said he wished to go with us, to see his wife and family.

Q. Did you consider him as a mutineer?

A. I considered him as an innocent man, and detained against his inclination.

Q. Ellison—relate all you know of him that day.

A. He appeared early under arms, and came to me insolently, saying, 'Mr Hallet, you need not mind, we are only going to put the captain on shore, and then you and the others may return on board,' meaning Mr Hayward and Mr Samuel, as no others at that time were ordered to quit the ship.

Q. M'Intosh—relate all you know of him.

A. He was employed in getting things from the store-room, and willing to procure things for us that we required.

Q. Did he show any inclination to come on board?

A. I did not myself observe it.

Q. Muspratt—relate all you know of him that day.

A. I do not remember to have seen him once.

Q. Burkett—relate all you know of him that day.

A. I have related the whole I know.

Q. Millward—relate all you know of him that day.

A. As I said before, I saw him and Morrison talking together, and shortly after saw him armed.

Q. Look round, and point out Morrison.

A. This is he. [*Pointing to Morrison.*]

Q. Do you know if Coleman, Norman, and M'Intosh were detained against their wills?

A. I have great reason to suppose they were.

Q. Did you speak to Byrne, so as to form an opinion of his mind?

A. He appeared pensive and sorrowful.

Q. Do you believe it proceeded from his disapprobation of the event that had taken place?

A. The cause I am totally ignorant of.

Q. Describe the situation of the commander of the *Bounty* when Heywood turned round, as you before said.

A. He was standing with his arms tied behind him; Christian holding the cord that bound him with one hand, and a bayonet at his breast with the other hand.

Q. Did you go down the main hatchway with Mr Heywood that morning?

A. I was below.

Q. Was Mr Heywood in his berth at that time?

A. I do not remember to have seen him during that morning, except at the time already related.

Q. At the time the boats were hoisting out, to whom did the mutineers give their arms?

A. Very few were given; those that were, were to their own party.

Q. When the boat put off from the ship, did you see or hear any person express any dissatisfaction at being left?

A. Yes: Coleman and Norman.

Q. per Morrison. You say you saw me under arms at the taffrail, and I did sneeringly say, 'Tell my friends, if they inquire, that I am somewhere in the South Seas.' Can you positively declare before God and this court that it was me and no other person you saw under arms, and to whom I delivered the said sneering message?

A. I have declared it, but did not remark that the message was said to any particular individual.

Q. Can you deny that I did lower down into the boat from the larboard quarter two cutlasses, two large jars of water, and five or six and twenty pieces of pork?

A. I remember four cutlasses lowered, and the other things you mention in the boat, but by whom I cannot say.

Q. Do you remember that I personally assisted you to haul your chest up the main hatchway, and if I was armed?

A. Concerning the chest, I do not remember, and have before said that I did not see you under arms till the boat was veered astern.

JOHN SMITH's evidence

Between five and six o'clock, on the 28th of April 1789, Thomas Hall told me I was wanted aft, on the quarter-deck; Captain Bligh then stood on the quarter-deck in his shirt, Christian holding him in his left hand, and a cutlass in his right. Christian ordered me to bring a bottle of rum, and serve every man under arms; and at the same time to bring up the captain's clothes. I did so, and put some clothes over Captain Bligh's shoulders, and then served the drams.

Court. Name who you served.

A. Christian first. I believe M'Koy and Williams were on the starboard side. I served several, but am not positive who; then I went on the quarter-deck and served Ellison, no more on the deck; I then went down with the bottle. By that time the captain was gone over the side. I saw Mr Samuel in the captain's cabin, getting his papers and things. There was a sentinel below, between the cabin and Mr Fryer's; Sumner and Quintal remained below until the captain was gone over the side. I then came up with wine in my hand, and went across the ship and put the wine into the boat, and we dropped astern.

Q. You say you served the drams by Christian's order?

A. Yes.

Q. Did you give a dram to Coleman?

A. Yes; some in a tin pot.

Q. To Mr Heywood?

A. No; he refused.

Q. Where was he standing?

A. By the windlass, with his back towards me, and his hands in his pockets.

Q. To Byrne?

A. No.

Q. To Morrison?

A. I don't know.

Q. To Norman?

A. No.

Q. To Ellison?

A. Yes.

Q. To M'Intosh?

A. No.

Q. To Muspratt?

A. No.

Q. To Burkett?

A. Yes.

Q. To Millward?

A. Yes.

Q. Did any person go into the boat after you?

A. Not to my knowledge.

Q. How long was the boat alongside after you went into it?

A. It dropped astern directly.

Q. Did Christian order any one to go into the boat?

A. No.

Q. Was you ordered to go into it?

A. No.

Q. Did you assist in hoisting out the launch?

A. No.

Q. You did not see her hoisted out?

A. No.

Q. In what station was you?

A. Captain's servant.

Q. Who ordered you to get the captain's clothes?

A. Christian—when I went down for the rum.

Q. How long after the mutiny began, before you served the drams?

A. Immediately after putting the captain's clothes on. I can't say how long.

Q. When you offered a dram to Coleman, where was he?

A. Forward upon the booms.

Q. Had he arms then?

A. No.

Q. You say when you offered a dram to Mr Heywood he had no arms?

A. No; he was neither talking nor doing anything.

Q. Did you see Morrison?

A. Yes.

Q. Where?

A. I can't tell; I did not offer him a dram.

Q. Had he any arms?

A. No.

Q. Did you see Norman?

A. Yes.

Q. What was he doing?

A. I don't recollect.

Q. What was Ellison doing?

A. Standing with a musket in his hand.

Q. In what part of the ship?

A. Before the mizen-mast.

Q. What was M'Intosh doing?

A. Standing by the booms, having no arms.

Q. Did you see Muspratt?

A. I don't recollect seeing him at all.

Q. Where was Burkett?

A. On the fore part of the quarter-deck.

Q. What was he doing?

A. He was under arms.

Q. What was Millward doing?

A. He stood with a musket in his hand on the after-ladder.

Q. per Morrison. Do you recollect when you came forward with the bottle that Coleman and I were talking together, and you gave Coleman a glass in a tin pot, and said, 'Morrison, you may as well have a drop, though I am ordered to serve none but the sentinels'?

A. I do not.

Q. per Muspratt. Do you know on that morning if any one came down abaft and got a bottle of rum to serve the ship's company besides yourself?

A. Not to my knowledge.

Q. per Millward. Do you recollect any person who took the case from you, and the other necessaries, handing up for the good of those going in the boat?

A. I do not recollect.

Captain Edwards's evidence

Court. Relate all you know concerning the prisoners belonging to the *Bounty*.

A. Before we came to anchor in Mattavai Bay, Coleman came on board. I was informed that others had sailed in a schooner that had been built by some of the *Bounty's* people. I likewise heard that one man had been murdered (the master-at-arms), and likewise an account that the *Bounty* had been twice at Otaheite, in possession of Captain Bligh; the last time, after some people being landed, she went away in the night, and was seen again in the morning in a north-west direction. Coleman was ready to give me any information. Stewart and Heywood, after we anchored, came on board before any boat was sent on shore. Mr Larkin brought them to me. I asked, 'What news?' and Mr Heywood said he supposed I had heard of the affair concerning the *Bounty*. I cannot recollect all the conversation, but he inquired if Mr Hayward was on board. I said he was; he desired to see him, and I desired Mr Hayward to come out of my state room. Mr Hayward came, and gave them a contemptuous look, and began to enter into a conversation concerning the *Bounty*. I called people to take the prisoners; some words passed, and Heywood said he would be able to vindicate his conduct. Byrne came on board the third day, alone. Ellison, Morrison, and Norman were sent on board by parties that were sent after them.

Q. per Byrne. Did you, or any under your command, commissioned, warrant, petty officers or seamen, bring me on board the *Pandora*?

A. No; I did not understand it so.

Q. Did you know at what part of the island I was when the *Pandora* anchored in Mattavai Bay?

A. Not exactly, but I heard some distance from the place.

Q. Was I not introduced to you by your officers?

A. Probably you was. [*Admitted that Byrne voluntarily surrendered himself.*]

Court. Did Byrne request an interview with you, saying he came from Papara, a distant part of the island, and that he had walked all night to join the ship?

A. I do not recollect the place, but I believe he did say he had walked all night.

LIEUTENANT LARKIN'S evidence

Court. Inform the court how the prisoners came on board the *Pandora*.

A. Coleman came before we came to anchor, voluntarily. Heywood next, and Byrne, both voluntarily.

Norman ⎞ Ellison ⎬ Morrison ⎠	Came round in one of our boats from the other side of the island, sent by Mr Saville (since lost).
M'Intosh ⎞ Muspratt ⎬ Millward ⎟ Burkett ⎠	Brought on board in one of our boats that was sent after them.

LIEUTENANT CORNER'S evidence

Court. Inform the court what you know of the prisoners being taken and carried on board the *Pandora*.

A. Norman ⎞ Came to me in company with another person
Morrison ⎬ named Brown (who had been left at Ota-
Ellison ⎠ heite) at Papara, when I was going in search of the schooner.

I landed about two o'clock in the morning; they were armed with hatchets and instruments that Brown had given them to defend themselves from the Indians; I confined them in the boat and went to secure the rest.

Q. Was you sent in pursuit in the *Pandora's* boat?

A. I was sent in pursuit of the schooner the evening the ship arrived. I got within a mile of her, when the schooner avoided us. We chased her, but I cannot say who was on board.

Q. Was the schooner in your possession before the prisoners surrendered themselves?

A. No.

Q. Did Norman, Morrison, and Ellison voluntarily surrender themselves?

A. They made no resistance; they came voluntarily with Brown.

Coleman, Norman, M'Intosh, and Byrne were acquitted. Mr Heywood, Morrison, Muspratt, Millward, Burkett, and Ellison were found guilty, and sentence of death was pronounced upon them; but the court at the same time informed Mr Heywood and Morrison that they should recommend them to the king for mercy, which His Majesty was afterwards graciously pleased to grant. Muspratt having requested that Norman, one of the prisoners, against whom there was no evidence, might be acquitted and examined in his favour, and this being refused by the court, his sentence was respited till the opinion of the twelve judges could be obtained upon the question. They decided that the evidence ought to have been received, and in consequence Muspratt was discharged.

The sentence of the court was afterwards executed upon Millward, Burkett, and Ellison. When they were brought upon the forecastle of the ship in which the execution was ordered, Millward addressed the ships' crews and spectators in the following words: 'Brother Seamen, you see before you three lusty young fellows about to suffer a shameful death for the dreadful crime of mutiny and desertion. Take warning by our example never to desert your officers, and should they behave ill to you, remember it is not their cause; it is the cause of your country you are bound to support.'

THE APPENDIX

To STEPHEN BARNEY, ESQUIRE, PORTSMOUTH

GREY'S INN SQUARE,
15th May 1794.

SIR,

I assure you I regard the publication of your minutes of the court martial as a very great favour done to myself, and I am the more sensible of the obligation from being convinced that they were not originally taken with an intent to publish. But they appear to be so full and satisfactory, that from your further kindness in permitting the extraordinary information which I have collected to be annexed as an appendix, the public, I trust, will at length be possessed of a complete knowledge of the real causes and circumstances of that most melancholy event, the mutiny on board the *Bounty*. It is unnecessary for me to add that I alone am responsible for the authenticity, or rather accuracy, of the information contained in the Appendix, as far at least as it has been obtained by me in the manner and from the persons described therein.

I have the honour to be, sir,

Your most obedient and obliged servant,

ED. CHRISTIAN.

———————

THE circumstances communicated in this Appendix have been collected by a person nearly related to Christian; and it is far from his intention or wish to insinuate a vindication of the crime which has been committed. Justice, as well as policy, requires that mutiny, from whatever causes produced or with whatever circumstances accompanied, should be punished with inexorable rigour. The publication of the trial and of these extraordinary facts, it is presumed, will in no degree impede the pursuit of justice, yet it will administer some consolation to the broken hearts which this melancholy transaction has occasioned. And whilst the innocent families and relations of twenty-one unhappy men are deeply interested in reducing to its just measure the infamy which this dreadful act has brought upon them, every friend to truth and strict justice must feel his attention awakened to the true causes and circumstances which have hitherto been concealed or misrepresented of one of the most remarkable events in the annals of the navy. It is the aim of the writer of this Appendix to state facts as they are, and to refrain as far as possible from invective and reproach.

It will naturally be asked, from whom and how have these facts been collected, and why have they been so long suppressed? It may be answered that the writer of this Appendix, with the other relations of the mutineers, entertained no distrust of the narratives published to the world, or the accounts which they received in private; and as they came from those whose sufferings had unquestionably been extreme and preservation almost miraculous; and thus carrying with them the stamp of even greater authenticity than the solemn declarations of a death-bed, they precluded all suspicion and inquiries among those who were most concerned in the horrid representation. Their lips were closed, they mourned in silence, and shuddering at the most distant allusion to this melancholy subject, they were of all persons the least likely to discover the real truth of the trans-action.

All the circumstances stated here could not be produced at the trial, as the court confined the witnesses as much as possible to the question, Who were actually engaged in the mutiny? for that being a crime which will admit of no legal justification, the relation of previous circumstances could not be material or legal evidence; yet what passed at the time of the mutiny was so immediately connected with what had happened previously in the ship, that in the testimony of most of the witnesses there will be found an allusion to, or confirmation of, what is here advanced.

Some time after the trial of the mutineers, the writer of this Appendix received such information as surprised him greatly, and in consequence of which he resolved to make every possible inquiry into this unhappy affair. The following circumstances have been collected from many interviews and conversations, in the presence and hearing of several respectable gentlemen: with Mr Fryer,[1] master of the *Bounty*; Mr Hayward,[2] midshipman; Mr Peckover,[3] gunner; Mr Purcell,[4] carpenter; John Smith,[5] cook; Lawrence Lebogue,[6] sail-maker; all these returned in the boat with Captain Bligh: and with Joseph Coleman,[7] armourer; Thomas M'Intosh,[8] carpenter's mate; Michael Byrne,[9] seaman; these are three of the four who were tried and honourably acquitted, even with Captain Bligh's testimony in their favour; and with Mr Heywood, midshipman, who has received His Majesty's pardon; and William Muspratt, discharged by the opinion of the judges in his favour upon a point of evidence.

---

[1] Now of the *Inconstant* man-of-war.
[2] Now lieutenant in the *Diomed*, East Indies.
[3] Lives at No. 13 Gun Alley, Wapping.
[4] Now of the *Dromedary*, West Indies.
[5] In London, but residence unknown.
[6] In Greenwich Hospital.
[7] In Greenwich Hospital.
[8] In the merchants' service, his mother keeps a public-house at North Shields.
[9] In Greenwich Hospital.

The writer of this has received letters also upon the subject from James Morrison, the boatswain's mate, who was pardoned. Mr Heywood is now serving again as midshipman, under Lord Howe in the *Queen Charlotte*, and is much respected by all who know him; and Morrison and Muspratt are also employed again in the king's service. Yet the writer of this Appendix thinks it necessary to assure the reader that no material fact here stated stands in need of their testimony or confirmation. The gentlemen who were present at different conversations with the persons just mentioned are: John Farhill, Esq., No. 38 Mortimer Street; Samuel Romilly, Esq., Lincoln's Inn; Mr Gilpin, No. 432 Strand; the Rev. Dr Fisher, Canon of Windsor; the Rev. Mr Cookson, Canon of Windsor; Captain Wordsworth, of the *Abergavenny* East Indiaman; Rev. Mr Antrobus, Chaplain to the Bishop of London; John France, Esq., Temple; John Losh, Esq., Temple; Rev. Dr Frewen, Colchester; and John Atkinson, Esq., *Somerset Herald*. Each of these gentlemen has heard the declaration of one at the least of the persons before mentioned; some have had an interview with five or six of them at different times, together with the writer of this Appendix, who is confident that every one of these gentlemen will bear testimony that what he has heard is not here exaggerated or misrepresented. There is no contradiction or variance whatever in the account given by the gentlemen and people of the *Bounty*, though they could not upon every occasion be all present together, and therefore cannot all relate exactly the same circumstances.

They declare that Captain Bligh used to call his officers 'scoundrels, damned rascals, hounds, hell-hounds, beasts, and infamous wretches'; that he frequently threatened them that when the ship arrived at Endeavour Straits 'he would kill one-half of the people, make the officers jump overboard, and would make them eat grass like cows'; and that Christian and Stewart, another midshipman, were as much afraid of Endeavour Straits as any child is of a rod.

Captain Bligh was accustomed to abuse Christian much more frequently and roughly than the rest of the officers, or as one of the persons expressed it, 'whatever fault was found, Mr Christian was sure to bear the brunt of the captain's anger.' In speaking to him in this violent manner, Captain Bligh frequently shook his fist in Christian's face. But the immediate cause of the melancholy event is attributed to what happened on the 26th and 27th of April; the mutiny broke out on the morning of the

28th of April 1789. The *Bounty* had stopped at Annamooko, one of the Friendly Islands; on the 26th Christian was sent upon a watering-party, with express orders from the captain by no means to fire upon the natives. Upon their return the captain was informed that the natives had stolen the cooper's adze. At this Captain Bligh was in a great rage and abused Christian much, saying to him, 'G—— damn your blood, why did not you fire—you an officer!' At this island the captain and ship's company had bought quantities of coconuts, at the rate of twenty for a nail. The captain's heap lay upon the deck, and on the morning of the 27th Captain Bligh fancied that the number was diminished, but the master, Mr Fryer, told him he supposed they were pressed closer from being run over by the men in the night. The captain then ordered the officer of the morning watch, Mr Christian, to be called. When he came the captain accosted him thus: 'Damn your blood, you have stolen my coconuts!' Christian answered, 'I was dry; I thought it of no consequence. I took one only, and I am sure no one touched another.' Captain Bligh then replied, 'You lie, you scoundrel, you have stolen one-half.' Christian appeared much hurt and agitated, and said, 'Why do you treat me thus, Captain Bligh?' Captain Bligh then shook his hand in his face and said, 'No reply!' and called him a thief and other abusive names. He then ordered the quartermasters to go down and bring all the coconuts both from man and officer, and put them upon the quarter-deck. They were brought. The captain then called all hands upon deck, and desired 'the people to look after the officers, and the officers to look after the people, for there never were such a set of damned thieving rascals under any man's command in the world before.' And he told the men, 'You are allowed a pound and a half of yams to-day, but to-morrow I shall reduce you to three-quarters of a pound.' All declare that the ship's company were before greatly discontented at their short allowance of provisions, and their discontent was increased from the consideration that they had plenty of provisions on board, and that the captain was his own purser.[1] About four o'clock on the same day Captain Bligh abused Christian again. Christian came forward from Captain Bligh, crying; tears were running fast from his eyes

[1] During the mutiny Captain Bligh said to Mr Young, 'This is a serious affair, Mr Young.' Mr Young replied, 'Yes, it is a serious affair to be starved. I hope this day to get a belly full.'

in big drops. Purcell, the carpenter, said to him, 'What is the matter, Mr Christian?' He said, 'Can you ask me and hear the treatment I receive?' Purcell replied, 'Do not I receive as bad as you do?' Christian said, 'You have something [1] to protect you, and can speak again; but if I should speak to him as you do, he would probably break me, turn me before the mast, and perhaps flog me; and if he did it would be the death of us both, for I am sure I should take him in my arms and jump overboard with him.' Purcell said, 'Never mind it, it is but for a short time longer.' Christian said, 'In going through Endeavour Straits I am sure the ship will be a hell.' He was heard by another person to say, when he was crying, 'I would rather die ten thousand deaths than bear this treatment. I always do my duty as an officer and as a man ought to do, yet I receive this scandalous usage.' Another person heard him say that flesh and blood cannot bear this treatment. This was the only time he ever was seen in tears on board the ship, and one of the seaman, being asked if he had ever observed Christian in tears before, answered, 'No, he was no milk-sop.' It is now certainly known that Christian after this had prepared to leave the ship that night upon a raft; those who came with Captain Bligh can only know it by circumstances which they afterwards recollected, and which were the subject of conversation in the boat. He gave away that afternoon all his Otaheite curiosities; he was seen tearing his letters and papers and throwing them overboard; he applied to the carpenter for nails, who told him to take as many as he pleased out of the locker; and the ship intending to stop at no other island, these could have been of no use to him, but in case of his escape to land. Mr Tinkler, a young boy, one of Christian's messmates, was hungry in the evening, and went below to get some pig which was left at dinner; this he missed, and after some search found it packed up with a bread-fruit in a dirty clothes' bag in Christian's cot. When the launch was hoisted out, the two masts were lashed to a plank, which they were obliged to untie. This was the raft or stage upon which he intended to leave the ship. These circumstances are remembered by those who came in the boat, but his design of going off upon the raft was frequently the subject of conversation afterwards in the ship. Norman, one

[1] By this he meant his warrant; the warrant-officers can only be punished by suspension and confinement, they cannot be broke and flogged like midshipmen.

of the four who were honourably acquitted, said to him after the mutiny, 'This is a hard case upon me, Mr Christian, who have a wife and family in England.'[1] Christian replied, 'It is a hard case, Norman, but it never would have happened if I could have left the ship alone.' Christian told them afterwards in the ship that he did not expect to reach the shore upon the raft, but he was in hopes of being seen and taken up by some of the natives in their canoes. The reason of his disappointment is said to have been owing to the people being upon deck in greater numbers than usual, looking at a volcano in the island of Tofoa.

All agree that there was no plot or intention to mutiny before Christian went upon his watch at four in the morning. The mutiny broke out at five o'clock, and all the mutineers were in bed when it began, except those who were in Christian's watch. How soon after four o'clock the conspiracy was entered into, before it was put in execution, does not appear. That there had been some agreement previous to the breaking out of the mutiny is manifest from the evidence of Mr Fryer, who was told by two of them, 'Sir, there is no one means to hurt you; no, that was our agreement, not to commit murder.' This statement cannot be reconciled with the testimony of Mr Hayward and Mr Hallet, who were both in Christian's watch, if the reader were not apprised of a circumstance which was not mentioned before the court martial; viz. that these gentlemen, who were very young at the time, viz. about fifteen, had both fallen asleep. The circumstance of the rest of the mutineers being in bed when the mutiny began proves that it had not been preconcerted with them, and it is remarkable that Mr Young was the only person among Christian's messmates who was concerned in it, and he was in bed when it broke out. On the 26th, before the ship left Annamooko, Christian and some other officers threw away their beads and trifles among the natives, as articles for which they would have no further occasion.

It appears from the testimony of every witness that the original intent was to put the captain on shore, with three other persons only, and if the smallest boat, which was hoisted out for that purpose had not been leaky, it is probable that this design would have been carried into execution; but by the time that the second cutter or boat was got into the water a great number desired to leave the ship and requested the launch.

[1] Norman's family live at Portsmouth.

It is agreed by all that every person who went into the launch went voluntarily, or might have continued on board if he had wished to stay, except the four who were first ordered into the small boat, and afterwards Mr Fryer, who was commanded to go in consequence of his design to retake the ship being over-heard. It is indeed expressly proved by Mr Hallet that the boatswain and carpenters told Christian they would prefer going in the boat to staying in the ship, and he said he did not wish them, or any other, to stay against their inclination, or to go; and that the most part went voluntarily. And Mr Hayward in his evidence has also deposed, 'I heard no one ordered to go into the boat, but Mr Hallet, Mr Samuel, and myself.' Although Mr Fryer himself wished to stay, from a very laudable motive, viz. that of retaking the ship, yet being obliged to go he earnestly requested that his brother-in-law Tinkler, then a young boy, might be permitted to follow him.[1] In such a dilemma the alternative was dreadful, yet those who went voluntarily into the launch were sure of getting to shore, where they expected to live until an European ship arrived or until they could raise their boat or build a greater, as one of the mutineers said of the carpenter, 'You might as well give him the ship as his tool-chest.' It is proved by Mr Hallet that they were veered astern in order to be towed towards the land, which was so near that it is said they might see them reach the shore from the masthead of the ship.

After the mutiny commenced it was between three and four hours before the launch left the ship, and one reason, besides the number of persons, why she was so deeply laden was that almost all Captain Bligh's property in boxes and trunks was put on board. A short time after it had quitted the ship Christian declared that he would readily sacrifice his own life if the persons in the launch were all safe in the ship again.'

At Annamooko, besides the cooper's adze being stolen, the natives, by diving, had cut and carried off a grapnel by which a boat was fastened. Captain Bligh, in order to compel the natives to restore it, had made them believe he would sail away with their chiefs whom he had on board. This was unattended

---

[1] It is worthy of notice that Lamb the butcher was a mutineer, but when he saw such a number going off in the launch, he actually laid down his arms and joined them; he afterwards died at Batavia. Martin, another mutineer, attempted to get into the launch, but was opposed by the carpenter, who said he would get him hanged when they got to England; and he was then ordered back by the people in the ship.

with success, as they assured him the grapnel had been carried away in a canoe belonging to another island; but the people of the island, who crowded round the ship to entreat the deliverance of their chiefs, and the chiefs themselves were greatly frightened and distressed before they were set at liberty. For Captain Bligh carried them out some distance to sea, and they were followed and taken back in canoes.[1] This unfortunate circumstance is supposed to have been the cause of the rough reception which the people in the launch met with at Tofoa. For Nageete, one of the chiefs who had been thus frightened, had come upon a visit from Annamooko, though ten leagues distant, and was one of the first persons they saw at Tofoa. He appeared at the first friendly, yet it is thought that he was glad of having this opportunity of resenting the treatment he had received in the ship at Annamooko.

Those who came in the boat, though they gave vent to no open complaints, yet sometimes made allusions in the hearing of the captain to what had passed previous to the mutiny. Captain Bligh was one day observing that it was surprising that this should have happened after he had been so kind to the people, by making them fine messes of wheat; upon which Mr Hallet replied, 'If it had not been for your fine messes and fine doings we should have had the ship for our resource [2] instead of the boat.'

In a misunderstanding about some oysters, between the captain and the carpenter, Captain Bligh told him, 'If I had not taken so much pains with you, you would never have been here'; the carpenter replied, 'Yes, if you had not taken so much pains with us, we should never have been here.'

In the evidence of Mr Peckover and Mr Fryer it is proved that Mr Nelson the botanist said, upon hearing the commencement of the mutiny, 'We know whose fault this is, or who is to blame; and oh! Mr Fryer, what have we brought upon our-

[1] When Mr Nelson told Mr Peckover that the ship is taken from us, Mr Peckover in his evidence says he answered, 'We were a long way from land when I came off deck' (thinking, as he declares, that the people in the canoes had followed and taken the ship); and so it was understood by Mr Nelson, who replies, 'It is by our own people.'
[2] It must be supposed that after a distance of time, although the ideas and impression are remembered, the exact words will be forgotten; but one person particularly recollects that Mr Hallet used the word 'resource' upon this occasion, because he afterwards fancied it was thus suggested to Captain Bligh's mind, as the name which he gave to the vessel purchased at Timor.

selves?' In addition to this, it ought to be known that Mr
Nelson, in conversation afterwards with an officer at Timor,
who was speaking of returning with Captain Bligh if he got
another ship, observed, 'I am surprised that you should think
of going a second time with one (using a term of abuse) who
has been the occasion of all our losses.'

In Captain Bligh's *Narrative* no mention is made of the two
little boats or cutters; the least boat would not hold more than
six, and the larger more than nine, persons. But after Captain
Bligh relates that he was brought upon deck, he proceeds thus
in the two next paragraphs:

'The boatswain was now ordered to hoist out the *launch*,
with a threat if he did not do it instantly to take care of
himself.

'The *boat* being out, Mr Heywood and Mr Hallet, midshipmen, and Mr Samuel were ordered into it' (p. 2).

Every reader must have supposed that the boat mentioned
in the latter paragraph was the same as the launch in the
former, and that these four was the first of the nineteen who
were ordered into it.

If the small boats had been distinctly mentioned in Captain
Bligh's *Narrative* it would have been manifest to all the world
that the mutiny could not have been the result of a conspiracy
of twenty-five of the people to turn the other nineteen into one
or both of them.

Indeed, many readers had the penetration to think that it
was incredible and almost beyond any calculation of probability that twenty-five persons could have been seduced to have
concurred in such a horrid plot, without a single one having the
virtue to resist the temptation and to disclose the design to
the captain.

In the *Narrative*, p. 8, there is this memorable paragraph:
'Notwithstanding the roughness with which I was treated, the
remembrance of past kindnesses produced some signs of remorse
in Christian. When they were forcing me out of the ship I
asked him if this treatment was a proper return for the many
instances he had received of my friendship? He appeared
disturbed at my question, and answered with much emotion,
"That, Captain Bligh—that is the thing; I am in hell—I am
in hell."' In Mr Purcell's evidence before the court this conversation is sworn to thus: 'Captain Bligh attempted to speak
to Christian, who said, "Hold your tongue, and I'll not hurt

you; it is too late to consider now. I have been in hell for weeks past with you." ' But all who were upon deck and overheard the whole of this conversation state it thus: 'Captain Bligh, addressing himself to Christian, said, "Consider, Mr Christian, I have a wife and four children in England, and you have danced my children upon your knee." Christian replied, "You should have thought of them sooner yourself, Captain Bligh; it is too late to consider now. I have been in hell for weeks past with you." ' Christian afterwards told the people in the ship that 'when Bligh spoke of his wife and children my heart melted, and I would then have jumped overboard if I could have saved you, but as it was too late to do that I was obliged to proceed.' One person who heard what passed immediately after Captain Bligh was brought upon deck says that Captain Bligh asked Christian, 'What is the meaning of all this?' And Christian answered, 'Can you ask, Captain Bligh, when you know you have treated us officers and all these poor fellows like Turks?'

Captain Bligh in his *Narrative* asserts, 'When we were sent away "Huzza for Otaheite!" was frequently heard among the mutineers' (p. 7). But every one of those who came in the boat, as well as all who stayed in the ship, declare that they neither heard nor observed any huzzaing whatever in the ship.

In Captain Bligh's *Narrative*, p. 11, there is the following paragraph: 'Had their mutiny been occasioned by any grievances, either real or imaginary, I must have discovered symptoms of their discontent, which would have put me upon my guard, but the case was far otherwise. Christian in particular I was on the most friendly terms with. That very day he was engaged to have dined with me; and the preceding night he excused himself from supping with me, on pretence of being unwell, for which I felt concerned, having no suspicion of his integrity and honour.'

It is said that the captain had his officers to dine with him in rotation, and Christian's turn might have fallen on the day of the mutiny, but in consequence of the charge of stealing the coconuts, the gentlemen (or most of them) had resolved not to dine again at the captain's table. Mr Fryer had not dined there for a long time before. It is true that Captain Bligh had asked Christian to supper, but it now appears he excused himself not to meditate the destruction of his benefactor, but his own flight.

It was proved at the trial that Christian, during the mutiny, told Mr Fryer, 'You know, Mr Fryer, I have been in hell on board this ship for weeks past'; and that he said to the captain, 'I have been in hell for weeks past with you'; but what particular period Christian referred to, or when the poignancy of his distress had begun to prey upon his mind, does not appear. But instances are mentioned of Christian's being hurt by Captain Bligh's treatment even at the Cape of Good Hope in their outward bound voyage. Christian had the command of the tent on shore at Otaheite, where Captain Bligh sometimes entertained the chiefs of the island, and before all the company used to abuse Christian for some pretended fault or other, and the chiefs would afterwards take an opportunity of observing to Christian, 'Titriano, Brie worrite beha' (i.e. 'Christian, Bligh is perhaps angry with you'). Christian would turn it off by saying, 'No, no.' But he afterwards complained to the officers of the captain's cruelty in abusing him before the people of the country, observing that he would not regard it if he would only find fault with him in private. There is no country in the world where the notions of aristocracy and family pride are carried higher than at Otaheite, and it is a remarkable circumstance that the chiefs are naturally distinguished by taller persons, and more open and intelligent countenances, than the people of inferior condition. Hence these are the principal qualities by which the natives estimate the gentility of strangers, and Christian was so great a favourite with them that according to the words of one person, 'they adored the very ground he trod upon.' He was *tyo*, or friend, to a chief of the first rank in the island, whose name, according to the custom of the country, he took in exchange for his own, and in whose property he participated. This chief dined one day with Captain Bligh and was told by him that his *tyo* Christian was only his *towtow*, or servant. The chief upbraided Christian with this, who was much mortified at being thus degraded in the opinion of his friend, and endeavoured to recommend himself again to the chief by assuring him that he, Captain Bligh, and all the officers were *towtows* of the King of Bretane.

These circumstances, although comparatively trifling, are such as to be distinctly remembered; but they prove that there could be little harmony where such painful sensations were so frequently and unnecessarily excited.

A regard to truth obliges the writer of this Appendix to add that Captain Bligh has told some of Christian's relations that after they sailed from Otaheite, Christian, when he was upon duty, had put the ship in great danger; from which Captain Bligh supposed that it had been his intention to cripple the ship that they might be obliged to return to Otaheite to repair. But no such circumstance is remembered by any person besides the captain.[1] Captain Bligh has also declared that the persons in the launch 'were turned out to certain destruction, because the mutineers had not the courage to embrue their hands in blood.' It has already been observed that it is proved before the court martial that most of the persons went into the launch voluntarily. And it is certainly true, that although the sufferings of the persons in the boat were distressful to the last degree, they were not the occasion of the death of Mr Nelson at Timor or of those who died at Batavia, for all recovered from the extremity to which they had been reduced by this unhappy voyage.

It is agreed that Christian was the first to propose the mutiny, and the project of turning the captain on shore at Tofoa to the people in his watch; but he declared afterwards in the ship, he never should have thought of it if it had not been suggested to his mind by an expression of Mr Stewart, who knowing of his intention of leaving the ship upon the raft, told him, 'When you go, Christian, we are ripe for anything.'

The mutiny is ascribed by all who remained in the ship to this unfortunate expression, which probably proceeded rather from a regard for Christian than from a mutinous disposition; for all declare that Stewart was an excellent officer and a severe disciplinarian, severe to such a degree as to be disliked by the seamen, though much respected for his abilities. Mr Stewart was in bed when the mutiny broke out, and afterwards was neither in arms nor active on the side of the mutineers; yet it ought not to be concealed that during the mutiny he was dancing and clapping his hands in the Otaheite manner, and saying it was the happiest day of his life. He was drowned

---

[1] They had sailed from Otaheite twenty-four days when the mutiny broke out; and as in those seas a constant trade wind blows from east to west; in order to return to Otaheite they must have been obliged to have gone into a high southern latitude before they could have gained the advantage of the variable winds. Their return to Otaheite would probably have taken up twice or thrice twenty-four days. If the mutiny had been plotted at Otaheite, it is not probable the execution of it would have been so long delayed.

in the wreck of the *Pandora*. This gentleman is spoken of by all in terms of great praise and respect. He is said to have been the best practical navigator on board, even superior in that character to Captain Bligh and Christian.[1] Soon after the launch had left the ship Christian told the people that he had no right to the command, and that he would act in any station they would assign him. But they all declared that he should be their captain, and after some persuasion from Christian they permitted Mr Stewart to be the second in command, though they were desirous, from Stewart's former severity, of preferring Mr Heywood; but being told by Christian that as the ship must be at watch and watch, he thought Mr Heywood, who was then only sixteen, too young and inexperienced for such a charge, with some reluctance they acceded to his recommendation of Mr Stewart. The other arrangements being settled, instead of insisting upon going back to Otaheite, they told Christian he might carry them wherever he thought proper. Christian advised them to go to an island called Tobooy, which was laid down in the charts by Captain Cook, though no European ship had ever landed there. This lies about seven degrees south of Otaheite, and it was chosen because it was out of the track of European ships.[2] When they arrived there, and with difficulty had made a landing, although it was full of inhabitants, they found no quadrupeds but a species of small rats with which the island was completely overrun. They stayed there a few days, and then resolved to sail for Otaheite for a shipload of hogs, goats, dogs, cats, and fowls to stock the island of Tobooy, which they had fixed upon for their settlement.[3]

When they had reached Otaheite, in order to acquire what they wanted more expeditiously, Christian told the chiefs and

[1] Though all acknowledge Captain Bligh's great skill and abilities in theory and in making observations, yet they all declare, that in the practical management of a ship he was not superior to Stewart or Christian. For the two last are thus classed and compared with the captain. Captain Bligh was the best artist on board; Stewart the best seaman; and Christian was the best in both characters united. Stewart was several years senior to Christian, both in age and in the service.

[2] One of the four acquitted said, 'Mr Christian was a fine scholar, he carried us like a shot to Tobooy, and told us within half an hour when we should make land.'

[3] They prevailed upon the king to give them a bull and a cow, which were kept tied up as royal curiosities; but the voyage back to Tobooy was very tempestuous, and the bull being old could not stand upon his legs, and died in consequence of the bruises from his falls. There is a breed of English cattle which run wild upon the mountains of Otaheite, but the natives cannot be persuaded to make use either of their flesh or milk.

people that Captain Bligh had returned to Captain Cook, who had sent Christian back to purchase for him the different articles which they wished to obtain.

The story was the more plausible as the people of Otaheite had been told by Captain Bligh that Captain Cook was still living, and that he had sent him for the bread-fruit. Such is still their love and veneration for the memory of Captain Cook that the natives even contended for the honour of sending their best hogs and animals to Toote. The ship by this artifice being soon filled, they returned with some Otaheite men and women to Tobooy. It was thought that the Otaheite men would be useful in introducing them to the friendship and good offices of the natives. At Tobooy they built a fort,[1] and having stayed there three months, and finding the inhabitants always inhospitable and treacherous, the people of the ship grew discontented; all hands were called up, and it being put to the vote what should be done, sixteen out of the twenty-five voted that they should go back to Otaheite. Christian, thinking that this was the general wish, said, '*Gentlemen, I will carry you and land you wherever you please; I desire no one to stay with me, but I have one favour to request, that you will grant me the ship, tie the foresail, and give me a few gallons of water, and leave me to run before the wind, and I shall land upon the first island the ship drives to. I have done such an act that I cannot stay at Otaheite. I will never live where I may be carried home to be a disgrace to my family.*'

Upon this Mr Young, the midshipman, and seven others declared, '*We shall never leave you, Mr Christian, go where you will.*' It was then agreed that the other sixteen should be landed at Otaheite and have their share of the arms and other necessary articles; and he proposed to the rest that they should go and seek an island, not before discovered, where they were not likely to be found, and having run the ship aground and taken out everything of value, and scuttled and broke up the ship, they would endeavour to make a settlement. They reached Otaheite on the 27th of September 1789, and came to an anchor in Matavai Bay about eleven o'clock in the forenoon, and the sixteen were disembarked with their portions of the

[1] Christian, having endeavoured to convince them of the necessity of building a fort for their protection, assured them that he would take his share of the labour, and calling for a pick-axe was the first who began the operations.

arms and other necessaries. Christian took leave of Mr Stewart and Mr Heywood, and told them he should sail that evening, and desired them if they ever got to England to inform his friends and country what had been the cause of his committing so desperate an act; but to guard against any obstruction he concealed the time of his sailing from the rest.

The natives came on board in crowds as usual, and about twelve o'clock at night he cut his cable and sailed from the bay. The people on board consisted of nine Englishmen, about twenty-five men, women, boys and girls of different ages from Otaheite, and two men from Tobooy. It does not appear that any selection was made of the Otaheiteans, who are always eager to be carried away in an English ship. The ship was seen standing off the island the next morning, but from that day, for the nineteen months the others lived at Otaheite, they never saw nor heard anything more of Christian, and upon the arrival of Captain Edwards in the *Pandora* they could give him no further account of the *Bounty* than what is here stated.[1]

During his short stay at Otaheite Christian was much pressed to go on shore to visit the king, but he declined it, saying, '*How can I look him in the face after the lie I told him when I was here last?*' These circumstances concerning the *Bounty* subsequent to the mutiny must necessarily be collected from the seven persons who were left in the ship, and who are now, or were lately, in England. These say that Christian was always sorrowful and dejected after the mutiny, and before he left them had become such an altered man in his looks and appearance as to render it probable that he would not long survive this dreadful catastrophe. Indeed it is impossible that he should

[1] Sixteen were left at Otaheite, one of whom, in a quarrel about their arms, was shot by another Englishman, who was put to death by the natives as an act of justice; the other fourteen surrendered themselves to Captain Edwards, or were taken by the people of the *Pandora*; four of them were lost when the *Pandora* was shipwrecked; four have been honourably acquitted; two have received His Majesty's pardon; one has been discharged by the opinion of the judges in his favour; and the remaining three have suffered death according to the sentence of the court martial. Millward, one of the three, was in bed when the mutiny broke out; the other two were in Christian's watch; Ellison, one of them, was a young boy at the time.   When the others went down to arm themselves he was left at the helm.   He was afterwards active in the mutiny.   He had got a musket in his hand, which Christian having observed said: 'You little monkey, what business have you with that?' and ordered it to be taken from him.

have appeared otherwise, if he deserved the character which all unite in giving him.

In the *Royal Jamaica Gazette,* dated 9th February 1793, which announced the arrival of Captain Bligh in the *Providence,* the following was one of the paragraphs, and it has been copied into all the English newspapers:

'Captain Bligh could gain no intelligence of the mutineer Christian and his accomplices who were on board the *Bounty.* When they returned to Otaheite, after executing their infernal project, the natives, suspecting some mischief from the non-appearance of the commander and the gentlemen with him, laid a plan to seize the vessel and crew, but a *favourite female* of Christian's betrayed the design of her countrymen. He put to sea in the night, and the next morning the ship was nearly out of sight.' It is immaterial to inquire who was the author of this paragraph, yet it cannot but be remarked that it is totally different from the account which has been given by those who stayed at Otaheite, and who can have no possible interest in concealing this circumstance, if in fact it had existed; nor can it be reconciled with probability, or the treatment and protection which the Englishmen experienced from the natives when the ship had left them.

As this paragraph contains an assertion that Christian had a *favourite female* at Otaheite, it is proper that it should be known that although Christian was upon shore, and had the command of the tent all the time that Captain Bligh was at Otaheite with the *Bounty,* yet the officers who were with Christian upon the same duty declare that he never had a female favourite at Otaheite, nor any attachment or particular connection among the women. It is true that some had what they call *their girls,* or women with whom they constantly lived all the time they were upon the island, but this was not the case with Christian.

Until this melancholy event no young officer was ever more affectionately beloved for his amiable qualities, or more highly respected for his abilities and brave and officer-like conduct. The world has been led to suppose that the associates in his guilt were attached to him only by his seducing and diabolical villainy. But all those who came in the boat, whose sufferings and losses on his account have been so severe, not only speak of him without resentment and with forgiveness, but with a degree of rapture and enthusiasm. The following are, word for word, some of the unpremeditated expressions used by the

gentlemen and people of the *Bounty* in speaking of this unfortunate mutineer:[1] '*His Majesty might have his equal, but he
had not a superior officer in his service.*' This probably had a
reference to his age, which was but twenty-three. '*He was a
gentleman and a brave man ; and every officer and seaman on board
the ship would have gone through fire and water to have served
him.*' '*He was a good and worthy gentleman, and was dear to
all who ever knew him ; and before the fatal day his conduct was
in every respect such as became an officer, a gentleman, and a man
of honour.*' '*He was adorned with every virtue, and beloved by
all.*' '*He was a gentleman every inch of him, and I would still
wade up to the arm-pits in blood to serve him.*' '*As much as I
have lost and suffered by him, if he could be restored to his country
I should be the first to go without wages in search of him.*' '*He
was as good and as generous a man as ever lived.*' '*Mr Christian
was always good-natured ; I never heard him say "Damn you"
to any man on board the ship.*' '*Everybody under his command
did their duty at a look from Mr Christian, and I would still go
through fire and water for him.*' These are respectively the
expressions of nine different persons, and it is the language of
one and all. Mr Hayward, in his evidence, no doubt with a
proper sentiment of the crime of mutiny, has used the words,
'*Christian and his gang*'; yet that gentleman has declared that
until the desperate act Christian deserved the character described
by the strongest of the above expressions.

Christian, having stayed at school longer than young men
generally do who enter into the navy, and being allowed by all
who knew him to possess extraordinary abilities, is an excellent
scholar, and every one acquainted with him from a boy till he
went on board the *Bounty* can testify that no young man was
ever more ambitious of all that is esteemed right and honourable
among men, or more anxious to acquire distinction and advancement by his good conduct in his profession. He had been an
acting midshipman but a short time in the service when Captain
Courtenay, the late brave commander of the *Boston* frigate,
entrusted him with the charge of a watch in the *Eurydice* all

[1] One of the seamen, being asked if they never mutinied afterwards in
the ship, and told Christian they had as good a right to the command as
he had, said: 'No, no man would ever have mutinied against Mr Christian;
no one ever thought of resisting his authority.' One method, it is said,
which he adopted to prevent riot and confusions in the ship was to draw
off secretly the spirituous liquors from the cask, and he then persuaded the
people they had drunk them to the bottom.

the way home from the East Indies. This, no doubt, was extremely flattering to him, and he declared to a relation who met him at Woolwich he had been extremely happy under Captain Courtenay's command, and at the same time observed that '*it was very easy to make one's self beloved and respected on board a ship ; one had only to be always ready to obey one's superior officers, and to be kind to the common men, unless there was occasion for severity, and if you are severe when there is a just occasion they will not like you the worse for it.*'[1] This was after the conclusion of the peace, and within a few days the ship was paid off; and being out of employ he wished to be appointed a mate of a West Indiaman, a situation for which he thought himself qualified. Whilst he was in treaty with a merchant in the city to go in that capacity in his ship, Captain Taubman, a relation of Christian's, came to London from the Isle of Man and suggested to Christian that it would be very desirable for him to serve under so experienced a navigator as Captain Bligh, who had been sailing-master to Captain Cook, and who was then in the merchants' service; and as Captain Taubman was acquainted with Captain Bligh, he offered to make an application to him in Christian's favour. The application was made, and Captain Bligh returned a polite answer, that he was sorry he could not take Christian, having then his complement of officers. Upon this Christian of his own accord observed that 'wages were no object, he only wished to learn his profession, and if Captain Bligh would permit him to mess with the gentlemen, he would readily enter the ship as a foremast-man until there was a vacancy among the officers'; and at the same time added, '*We midshipmen are gentlemen, we never pull at a rope ; I should even be glad to go one voyage in that situation, for there may be occasions when officers may be called upon to do the duties of a common man.*'

To this proposal Captain Bligh had no objection, and in that character he sailed one voyage, and upon his return spoke of Captain Bligh with great respect. He said that although he had his share of labour with the common men, the captain had been kind to him in showing him the use of his charts and instruments; but at the same time he observed that Captain

---

[1] Christian always spoke of Captain Courtenay as an officer and a gentleman, with the greatest affection and gratitude. The gentlemen and people on board the *Eurydice*, the writer of this Appendix has been assured, declare that Christian was the last person whom they would have expected to have committed such a crime.

Bligh was very passionate, yet he seemed to pride himself in knowing how to humour him. In the next voyage Captain Bligh took him out as his second mate, and before his return the captain was chosen to command the *Bounty*.[1] Christian, wishing to go upon a voyage where so much service would be seen, in which he would complete his time as a midshipman, and if it had been successful he would no doubt with little difficulty upon his return have been raised to the rank of lieutenant, was recommended to the Admiralty by Captain Bligh himself as one of his officers; and as it was understood that great interest had been made to get midshipmen sent out in this ship, Christian's friends thought this recommendation, as they do still, a very great obligation. Captain Bligh had no lieutenant on board, and the ship at the first was divided into two watches, the charge of which was entrusted to the master and the gunner; but after they had sailed about a month the captain divided the ship into three watches, and gave the charge of one to Christian, on whom Captain Bligh has always declared he had the greatest reliance. Such was his introduction to, and connection with, Captain Bligh; and every one must sincerely lament that what in its commencement had been so honourable to both, should in its event and consequences have proved to both so disastrous and fatal.

The writer of this Appendix would think himself an accomplice in the crime which has been committed if he designedly should give the slightest shade to any word or fact different from its true and just representation, and lest he should be supposed to be actuated by a vindictive spirit, he has studiously forborne to make more comments than were absolutely necessary upon any statement which he has been obliged to bring forward. He has felt it a duty to himself, to the connections of all the unfortunate men, and to society to collect and lay before the public these extraordinary circumstances.

The sufferings of Captain Bligh and his companions in the boat, however severe they may have been, are perhaps but a small portion of the torments occasioned by this dreadful event;

[1] Upon Christian's return from the second voyage to the West Indies with Captain Bligh, he had no opportunity of a personal interview with his friends, and he made no complaint by letter. But a person, who had sailed with Captain Bligh and Christian, both to the West Indies and the South Seas, being asked if Captain Bligh's treatment of Christian had always been the same, said: 'No, it would not long have been borne in the merchant service.'

and whilst these prove the melancholy and extensive consequences of the crime of mutiny, the crime itself in this instance may afford an awful lesson to the navy, and to mankind, that there is a degree of pressure beyond which the best formed and principled mind must either break or recoil. And though public justice and the public safety can allow no vindication of any species of mutiny, yet reason and humanity will distinguish the sudden unpremeditated act of desperation and frenzy from the foul, deliberate contempt of every religious duty and honourable sentiment; and will deplore the uncertainty of human prospects when they reflect that a young man is condemned to perpetual infamy, who, if he had served on board any other ship, or had perhaps been absent from the *Bounty* a single day, or one ill-fated hour, might still have been an honour to his country and a glory and comfort to his friends.

AN
ANSWER

to

CERTAIN ASSERTIONS

contained in

THE APPENDIX TO A PAMPHLET

entitled

Minutes of the Proceedings on the Court Martial held at Portsmouth, 12th August 1792, on Ten Persons charged with Mutiny on Board his Majesty's Ship the *Bounty*

BY CAPTAIN WILLIAM BLIGH

LONDON:

Printed for G. Nicol, Bookseller to His Majesty,

Pall-Mall

1794

AN ANSWER TO ASSERTIONS

It is with no small degree of regret that I find myself under the necessity of obtruding my private concerns on the public. A pamphlet has appeared under the title of *Minutes of the Proceedings on the Court Martial, held at Portsmouth, 12th August 1792, on Ten Persons charged with Mutiny on Board His Majesty's Ship the 'Bounty'; with an Appendix, containing a full Account of the real Causes, etc. etc.* This Appendix is the work of Mr Edward Christian, the brother of Fletcher Christian, who headed the mutineers of the *Bounty*, written apparently for the purpose of vindicating his brother's conduct at my expense.

The respect I owe to that public in whose service I have spent my life, as well as regard to my character, compel me to reply to such parts of Mr Christian's Appendix as might if unnoticed obtain credit to my prejudice.

Of the minutes of the court martial thus published, it is necessary to observe that they differ from the minutes lodged in the Admiralty Office, and in some places materially. One instance of this will appear among the proofs, which are here submitted to the public.

The information which furnished Mr Edward Christian with materials for his Appendix, he states to 'have been collected from many interviews and conversations, in the presence and hearing of several respectable gentlemen.' He then mentions the names of all the persons with whom these conversations were held, without distinguishing the particular information given by any individual.

The mixing together the names of men whose assertions merit very different degrees of credit, and blending their evidence into one mass, is liable to two objections: firstly, the impossibility of tracing the author of any particular assertion; and secondly, the danger, which to a reader is unavoidable, of supposing that the statements made by those who were actually accomplices in the mutiny, came from men of respectable character with whom he has thus associated them.

One of the hardest cases which can befall any man is to be reduced to the necessity of defending his character by his own assertions only. As such, fortunately, is not my situation, I have rested my defence on the testimony of others, adding only such of the written orders issued by me in the course of the voyage as are connected with the matter in question; which orders being issued publicly in writing, may be offered as evidence of unquestionable credit.

These testimonials, without further remark from me, I trust will be sufficient to do away any evil impression which the public may have imbibed from reading Mr Edward Christian's defence of his brother.

LIST OF PROOFS

I. Orders issued upon our arrival at Otaheite, to regulate our intercourse with the natives.—25th October 1788.

II. Orders respecting the confinement of three men who had deserted from the ship.—24th January 1789.

III. Letter from the deserters before-mentioned.—26th January 1789.

IV. Examination respecting the loss of His Majesty's ship the *Bounty* by the High Court of Judicature at Batavia.—13th October 1789.

V. Descriptive list of the mutineers.—28th April 1789.

VI. Orders given to Mr John Fryer, the master, on leaving him at Batavia.—14th October 1789.

VII. Letter from Mr Peter Heywood, midshipman, to Mrs Bligh.—14th July 1792.

VIII. Extract from Mr Peter Heywood's defence, on his trial by a court martial, held 12th August 1792, at Portsmouth.

IX. Letter from Mr Peter Heywood to Mr Edward Christian; published in the *Cumberland Packet and Whitehaven Advertiser*.—20th November 1792.

X. Letter published in *The Times*, 16th July 1794, from Mr Edward Harwood, late surgeon of His Majesty's Ship *Providence*.

XI. Affidavit of Joseph Coleman.—31st July 1794.

XII. Affidavit of John Smith.—1st August 1794.

XIII. Affidavit of Lawrence Lebogue.—2nd August 1794.

XIV. Letter from Lieutenant Hallet.—1st August 1794.

XV. Letter from Mr Edward Lamb, commander of the *Adventure*, in the Jamaica trade.—28th October 1794.

No. I

Rules to be observed by every person on board, or belonging to the 'Bounty,' for the better establishing a trade for supplies of provisions, and good intercourse with the natives of the South Sea, wherever the ship may be at.

1. At the Society, or Friendly Islands, no person whatever is to intimate that Captain Cook was killed by Indians; or that he is dead.

2. No person is ever to speak, or give the least hint, that we have come on purpose to get the bread-fruit plant, until I have made my plan known to the chiefs.

3. Every person is to study to gain the goodwill and esteem of the natives; to treat them with all kindness; and not to take from them by violent means anything that they may have stolen; and no one is ever to fire but in defence of his life.

4. Every person employed on service is to take care that no arms or implements of any kind under their charge are stolen; the value of such thing being lost shall be charged against their wages.

5. No man is to embezzle, or offer to sale, directly or indirectly, any part of the king's stores of what nature soever.

6. A proper person or persons will be appointed to regulate trade and barter with the natives, and no officer or seaman, or other person belonging to the ship, is to trade for any kind of provisions or curiosities; but if such officer or seaman wishes to purchase any particular thing he is to apply to the provider to do it for him. By this means a regular market will be carried on, and all disputes which otherwise may happen with the natives will be avoided. All boats are to have everything handed out of them at sunset.

Given under my hand, on board the *Bounty*,

    Otaheite, 25th October 1788.

                          Wm. Bligh.

No. II

All prisoners are to be kept upon deck in fair weather; and the sentinel to report their state in the night, every half-hour. The key of their irons is to be taken care of by the master.

The mate of the watch is to be answerable for the prisoners. When they are released for a while, out of necessity, he is to see them again securely confined.

The mate of the watch is to have the charge of a brace of pistols and one cartouche box, to be kept in the binnacle.

The mate of the watch is to take care the sentinels do not lounge or sit down.

No canoe is to come on board after eight o'clock at night, or any to go under the bows of the ship upon any pretence; but whatever is handed in or out of the ship is to be at the gangways.

All boats when moored to have everything handed out of them at sunset, and the sentinel is to report the state of the prisoners every half-hour, after the watch is set.

Given under my hand, in Oparré harbour,
on board the *Bounty*, 24th January 1789.

WM. BLIGH.

No. III

DESERTERS' LETTER, DATED ON BOARD THE 'BOUNTY,' AT OTAHEITE, 26TH JANUARY 1789

SIR,

We should think ourselves wholly inexcusable if we omitted taking this earliest opportunity of returning our thanks for your goodness in delivering us from a trial by court martial, the fatal consequences of which are obvious; and although we cannot possibly lay any claim to so great a favour, yet we humbly beg you will be pleased to remit any farther punishment, and we trust our future conduct will fully demonstrate our deep sense of your clemency and our steadfast resolution to behave better hereafter.

We are, sir,
Your most obedient, most humble servants,[1]

C. CHURCHILL,
WM MUSPRATT,
JOHN MILLWARD.

TO CAPTAIN BLIGH [*copy*]

---

[1] These three persons, who were afterwards mutineers, had run away with the large cutter and a chest of fire-arms; and this is what Millward, on his trial by the court martial, calls 'the former foolish affair.'

No. IV

TRANSLATION OF AN EXAMINATION BEFORE A COURT OF INQUIRY, AT BATAVIA, INTO THE LOSS OF THE 'BOUNTY'

This day, the 13th October 1789, came before Nicholas Van Bergen Vander Gryp, notary public of the Noble High Regency of Netherland India, residing in the town of Batavia. Present, the hereafter to be named witnesses: John Fryer, master; Thomas Denman Ledward, surgeon; William Cole, boatswain; William Peckover, gunner; William Elphinstone, master's mate; Thomas Hayward and John Hallet, midshipmen; John Samuel, secretary; and the sailors, Robert Tinkler, Peter Linkletter, Lawrence Lebogue, George Simpson, John Smith, and Robert Lamb; all here present declare, with previous knowledge of Mr Nicholas Englehard, superior marchand and sabandhaar and licence-master in this place, and by interpretation of Mr Peter Aeneas Mackay, sub-marchand, in the service of the Noble Company. That the truth is they have been together, serving on board His Britannic Majesty's ship the *Bounty*, commanded by the requirant.

That on the 28th April 1789 that the greatest number of the ship's company, consisting of twenty-five persons, by the break of day were mutineers, and before anybody had discovered or got notice of it had already secured the requirant, binding his hands behind his back and forcing him to come on deck in his shirt, where he was kept under a guard behind the mizen-mast. That the boatswain and the others were forced by the mutineers to assist in hoisting out the launch, which being done they were forced to go into her, and the last of all the requirant; after which they were veered astern on the ship by a rope, and soon after cast adrift in the wide ocean.

That there were in all nineteen souls in the launch, with a small quantity of bread and water and no fire-arms.

That it has been impossible to foresee what has happened to them, as they had sailed homewards from the Friendly Islands with a great cargo of plants in the best order.

That there was no possibility to retake the ship, or do more for the welfare of the king's service than what had been done by the requirant, who had been tied and kept apart from the attestants until he was let down in the launch.

That there were heard at the time several expressions and huzzas in the ship, which makes them believe that the mutineers are returned to Otaheite.

That on the night of the 28th they arrived at the island of Tofoa, one of the Friendly Islands, and remained there until the 2nd of May 1789, seeking provisions and water. That they were attacked that day by the natives, whereby one man, John Norton, was killed and they narrowly escaped.

That they, after having suffered all distress and misery, arrived the 14th June following at Coupang, in Timor, and that there David Nelson, gardener, died of a fever.

That they sailed from Coupang on the 20th August following, in a schooner for that purpose purchased, and arrived here at Batavia the 1st of October 1789, where that vessel has been sold on the 10th of that month; that likewise on the 10th of October died in the hospital, Thomas Hall.

Alleging that all above-mentioned to be the truth and verity, offering to confirm this given attestation with solemn oath.

Thus acted and passed in presence of Hermanus Abraham Simonsz and Francis Abraham Simonsz, clerks, as witnesses.

The minute of this act is in form signed, and put on stamp paper of twelve styvers.

Was signed N. BERGEN V. D. GRYP, Notary.

This day, the 15th October 1789, are heard by us Gose Theodore Vermeer and Jacobus Martinus Balze, members in the Honourable Court of Eschevans Commissaries, being qualified thereto by that court, assisted by the sworn clerk, Johannis Lohr, all the above attestants named in this act, and under translation of the sworn translator in the English language, Louis Wybrand Van Schellebeck, on the repetition of this their depositions, in which they declare to persist, with demand only that for more elucidation the following changes may be made to it.

That the affair has happened in the vicinity of the Friendly Islands, near the island of Tofoa.

That the whole of the ship's company at the time of the mutiny consisted of forty-four persons, of which twenty-five have mutinied.

That after they were overpowered they heard the mutineers

say, 'We shall in a short time return to the Society Islands';[1] and that the attestants, by homeward-bound, mean England.

On which, to prove the veracity of this their deposition, they give their oath, in the Protestant form.

Further is, by us commissaries, in our qualifications, and on request of the requirant, resolved of this act to give an account *in forma dupla*; of the same tenor and date, and both signed by the deposants, and authenticated by our common signature.

JOHN FRYER,
T. D. LEDWARD,

(*Signed*)
  G. T. VERMEER,
  J. BALZE.

WM COLE
WM PECKOVER,
WM ELPHINSTONE,
THOS. HAYWARD,
JOHN HALLET,
JOHN SAMUEL,
ROBT TINKLER,
PETER LINKLETTER, × his mark.
L. LEBOGUE, × his mark
GEORGE SIMPSON,
JOHN SMITH, × his mark
ROBT LAMB.

NOTE.—*By the desire of the court I was not present at these examinations. The originals are lodged in the Admiralty Office.*

No. V

Description of the pirates remaining on board His Majesty's armed vessel, 'Bounty,' on the 28th April 1789. Drawn up at Timor. Copies of this list were forwarded from Batavia to Lord Cornwallis, then Governor-General of India, at Calcutta ; to Governor Philips, at New South Wales ; and one was left at Batavia, with the Governor-General of the Dutch possessions in India.

Fletcher Christian, master's mate, aged twenty-four years, five feet nine inches high, blackish, or very dark brown complexion, dark brown hair, strong made, a star tattooed on his

---

[1] This fact, and the huzzaing mentioned in the preceding page, are denied by Mr Edward Christian in a very pointed manner (see his Appendix, p. 69); yet he professes to have received his information from 'every one of those who came in the boat,' the very persons who had affirmed both circumstances on their oaths in this instrument.

left breast, tattooed on his backside; his knees stand a little out, and he may be called rather bow-legged. He is subject to violent perspirations, and particularly in his hands, so that he soils anything he handles.

George Stewart, midshipman, aged twenty-three years, five feet seven inches high, good complexion, dark hair, slender made, narrow chested, and long neck, small face, and black eyes; tattooed on the left breast with a star, and on the left arm with a heart and darts, is also tattooed on the backside.

Peter Heywood, midshipman, aged seventeen years, five feet seven inches high, fair complexion, light brown hair, well proportioned; very much tattooed; and on the right leg is tattooed the three legs of Man, as it is upon that coin. At this time he has not done growing; and speaks with the Manx, or Isle of Man, accent.

Edward Young, midshipman, aged twenty-two years, five feet eight inches high, dark complexion, and rather a bad look; dark brown hair, strong made, has lost several of his fore teeth, and those that remain are all rotten; a small mole on the left side of the throat, and on the right arm is tattooed a heart and dart through it, with E. Y. underneath, and the date of the year 1788 or 1789.

Charles Churchill, ship's corporal, aged thirty years, five feet ten inches high, fair complexion, short light brown hair, top of the head bald, strong made; the forefinger of his left hand crooked, and his hand shows the marks of a severe scald; tattooed in several places of his body, legs, and arms.

James Morrison, boatswain's mate, aged twenty-eight years, five feet eight inches high, sallow complexion, long black hair, slender made; has lost the use of the upper joint of the forefinger of the right hand; tattooed with a star under his left breast, and a garter round his left leg, with the motto of 'Honi soit qui mal y pense'; and has been wounded in one of his arms with a musket-ball.

John Mills, gunner's mate, aged forty years, five feet ten inches high, fair complexion, light brown hair, strong made, and raw-boned; a scar in his right arm-pit, occasioned by an abscess.

John Millward, seaman, aged twenty-two years, five feet five inches high, brown complexion, dark hair, strong made; very much tattooed in different parts of the body, and under the pit of the stomach, with a *taoomy* of Otaheite.

Matthew Thompson, seaman, aged forty years, five feet eight inches high, very dark complexion, short black hair, slender made, and has lost the joint of the great toe of his right foot; and is tattooed in several places of his body.

William M'Koy, seaman, aged twenty-five years, five feet six inches high, fair complexion, light brown hair, strong made; a scar where he has been stabbed in the belly, and a small scar under his chin; is tattooed in different parts of his body.

Matthew Quintal, seaman, aged twenty-one years, five feet five inches high, fair complexion, light brown hair, strong made; very much tattooed on the backside and several other places.

John Sumner, seaman, aged twenty-four years, five feet eight inches high, fair complexion, brown hair, a scar on the left cheek, and tattooed in several places.

Thomas Burkett, seaman, aged twenty-six years, five feet nine inches high, fair complexion, very much pitted with the small-pox, brown hair, slender made, and very much tattooed.

Isaac Martin, seaman, aged thirty years, five feet eleven inches high, sallow complexion, short brown hair, raw-boned, tattooed with a star on his left breast.

William Muspratt, seaman, aged thirty years, five feet six inches high, dark complexion, brown hair, slender made, a very strong black beard, with scars under his chin; is tattooed in several places of his body.

Henry Hillbrant, seaman, aged twenty-five years, five feet seven inches high, fair complexion, sandy hair, strong made; his left arm shorter than the other, having been broke; is an Hanoverian born and speaks bad English; tattooed in several places.

Alexander Smith, seaman, aged twenty-two years, five feet five inches high, brown complexion, brown hair, strong made; very much pitted with the small-pox, and very much tattooed on his body, legs, arms, and feet. He has a scar on his right foot, where it has been cut with a wood axe.

John Williams, seaman, aged twenty-five years, five feet five inches high, dark complexion, black hair, slender made; has a scar on the back part of his head; is tattooed and a native of Guernsey; speaks French.

Richard Skinner, seaman, aged twenty-two years, five feet eight inches high, fair complexion, very well made, and has scars on both ankles and on his right shin; is very much tattooed.

Thomas Ellison, seaman, aged seventeen years, five feet three inches high, fair complexion, dark hair, strong made; has got his name tattooed on his right arm and dated 25th October 1788.

William Brown, assistant botanist, aged twenty-seven years, five feet eight inches high, fair complexion, dark brown hair, slender made; a remarkable scar on one of his cheeks, which contracts the eyelid and runs down to his throat, occasioned by the king's evil; is tattooed.

William Byrne, seaman, aged twenty-eight years, five feet six inches high, fair complexion, short fair hair, slender made; is almost blind and has the mark of an issue on the back of his neck; plays the violin.

Joseph Coleman, armourer, aged forty years, five feet six inches high, fair complexion, grey hair, strong made; a heart tattooed on one of his arms.

Charles Norman, carpenter's mate, aged 26 years, five feet nine inches high, fair complexion, light brown hair, slender made, is pitted with the small-pox, and has a remarkable motion with his head and eyes.

Thomas M'Intosh, carpenter's crew, aged twenty-eight years, five feet six inches high, fair complexion, light brown hair, slender made; is pitted with the small-pox and is tattooed.

The four last are deserving of mercy, being detained against their inclinations.

WM BLIGH.

NOTE.—*This description was made out from the recollection of the persons with me, who were best acquainted with their private marks.*

No. VI

ORDERS TO MR J. FRYER, MASTER OF THE 'BOUNTY,' ON MY
LEAVING HIM AT BATAVIA

SIR,

Whereas from a representation of the physician-general it appears that my life is in great danger if I remain here until the fleet for Europe sails, and that only myself and two others can be taken in the packet, which departs on Friday, the 16th instant.

I therefore impower you to take the command of the remaining officers and men, and order you to follow me to the Cape of

Good Hope by the first ships his excellency the governor-general small permit you to embark in; and as his excellency has been pleased to order that the people may be taken care of at the convalescent hospital, about four miles from town, where is a good air and the best of treatment, you are hereby required to see that every one remains there.

You are not to permit any of those who remain in town to be wandering about between the hours of nine in the morning and four in the afternoon.

You are, upon embarkation, or at a proper time, to get a knowledge of what charges are against His Majesty's subjects; and upon fairly and duly considering them, you are to draw bills for the amount on the commissioners for victualling His Majesty's navy (if it cannot be done as hereafter expressed), giving them a letter of advice, at the same time certifying that I sailed to the Cape of Good Hope before you in a packet that could not take any more men; my health being so exceedingly impaired as to render my existence very doubtful, and that the governor-general could not give us all a passage in one ship.

I have agreed with the sabandhaar that all debts on the government account, incurred for victualling or passage money, shall be presented to him; and then on your certifying the justness of it, and another signing officer, such account shall stand over until presented to government in England—that of all such accounts you are to secure copies, and to send them, by different opportunities, to me in England, signed as before mentioned, to the care of Messrs Marsh and Creed, agents, Norfolk Street, Strand. You are, for further security, to send one to your agent.

That before the departure of the people you are to allow each seaman one month's pay to buy warm clothing to pass the Cape of Good Hope with, and you may also give the officers one month's pay for the same use, except yourself and doctor.

I shall leave with you the money I received on the sale of the schooner—177 ducatoons, or 295 rix-dollars, for the expenditure of which you must produce regular vouchers; but you are to pay no account without consulting the sabandhaar, that such account is at a moderate price.

The board and lodging for yourself and doctor, you may consider to be paid at one rix-dollar per day; and for the boatswain, gunner, Mr Elphinstone, Mr Hayward, and Mr Hallet one rupee per day; and the charges for the seamen in the hospital from the 13th October, you must pay as demanded, allowing for your brother, Robert Tinkler, at the same rate, to be put into the general account.

Should it be demanded of you to pay the passage money for every individual before you sail, you are to draw bills on the treasurer of His Majesty's navy for the amount.

Before the ships are ready for sea, you are from time to time to apply to the sabandhaar, Mr Englehard, who will assist you for the good of His Majesty's service; and through him, or as circumstances may point out, you are to make all necessary application to the governor-general.

The remaining men and officers you are to take according to the ships they are put into, not separating Mr Hayward and Mr Hallet. The carpenter you must apply for to come with you, and is to be considered a prisoner at large in the ship.

On embarkation, you are to see that both officers and men conduct themselves with propriety and regularity.

On your arrival at the Cape of Good Hope, you are forthwith to join me; but should I not be there before the ship you sail in departs for Europe, you are to make the best of your way, in the same ship, and give an account of your transactions to the Admiralty.

While you remain here you are to examine into the situation of the people in the hospital twice a week; and if they are not properly treated, you must represent the same to the sabandhaar.

The carpenter having applied to me for clothes, you are to supply him with a month's pay to purchase the necessary articles he is in want of, and to see he is not ill-treated.

Given under my hand, at Batavia, 14th October 1789,

To Mr. J. Fryer, Master in His
Majesty's navy.

WM BLIGH.

No. VII

HIS MAJESTY'S SHIP 'HECTOR,' PORTSMOUTH,
14th July 1792.

DEAR MADAM,

As I make no doubt you have already heard of my arrival here as a prisoner, to answer for my conduct done on the day that unfortunate mutiny happened, which deprived Captain Bligh of his ship, and, I then feared, of life; but thank God it is otherwise and I sincerely congratulate you, madam, upon his safe and miraculous arrival in England. I hope ere this you have heard of the cause of my determination to remain in the ship; which being unknown to Captain Bligh, who, unable to conjecture the reason, did, as I have had reason to fear (I must say naturally), conclude, or rather suspect me to have likewise been a coadjutor in that unhappy affair; but God only knows how little merited so unjust a suspicion (if such a suspicion ever entered his breast); but yet my thorough consciousness of not having ever merited it makes me sometimes flatter myself that he could scarcely be so cruel; and, ere long, let me hope I shall have an equitable tribunal to plead at; before which (through God's assistance) I shall have it in my power to proclaim my innocence and clear up my long injured character before the world. I hear he is gone out again; if so, may he have all the success he can wish. Alas, madam! I yesterday heard the melancholy news of the death of your best of parents. I heartily condole with you for his loss, for in him I lost the most kind friend and advocate, whose memory I shall for ever revere with the highest veneration.

I have one request to ask of you, madam, which is that you will be so obliging as to inquire whether Mrs Duncan, in Little Hermitage Street, hath in her possession the clothes (which, if you remember) I left with her in 1787, and gave you an order by which you might at any time get them from her; so that if they are still there, you will be so good as to send them down here, directing them (*for me, on board His Majesty's ship 'Hector,' to the care of Sergeant William Clayfield, marines, Portsmouth, or elsewhere*); but if you can hear no tidings of them or her, you will honour with a few lines your much obliged,

Obedient humble servant,

P. HEYWOOD.

No. VIII

Extract from Mr P. Heywood's defence, on his trial by a court martial, held 12th August 1792, at Portsmouth. Copied from the minutes of the court martial, lodged in the Admiralty Office.[1]

Captain Bligh, in his *Narrative*, acknowledges that he had left some friends on board the *Bounty*, and no part of my conduct

---

[1] This part of Mr Heywood's defence does not appear in the minutes of the court martial published, or in Mr Edward Christian's Appendix.

could have induced him to believe that I ought not to be reckoned of the number. Indeed, from his attention to and very kind treatment of me personally, I should have been a monster of depravity to have betrayed him. The idea alone is sufficient to disturb a mind where humanity and gratitude have, I hope, ever been noticed as its characteristic features.

No. IX

The following letter, signed P. Heywood, with the Remarks, appeared in the 'Cumberland Packet, or Ware's Whitehaven Advertiser,' 20th November 1792, about three months after the court martial.

WE HAVE THE FOLLOWING IMPORTANT INFORMATION FROM THE MOST UNQUESTIONABLE AUTHORITY

The late most interesting trial at Portsmouth of the unfortunate mutineers of the *Bounty* will be shortly published by a gentleman of respectability who was employed before the court martial. That publication will astonish the world, and the public will then correct the erroneous opinions, which from certain false narratives they have long entertained; and will be enabled to distinguish between the audacious and hardened depravity of the heart, which no suffering can soften, and the desperation of an ingenuous mind, torn and agonized by unprovoked and incessant abuse and disgrace.

Though there may be certain actions which even the torture and extremity of provocation cannot justify, yet a sudden act of frenzy, so circumstanced, is far removed in reason and mercy from the foul, deliberate contempt of every religious and virtuous sentiment and obligation excited by selfish and base gratifications.[1]

For the honour of this county we are happy to assure our readers that one of its natives, FLETCHER CHRISTIAN, is not that detestable and horrid monster of wickedness which with extreme and perhaps unexampled injustice and barbarity to him and his relations he has long been represented; but a character for whom every feeling heart must now sincerely grieve and lament.

[1] The great resemblance between the last page of Mr Edward Christian's Appendix and this paragraph is very remarkable, if they were written by different persons.

When Mr Heywood, the midshipman, had received His Majesty's free pardon, he felt it his duty to write to Mr Christian's brother the following letter:

GREAT RUSSELL STREET,
5th Nov. 1792.
SIR,

I am sorry to say I have been informed you were inclined to judge too harshly of your truly unfortunate brother, and to think of him in such a manner, as I am conscious, from the knowledge I had of his most worthy disposition and character (both public and private), he merits not in the slightest degree; therefore I think it my duty to undeceive you and to rekindle the flame of brotherly love (or *pity* now) towards him, which I fear the false reports of slander and vile suspicion may have nearly extinguished.

Excuse my freedom, sir; if it would not be disagreeable to you I will do myself the pleasure of waiting upon you, and endeavour to prove that your brother was not that vile wretch void of all gratitude, which the world had the unkindness to think him: but, on the contrary, a most worthy character ruined only by having the misfortune, if it can be so called, of being a young man of strict honour, and adorned with every virtue, and beloved by all (except one, whose ill report is his greatest praise) who had the pleasure of his acquaintance.

I am, sir, with esteem,
Your most obedient humble servant,
P. HEYWOOD.

This character every officer and seaman, except one, on board the *Bounty*, who has yet arrived in England, now unites in bestowing upon him. The mystery of this transaction will soon be unravelled, and then the shame and infamy of it will be distributed in the just proportions in which they are and have been deserved.

No. X

Taken from 'The Times,' 16th July 1794

TO THE CONDUCTOR OF 'THE TIMES'

SIR,

A publication has lately made its appearance, entitled 'Minutes of the Proceedings of the Court Martial, held at

Portsmouth, 12th August 1792, on Ten Persons charged with Mutiny on Board his Majesty's Ship *Bounty*; with an Appendix, containing a full Account of the real Causes and Circumstances of that unhappy Transaction, the most material of which have hitherto been withheld from the Public; written by *Edward Christian*.' The obvious tendency of which is to palliate the conduct of Fletcher Christian, his brother, and ultimately to asperse the character of Captain Bligh. As if anything could be advanced in extenuation of a crime, at the bare recital of which humanity shudders; a crime marked by such circumstances as to be unexampled in the annals of nautical history. This publication, Mr Editor, is disgraced by gross representations and low malevolence, of which innumerable instances could be adduced were long details admissible in a newspaper. The shafts of envy are ever levelled against conspicuous merit, but they recoil with redoubled force on the impotent adversary. Captain Bligh's general conduct during the late expedition, which was crowned with the most ample success, his affability to his officers, and humane attention to his men, gained him their high esteem and admiration, and must eventually dissipate any unfavourable opinion hastily adopted in his absence. I trust that this imbecile and highly illiberal attack, directed by the brother of the arch-mutineer, will be received by the world with that indignation and contempt it so justly deserves.

I remain, sir, your humble servant,

ED. HARWOOD.

(Late Surgeon of His Majesty's ship, *Providence*, Captain Bligh.)

No. XI

Affidavit of Joseph Coleman

I, Joseph Coleman, late belonging to His Majesty's armed vessel *Bounty*, William Bligh, Esq., commander, voluntarily do make oath:

That Mr Edward Christian sent for me, and asked me concerning the mutiny in the *Bounty*, and about Captain Bligh; and I said, I knew nothing of him, but that he was a very good man to me.

I told Mr Christian that I never heard Captain Bligh say he

would make his officers jump overboard and eat grass like cows.

I told him that after the ship was taken, I heard the mutineers say he swore and damned them; but not that I heard him do it myself.   I said, I could never agree with the mutineers.

I never saw Captain Bligh shake his hand in Christian's face, or heard him damn him for not firing at the Indians.

I do not remember anything about the heap of coconuts being taken away, but by hearsay from the mutineers, after the ship was taken, and we came home.

I never heard, or told Mr Edward Christian, about his brother's expression, that 'he had been in hell for weeks past with you.'

I never knew or heard that Captain Bligh and Fletcher Christian had any words at the Cape or before the mutiny.

I never told, or heard, of Captain Bligh telling the chiefs at Otaheite that Christian was a *towtow* (or servant).

I never knew anything of Christian intending to make a raft to quit the ship.

I never told Mr Christian that Stewart clapped his hands and said it was the happiest day of his life.

I remember Christian having a girl, and of her going with him to the island Tobooy, and lived with him.

I said, I never could be easy with the mutineers, because they knew I was kept against my will.   Morrison threatened to blow my brains out.

I remember that Muspratt, Churchill, and Millward deserted with the cutter and arms while at Otaheite, and that they said many others intended to remain among the islands.

I remember that one of our cables was almost cut through at Otaheite, and that afterwards the captain had always a sentinel on the bowsprit.

I know the captain never suffered any man to hurt the Indians, or insult them.

I know we were at short allowance of bread, and that we were at two-thirds allowance of that article; but I remember that by the consent of every one we had only grog every other day while at Otaheite, and that was that we might not be in want in case we could not get through Endeavour Straits, and we did not want it so much at Otaheite, because we had plenty of coconut milk.

I never said more to Mr Christian than that his brother

behaved very well to me after the mutiny, and that I knew no harm of him before the mutiny.

I never said that Christian or Stewart was equal to Captain Bligh in abilities; I never thought of such a thing.

his

JOSEPH X COLEMAN.

mark

Sworn before me, at the Public Office in Great Marlborough Street, this 31st day of July 1794.

JOHN SCOTT.

(*A copy*)

No. XII

John Smith's Affidavit

I, John Smith, late belonging to His Majesty's armed vessel the *Bounty*, William Bligh, Esq., commander, maketh oath, that Mr Edward Christian sent for me and asked me how his brother (who was the mutineer in the *Bounty*) had behaved in the ship.

I said his brother was well liked in the ship, as far as I knew, by the people.

I never knew Christian and Captain Bligh have any words particular.

On the day before the mutiny happened I was sent by the captain to ask Christian to dine with him, but he said, 'I am so ill I cannot wait on the captain'; and I was sent again in the evening to ask Christian to supper, and he said he was so ill that he could not come.

When in working the ship, and things had been neglected to have been done at other times that the captain had ordered, I have known the captain to be angry and damn the people, as is common; but the captain immediately afterwards always behaved to the people as if nothing had happened.

I never heard the captain damn the officers, and call them names, and threaten to make them jump overboard, kill half of them, and make them eat grass like cows. I never heard any such a thing.

I never saw the captain shake his hand in Christian's face, and I never heard of it even that he did; or in any of their faces.

I never heard that the captain damned Christian for not firing at the Indians for stealing an adze.

I did not hear Christian say to the captain, 'I am in hell, I am in hell,' because I was below; but I never understood but that he did say so. The captain said so in the boat, and had it in his *Narrative*, which I never heard any one deny.

I never told Mr Edward Christian anything about the coconuts, or did I know anything about it, any more than that the captain found fault at a heap of coconuts being taken away; and I never knew or heard that such a thing could be the cause of the mutiny.

I never knew or heard of any words that the captain had with Christian at the Cape of Good Hope, but I always understood he was on good terms with the captain, and remember he used to dine with him every third day, and did so until the day of the mutiny, and frequently supped with the captain besides.

I never heard, or told Mr Edward Christian, that Captain Bligh told the people of Otaheite that his brother was a *towtow* (or servant), or ever heard of such a thing.

I never knew anything that Christian intended to make a raft, or ever heard of it until the mutineers arrived in the *Pandora*, and I never told Mr Edward Christian about it.

I never told Mr Edward Christian that his brother never kept a girl, for I remember he had a girl, and she was called 'Tittriano's girl,' which was the name Christian went by.

I never told Mr Edward Christian that his brother, or Stewart, was equal to Captain Bligh in abilities, nobody could say such a thing as that. I always saw Captain Bligh instructing him.

I never said to Mr Edward Christian anything about his brother's abilities, or anything respecting his qualifications, or the praises which he in his Appendix says were repeated by one and the other.

I remember that Christian always had leave to have grog out of Captain Bligh's case whenever he wanted it, and I always gave it him, and Mr Nelson the gardener, when they chose to ask for it.

I know that we were never at short allowance of provisions except bread, and that was one-third short; but I remember that at Otaheite all hands, by their own consent, had their grog but every other day, on account of the danger of going through Endeavour Straits, where we might lose our passage; and the want of grog at Otaheite we did not mind, because we had plenty of fine coconut milk, and the finest fresh pork, bread-fruit, and other things of the country.

Mr Edward Christian asked me how Captain Bligh was liked in the *Providence*, and if nothing had happened; and I told him nothing had happened, and all was well, and the captain very much liked.

I know the captain was always very kind to the Indians, and would not suffer any man to hurt or insult them.

This is all that I said to Mr Christian, the brother of Christian the mutineer on board the *Bounty*; and Mr Christian had no right to make use of my name in the manner he has done in his late publication.

I know that three of the mutineers, Muspratt, Churchill, and Millward, while at Otaheite run away with the cutter and arms.

I remember our cable being cut nearly through at Otaheite, in a stormy night, and that Captain Bligh afterwards ordered a sentinel on the bowsprit.

JOHN SMITH.

Sworn before me at Guildhall,
London, this 1st August 1794.

WATKIN LEWES.

(*A copy*)

No. XIII

Lawrence Lebogue's Affidavit

I, Lawrence Lebogue, late sail-maker on board His Majesty's armed vessel, William Bligh, Esq., commander, do voluntarily make oath:

That I was sent for by Mr Edward Christian to a public-house, and asked whether Captain Bligh did flog his people and why he kept them at short allowance; but the most of his questions were about Captain Bligh's behaviour to the officers of the *Providence*, and how he behaved to them, and if I thought they liked him.

I told him that Captain Bligh made no distinction, every

officer was obliged to do his duty, and he showed no more
favour to one man than another. I was sure every person in
the *Providence* would speak well of Captain Bligh—he was a
father to every person.

I said I knew Captain Bligh was a very great friend to Christian
the mutineer; he was always permitted to use the captain's
cabin, where I have seen the captain teaching him navigation
and drawing. He was permitted to use the captain's liquor
when he wanted it, and I have many times gone down at night
to get him grog out of the captain's case.

I have heard the captain damn the people, like many other
captains; but he was never angry with a man the next minute,
and I never heard of their disliking him.

I never heard of the captain abusing his officers, nor ever
said to Mr Edward Christian that he threatened to make them
jump overboard, or eat grass like cows, or shake his hand in
their faces.

I said Captain Bligh was not a person fond of flogging his
men; and some of them deserved hanging who had only a dozen.

I said we were never at short allowance but in bread, and that
we were at two-thirds, because we did not know how long it
would be before we got a supply, as we had to go through a
terrible passage near New Guinea. And for fear of being in
want of spirits the ship's company had agreed, while at Otaheite,
to have their grog but every other day, because they had plenty
of fine coconut milk and all they cared about.

I remember that a heap of coconuts, which the captain had
ordered to be saved as a rarity until we got to sea for a day or
two, when we should enjoy them, was taken away; and that the
captain told the officers they had neglected their duty and
disobeyed his orders; and that all the coconuts, on that account,
were brought upon deck; and the matter ended with their being
divided.

I never heard nor told Mr Edward Christian anything about
'I have been in hell,' which he speaks of.

I never knew, or heard, that Christian was ever found fault
with by Captain Bligh at the Cape of Good Hope, and I always
thought they were very good friends until the mutiny.

I remember very well that the captain came on deck one
night and found fault with Christian because in a squall he had
not taken care of the sails.   It was after we left Wytootackee.[1]

[1] Mr Edward Christian declares no one ever knew of this circumstance.

I never knew that Christian intended to go away on a raft; or could he have made one without its being known by every person.

I remember Christian had a girl, who was always with him.

I never heard anything at Otaheite that Captain Bligh had told the chiefs Christian was a *towtow*; I know the chiefs did not think so of any of the officers.

I never knew Captain Bligh find fault with Christian for not firing at the Indians at Anamooka.

I was the only person mentioned who sailed with Captain Bligh to the West Indies and to the South Seas, as Christian did, and I never told Mr Edward Christian that his brother could not have borne Captain Bligh's conduct much longer, because I knew Captain Bligh was always a friend to Christian, when he sailed with him to the West Indies as well as afterwards.

I know that three of the mutineers deserted with one of the boats and an arms chest with arms at Otaheite, because they wished to stay among the islands. Muspratt, Churchill, and Millward were the three, and they said many others intended to do it.

I remember one of our cables being almost cut through in a dark stormy night, which we thought was to let the ship go on shore; and that after that the captain ordered a sentinel on the bowsprit. This was at Otaheite.

Mr Christian asked me if I thought Captain Bligh could hurt his brother if he ever came home. I said Captain Bligh had such a forgiving temper that I did not think he would—unless the law of his country would hurt him. I said Captain Bligh was the best friend Christian ever had.

I remember that Christian was drinking with the carpenter, William Purcell, at twelve o'clock at night, although Christian was to be up at four o'clock in the morning to keep his watch, and that when the mutiny broke out that morning I saw a musket at Purcell, the carpenter's, cabin door.

Sworn to the truth of the fore-
going narrative, 2nd day of
August 1794, at Guildhall,
London.

The mark of
X
LAWRENCE LEBOGUE

WATKIN LEWES.
(*A copy*)

No. XIV

From Lieutenant John Hallet to Captain Bligh

Dear Sir,

I have just read a publication, by Mr Edward Christian, respecting the mutiny on the *Bounty*, and have made a few remarks thereon, which I have transmitted to you and beg that you will make any use of them you please.

I am, dear sir,

Your obedient humble servant,

John Hallet, Junior.

Having been long confined by a severe illness, and having consequently not mixed with the world since my return in February last from Jamaica, it was but lately that the minutes of the court martial, held in 1792, on ten persons charged with mutiny on board the *Bounty*, together with an Appendix to those minutes, published by Mr Edward Christian, reached my hands. As I was on board the *Bounty* at the time of the mutiny, and as my name is not wholly unimplicated in the Appendix, I cannot but consider myself bound, in justice to my own character as well as to that of Captain Bligh, to advance my mite towards the confutation of the very malevolent assertions and insinuations conveyed to the public through the medium of that Appendix. I will by no means affirm that I never heard Captain Bligh express himself in warm or hasty language when the conduct of his officers or people has displeased him; but every seafaring gentleman must be convinced that situations frequently occur in a ship when the most mild officer will be driven, by the circumstances of the moment, to utter expressions which the strict standard of politeness will not warrant; and I can safely assert that I never remember to have heard Captain Bligh make use of such illiberal epithets and menaces as the Appendix attributes to him. I must likewise declare that I always considered Captain Bligh as being a friend to Christian, and I have frequently heard Fletcher Christian assert that he had conducted himself as such. I remember a complaint of some coconuts having been stolen, but I did not hear that Captain Bligh accused any individual of the theft.

As to the insinuation of the people being at short allowance of provisions, I remember being at two-thirds allowance of bread, but at and from Otaheite there was full allowance, and fresh pork was thrown overboard because it could not be eaten while it was good, and during our stay there we were at half-allowance of grog. Whether the mutiny was preconcerted or not is a question which can be solved only by those who were concerned in it, because any officer or man apprised of the circumstances, and not being a party in it, must have been compelled, if not by his duty at least by the desire of self-preservation, to have counteracted the plot by his informations and exertions.

Much stress is laid on the most part having gone voluntarily into the boat; in answer to which I would only ask any person, endued with a proper sense of honour, if he would not rather commit himself to the evident danger of the boat than incur the risk of an ignominious death, or the stigma of being arraigned as a pirate?

The Appendix charges Mr Hayward and myself with the imputation of being asleep in our watch. With regard to myself, I deny the accusation; and with regard to Mr Hayward (who is now absent on service), I have reason to believe it is equally false, as I had conversed with him a few minutes before. Besides what immediately belonged to Captain Bligh, every person in the boat had some useful articles, and many general necessaries were included.

I am likewise accused of uttering some dissatisfaction to Captain Bligh in the boat, to which Mr Edward Christian seems desirous of attaching much criminality. I can only say that I do not remember to have used such words imputed; and even if I had uttered them, they are such as would bear an interpretation diametrically opposite to that put upon them. And it is worthy of observation that by the kind addition of a note, my whole offence is concentrated in the innocent word 'resource.'

As to Mr Christian's ability as an artist, or a seamen, I never considered them to bear any competition with those of Captain Bligh; and he certainly could not be called a fine scholar, as he did not appear to have received any portion of classical education, and was ignorant of all but his native language.

My situation in the *Bounty*, together with a proper regard to truth and the introduction of my name in the Appendix, has compelled me to advance so much, uninfluenced by any personal animosity to Mr Fletcher Christian, whose memory I wish had been quietly committed to oblivion; as I am convinced that the stain will be deeper impressed on his name by the endeavours which his friends have exerted in vindication of his character.

JOHN HALLET, JUNIOR.

MANCHESTER BUILDINGS,
  1st *August* 1794.

No. XV

Letter from Mr Edward Lamb, commander of the 'Adventure,' in the Jamaica trade, to Captain Bligh

ST GEORGE'S PLACE, ST GEORGE'S IN THE EAST,
28th October 1794.

DEAR SIR,

Upon my arrival from Jamaica I saw a pamphlet published by Mr Edward Christian, who in order to lessen the guilt of his brother, Mr Fletcher Christian, wishes to make the public believe that the mutiny on board His Majesty's ship the *Bounty* proceeded from your treatment of his brother and the other mutineers. I was much surprised at what Mr Edward Christian has introduced in page 78 in the Appendix, as he insinuates that your bad behaviour to Mr Fletcher Christian commenced during his last voyage with you to Jamaica, in the ship *Britannic*, when I was chief mate and eyewitness to everything that passed. Mr Edward Christian must have been misinformed, and known very little either of his brother's situation, abilities, or the manner in which he conducted himself during that voyage. He mentions his being second mate with you, when, in fact, he was no officer. I recollect your putting him upon the articles as gunner, telling me, at the same time, you wished him to be thought an officer, and desired I would endeavour to make the people look upon him as such.

When we got to sea and I saw your partiality for the young man, I gave him every advice and information in my power, though he went about every point of duty with a degree of indifference that to me was truly unpleasant; but you were blind to his faults, and had him to dine and sup every other day in the cabin, and treated him like a brother in giving him every information. In the Appendix it is said that Mr Fletcher Christian had no attachment amongst the women at Otaheite; if that was the case, he must have been much altered since he was with you in the *Britannic*; he was then one of the most foolish young men I ever knew in regard to the sex. You will excuse the liberty I have taken in addressing you upon so unpleasant a subject, but I could not pass over many assertions in the Appendix without feeling for a man whose kind and uniform behaviour to me, through the whole voyage to Jamaica, was such as to lay me under an everlasting obligation, and I shall still think myself fortunate in having engaged with such an attentive officer and able navigator as yourself.

I have no pique at Mr Fletcher Christian, but finding Captain Bligh's character suffering in the opinion of the public, I think it my duty to offer my services in the vindication of it, so far as comes within my knowledge; therefore, can I render him any service, he may command me.

I remain, sir,

Your most obliged and humble servant,

EDWARD LAMB.

To Captain William Bligh.

I submit these evidences to the judgment of the public without offering any comment. My only intention in this publication is to clear my character from the effect of censures which I am conscious I have not merited. I have therefore avoided troubling the public with more than what is necessary to that end, and have refrained from remark lest I might have been led beyond my purpose, which I have wished to limit solely to defence.

WILLIAM BLIGH.

3rd December 1794.

A SELECTION
OF THE CORRESPONDENCE
of
CAPTAIN WILLIAM BLIGH
Relative to
THE VOYAGE AND MUTINY
of
THE 'BOUNTY'

BLIGH TO SIR JOSEPH BANKS

NO. 4 BROAD STREET, ST GEORGE'S EAST,
6th August 1787.

SIR,

I arrived yesterday from Jamaica and should have instantly paid my respects to you had not Mr Campbell told me you were not to return from the country until Thursday. I have heard the flattering news of your great goodness to me, intending to honour me with the command of the vessel which you propose to go to the South Seas, for which, after offering you my most grateful thanks, I can only assure you I shall endeavour, and I hope succeed, in deserving such a trust. I await your commands, and am, with the sincerest respect,

Yours, etc.,
WM BLIGH.

DR RICHARD BETHAM [1] TO BLIGH

DOUGLAS,
21st September 1787.

MY DEAR SIR,

My health has been so very bad of late that it has even prevented my writing to my friends so frequently as I could have

[1] Dr Betham was Bligh's father-in-law.

wished, for of all things writing is become exceedingly irksome to me. I cannot, however, suffer you to leave England without expressing my best wishes for your health and safety during the long voyage you are going to undertake and that it may turn out prosperous and for your interest and advantage. I own I have a different idea of it from what I had conceived before I was acquainted with the circumstances of the vessel and the manner in which it is fitted out.

Government I think have gone too frugally to work; both the ship and the complement of men are too small, in my opinion, for such a voyage.[1] Lord Howe may understand navy matters very well, but I suppose mercantile projects are treated by him with contempt. Yet, in my opinion, the bringing the bread-fruit tree into the West India Islands must be as beneficial to them as the bringing the potato plant from Virginia by Sir Walter Raleigh to be cultivated in Great Britain have been of benefit to us and to all Europe. Philosophers are better judges in these matters than admirals, and Sir Joseph Banks is a much superior man to my Lord Howe. However, I'm most solicitous about the success of the voyage on your account, that it may not only be the means of your promotion, but attended with such emoluments as may enable you to live comfortably after the toils of the sea are past. . . .

I always imagined you would have been made master and commander on your going out, and some navy officers here persuaded me that you will have a commission for that purpose to be opened with your instructions in a certain latitude at sea —as no promotions in time of peace are made at land. But be this as it may, I hope to hear from you from the Madeiras; after which I fancy we shall not have another opportunity till you are upon your return by the East Indies. . . .

. . . Adieu, my dear sir, Heaven bless you and protect you in the course of this long voyage, and that you may return safe and well to your family and friends is and will be the constant prayer of your most affectionate father-in-law. I beg my love to Betty and the two little girls Campbell. Annie [2] and Betty, who is exceedingly well, all desire their love to you and your

---

[1] See also Lord Selkirk to Banks, 14th September 1787 (Mitchell Library MSS.), where the former bitterly complains: 'Only twenty-four able seamen, and twenty-one of all others, without a lieutenant or any marines, with only a surgeon, without a surgeon's mate.'

[2] There was an Anne Betham, who was the intimate friend of Charles and Mary Lamb.

friends and acquaintances here, Mr and Mrs Wilson in particular. Mrs Young, etc., beg to be remembered to you, and wish you health and success in your voyage. Once more adieu. Believe me, with sincerest esteem and affection,

Yours, etc.,
RICHARD BETHAM.

BLIGH TO SIR JOSEPH BANKS

'BOUNTY,' SPITHEAD,
Monday, 5th November 1787.

SIR,

I have been very anxious to acquaint you of my arrival here, which I have now accomplished with some risk. I anchored here last night, after being drove on the coast of France in a very heavy gale. However, by persevering, I am now in readiness, or will be in three days, to receive my final orders. I once before made an attempt to get here, but was glad to go into the Downs again, although of all other places it is one of the most disagreeable to be in. I think I cannot have much worse weather in going round Cape Horn, and it is with pleasure I tell you I think the ship very capable. This also is another consolation to me, for my ideas of making a ship fit for sea and of those above were very different, and my conduct in troubling the Navy Board for alterations cannot be reprehensible, for had I not got ye masts, yards, and tops all altered I should not be getting ready to go into the harbour. The master is a very good man, and gives me every satisfaction,[1] and I think between this and the latitude of 60 south I shall have them all in very good order. The conduct of Nelson and the gardener[2] is very satisfactory, and we all seem embarked heartily in one cause, which I shall cherish as much as possible. I shall take eighteen months' provisions, which, with other supplies, will do very well, and my present intention is that, as I shall be late round Cape Horn, not to depend on touching there, but complete my water, if convenient, at Falkland Islands, for if I get the least slant round the Cape I must make the most of it. Lord Howe, when I took leave of him, behaved very flatteringly to me, but he took from me a Mr Brown you recommended, and was the

---

[1] He had good reason for changing his opinion of Fryer before the voyage was over.
[2] Brown.

best uncommissioned officer I had. He was sent to the *Ariel*, commanded by a Lieutenant Moorsom, designed for some private service, who, I am informed, is to be made a master and commander. My surgeon,[1] I believe, may be a very capable man, but his indolence and corpulency render him rather unfit for the voyage. I wish I may get him to change. The wind and weather is now very bad, and I fear will continue so for some days; but I assure you, sir, I will lose no time in proceeding on my voyage. As we have effectually got rid of that troublesome application about Mr Lockhead, and if I find no possibility of getting rid of my surgeon, I think it would be very proper for me to endeavour to get some young man as surgeon's mate, and enter him as A.B., for I am aware how improper any application for one publicly would be at this crisis. I have just now waited on Lord Hood,[2] who has not yet received any orders concerning me. The commissioner promises me every assistance, and I have no doubt but the trifles I have to do here will be soon accomplished. I shall take a pleasure of informing you of my progress as I go on, and I hope by the time my business is over here the wind will turn favourable. At present I could not move with it. I am particularly happy at receiving your letter of the 25th, and I trust nothing can prevent me from completing my voyage much to your satisfaction. Difficulties I laugh at whilst I have your countenance, and shall be always sufficiently repaid whilst I am admitted to subscribe myself,

Yours, etc.,
WM BLIGH.

Sir Joseph Banks has endorsed this letter: 'I offered my interest to any surgeon's mate who would go out as able seaman with C. Bligh.'

BLIGH TO DUNCAN CAMPBELL [3]

'BOUNTY,' AT SEA,
28th November 1787.

. . . I have found that Captain Cook and Clerk had a great many coals allowed them by the Government, and as I am at

---

[1] Thomas Huggan. That Bligh's fears were only too well founded is shown by many private entries in his private log-book. Huggan died from the effects of intemperance six weeks after the *Bounty* arrived at Otaheite.

[2] Viscount Hood was one of the Lords of the Admiralty.

[3] Duncan Campbell, West Indian merchant, uncle of Mrs Bligh.

upwards of £42 expense for what is on board, I have solicited
Mr Nepean from whom I have received obliging and kind letters,
to assist me in getting an allowance for the same as they are
for the use of the plants and forge.   I shall be very much obliged
to you, sir, if in the course of conversation you can back my
solicitation with Mr Nepean and then I think it will certainly
be allowed as Mr Stephens to whom also I have wrote promised
if I could find a precedent I should be reimbursed. . . .

Yours, etc.,

WM BLIGH.

BLIGH TO DUNCAN CAMPBELL

'BOUNTY,' OFF ST HELEN'S,

10th December 1787.

. . . If there is any punishment that ought to be inflicted on
a set of men for neglect, I am sure it ought on the Admiralty
for my three weeks' detention at this place during a fine fair
wind which carried all outward bound ships clear of the Channel
but me, who wanted it most.   This has made my task a very
arduous one indeed for to get round Cape Horn at the time I
shall be there.   I know not how to promise myself any success
and yet I must do it if the ship will stand it at all or I suppose
my character will be at stake.   Had Lord Howe sweetened this
difficult task by giving me promotion I should have been satisfied, but he has done it with a Lieutenant Moorsom of the *Ariel*,
bound on a surveying voyage to the East Indies, who was made
a lieutenant on 5th January 1784, whose difficulties are not
likely to be any way equal to those I am to encounter.

The last time I was here I wrote to Sir J. Banks about it and
Mr Nepean and from them both I had the most flattering letters
that if Moorsom got promoted Lord Howe could not object to
me—but to-day I have read a letter from Sir J. Banks wherein
he says: 'I only write this to assure you that though it was
impossible to get your name into the king's promotion as that
was designed entirely as a reward to those who had engaged
in the war equipment, no opportunity on my part shall be omitted
in which it may be urged with propriety, and the circumstance
of that very promotion among others shall not fail to be used as
an argument.'   But Mr Moorsom was not engaged in a war
equipment any more than I was.   The hardship I make known

I lay under is that they took me from a state of affluence from your employ with an income of five hundred a year to that of lieutenant's pay four shillings per day to perform a voyage which few were acquainted with sufficiently to ensure it any degree of success. . . .

Yours, etc.,

WM. BLIGH.

BLIGH TO DUNCAN CAMPBELL

'BOUNTY,' OFF ST HELEN'S,
22nd December 1787

. . . My absence is quite a secret to Sir J. Banks and every one except Lord Hood who has (although a stranger to me) behaved with the greatest kindness and attention. I had wrote to Sir J. B. and told him that as my orders were not sufficiently discretional, but enjoined me to make my passage round Cape Horn, I thought it hard at this late period of the year, and by return of post I received directions to do as I thought best. It is impossible to say what may be the result—I shall endeavour to get round, but with heavy gales, should it be accompanied with sleet and snow my people will not be able to stand it, and I shall not then hesitate to go to the Cape of Good Hope. Indeed I feel my voyage a very arduous one, and have only to hope in return that whatever the event may be my poor little family may be provided for. . . . My little ship is in the best of order and my men and officers all good and feel happy under my directions.

If I accomplish my passage round Cape Horn, I have no doubt of being home in the two years, but on the contrary it may make six months longer.

Yours, etc.,

WM. BLIGH.

BLIGH TO DUNCAN CAMPBELL

'BOUNTY,' OFF ST HELEN'S,
23rd December 1787.

. . . My little ship is in the best of order and my men and officers all good and feel happy under my directions.

If I accomplish my passage round Cape Horn, I have no

doubt of being home in the two years, but on the contrary it may make six months longer.

> Yours, etc.,
> WM BLIGH.

BLIGH TO SECRETARY STEPHENS

> 'BOUNTY,' at TENERIFFE,
> *9th January* 1788.

SIR,

I request you will be pleased to inform the Lords Commissioners of the Admiralty that I arrived here on the 6th instant to take in wines for the ship's company, which will be completed this day, and some damages done to my boats in a heavy gale of wind on the 27th December, and also the ship being repaired. I shall sail to-morrow and proceed on my voyage with the utmost dispatch, according to their lordships' directions.

> I have, etc.,
> WM BLIGH.

BLIGH TO DUNCAN CAMPBELL

> TENERIFFE,
> *12th January* 1788.

. . . I have the happiness to tell you my little ship does wonderfully well, but it would have been an end to our voyage if I had not profited by your experience and good advice. I have her now the completest ship I believe that ever swam, and she really looks like one fit to encounter difficulties, and is looked at as such, knowing our voyage. I shall sail to-morrow morning, and of course this must be my farewell letter to you. God grant my next to you may be from a desirable port, wind and time must point out where I am to touch next. . . . Having much to think of and little or no assistance my mind is pretty well employed, and as my pursing depends on much circumspection and being ignorant in it with a worthless clerk, I have some embarrassment, but as I trust nothing to any one and keep my accounts clear, if I fail in rules of office I do not doubt of getting the better of it. . . . My men are all well and cheerful and . . .[1] behave very well. Tom Ellison [2] improves and will make a very good seaman. . . .

> Yours, etc.,
> WM BLIGH.

[1] MS. is torn here.   [2] Afterwards executed for mutiny.

BLIGH TO DUNCAN CAMPBELL

'BOUNTY,' AT SEA,
17th February 1788.

. . . We are all in good spirits and my little ship fit to go round a half-score of worlds. My men all active good fellows, and what has given me much pleasure is that I have not yet been obliged to punish any one. My officers and young gentlemen are all tractable and well disposed, and we now understand each other so well that we shall remain so the whole voyage, unless I fall out with the doctor, who I have trouble to prevent from being in bed fifteen hours out of the twenty-four. I am at present determined to push round the Cape Horn without touching anywhere as I have plenty of water, but that must depend on the winds. We laid in a good stock of wines at Teneriffe and our allowance among four is a bottle every day and one bottle of porter, this with fine sour krout, pumpkins, and dried greens and a fresh meal five times a week, I think is no bad living. My men are not badly off either, as they share in all but the poultry, and with much content and cheerfulness, dancing always from four until eight at night. I am happy to hope I shall bring them all home well. Tom Ellison is a very good boy and will do very well. . . .

Yours, etc.,
WM BLIGH.

BLIGH TO SECRETARY STEPHENS

'BOUNTY,' CAPE OF GOOD HOPE, FALSE BAY,
24th May 1788.

SIR,

You will please to acquaint the Lords Commissioners of the Admiralty that after experiencing the worst of weather for thirty days between the latitude of 58° oo′ S. and 61° oo′ by constant gales of wind from SW. to NW. off Cape Horn, I have been under the absolute necessity of bearing away for this place, as I found it totally impracticable to get round the land and make the passage to Otaheite, agreeable to their lordships' first orders.

I hope their lordships will observe that it was not possible to make more of the season than I have done. I left Spithead on the 23rd December; Teneriffe on the 10th January; doubled Staten Land on the 23rd March, from which time the weather was exceedingly tempestuous, particularly the last three weeks, when the snowstorms became so violent we were scarce ever doing better than lying to and drifting before the wind. In this situation my people at last began to be affected with severe rheumatisms, and I had three accidents from the violent motion of the ship—two men fell and dislocated their shoulders and one broke a rib. The ship began to be leaky, but in all other respects as good a vessel as could possibly be. This increased our labour, and seeing no prospect of success I conceived it would be hazarding the object of the voyage, and my conduct reprehensible under the discretionary orders I was honoured with, to persist any longer, as I had not a moment's time to spare to proceed and refit at the Cape of Good Hope, and to be in time to pass the intricate parts of the voyage and to secure a completion of it. From these considerations I bore away on the 22nd April, repassed Staten Land on the 23rd, and, without ever being in any port from the time of leaving Teneriffe, I arrived here this day, with every man and officer in as good health as when they left England, notwithstanding for these last three months we have never been able to have our hatches open for six hours together.

I shall refit with the utmost dispatch, and proceed on the voyage by New Holland and New Zealand.

I have informed their lordships by letter of this date of my proceedings by a Dutch ship, and an opportunity offering by a French packet, *Havre de Grace*, I thought it my duty to take that conveyance also (to) send a duplicate of my first letter.

I have, etc.,
WM BLIGH.

BLIGH TO DUNCAN CAMPBELL

CAPE TOWN,
10th June 1788.

. . . I am satisfactorily repaid for all my trouble by bringing them all safe here without a single complaint. A Dutch ship came in to-day, having buried thirty men and many are sent to the hospital, although they have only been out since the last of January. This is a credit I hope will be given to me as my ship is not roomy or of size to be comfortable. Indeed, had I not been very conversant in these matters, I believe, poor fellows, they would scarce ever have got here. At one time when they saw no prospect of success they began to be low spirited, but I soon drove that away by assuring them if we failed I would soon be at the Cape of Good Hope, where they would have every comfort. This, with a fiddle playing every night from six to eight and their fun in attempting to dance on the fore-hatch, kept them in health and good humour, wishing for the time to come. Upon the whole, no people could live better. I fed them with hot breakfasts of ground wheat and sugar—portable soup and krout equal to cabbage made a valuable meal. Pease also mixed with the two former articles was equal to the greatest dainty and I supplied half their allowance of salt meat by giving them flour and raisins in lieu. I assure you I have not acted the purser with them for profits was trifling to me while I had so much at stake. I do not repine, but if the cruel inattention of the Admiralty had not detained me I should certainly have made my passage round the land. . . .

Yours etc.,
Wm Bligh.[1]

Bligh to Secretary Stephens

'Bounty,' in False Bay, Cape of Good Hope,
20th June 1788.

Sir,

This is the third letter since my arrival at this port that I have transmitted to you of my proceedings hitherto in the voyage; [2] the former ones were fully on the cause of my coming here. I therefore beg you will acquaint the Lords Commissioners of the Admiralty that His Majesty's ship under my command requiring much caulking and refitting has rendered it not practicable, consistent with the good of the service, for me to sail before the 26th instant, when I shall proceed on my voyage to Otaheite. As the conveyance of letters from this to England in foreign ships is very uncertain, it may not be improper (having had no other opportunity) to acquaint their lordships that the reason

---

[1] Bligh had no further opportunity of communicating with his family or friends until he reached Timor after the mutiny and the boat voyage.

[2] One of these letters, apparently written between 24th May and 20th June, is missing.

of my bearing away for this place is occasioned by my meeting with very tempestuous weather off Cape Horn, where I remained thirty days endeavouring to perform my passage that way. I left it on the 22nd of April, and arrived here the 24th May.

I have, etc.,

WM BLIGH.

BLIGH TO SECRETARY STEPHENS

'BOUNTY,' IN FALSE BAY, CAPE OF GOOD HOPE,
28th June 1788.

SIR,

You will please to acquaint the Lords Commissioners of the Admiralty that I am now ready for sea, with his Majesty's ship under my command, and shall sail and execute their Lordships' directions with the utmost dispatch. My route will be by the south part of New Holland and New Zealand. My people are in perfect health, and ship thoroughly refitted. This is the fourth letter I have had the honour to write to acquaint their lordships of my proceedings.

I have, etc.,

WM BLIGH.

BLIGH TO HIS WIFE

COUPANG, IN TIMOR,
19th August 1789.

MY DEAR, DEAR BETSY,

I am now in a part of the world that I never expected; it is, however, a place that has afforded me relief and saved my life, and I have the happiness to assure you I am now in perfect health. That the chance of this letter getting to you before others of a later date is so very small, I shall only just give you a short account of the cause of my arrival here—what an emotion does my heart and soul feel that I have once more an opportunity of writing to you and my little angels, and particularly as you have all been so near losing the best of friends, when you would have had no person to have regarded you as I do, and you must have spent the remainder of your days without knowing what was become of me, or what would have been still worse, to have known I had been starved to death at sea or destroyed by Indians—all these dreadful circumstances I have combated with success, and in the most extraordinary manner that ever happened, never despairing from the first moment of my disaster but that I should overcome all my difficulties. Know then, my own dear Betsy, I have lost the *Bounty*. . . .[1] The secrecy of this mutiny is beyond all conception, so that I cannot discover that any that are with me had the least knowledge of it. Even Mr Tom Ellison took such a liking to Otaheite that he also turned pirate so that I have been run down by my own dogs. I, however, have every expectation to get the better of everything. . . . My misfortune I trust will be properly considered by all the world. It was a circumstance I could not foresee. I had not sufficient officers, and had they granted me marines, most likely the affair would never have happened—I had not a spirited or brave fellow about me, and the mutineers treated them as such. My conduct has been free from blame, and I showed every one that, tied as I was, I defied every villain to hurt me; Hayward and Hallet were mate and midshipman of Christian's watch, but they alarmed no one, and I found them on deck seemingly uncerned [unconcerned] until they were ordered into the boat. The latter has turned out a worthless impudent scoundrel, but I beg of you to relate nothing of them until I come home.

I know how shocked you will be at this affair, but I request of you, my dear Betsy, to think nothing of it; all is now past and we will again look forward to future happiness; nothing but true consciousness as an officer that I have done well could support me. I cannot write to your uncle or any one, but my public letters, therefore tell them all that they will find my character respectable and honour untarnished. I have saved my pursery books so that all my profits hitherto will take place and all will be well. Give my blessing to my dear Harriet, my dear Mary, my dear Betsy, and to my dear little stranger,[2] and tell them I shall soon be home.

Remember [me] to your father and Annie Campbell and Mrs C., and give affectionate respects to your uncle and family. To you, my love, I give all that an affectionate husband can give—love, respect, and all that is or ever will be in the power of your ever affectionate friend and husband,

Wm Bligh.

[1] Then follow the details as given in the letters to Sir Joseph Banks.
[2] Bligh's 'little stranger' turned out to be twin daughters, Frances and Jane Bligh.

BLIGH TO DUNCAN CAMPBELL

BATAVIA,
13*th October* 1789.

DEAR SIR,

By the account that I enclose to you, you will see what hardships and difficulties I have undergone since I had the happiness to see you. . . .

It will very naturally be asked what could be the reason for such a revolt, in answer to which I can only conjecture that they have ideally assured themselves of a more happy life among the Otaheiteans than they could possibly have in England, which, joined to female connections, has most likely been the leading cause of the whole business.

My health has been much impaired, but conscious of my honour and integrity with a self-acquittal of every particle of disgrace. It has buoyed my spirits up in a most amazing degree—I have done more than ever man did; no man shares with me in what honour I may receive, for I have none that merit it; they, however, shall never bear any part of my misfortune. I have saved their lives most miraculously, and now to save my own I am obliged to fly from Batavia in the packet which sails on the 15th, and leave all my people behind me except my clerk and servant—I have been since here almost dead with a fever, but it seems to be at present tolerably removed—I am still, however, in a precarious state and scarce can write to you my head is so distracted, the sea air I hope will again re-establish my health.

I leave this account to be transmitted to you by the next ship that sails, but I hope to arrive in England long before it.

Should it please God not to give me life to return, let it be remembered there is no one here that is deserving of any attention from their country but my clerk,[1] who has shown much resolution and behaved well—also a young man, a Mr Hayward, but let this remain among ourselves until I return or not——

I think I see you feel for my situation, but let it be in no other point than for my health; my character and honour is spotless when examined, and I shall stand to be tried, despising mercy or forgiveness if it can be found I have been guilty even of an error in judgment. Happy it is for me that my clerk, while I was bound, saved my Journals and every kind of voucher, but everything else was lost. . . .

Mr Samuel.

I write to my dear Mrs Bligh, to your care, also by this opportunity, but she will require some information from you. My head is now distracted. . . .

Your . . . servt.,

WM BLIGH.

BLIGH TO SIR JOSEPH BANKS

CAPE TOWN,
16th December 1789.

. . . In this, you will find, sir, the misfortunes of a man who pledges his honour to you, could not be foreseen or guarded against, whose conduct will bear the test of the minutest inquiry, and who only regrets that you should see him so unsuccessful. But although I have failed in the completion of my undertaking I had accomplished most assuredly the most difficult part of it. My sufferings have been very great, but through the whole, that no dishonour could be reflected on your recommendation I have endeavour'd to make the remaining part of my voyage of some avail—even in my distressed situation. I went in search of Fiji Islands and discovered them or a number of others through which I sailed, and have made decent survey of them with respect to their situation. I have also done the same on the coast of New Holland, from the latitude 13° S. to the north of Captain Cook through the Prince of Wales's Islands in latitude about 10° 30′ S.—I was fearful having no arms to go near to New Guinea, otherwise I would have discovered how far Endeavour Straits was an eligible pass for shipping, but that, perhaps, is already done. . . .[1]

BLIGH TO SIR JOSEPH BANKS

LONDON,
Undated.

SIR,

It is peculiarly distressing that I am to be the person to inform you of the failure of an expedition, in which I had the honour to have your confidence and regard; but, sir, I undertook it zealously, and I trust you will find I have executed faithfully, securing every object but my return with the wonderful success I had acquired.

[1] Enclosed in this letter was an account of the mutiny. See letter of 13th October 1789.

If there is any one disposed to look unfavourably on the unhappy circumstance, I see with pleasure it can only be on the loss of the ship; for the intention of the voyage was completed. Your plants were secured in the highest perfection—everything in that particular even more than you could have imagined, and equal to that the world expected from your honouring the expedition with your countenance and direction, and in this rests the greatest satisfaction I am now possessed of.

As an officer and a navigator I have ever looked with horror on neglect and indolence, but I have never yet crossed the seas without that foresight which is necessary to the well-being of the voyage; but in the present instance I must have been more than a human being to have foreseen what has happened.

It is with a view that you may readily understand the whole of my misfortune that I present to you the following sheets, where you will find a series of distresses that are not made the most of; but simply a recital of facts as they happened and which I hope will show you that to the last I never lost that presence of mind, or professional skill, which you have been pleased to allow was the first cause of my being honoured with your notice.

I have the honour to be, etc.,
WM BLIGH.

BLIGH TO SECRETARY STEPHENS

BATAVIA,
15th October 1789.

SIR,
I beg you will present the enclosed account [1] of my transactions and of the loss of His Majesty's ship *Bounty* under my command unto the Lords Commissioners of the Admiralty, by which their lordships will please to observe I have begun the account from the arrival of the ship at the Cape of Good Hope after my return from Cape Horn.

I left at Timor, to be sent by the first vessel that sailed, other accounts for their lordships' inspection.

I have, etc.,
WM BLIGH.

[1] This account which differs little from that sent to Sir Joseph Banks has not been reprinted. See *post*, p. 310.

Bligh to Sir Joseph Banks

Batavia,
13th October 1789.

Dear Sir,

I am now so ill that it is with the utmost difficulty I can write to you; but as I hope to be in England before you can receive it, the necessary information which perhaps may be omitted in this letter will be of no consequence.

I have, however, for your satisfaction, enclosed to you a short account of my voyage. It is nearly a copy of what I have given to the Governor of Coupang and the Governor-General here, because my weak habit of body at present will not allow me to do more.

You will now, sir, with all your generous endeavours for the public good, see an unfortunate end to the undertaking; and I feel very sensible how you will receive the news of the failure of an expedition that promised so much. The anxious and miserable hours I have passed is beyond my description; but while I have health the strange vicissitude of human affairs can never affect me. Unhappily, I have lost it at present, for on my arrival here I was seized with a fever, which, fixing in my head, it made me almost distracted; but now I am better, and am to sail in the packet on Thursday next, which will save my life.

You will find that the ship was taken from me in the most extraordinary manner, and I presume to say it could not have been done in any other way. I can, however, sir, promise to you that my honour and character is without a blemish, and I shall appear as soon as I possibly can before the Admiralty that my conduct may be inquired into, and where I shall convince the world I stand as an officer despising mercy and forgiveness if my conduct is at all blameable.

Had I been accidentally appointed to the command the loss of the ship would give me no material concern; but when I reflect that it was through you, sir, who undertook to assert I was fully capable, and the eyes of every one regarding the progress of the voyage, and perhaps more with envy than with delight, I cannot say but it affects me considerably. To those, however, who may be disposed to blame, let them see I had, in fact, completed my undertaking. What man's situation could be so peculiarly flattering as mine twelve hours before the loss of the ship? Everything was in the most perfect order, and we were well stored with every necessary both for service and health. By early attention to those particulars I acted against the power of chance in case I could not get through Endeavour Straits, as well as against any accident that might befall me in them; and to add to this, I had most successfully got my plants in a most flourishing and fine order, so that upon the whole the voyage was three-quarters over, and the remaining part no way doubtful. Every person was in the most perfect health, to establish which I had taken the greatest pains, and bore a most anxious care through the whole course of the voyage.

I even rejected carrying stock for my own use, and throwing away the hencoops and every convenience I roofed a place over the quarter-deck and filled it with plants, which I looked at with delight every day of my life.

I can only conjecture that the pirates (among whom is poor Nelson's assistant) have ideally assured themselves of a more happy life among the Otaheiteans than they could possibly have in England, which, joined to some female connections, has most likely been the leading cause of the whole business.

If I had been equipped with officers and marines the piracy could never have happened.

I arrived here on the 1st instant, and solicited the governor-general to be allowed a passage in the first ship that sailed for Europe, but he had told me that he could not possibly send us all in one ship, but has consented, as granting me a favour, to be allowed to go in the packet, for the physician-general has represented my life in danger if I remain here.

I am, etc.,
WM BLIGH.

[Enclosure]
BLIGH TO SIR JOSEPH BANKS [1]

On the 16th August 1787 I received my commission to command His Majesty's armed vessel *Bounty* (for that was her establishment), and to fit her out with the utmost dispatch for remote parts.

The burden of this ship was nearly 215 tons, her extreme length on deck 90 ft. 10 in., and breadth, from outside to outside

[1] This letter was sent to Sir Joseph Banks on 13th October 1789.

RELATIVE TO VOYAGE AND MUTINY 311

of the bends, 24 ft. 3 in., a flush deck, and a pretty figure-head of a woman in a riding-habit.

The complement of men and officers:

(*Here follows list previously transcribed.*) [1]

Out of the number forty-five is one borne not actually on board, his pay going to the support of widows, so that the real number on board were forty-four seamen and officers, likewise one botanist and an assistant, the whole being forty-six.

On the 4th October I was fully victualled and stored for eighteen months, and on the 20th November 1787 I received my final orders to proceed on my voyage, the purport of which was as follows:

The king, upon a representation from his subjects in the West Indies that the introduction of the bread-fruit tree among them would be of universal good to constitute an article of food, and that such having been signified to be His Majesty's pleasure unto the Lords Commissioners of the Admiralty by Lord Sydney, one of his principal secretaries of state; I was therefore directed to sail forthwith round Cape Horn for the Society Islands, in latitude about 18° S. and longitude 210° E. of Greenwich, and there, with the necessary articles I was furnished with, to procure of the natives as many plants as I could stow on board the ship.

Having completed this I was to proceed through Endeavour Straits (which separate New Guinea from New Holland), and from thence to Prince's Island, in the Straits of Sunda, leaving to my discretion to touch at Java or any other island for refreshment and water as I might think proper.

From Prince's Island I was to proceed discretionally to St Vincent's, one of the Windward Islands, and depositing one-half of my plants there, I was to go immediately to Jamaica, and having given the remainder there to persons appointed to receive them, I was then, with such plants as were directed by His Majesty to be put on board, to return to England.

This was the sole design of my voyage, to complete which I sailed from Spithead on the 23rd December 1787.

On the 23rd March 1788 I doubled Staten Land,[2] and attempted to make my passage round Cape Horn, between the latitude of 59° S. and 61° S., but I met with such dreadful tempestuous weather and mountainous seas, with hail and snow storms, that, although I tried it for thirty days, I could not accomplish it.

---

[1] See page 4, *ante.* [2] Staten Island.

I therefore (as my people were getting ill, and I had the honour to have the most discretionary orders to do as I thought best for the good of the voyage) determined to bear away for the Cape of Good Hope on the 22nd of April and repassed Staten Land the next day.

On the 24th May anchored at the Cape of Good Hope, and having refitted and completed my stores and provisions, I sailed on the 1st July 1788, arrived at Van Diemen's land on the 20th August, and having completed wooding and watering I sailed from thence on the 4th September.

On the 19th September, after having passed the south part of New Zealand, I discovered very dangerous rocky islets never known before. They extend three and a half miles east and west and one and a half north and south. They lie from the Traps, off the south end of New Zealand, S. 89° E., distant 146 leagues. Their latitude is 47° 44′ 30″ S.; longitude, 179° 09′ E.

On the 26th October I anchored in Matavai Bay, Otaheite; sailed the 25th December and anchored in Toahroah Harbour, three miles distance from the bay. I remained here until the 4th April when I sailed with 1,015 bread-fruit plants and many fruit kind, in all 774 pots, 39 tubs, and 24 boxes. Latitude of this harbour, 17° 31′ 26″ S.; longitude, per observation, sun and moon, and stars each side of the moon, 210° 31′ 37″ E.; variation compass, 5° 31′ E.

I left these happy islanders in much distress, for the utmost affection, regard, and good fellowship remained among us during my stay. The king and all the royal family were always my guests, and their good sense and observations, joined with the most engaging dispositions in the world, will ever make them beloved by all who become acquainted with them as friends.

On the 12th April I discovered an island, called by the natives Wytootackee, whose chief was named Comackaiah, as I was informed by people in a canoe that came off to me. Their language seemed to prove them nearly the same people as at Otaheite. This island is about ten miles in circuit in latitude 18° 52′ S. It has eight small keys lying joined by a reef to the SSE. of it, and one to the WSW. The southernmost key lies in latitude 18° 58′ S.; the longitude, by observation, is 200° 19′ E. of Greenwich; variation compass, 8° 14′ E.

On the 18th of April I saw Savage Island in 19° 02′ S., and longitude, by my observation, 190° 18′ E. of Greenwich.

On the 21st of April I made the Friendly Islands, and on the 23rd following I anchored in Annamooca Road (called by Tasman Rotterdam). On the 26th, having completed my water and got on board some wood, I sailed.

This island lies in latitude 20° 16′ S., 185° 30′ E.

On the 28th of April in the morning, the north-westernmost of the Friendly Islands, called Tofoa, bore NE. ten leagues, and I had directed my course to the WNW., with a ship in most perfect order, and all my plants in a most flourishing condition, all my men and officers in good health, and, in short, everything to flatter and ensure my most sanguine expectations and success.

But I am now to relate one of the most atrocious and consummate acts of piracy ever committed.

At dawn of day Fletcher Christian, officer of the watch, Charles Churchill, ship's corporal, Thomas Burkett, seaman, and several others came into my cabin, and while I was asleep seized and tied my hands behind my back with a strong cord, and with cutlasses and a bayonet fixed at my breast threatened instant death if I spoke or made the least noise. I nevertheless called out so loud that every one heard me and were flying to my assistance, but all my officers, except those concerned, were kept in their cabins by armed sentinels, and the arms chest was in their possession. I was now hauled upon deck in my shirt, and hands tied behind me, held by Fletcher Christian and Charles Churchill with a bayonet at my breast, and two men, Alex. Smith and Thomas Burkett, behind me with loaded muskets cocked and bayonets fixed. Under this guard I was kept abaft the mizen-mast. The different hatchways were all guarded by armed men in the same manner, and those who were to be sent out of the ship, and some of the mutineers who could be spared, hoisted the boats out. Among these was the boatswain, who, with some others, got sails, twine, rope, grapnel, and a small cask of water into the boat, about which there were many altercations among the mutinous crew, and exerting myself in speaking loud to try if I could rally any with a sense of duty in them, I was saluted with: 'Damn his eyes! Blow his brains out.'

Being confined and kept apart from every one, Mr Samuel, my clerk, secured to me a quadrant and compass, some clothes, my journals, and a few material ship's papers, but all my valuable instruments, with a timepiece of three hundred and fifty guineas value, a valuable collection of books, maps, and drawings with all my remarks and observations for fifteen years past were kept from me.   He also secured about one hundred and fifty pounds of bread.

The officers and men being now drove into the boat one by one, I was told by Christian, 'Sir, your officers are now in the boat and you must go with them.'   I was then taken hold of under a guard and forced over the gangway into the boat which waited only for me, and untying my hands I was veered astern by a rope. A few pounds of pork were now thrown to us, being nineteen in number, and each began to solicit some of their little valuables that were left behind them.   I desired only some firearms, and even at last solicited two, but we received insolence and were told I should have none.   Four cutlasses were, however, thrown into the boat and we were cast adrift and rowed with all our strength for the land.

The size of the boat was twenty-three feet from stem to stern, and rowed six oars and was so deeply lumbered that they believed we could never reach the shore and some of them made their jokes of it.   However, by seven o'clock in the evening I got safe under Tofoa but could find no landing, and therefore kept the boat under the land all night paddling with two oars to preserve our station.

29th. Endeavouring to find landing to increase our stock of water and to get some coconuts and provisions.

30th. Found landing at the NW. part of the island in a cove, latitude 19° 41′ S., as I observed it.   Went in search of water, but found only a few quarts in holes of the rocks; suffered much fatigue and distress.   I should now have proceeded, as I intended, for some of the islands where I had a knowledge of the chiefs for I was well acquainted here, but the wind and the sea was too stormy to venture out.   Part of us slept in the boat, and others, with myself, on shore, and as we saw no natives we felt our distress the more because we wanted not to use any of our own stock.

1st May. Party out as yesterday and found out the residence of the natives who brought supplies of coconuts and bread-fruit, besides shells of water, all of which I bought for buttons which we cut off our clothes.   They all left us at sundown.   Weather so windy could not proceed to sea.

2nd. In the morning two chiefs—Eegyeefow, and the other, Maccaacabou—came down, also two canoes came in and another chief called Vageetee, and having inquired our situation and my determination to proceed to Paulehow, their king (Eegyeefow) agreed as soon as it moderated to go with me. This readiness gave me pleasure, but in a few hours I had as much uneasiness. The natives began to be very troublesome, and showed signs of hostilities towards us. We, however, thought they would go off at sundown, as they had done before, and that then I could leave the place without any risk, but it proved to the contrary, for three canoes were now come in, and places were fixed on for their residence during the night and fires made.

I therefore determined to do our best while it was light, and directed some provisions we had bought to be put in the boat. The chiefs desired I would stay, notwithstanding they perceived that I saw all their people were arming with clubs and stones. We were now all on the go, and taking one of the chiefs by the hand with a cutlass in the other, and my people with sticks, we proceeded down to the boat, when we were attacked by a multitude of Indians, in the course of which I lost a very worthy good man,[1] and the rest of us more or less bruised and wounded.

As I hauled out to our grapnel I hoped they could no longer annoy us, but here I was mistaken, for they launched their canoes and gave battle to us, or rather stoned us, until I got a league from the land. I could not return their salute but with such stones as lodged in the boat. I therefore, as the only thing left for to save our lives, exhorted every one to persevere in rowing, and throwing overboard some clothes which beguiled them and they lost time in taking up, together with the night coming on, we very miraculously escaped. Taking this as a real sample of their natural disposition, there were little hopes to expect much where I was going, for I considered their good behaviour hitherto owing to a dread of our firearms, which now knowing us to have none would not be the case, and that supposing our lives were safe, our boat, compass, and quadrant, would all be taken from me, and thereby I should not be able to return to my king and country to give an account of the transaction.

I was now solicited by every person to take them towards home, and when I told them no hopes of relief remained for us but what I might find at New Holland until I came to Timor, a distance of 1,200 leagues, where there was a governor, but that I had no idea at what part of the island the settlement was, they all agreed to live on one ounce of bread per day and one gill of water.

[1] The quartermaster, John Norton.

I therefore, after recommending this promise for ever to their memory, bore away for New Holland and from thence to Timor, a distance of 1,200 leagues across a sea where the navigation is dangerous and not known, and in a small boat deep-loaded with eighteen souls, without a single map, and nothing but my own recollection and general knowledge of the situation of places, assisted by a table in an old book of latitude and longitude to guide me.

Our stock of provisions at first consisted of 150 pounds of bread (part of which afterwards got damaged and lost), 28 gallons of water, 20 pounds of pork, 3 bottles of wine, and 5 quarts of rum.

It may be asked what could be the cause for such a revolution. In answer to which I have only to give a description of Otaheite, which has every allurement both to luxury and ease and is the Paradise of the world.

The women are handsome and mild in their manners and conversation, with sufficient delicacy to make them admired and beloved, and the chiefs have acquired such a liking to our people that they rather have encouraged their stay among them than otherwise, and even made promises of large possessions to them.

Under these and many other attendant circumstances equally desirable, is it to be wondered at that a set of sailors void of connections (or, if they have any, not possessed of natural feelings sufficient to wish themselves never to be separated from them) should be led by such powerful ties.

But equal to this, what a temptation is it to such wretches when they find it in their power (however illegally it can be got at) to fix themselves in the midst of plenty in the finest island in the world, where they need not labour, and where the allurements of dissipation are more than equal to anything that can be conceived.

Desertions have happened more or less in every ship that has been at the Society Isles, but it has ever been in the commander's power to make the chiefs return their people. They therefore knew such a plan could never succeed, and perhaps suggested that never so small a ship and so eligible an opportunity would offer to them again.

Christian was the officer on deck, and the whole watch being concerned except two midshipmen, who knew not what their officer was about, it is not surprising that the business was speedily done, all the able men being concerned, and also the greatest number, as may be seen by the following list.

People who came in the boat. (Here follows list previously transcribed.)

People who remained in the ship. (Here follows list previously transcribed.)

To return now to my proceedings in the boat. I steered to the WNW., as I formerly had heard from the Friendly Island people that land lay in that quarter.

The weather very boisterous, and obliged to keep right before the sea which at times ran into us and nearly filled the boat, and were obliged to throw all spare clothes overboard and every article we could possibly do without.

On the 4th May, latitude 18° 58′ S., longitude 182° 16′ E., I discovered land, an island, WSW. 4 or 5 leagues.

On the 6th discovered ten other islands, and that day at noon was in latitude 17° 53′ S. and longitude 179° 43′ E. Many shoals.

On the 7th discovered other islands; at noon latitude 16° 33′ S., 178° 34′ E., were chased by two large canoes but got clear of them by rowing. At night torrents of rain, with thunder and lightning; caught six gallons of water.

On the 9th fair weather, kept steering to the WNW. and W.

On the 10th very heavy rains, hard gales, and a high sea unto the 14th; suffered much cold in the nights, being constantly wet.

On the 14th discovered land—five islands—and were at noon in latitude 13° 29′ S., 169° 31′ E.; steered to WSW.

On the 15th discovered an island, latitude at noon 13° 4′ S., longitude 167° 35′ E. Very fresh gale and high sea with rain; constantly wet and constantly bailing. Distressed for want of light to see to steer by, the weather being stormy, with thunder, lightning, rain, and a high sea keeping the boat before it to the 21st when we had more dreadful weather, and the rain fell so heavy that we could scarce keep the boat from filling.

To the 24th the weather and sea continued very bad, and we now dreaded the nights for we were all benumbed with cold, and what added to our distress in the weak situation we were in, one of us in turns was obliged to be constantly bailing the boat in all this dreadful weather, being continually wet, and never having a dry rag about us. The resource I directed to be taken was, in the intervals when the rain ceased to strip naked and wash and wring all our clothes in the sea, which was a great refreshment.

To the 28th the weather better, when at midnight I fell in with most dreadful breakers, but I was able to stand away clear of them. As I knew I was near the coast of New Holland, I considered this to be the reef of that coast, and I therefore stood to the west again in the morning to search for a passage within it. At nine in the morning I saw the reef again, and soon after standing along it to the northward I discovered an opening which I safely entered and got into smooth water.

At noon latitude 12° 46′ S., 145° 02′ E. The entrance I came in at SW., about two leagues.

At a quarter-past five in the afternoon I got into a bay on an island about a quarter-mile from the main, and finding it uninhabited I determined on searching for supplies. Night came on. We, however, got a few oysters from the rocks which gave us a tolerable good meal.

As our boat was only large enough to admit one-half of us to rest at a time, I consented that one party should sleep on shore, but, unfortunately, having no materials we could not light a fire.

29th May. At dawn of day we went in search of water and what else we could get, and happily, by digging, found fine fresh water and plenty of it. Oysters were the only supply besides, of which, with our allowance of bread, we made very good stews. When the sun came out strong I was enabled to kindle a fire by a small magnifying glass, and we then made tinder and matches to supply our wants in future.

All hands were very weak, which with dizziness in the head and a dreadful tenesmus were the only complaints. At night part of us slept on shore.

30th May. I now determined, as the people were a little refreshed, to proceed on. I therefore by noon got our small watercasks filled, and having found some fern-root that I thought wholesome and very conducive to prevent thirst, I ordered a parcel into the boat. Birds could have easily have been got here if I had had arms. On that account every one we saw recalled to us our miserable situation, but Providence has been graciously kind to us, for we frequently caught by hand seafowls, which made great additions to our dinners of bread. The frequent supply of water was also a great blessing, but I had not vessels to contain a sufficient allowance: it therefore happened that nearly half a pint of water was what each person received in the course of the day, issued at eight in the morning, at noon, and sunset, with one-twenty-fifth of a pound of bread at breakfast and the same at dinner.

I found the latitude of this place 12° 39' S., 144° 44' E. The main appeared with a variety of high and low land, interspersed with wood and the more interior parts mountainous.

31st. At four in the afternoon, having performed divine service, I sailed. Saw twenty natives armed with spears, come down on the shore opposite to us. They were black and waved to us to come to them.

I steered along shore to the NNW. and NW. by N. in the direction of the coast. Saw several islands, and at eight in the morning passed through a cluster and saw more natives armed in the same manner and made the same signs. I, however, did not land.

The appearance of the country all changed, being very low and mostly sandhills. Landed on an island, and gathered shell-fish, oysters, and clams; also water, in the hollow of a rock, which enabled us to fill our sea store.

From the heights of this island I saw a small key to the NW. by N. As my present situation was, therefore, too near the main, having discovered at this place the natives to have canoes, I again prepared to sail, so as to reach the key before night. At noon dined on stewed oysters and clams. Found the latitude of this island 11° 58' S., 144° 29' E.

1st June. With a continuance of fine weather this evening I landed and spent the night at the key above-mentioned, could get no supplies of any kind. Some of my people were taken ill with vomitings and dizziness, besides a most dreadful tenesmus afflicted many of them, who had not been at stool for three weeks, and some more.

At noon I found the latitude of this key 11° 47' S., longitude 144° 24' E.

2nd June. This afternoon it came on strong gales, and my people being again ill I preferred giving them a good night's rest to going to sea. At dawn of day I sailed; people much better. Passed several islands, the coast sandy and barren. At noon, latitude 11° 18' S., 144° 20' E. I saw what I considered to be Cape York, bearing W½N. 3 leagues.

3rd. At night I again stopped on an island, whose latitude is 10° 52' S., 141° 05' E., by corrected longitude from Cape York, whose true situation is 141° 15′ E. My account, therefore, yesterday was 3° 05′ wrong.

4th. At dawn of day I again sailed and followed the direction of the coast to the NW.; saw many islands and breakers. At noon I was in 10° 31′ S. and 140° 40′ E. I now found I had doubled the north part of New Holland.[1]

At five o'clock this evening I left New Holland and steered accordingly for Timor, the latitude of which I was not very certain of. However, I determined to make it in the latitude of about 9° 30′ S.

On the 12th June, at three in the morning, I saw the island of Timor, bearing WNW.

At daylight, finding I was on the SE. end of it, I went to the south of the island, laying-to at night lest I might pass any settlement, for I was not certain where the governor resided.

On the 14th, in the afternoon, after having passed through a very heavy breaking sea and shoal water, I discovered an opening into which I entered and anchored at three o'clock, which I since find to be a bay on Timor, opposite to Pulo Samow, in the south entrance, the island Rotty being in sight to the SW. by S.

Saw some Malays on the shore. Sent two men after them, and they brought several men to me. One of them agreed to be my pilot, and I agreed to give ten half-ducatoons to conduct me to the governor.

This being settled we rowed along shore conducted by him, and on the morning, at dawn of day, I anchored off Coupang, and waited for leave to come on shore. At sunrise I was desired by a soldier to come on shore, and I was conducted to a gentleman's house (Captain Spikerman), who, upon my application, ordered breakfast and victuals for all hands; the governor, from severe indisposition, not being able to see me just at that time. The surgeon, a Mr Max, gave us every kind assistance in dressing our sores, and all who saw us were ready to contribute to the comfort of such poor distress'd creatures, one half of whom could not have survived a week longer, and some, perhaps, not a few days.

The governor, with much goodness, became anxious about us, and although his illness was very severe, I had it in my power to see him by eleven o'clock, and was received in a most affection-

[1] He had passed Cape York and was in Torres Straits.

ate and peculiar manner of kindness, which will ever endear him to my memory.

Orders were instantly given for our accommodation and supplies, and I had full power to see my people taken care of.

Thus happily ended, through the blessing of Divine Providence, without accident, a voyage of the most extraordinary nature that ever happened in the world, let it be taken either in its extent, duration, or so much want of the necessaries of life.

I remained at Coupang until the 20th August 1789,[1] during which time I had the misfortune to lose Mr David Nelson (botanist), whose good conduct in the course of the whole voyage and manly fortitude in our late disastrous circumstances deserves this tribute to his memory. He died of a fever on the 20th July.

I have not given so full an account to the Admiralty. You will please, therefore, to attend to it in that particular.

[1] Bligh arrived at Batavia on 1st October 1789, and sailed for the Cape of Good Hope on 16th October, arriving on 16th December. He left the Cape on 2nd January 1790, and arrived at Portsmouth on 14th March.